TREE AND SERPENT WORSHIP

OR

ILLUSTRATIONS OF MYTHOLOGY AND ART IN INDIA

IN THE

First and Fourth Centuries after Christ

FROM THE SCULPTURES OF THE BUDDHIST TOPES

AT

SANCHI AND AMRAVATI.

TREE AND SERPENT WORSHIP:

OR

ILLUSTRATIONS OF MYTHOLOGY AND ART IN INDIA

IN THE

First and Fourth Centuries after Christ.

FROM THE SCULPTURES OF THE BUDDHIST TOPES

AT

SANCHI AND AMRAVATI.

PREPARED UNDER THE AUTHORITY OF THE SECRETARY OF STATE FOR INDIA IN COUNCIL

WITH

INTRODUCTORY ESSAYS AND DESCRIPTIONS OF THE PLATES

By

JAMES FERGUSSON, ESQ., F.R.S., M.R.A.S.,

AUTHOR OF "PICTURESQUE ILLUSTRATIONS OF INDIAN ARCHITECTURE," HISTORY OF ARCHITECTURE,"

ETC. ETC. ETC.

GYAN

Published by

Gyan Publishing House
5, Ansari Road
Daryaganj, New Delhi-110002
Phone: 011-47034999, 9811692060
E-mail: books@gyanbooks.com

Distribution Network
gyanbooks.com
India, USA, Canada, UK, Australia, France

ISBN : 978-81-212-2888-6 (HB)
First Published, 1968

2nd Impression 2021

Printed at: Gyan Press, Delhi.

Tree and Serpent Worship
Author: James Fergusson

TREE AND SERPENT WORSHIP:

OR

ILLUSTRATIONS OF MYTHOLOGY AND ART IN INDIA

IN THE

First and Fourth Centuries after Christ.

FROM THE SCULPTURES OF THE BUDDHIST TOPES

AT

SANCHI AND AMRAVATI.

PREPARED UNDER THE AUTHORITY OF THE SECRETARY OF STATE FOR INDIA IN COUNCIL.

WITH

INTRODUCTORY ESSAYS AND DESCRIPTIONS OF THE PLATES

BY

JAMES FERGUSSON, Esq., F.R.S., M.R.A.S.,

AUTHOR OF "PICTURESQUE ILLUSTRATIONS OF INDIAN ARCHITECTURE," "HISTORY OF ARCHITECTURE," ETC. ETC. ETC.

LONDON:

INDIA MUSEUM,

1868.

Wm. H. ALLEN AND CO., 13, WATERLOO PLACE, S.W.

Publishers to the India Office.

FRONTISPIECE,

LIEUT COL MAISEY, DEL. W GRIGGS, LITH

1 2 3 4 5 6 7 8 9 10

SCALE OF FEET

ELEVATION OF NORTHERN GATEWAY SANCHI.

PREFACE.

The story of this book is simple, but it seems necessary it should be told in order that much which it contains may be appreciated at its true value, and not taken for what it does not pretend to be.

When in the autumn of 1866 arrangements were being made in this country for the great Paris Exhibition, to be held in the following year, Mr. Cole suggested to me that it would afford an excellent opportunity for forwarding my designs for a dissemination of knowledge of Indian art and architecture. Having then just completed my "History of Architecture," and having consequently the requisite leisure, I fell readily into his views; and after due consideration it was arranged that I should exhibit a large collection of Photographs of Indian Architecture which I possessed, together with others to which I had access. It was felt, however, that a mere collection of Photographs, without some more prominent object to draw attention to them, would hardly answer the purpose. I therefore proposed that, in addition, some casts of Indian sculpture or architectural fragments should be added, not only to give a character to the exhibition, but also to enable students to judge of the merit of the objects from specimens of the true dimensions.

I next examined, among other places, the collection in the India Museum, then at Fife House, for the purpose of obtaining the requisite models for casting; and after carefully going over the whole, fixed on four examples of sculpture from the Amravati Tope as those best suited for my purpose. I had long been familiar with these marbles, as they had been sent to this country by Colonel Mackenzie before 1820, and were the principal ornaments of the old Museum in Leadenhall Street. I had often admired them when there, and considered them so curious and so interesting that, had an opportunity occurred, I would have thought it well worth while to make a voyage to India specially for the purpose of exploring the Tope, and of examining the numerous antiquities I knew to exist in its neighbourhood. I was therefore not a little astonished at being informed that a large collection of marbles from the same monument were stored in the coach-houses of the establishment.

On investigation I found that Mr.—now Sir Walter—Elliot, when Commissioner in Guntûr in 1845, had excavated a considerable portion of the monument, and sent down to Madras the results of his explorations. They lay there, exposed to the wind and rain, for ten or twelve years, and then were sent home, and after a short sojourn in the Docks, were deposited where I found them, in consequence of there being no space in the Museum itself for their exhibition.

This most unexpected discovery made a considerable alteration in the plan of campaign. It was now determined, instead of casting any, to send four or five specimens of the marbles themselves to Paris, and to bring out and photograph the whole to the same scale, so as to enable them to be pieced together, and a restoration of the monument was thus effected. In this project I was warmly seconded by Dr. Forbes Watson, the Director of the Museum, who lent me every assistance which the means at his disposal afforded, and notwithstanding numerous difficulties,—it was mid-winter, and the snow on the ground the greater part of the time—the task was successfully accomplished, in consequence of the intelligence and untiring zeal of Mr. Griggs, the photographer attached to the establishment.

As soon as a complete set of the photographs was obtained, I set to work to piece them together, and by processes explained in the text obtained two elevations of the outer Rail, shown on a reduced scale in Plates XLVIII. and XLIX., and one of the inner Rail, Plate LXXV., all which were exhibited in Paris with the marbles, and some 500 other Photographs of Indian architectural objects. During the three or four months, however, which I had spent poring over these Photographs, I had not only become familiar with their forms, but had acquired a considerable amount of unexpected knowledge of ancient Indian art and mythology. The greater part of this was quite new to me, but seemed of sufficient importance to justify me in making it public; and in pursuance of this object, I exhibited the Photographs and read a paper on the subject to the Royal Asiatic Society in June 1867, which afterwards was printed in their Journal, vol. III. of new series, p. 132, et seqq. This paper, however, was very far from exhausting the subject, or from illustrating the monument to the extent which seemed desirable, and I in consequence appealed to the Secretary of State for India in Council for assistance to enable me to publish the whole of the Photographs, with such explanations as might seem desirable. Sir Stafford Northcote entered warmly into the project, and the Council most liberally granted the permission and funds necessary for its execution, in the section of the India Museum devoted to the reproduction of works of artistic value.

It was then intended that the work should consist of thirty or thirty-two Photographic Plates and eighteen or twenty Lithographs, with the accompanying explanations, but should be confined wholly to the Amravati Tope. It was then also agreed that the price should be limited to three guineas, on the principle adopted in the Department, that the public should obtain this and other similar works at prices calculated only to cover the cost of production. In the course, however, of the investigations required for carrying out this project, I lighted on a beautiful series of drawings of the Sanchi Tope, made in 1854 by Lieutenant-Colonel Maisey, of the Bengal army, and which were then in the Library of the India Office; and at the same time received from Lieutenant Waterhouse, R.A., a set of Photographs of the same monument. The sculptures of this Tope bore so directly on the subject in hand, that, having now ample means of illustrating the Sanchi Tope also, I determined to publish it as a sequel to that at Amravati. As the work progressed, however, it became apparent that this was in reality putting the cart before the horse. That at Sanchi was the oldest of the two Topes; and it would be reading the book backwards to publish first the more modern example. I in consequence again applied to the India Council, and my proposal being met in the same liberal spirit, the work has assumed its present form and price.

When this stage was reached it became a very serious question what form the text of the work ought to assume. The great danger to be avoided was apparently the assumption that the Tree and Serpent Worship portrayed in the illustrations of this work should be considered as a mere local Indian superstition. In order either to enlist the sympathy of European scholars, or to place it on its true basis, it seemed indispensable to explain how far that form of worship had prevailed in other countries, and to what extent it underlaid or influenced other forms of faith. To do this fully and completely was quite incompatible with the scope of the present work, even if I had been qualified to attempt it. At the same time, however, I could not but feel that to have made the text a mere description of the two Topes, and to announce it as such, was simply to seal the book against general readers, and to relegate it to the small and I fear diminishing body of enthusiasts who are supposed to delight in grubbing in the despised local antiquities of India. On the other hand, to treat it from a scientific and more cosmopolitan point of view required an author who not only knew Sanskrit and Pali sufficiently well to read the ordinary texts, but who could also decipher inscriptions and pronounce on paleographic puzzles. He ought also to have devoted some years study at least to the Western branch of the subject, from the early Grecian to its latest Finnish developments.

To none of these accomplishments can I make the smallest possible pretensions. My knowledge of Indian languages is confined to the vernacular dialects, and I had never devoted any special attention to Tree or Serpent Worship in the West before I undertook this work. I am therefore wholly dependent on translations, which are seldom complete and not always trustworthy, for my knowledge of the Eastern branch of the subject, and to a moderate course of reading for the Western. A more cautious or prudent man, aware of the numerous pitfalls which such a course must lead him across, would have declined the undertaking altogether; and all I can plead in excuse for my temerity is, that in all instances I have tried to write well within what I believe to be my real knowledge. So much indeed is this the case that my impression is, that the work is more open to criticism for what it omits than for what it contains, and I in consequence lay myself open to the reproach of seeming ignorant of what it may be assumed ought to be known to every one treating of such a subject. It would have been far easier to write an introduction twice or three times as long, and to have left it to the reader to discriminate between the wheat and the chaff; but I have thought it better to put forward only what I felt I could substantiate, and to leave the fuller development of the subject to more competent scholars.

At the same time, though fully aware of my shortcomings in a literary point of view, I felt that I probably was as competent as any other person I could name to treat of the subject of the Topes and their sculptures from an architectural or archæological point of view. Long personal familiarity with Indian monuments, and loving study of them, extending through half a lifetime, had given me a readiness in discriminating their peculiarities, which I am sorry to think very few possess; and I felt, therefore, some confidence in undertaking this part of the work.

Whether I was justified in this or not, others must judge; but at all events, I felt and feel to be only too true, that if I did not undertake it there was no one else, so far as I knew, who possessed the leisure, combined with the love of the subject, necessary for the task. Unless I availed myself of the opportunity, I could not but fear that the illustrations of the work might lie dormant for another half century—as those of the Mackenzie Collection have done—or at least for another quarter of a century, as has been the fate of those presented to the nation at so much trouble and expence by Sir Walter Elliot.

There was still another course open, which was to delay the appearance of the work till this time next year. Another twelve months' study and preparation might have enabled me to make my text much more complete than it now pretends to be; but even then it would not have been perfect. Personally I should no doubt have gained considerable credit to my own reputation by such a course, but so convinced do I feel that the illustrations of this work are in themselves—wholly irrespective of the text—the most valuable contribution that has been offered to the students of Indian antiquities for many years past, that I at once abandoned any such idea. The text has gone on *pari passu* with the plates, and my last sheet was sent to press before the last lithograph was ready for proving. The work has not consequently been delayed one hour for anything I have done, and I am sure I have been right in acting thus. Still I might have been induced to delay the appearance of the work if I had been able to enlist the co-operation of persons in India who have local opportunities of acquiring knowledge regarding the subject. I have, however, found it so difficult to explain by correspondence, with strangers, what it is exactly that I wanted to know, and still more difficult to disabuse their minds from the idea that it was not a mere antiquarian crotchet on my part, that I am afraid that very little would be gained in that respect by delay. The real way to interest strangers is to show them what has been done, and to let them see what still remains undone. When this is once brought home to them, I feel convinced that there are hundreds of intelligent officers and others in India who both can and will at once supply the required information.

In the meanwhile, however, I must not be understood as complaining. General Cunningham, Colonel Meadows Taylor, Professor Cowell, Dr. Balfour, and Dr. Best, have contributed most important appendices to this work. Dr. Reinhold Rost has afforded me most valuable assistance in passing the sheets through the press, while Prinee Frederick of Schleswig Holstein, and many others, have given me most useful information and aid. Still the subject, in its present form at least, is new, and it will require the co-operation of a considerable number of qualified individuals before it can be placed on an intelligible and secure basis.

This last is the fact to which, in conclusion, I would wish especially to direct attention. If this work is really of the importance and interest which from its illustrations I believe it really is, the very limited number of copies to which this edition extends will soon be exhausted, and the work must appear again either in a similar or a more popular form. Whether in that event it will also be more complete or perfect depends more on others than on myself. If those who are more competent, or who have special opportunities of gaining knowledge, will aid either by criticisms or communications to the public press, or by imparting information to me privately, a great deal may easily be done. I urge this the more earnestly, because it seems to be only by such co-operation, either in such a book as this, or under some more competent leadership, that we shall be able to follow the worship of the Tree or the Serpent through all their ramifications, or to trace them back to their source. My conviction, too, is that the subject will well repay any trouble that may be bestowed upon it, for if I mistake not it is the oldest—it was at one time the most prevalent, and it is now the most curious of all those forms of worship through which man ever attempted to approach or to propitiate the Divinity.

J. F.

20 Langham Place, November 1868.

NOTE.

THE difficulty as to the correct mode of spelling Indian names has presented itself with more than usual prominence in the following pages. The rule which it has been attempted to follow is, in the first instance, to leave all names which are already familiar to the English ear in the forms in which they have been adopted into our literature. Thus, such names as Cashmere, Cambodia, Karlee, Ellora, Amravati, &c., have been left as they are usually written. Such familiar terms as Râjâ, Nâga, Hindû, &c., which occur at every page in the latter part of the work, and regarding the pronunciation of which there can be no doubt, are written without any accents. All other Indian proper names are accented according to the method of transliteration most usually adopted by Indian scholars. This is done not only to indicate to the English reader the correct mode of pronouncing the word, but also to prevent any ambiguity as to the word or person intended.

It has been a little difficult to follow out these rules strictly on all occasions, but this is at least what has been attempted throughout.

CONTENTS.

INTRODUCTORY ESSAY.

PART I.—WESTERN WORLD.

PART II.—EASTERN ASIA.

THE TOPE AT SANCHI.

THE TOPE AT AMRAVATI.

CONCLUSION.

APPENDIX.

LIST OF ILLUSTRATIONS.

PHOTOGRAPHS AND LITHOGRAPHS.

SANCHI.

NOTES

ON

TREE AND SERPENT WORSHIP.

INTRODUCTION.

PART I.—WESTERN WORLD.

THERE are few things which at first sight appear to us at the present day so strange, or less easy to account for, than that worship which was once so generally offered to the Serpent God. If not the oldest, it ranks at least among the earliest forms through which the human intellect sought to propitiate the unknown powers. Traces of its existence are found not only in every country of the old world; but before the new was discovered by us, the same strange idolatry had long prevailed there, and even now the worship of the Serpent is found lurking in out-of-the-way corners of the globe, and startles us at times with the unhallowed rites which seem generally to have been associated with its prevalence.

Although the actual worship of Trees is nearly as far removed from our ordinary forms of faith as Serpent Worship, still it can hardly be considered as more than an exaggerated perversion of many of the ideas now current; and we can hardly wonder that in an early stage of human civilization, it may have assumed considerable importance. There is such wondrous beauty in the external form of trees, and so welcome a shelter beneath their over-arching boughs, that we should not feel surprise that in early ages groves were considered as the fittest temples for the gods. There are also, it must be remembered, few things in nature so pleasing to the eye as the form or the colour of the flowers which adorn at seasons the whole vegetable kingdom, and nothing so grateful to the palate of the rude man as the flavour of the fruits which trees afford. In addition to these were the multifarious uses to which their wood could always be applied. For buildings, for furniture, for implements of peace or war, or for ornament, it was indispensable. In ancient times it was from wood alone that man obtained that fire which enabled him to cook his food, to warm his dwelling, or to sacrifice to his gods. With all their poetry, and all their usefulness, we can hardly feel astonished that the primitive races of mankind should have considered trees as the choicest gift of the gods to men, and should have believed that their spirits still delighted to dwell among their branches, or spoke oracles through the rustling of their leaves.

On the other hand, when it comes to be more closely examined, the worship of the Serpent is not so strange as it might at first sight appear. As was well remarked by an ancient author,* "The serpent alone of all animals without legs or arms, or any of the "usual appliances for locomotion, still moves with singular celerity;" and he might have added—grace, for no one who has watched a serpent slowly progressing over the ground, with his head erect, and his body following apparently without exertion, can fail to be struck with the peculiar beauty of the motion. There is no jerk, no reflex motion, as in all other animals, even fishes, but a continuous progression in the most graceful curves. Their general form, too, is full of elegance, and their colours varied and sometimes very beautiful, and their eyes bright and piercing. Then, too, a serpent can exist for an indefinite time without food or apparent hunger. He periodically casts his skin, and, as the ancients fabled, by that process renewed his youth. Add to this his longevity, which, though not so great as was often supposed, is still sufficient to make the superstitious forget how long an individual may have been reverenced in order that they may ascribe to him immortality.

Though these qualities, and others that will be noted in the sequel, may bave sufficed to excite curiosity and obtain respect, it is probable that the serpent never would have become a god but for his exceptional power. The destructive powers of tigers or crocodiles are merely looked upon as ordinary exaggerations of a general law, but the poison fang of the serpent is something so exceptional, and so deadly in its action, as to excite dread, and when we find to how few of the serpent tribe it is given, its presence is only more mysterious. Even more terrible, however, than the poison of the Cobra is the flash-like spring of the Boa—the instantaneous embrace and the crushed-out life—all accomplished faster almost than the eye can follow. It is hardly to be wondered at that such power should impress people in an early stage of civilization with feelings of awe; and with savages it is probably true that most religions sprung from a desire to propitiate by worship those powers from whom they fear that injury may be done to themselves or their property. Although, therefore, fear might seem to suffice to account for the prevalence of the worship, on looking closely at it we are struck with phenomena of a totally different character. When we first meet Serpent Worship, either in the Wilderness of Sinaï, the Groves of Epidaurus, or in the Sarmatian huts, the Serpent is always the Agathodæmon, the bringer of health and good fortune. He is the teacher of wisdom, the oracle of future events. His worship may have originated in fear, but long before we become practically acquainted with it, it had passed to the opposite extreme among its votaries. Any evil that ever was spoken of the serpent, came from those who were outside the pale, and were trying to depreciate what they considered as an accursed superstition.

If fear were the only or even the principal characteristic of Serpent Worship, it might be sufficient, in order to account for its prevalence, to say, that like causes produce like effects all the world over; and that the serpent is so terrible and so unlike the rest of creation that these characteristics are sufficient to explain everything. When more narrowly examined, however, this seems hardly to be the case. Love and admiration,

* Sanchoniathon quoting Taatus ap Eusebium, Præp. Evangel. 40.

more than fear or dread, seem to be the main features of the faith, and there are so many unexpected features which are at the same time common to it all the world over, that it seems more reasonable to suspect a common origin. In the present state of our knowledge, however, we are not in a position to indicate the locality where it first may have appeared, or the time when it first became established among mankind.

In so far as such glimmerings as we possess enable us to guess the locality of its origin, I would feel inclined to say that it came from the mud of the Lower Euphrates, among a people of Turanian origin, and spread thence as from a centre to every country or land of the Old World in which a Turanian people settled. Apparently no Semetic, or no people of Aryan race, ever adopted it as a form of faith. It is true we find it in Judea, but almost certainly it was there an outcrop from the older underlying strata of the population. We find it also in Greece, and in Scandinavia, among people whom we know principally as Aryan, but there too it is like the tares of a previous crop springing up among the stems of a badly-cultivated field of wheat. The essence of Serpent Worship is as diametrically opposed to the spirit of the Veda or of the Bible as is possible to conceive two faiths to be; and with varying degrees of dilution the spirit of these two works pervades in a greater or less extent all the forms of the religions of the Aryan or Semetic races. On the other hand, any form of animal worship is perfectly consistent with the lower intellectual status of the Turanian races, and all history tells us that it is among them, and essentially among them only, that Serpent Worship is really found to prevail.

Human Sacrifices.

The almost universal association of human sacrifices with the practice of Serpent Worship would render it extremely desirable to ascertain, if it were possible, how far the connexion between the two is real, or to what extent the juxtaposition may be only accidental. The subject is, however, very seriously complicated by the circumstance of the very different form which the rite took in various ages, and the different points of view from which it must consequently be at times regarded.

In its earliest and simplest form, human sacrifice seems merely to have been regarded in the nature of a tithe. A cannibal savage shared with his cannibal god the spoils of victory as he did the products of the chase, or he sought to sanctify his revenge or his sensuality by making his deity a participator in his crimes. Another form arose from the idea that death was only a change, and that the future state was little more than a continuation of this world. It became consequently necessary for his enjoyment of it, that a man should be accompanied by his cattle, and his slaves, male and female, and in its most refined form the wife voluntarily sacrificed herself to rejoin her beloved husband. A third form sprung from a higher and more religious motive: it arose from a conviction of man's own unworthy and sinful nature as compared with the greatness and goodness of God, and the consequent desire to atone for the one by the sacrifice of whatever was most dear, and to propitiate the favour of the deity by offering up whatever was most precious and most beloved—even one's own, and it might be only, child. A fourth form, equally compatible with the highest civilisation, was the national sacrifice of one to atone for the sins of the many. Serpent Worship is associated in a greater or less degree with all these forms of the human rite, and so much so that it is nearly correct to say that wherever human sacrifices prevailed, there Serpent Worship is found also, though the converse does not appear so capable of proof. Serpent Worship did continue to exist when, at least, human sacrifices had ceased to be performed, though even then it is not quite clear whether it was not only from the disuse of one part of what had once been associated.

In Egypt human sacrifices never assumed the position of a religious or domestic institution. The victorious king dedicated the prisoners taken in war to the gods, but beyond this it does not seem to have been carried; and Serpent Worship in Egypt seems likewise to have been sporadic and of little importance.

In Judea, so long as any traces of Serpent Worship prevailed, the idea of human sacrifices seems to have been familiar, but after Hezekiah's time we simultaneously lose all traces of either.

So long as Greece was Pelasgic, Serpent Worship and human sacrifices went hand in hand, but with the return of the Heraclidæ, the latter went out of fashion, though the former still lingered long, but in a modified form. In Rome, on the other hand, as we shall presently see, the worship of the Serpent was a later introduction, but as it strengthened, so did the prevalence of human sacrifices; and till Christianity put a stop to them they certainly were considered an important means of appeasing the wrath or propitiating the favour of the gods. It may, in Rome, have been to some extent derived from Etruria, or encouraged by the example of Carthage, where human sacrifices certainly prevailed till the destruction of the city, and wherever Moloch—"horrid king"—was worshipped; and in all these instances the practice seems to have risen and fallen with Serpent Worship.

In Mexico and Dahomey, where in modern times human sacrifices have been practised to an extent not known elsewhere, there too Serpent Worship was and is the typical and most important form of propitiation; while in India, there can be little doubt but that the two existed together from the earliest time. The sacrifice of men could not, however, stand before the intellectual acumen of the Aryan, and was utterly antagonistic to the mild doctrines of the Buddhist. It consequently was abolished wherever it was possible to do so; but the more innocent worship of the Serpent cropped up again and again wherever neglected, and remained in many places long after the sister form had practically lost its meaning. Both still exist in India at the present day, but not apparently practised together or by the same tribes. It is not, however, by any means clear whether the dissociation is real, or whether we merely assume it is so in consequence of our ignorance of the subject. Human sacrifices, especially among the Khonds, have attracted the attention both of governments and of individuals. No one has turned his attention to the modern forms of Serpent Worship.

Notwithstanding all these coincidences—and they might easily be extended—it must not be overlooked that nowhere can we trace any direct connexion between the two forms of faith. No human sacrifice was anywhere made to propitiate the serpent, nor was it ever pretended that any human victim was ever devoured by the snake god. In all instances the serpent is the Agathodæmon, the bringer of health or good fortune, the protector of men or of treasure, and nowhere was it sought to propitiate him by sacrifice of life beyond what was necessary for food, or to appease him by blood offerings.

When the subject has been more thoroughly investigated than has hitherto been the case, it may be possible to trace a more direct connexion between the two forms of faith than we are now able to do. At all events we shall then be in a position to say whether it was a real partnership or only an accidental juxtaposition. In the meanwhile, all that is required in this place is to draw attention to the subject, and to point out a coincidence which is so remarkable that when investigated it may hereafter lead to the most important results.*

Egypt.

In an attempt to investigate any form of ancient mythology from an historical point of view, we naturally turn first to Egypt; for not only was Egypt the earliest civilized of all the countries of the ancient world, in so far at least as we at present know, but she was pre-eminently the parent of all idolatries. With the Egyptians all knowledge was considered as divine, and whatever they saw, they worshipped. Their gods had been kings; their kings were gods; and all the animal kingdom was considered worthy of worship in a greater or less degree. From bulls to beetles, or from crocodiles to cats, it made little difference; all came alike to a people so essentially religious as the Egyptians seem to have been. It is little wonder, therefore, that Serpents, and it may be Trees, should be included in their multifarious Pantheon, and it is easy to detect numerous instances of the honours bestowed on both. Still it would be straining the argument beyond its legitimate issue to describe the Egyptians as in any sense an essentially Tree or Serpent worshipping people. The serpent was worshipped on the banks of the Nile among other animals, perhaps in some instances with a certain degree of pre-eminence;† but on the whole the accounts are hardly sufficient to enable us to say that the serpent was more honoured than his associated animal gods. At the same time it must be admitted that the serpent very frequently appears in the sculptures of the Temple walls, and frequently in a place of honour, as on the brow of the king, or as a prominent ornament of his dress, but hardly ever there with that pre-eminence he attained in other countries.

The relative position of Tree Worship among the Egyptians seems to be almost the same. It is true that the important part which the Tamarisk (Ἐρίκη) plays in the legend of Isis and Osiris, as told by Plutarch,‡ might tend to a somewhat different conclusion, and the prominence given to the other tree (Μηθίδη), which marked and shaded the tomb of Osiris in the same legend, might lead to the conclusion that a form of Tree Worship prevailed in Egypt before the multifarious Theban pantheon was elaborated. The authority, however, for these facts is not such as can be relied upon, and the sculptures again do not favour the belief that Trees were considered as divine on the banks of the Nile, though they may justify the belief that the sycamore was sacred to the goddess Netpe, and the persea to Athor.§

---

* As human sacrifices bardly form part of the subject of the work, I have not thought it necessary to encumber the text of this section with notes or references. The subject has been exhaustively treated by Kalish, in his Commentary on Leviticus XXIII. p. 381 to 416. I am also much iudebted to an unpublished essay by Sir John Acton, where the whole question is treated with his usual depth of learning.

† Herodotus, II. 74. Ælian, de Animal. XVII. 5. Clemens Alex. III. 2. p. 93.

‡ Plutarch, de Iside et Osiri, 11. Wilkinson's Ancient Egyptians, vol. V. p. 261, et seq.

§ Wilkinson, vol. IV. p. 391, plates 36 and 54, &c.

The great test of such a subject in Egypt are the sculptures which cover the walls of the Temples. These are the Bible of the Egyptians, in so far at least as we know it. Any one studying these with that object might easily pick out fifty or a hundred examples which would tend to show that the Egyptians were both Tree and Serpent worshippers; but, on a fair review of the whole subject, these would probably be found to be only a fractional part of the nature worship of the Egyptians, and neither the most prominent nor the most important.* In spite, therefore, of the passages in classical authors which may be quoted against this view, it would probably be incorrect to include the ancient Egyptians among the votaries either of the Serpent or of Trees.

Judea.

The earliest distinct allusion which we have to those mysterious properties which the ancients attributed to certain Trees, is to be found in the second and third chapters of Genesis. The planting of the Trees of Life and Knowledge in the Garden of Eden is there described in minute detail, and judging from subsequent forms of the story, their custody seems to have been intrusted to the serpent. Taken by itself, this narrative has always appeared one of the least intelligible parts of the Pentateuch, and numberless theories have been formed to account for what seemed so completely outside the range of ordinary human experience. With the knowledge we now possess, it does not seem so difficult to understand what was meant by the curse on the serpent, or the prohibition to eat the fruit of the trees. When the writers of the Pentateuch set themselves to introduce the purer and loftier worship of the Elohim, or of Jehovah, it was first necessary to get rid of that earlier form of faith which the primitive inhabitants of the earth had fashioned for themselves. The serpent, as the principal deity of that early religion, was cursed "above all cattle, and above every beast of the field;"† and in future there was to be for ever enmity between the serpent and "man of woman born." The confusion of ideas on this subject seems to have arisen from the assumption that the curse was directed at the reptile as such, and not rather at a form of worship which the writers of the Pentateuch must have regarded with horror, and which they thought it necessary to denounce in the strongest terms and in the form they believed would be most intelligible by those to whom it was addressed. The tree it was not necessary should be cursed; the fruit of the tree of knowledge had been eaten, and no further result could be obtained by access to it, while the tree of life was guarded by a cherub with a flaming sword, and all approach prevented. Its fruits could not then be obtained, nor have they to the present day.

The two chapters which refer to this, however,—as indeed the whole of the first eight of Genesis,—are now generally admitted by scholars to be made up of fragments of earlier books or earlier traditions belonging, properly speaking, to Mesopotamian rather than to Jewish history, the exact meaning of which the writers of the

* On such a monument, for instance, as the Sarcophagus of Menepthah, in Sir John Soane's Museum, where the Serpent occurs more frequently than on any monument of the same extent I am acquainted with, and in a more important character, there is not one instance in which it can be said he is being worshipped. He is the representative of heaven—is a good or evil genius—a protector or destroyer—a mere hieroglyphic—anything, in short, but never a god.—See Bonomi's published account of the Sarcophagus: Longman, 1864.

† Genesis, iii. 14.

Pentateuch seem hardly to have appreciated when they transcribed them in the form in which they are now found. The history of the Jews and of the Jewish religion commences with the call of Abraham, and from that time forward the worship of Serpents and Trees took an infinitely less important position, though still occasionally cropping up, often when least expected, but apparently not as a religion of the Jews, but as a backsliding towards the feelings of the pre-existing races among whom they were located.

There is apparently no mention of serpents, either in the Bible or in any of the traditions in connexion with Abraham or his immediate descendants; but that Patriarch "planted a grove at the well of the covenant (Beersheba), and called there "on the name of the Lord" *—a circumstance the more worthy of note, as it is the earliest mention of a form of worship to which continual allusions are afterwards made in Jewish history. The oak, or rather the terebinth tree, under which Abraham is said to have entertained the angels at Mamre, became an object of extreme veneration to his descendants, and, if we may trust Eusebius, was worshipped down to the time of Constantine.† The pious zeal of that emperor led him to desecrate its altars, and apparently to cut down the sacred tree to make way for a Christian church which he erected on the spot, and which was then or afterwards dedicated to St. George.‡

With the time of Moses the indications became more distinct and palpable. We gather from the context in the Bible,§ and still more from the narrative of Josephus,‖ that the tree or bush on Horeb, from which the Lord appeared to Moses as a flame, had been considered sacred before that event. It was, indeed, apparently in consequence of its sanctity that it was chosen for the delivery of the oracle, while the conversion on that occasion of Moses' rod into a serpent brings these two names into the juxtaposition in which they are so frequently found. This miracle on Horeb would, however, be more impressive and more to the point were it not that it was repeated by Aaron before Pharaoh, and copied by the Egyptians;¶ but at the burning bush it stands alone, and without any apparent motive for its exhibition there, except the appropriateness of the combination.

With the Brazen Serpent in the Wilderness ** we tread on surer ground; it is the first record we have of actual worship being performed to the Serpent, and it is also remarkable, as the cause of this adoration is said to have been its healing powers. From the readiness with which this explanation was adopted by the Jews, it would seem as if that characteristic had been ascribed to the Serpent before that time. We now, however, learn it for the first time, though we afterwards become so familiar with it in Greek mythology, where the Serpent himself represents Æsculapius, and is the indispensable concomitant of Hygieia.

From this time we lose sight of the worship of the Serpent from the narrative of the Bible, till it somewhat unexpectedly reappears in the time of Hezekiah. We then learn that the brazen image that Moses had set up, had for more than five centuries

* Genesis, xxi. 33.

† Eusebius, Vita Constantini, III. 53.

‡ The oak now pointed out at Hebron as Abraham's tree is in quite another locality.

§ Exodus, iii. 5.

‖ Josephus, Antiq. Ju. II. 12. 1.

¶ Exodus, vii. 8.

** Numbers, xxi. 9.

been preserved in the Temple, and that "unto those days the children of Israel did burn incense to it." * It was only then, after six centuries of toleration, that it was resolved to put an end to this idolatry, together with the kindred worship of the Groves. In the intermediate period there is hardly any expression that countenances the belief that the worship of Serpents generally prevailed among the Jews, unless it be one in the Wisdom of Solomon, where it is said, "They worshipped serpents void of reason,"† in strange contrast with the New Testament expression, "Be ye wise as serpents."‡

Neither in the Bible, however, nor in the Talmud,§ is there anything that would justify the assertion that Serpent Worship, even in the most modified form, prevailed among the Jews after its abolition by Hezekiah. It cropped up again, as we shall presently see, in the Christian sect of Ophites, but probably in this instance the superstition was derived from Persia.

The case is different with the worship of Trees or Groves. The first form of this appears to have arisen from the veneration paid to natural groves, and the worship offered therein to Baal ‖ and other foreign gods, but the Grove or Asherah is also frequently an image, no doubt like that emblem so often represented on the Assyrian sculptures.¶ This is an artificial tree, such as might have been placed alongside of the Brazen Serpent within the Temple at Jerusalem.**

It hardly admits of doubt but that this worship of the Asherah or of Groves was a true and essential form of Tree Worship, but it seems to have been local, and entirely opposed to the spirit of the Jewish religion. As a rule it is reprobated by their chroniclers and prophets, and eventually disappears. Had it ever been really adopted by the Jewish legislators, we might perhaps be able to ascertain more correctly its origin and affiliations. Possibly we may do so when the Assyrian antiquities are more completely investigated than they now are. For the present we must rest content with the knowledge that both Trees and Serpents were worshipped in Judea, and hope that some new light may some day be thrown on the subject.

Even, however, if in abeyance, we can hardly suppose that Serpent Worship was extinguished in Judea, inasmuch as immediately after the Christian era we found it bursting forth again with wonderful exuberance in the sects of the Nicolaitans, the Gnostics, and more especially that called the Ophites (Οφῖται). Of the latter, Tertullian tells us, "they even prefer the Serpent to Christ, because the former brought the know-" ledge of good and evil into the world. They point also to his majesty and power, " inasmuch as when Moses raised the Brazen Serpent in the Wilderness, whoever " looked on it was healed; and they even quote the Gospels to prove that Christ " was an imitation of the serpent, because it is said, 'As Moses lifted up the " 'serpent in the wilderness, so must the Son of Man be lifted up'" (John, iii. 14).††

* 2 Kings, xviii. 4.

† Wisdom, xi. 15.

‡ Matthew, x. 16.

§ I make the assertion on the authority of Mr. Deutsch, of the British Museum, who has kindly looked through the Talmud for me with reference to the question.

‖ 2 Kings, xvii. 16.

¶ Lord Aberdeen's black stone, History of Architecture, W.C. 75; see also British Museum Sculptures, and Layard's and Botta's plates, *passim*.

** 1 Kings, xvi. 33; 2 Kings, xxi. 3, xxiii. 4 & 6; Isaiah, xvii. 8, xxvii. 9, &c.

†† Tertullian, de Prescript. Hereticorum, c. xlvii.

Epiphanius describes these ceremonies in the following terms: "They keep a living "serpent in a chest, and at the time of the mysteries entice him out "by placing bread before him. The door being opened he issues forth, "and having ascended the table folds himself above the bread.* This "they call a perfect sacrifice. They not only break and distribute "this among the votaries, but whosoever wishes it may kiss the "serpent. This the wretched people call the Eucharist. They "conclude the ceremonies by singing a hymn through him to the "Supreme Father."†

No. 1.

CISTA, FROM A ROMAN COIN OF ADRAMYTTIUM.

There are other paragraphs to the same effect, and the representations of serpents and Serpent Worship in the so-called Gnostic form are too numerous and too familiar to require further notice here.‡

We have no means of knowing how long this worship of the Serpent continued to prevail in Syria—most probably down to the seventh century, when the Mahomedan invasion swept away a large mass of the parasitic superstitions which had fastened themselves on Christianity; but the literature of that age is so mixed up with fables and misrepresentations, that it is very difficult to write confidently about anything it describes.

Except the instance above alluded to, of the Terebinth at Mamre, I am not aware of any authentic instance of direct Tree Worship in Syria after the Christian era, but there may be, though, as they have not hitherto been looked for, they may still remain unknown.

---

* Pigraque labetur circa do aria serpens.—Ovid, Amor. Eleg. lib. ii.

† Epiphanius, lib. i. Hæres: XXXVII. p. 267, et seq.

‡ Though not bearing directly on the subject, the "Legend of the True Cross" is a curious example of a cognate superstition. Like most Mediæval legends, it is so childish that it would be hardly worth while to allude to it, but it contains an earlier oriental element, which may be considered as throwing some light on the old form of worship.

The legend relates that when Adam was on his death-bed, he sent Seth to try and regain admission to Paradise. This, of course, was impossible, but he was allowed by the angel who guarded it to look in at the gate. He saw, among other things, the tree which bad borne the fatal fruit, its roots then extending to hell, but its upper branches reaching to heaven. The angel gave him three seeds, recommending him to place them in Adam's mouth, when he died. He did so, and they produced three trees, a cedar, a cypress, and a pine. These afterwards united into one, and their branches performed many miracles. Solomon cut down the tree, and tried in vain to use its trunk to support the roof of his palace. It disdained such a use, and was consequently thrown across the Brook Cedron to be trodden upon. It was rescued from this ignominy by the Queen of Sheba, and buried below the Pool of Bethesda, which owed its healing properties to its virtues. It came to the surface when wanted for the Cross, and afterwards was buried in Calvary, where it was recognized by the Empress Helena in consequence of its miraculous healing powers. It was taken to Persia by Chosroes, and recovered by Heraclius, and afterwards, as is well known, throughout the middle ages a piece of the wood of the True Cross was prized by emperors and kings beyond all other earthly possessions. So great, indeed, was the demand that it was endowed with the property of self-multiplication, but even this did not suffice to bring it into contempt, and as late as 1248 Philip Augustus erected the Sainte Chapelle to enshrine a morsel of the wood of the tree of Paradise. The Sainte Chapelle may thus be considered as the last, as it probably is among the most beautiful, temples ever erected to Tree Worship.

All this is so silly that the only excuse for alluding to it is, that throughout the earlier past there runs a thread of oriental myth different from the clumsy inventions of ordinary mediæval miracle mongers, and this, if properly investigated, might perhaps throw some light on the feelings with which sacred trees were regarded in ancient times, and tell us something of the causes which led to their being so universally worshipped.[1]

[1] The following authorities for the legend are quoted by S. Baring Gould, in his "Myths of the Middle Ages," from which the above is abridged; Vita Christi, Troyes, 1517; Legenda Aurea de Jacques de Voragine; Geschiedenis van het Heylighe Cruys; Speculum Historiale, by Gottfried von Viterbo, &c.

Phœnicia.

In addition to the Tyrian coins and other monuments which in themselves would suffice to prove the prevalence of Serpent Worship on the seaboard of Syria, we have a direct testimony in a quotation from Sanchoniathon, an author who is supposed to have lived before the Trojan war.* This passage is in itself so curious as throwing light on the feelings of the ancients on this subject, that it may be worth while to quote it nearly entire. "Taautus attributed a certain divine nature to dragons and "serpents, an opinion which was afterwards adopted both by the Phœnicians and "Egyptians. He teaches that this genus of animals abounds in force and spirit more "than any other reptiles; that there is something fiery in their nature; and though "possessing neither feet nor any external members for motion common to other "animals, they are yet more rapid in their motion than any others. Not only has "it the power of renewing its youth, but in doing so receives an increase of size and "strength, so that after having run through a certain term of years it is again "absorbed within itself. For these reasons this class of animals were admitted into "temples, and used in sacred mysteries. By the Phœnicians they were called the good "dæmon, which was the term also applied by the Egyptians to Cneph, who added to "him the head of a hawk to symbolize the vivacity of that bird."

After this, Eusebius or Philo go on to quote several other authors to the same effect, among others the Magian Zoroaster, who describes the hawk-headed deity as "the chief, the best, and most learned of the gods"; but from the context it appears that there is here some confusion between the Serpent god and the eagle-headed deity of the Assyrians, who is generally supposed to represent Nisroch,† and whose image so frequently occurs in the Sculptures. It scarcely admits of a doubt but that this eagle-headed deity of the Assyrians became the Garuḍa of the Hindu mythology, who, before the time when Eusebius wrote, had taken so important a position in the Serpent Worship of the Hindus, as we shall afterwards see, but it is still not clear how the confusion between the two objects crept into the passage as we now find it. Eusebius certainly understood the quotation as applying to the serpent, but the ascription to the serpent of these qualities cannot, I fear, be relied upon. It suffices to show, however, what importance the Christian writers of the fourth century were inclined to attribute to the Serpent Worship of the Gentiles.

The coins of Tyre represent in some instances a tree with a serpent coiled round its trunk, and on either hand two rude stone pillars (Petræ Ambrosiæ?) or an altar with two serpents rising from the angles of its base. Others represent the serpent coiled around a rude stone obelisk, with the Tyrian Hercules contending with a serpent.‡

Taken in conjunction with the above quotation, these, with others that might be quoted, suffice to show that the serpent was honoured, perhaps worshipped, in Tyre from an early period down to the time of Alexander. More, probably, might be found if looked for, but they are not necessary for our present purpose.

---

* Eusebius, Præ. Evan. I. 9. (p. 66, Gaisford). See also Müller's Fragmenta, III. 572.

† Layard, Nineveh and its remains, abridged edition, p. 46.

‡ Maurice, vol. VI. pl. 5. p. 273.

Mesopotamia.

As hinted above, the Garden of Eden was supposed to have been situated somewhere on the Lower Euphrates, and the story of the earlier patriarchs down to Noah (Xisuthrus) being common to the narratives of Berosus and Moses, we naturally turn to Babylonia in the hope of being able to point out the mythical relations of that strange faith which is first mentioned as existing in that country. Unfortunately, long before the Greeks or any foreign travellers visited Babylonia, the great wave of the dominion of the Semitic Assyrian had passed over it, and nearly obliterated all traces of the earlier Chaldean forms, and as strangers ignorant of the language, it is hardly to be expected that they would have dug up the fossil remains of an extinct religion. The earliest native historian (Berosus) lived after the time of Alexander (B.C. 270 ?), so that he too was likely to pass over what had been so long forgotten. The one chance that now remains to us for recovering it is from the cuneiform inscriptions. Serpent Worship, so far as I know, has not yet been looked for among them, and till they are examined with special reference to the inquiry, it is impossible to say where it may or may not be found. In the meanwhile, Sir Henry Rawlinson informs us, that Hea, or Hoa, the third person in the Babylonian trinity of great gods, may be considered as the serpent deity, "since there are very strong "grounds for connecting him with the serpent of Scripture, and the paradisaical "traditions of the tree of knowledge and the tree of life."*

The only direct testimony we have of Serpent Worship in Babylon is in that part of the Book of Daniel which is now printed separately in the Apocrypha,† though it is difficult to understand why this should be so. The story told there of the fraud of the priests and the indignation of the people at the destruction of their god all bear so strong an impress of probability that it is difficult to doubt their truth.

The story as it stands, except in its catastrophe, is not unlike one related by Ælian,‡ as occurring in Egypt, in the days of Ptolemy Euergetes. The description of the serpents of Metele is nearly identical with this of Babylon, but there the only result was that the prying priest went mad, and for all we know the serpent continued to receive his daily dole for long afterwards.

Herodotus, strange to say, deserts us in this difficulty, and the only indication in Diodorus is in his description of the three statues that adorned the great Temple of Belus; that of Rhea being accompanied by two very large silver images of serpents, each weighing 30 talents; and that of Juno, standing with her right hand resting on a serpent's head.§

No mention of Tree Worship has, so far as known, been brought to light in Babylonia, but in Assyria it is among the most common forms of idolatrous veneration. The representations of this on Lord Aberdeen's black stone has already been alluded to, and it occurs at least twenty times as a principal object in Layard's plates, and very frequently also in Botta.‖

---

* Herodotus translated, &c., by Geo. Rawlinson, vol. I., p. 600.

† Story of Bel and the Dragon, v. 23, et seq.

‡ Ælian, de Animal. XVI. 39.

§ Diodorus, II. 9. 5.

‖ Monument de Ninive, 5 vols. folio. Paris, 1846–50.

It can hardly be doubted but that this is the Asherah or Grove so frequently mentioned in the Bible, and is a true form of Tree Worship; but no thorough investigation has yet been made by any one competent to the task, in order to ascertain how and where it arose, or what the exact ideas were which it represented. Judging *à priori*, I would feel inclined to suggest that the Serpent Worship was a peculiarity of the Turanian Babylonians of the old Chaldean Empire—Tree Worship that of the Semitic Assyrians; but a great deal has yet to be done before this can be either positively affirmed or rejected, and the reasons for even suggesting it will be more easily understood when our present task is further advanced.

Greece.

In attempting to explain the phenomena presented by the architectural history of Greece, it seems necessary, as a basis for any reasoning on the subject, to assume the existence in that country of two distinct and antagonistic races at one period of the story. The one race is represented by the tombs, or so-called treasuries, of Mycenæ and Orchomenos, and the megalithic polygonal masonry of the walls of the most ancient cities. To the other belongs the chaste intellectual refinement of the Doric order, while between the two intervenes the elegant and ornate Ionic as a compromise combining the peculiarities of each.

The first class of buildings have been ascribed to the Pelasgi; and though considerable difference of opinion exists as to the exact ethnological position of those people, and whence they came, there seems no valid objection to assuming that they were a people of a race entirely different to the Hellenes, who afterwards superseded them. If not of purely Turanian race, they must have been so closely allied to that family that, till the contrary is shown, they may be considered as belonging to it.

The same distinction seems indispensable in treating of the mythology of ancient Greece. Assuming the Veda and the Zend Avesta to be exponents of the religious feelings of the Aryans, it is impossible to understand—if language is any test in such a matter—how a people speaking a tongue so purely Aryan as the Greek, could so completely have relapsed into a Turanian ancestral worship as we find that of Greece in its great age. Unless a great substratum of the inhabitants of Greece belonged to the Turanian family, their religion, like their language, ought to have presented a much closer affinity to the earlier scriptures of the Aryan race than we find to be the case. The curious anthropic mythology of the Grecian Pantheon seems only explicable on the assumption of a potential Turanian element in the population, though the study of the language fails to reveal to us its existence.

Such an hypothesis is still more indispensable when we refer to the Tree and Serpent Worship that certainly prevailed to a greater or less extent during the whole period of Grecian history, though of course more prominently during the earlier part. Here again it is necessary to make a further distinction. All the earlier myths refer to the destruction of serpents or of serpent races. This continues down to the return of the Heraclidæ; after that time, when Hellenic supremacy was assured, we meet with a kindlier feeling. The serpent then became the oracle—the guardian of the city, or the healing god,—the Agathodæmon in short. In Greece, as everywhere else, when a new faith once feels secure in its position, it no longer objects to the forms which it superseded, and these by degrees crop up again, and eventually become part at least of the outward faith of people whose real sentiments may, nevertheless, be most diametrically opposed to such superstition.

One of the oldest and most celebrated myths of Greece relates the destruction of the dragon* Python by Apollo, and his taking possession of the oracle which the serpent guarded.† Cadmus fought and killed the dragon that devoured his men, and sowing its teeth raised soldiers for his own purposes. In Indian language, he killed the Naga Raja of Thebes, and made sepoys of his subjects. The tradition of the close of the career of Cadmus and his wife is even more suggestive of Serpent Worship than the events of their life. Their conversion into serpents as a cure for ills that had become unbearable, and the respect with which it is represented they were afterwards regarded, point to a form of faith that must have been at that time familiar to the inhabitants of Greece.‡

The Argonautic Expedition was undertaken to recover a fleece that hung on a sacred tree, guarded by a dragon that Jason and his companions would have been unable to cope with, unless they had been aided by the enchantments of Medea. But the great destroyer of serpents in those days was Hercules. Most appropriately was he represented as strangling two serpents sent by Juno to destroy him while he was yet in his cradle. His adventures in the Garden of the Hesperides is the pagan form of the myth that most resembles the precious serpent-guarded fruit of the Garden of Eden, though the moral of the fable is so widely different. His fight with the many-headed Lernean Hydra, on the other hand, suggests the origin in the West of many-headed serpents with which we are becoming so familiar in the East. In the earlier representations, apparently, he had only seven heads, but afterwards, as was also the case in India, they were indefinitely multiplied. A still earlier, perhaps the earliest, mention of this mythological animal is in Homer, who speaks of a three-headed snake as adorning the baldrick of the buckler of Agamemnon.§ As a Grecian peculiarity, this many-headedness might be passed over, but it is interesting as bearing on the subject we have specially in hand.

Though generally represented as the destroyer of Serpents, Hercules, on the other hand, is said to have been the progenitor of the whole race of Serpent-worshipping Scythians, through his intercourse with the Serpent Echidna.|| There is nothing, however, inconsistent in this. The age in which he is said to have lived was one of transition between two civilizations. An old Turanian Serpent-worshipping race were, in Greece, passing away, to make place for one of Aryan form. Hercules was the popular embodiment of all the favourite myths of the age; and to him consequently was ascribed the destruction of the old faith wherever it was destroyed, as well as its perpetuation wherever it was known to have been preserved.

---

* There seems to be no real or scientific difference in Greek between the word Δράκων and Ὄφις. Generally, however, Draco is applied to the larger, and serpent to the smaller kinds of snakes. Draco would hardly be applied to an asp or cobra; nor Ophis to one of the great guardian serpents so frequently alluded to. I can hardly admit, however, the popular definition :—Anguis aquarum, Serpens terrarum, Draco templorum.

† Python terræ filius draco ingens. Hic ante Apollinem ex oraculo in Monte Parnasso responsa dare solitus erat.—Hyginus, fab. 140. If we may trust Lucian, de Astrologia, p. 544, at Delphi a virgin delivers the oracle, (hence, the symbol of the constellation Virgo,) and a dragon speaks from under the tripod, because the constellation Draco appears among the stars.

‡ Ovid's Metamorph. III. 1. and IV. 9.

§ Iliad, XI. 38.

|| Herodotus, IV. 9.

After the return of the Heraclidæ, serpents—as hinted above—seem to have been kept at Delphi and in the caves of Trophonius;* in both instances, apparently, for oracular purposes. But the great centre of Serpent Worship was Epidaurus, where stood the famous temple of Æsculapius and the grove attached to it, in which serpents were kept and fed down to the time of Pausanias. Some of these, according to him, were of great size, measuring, he says, 30 cubits in length.† It is not, however, clear whence the myth of Æsculapius came, and when it was introduced into Greece. There was a temple dedicated to this god in Alexandria,‡ in which a huge serpent was kept; but this worship is as likely to have been taken there by the Greeks as brought thence, though the name and many features may be thought to betray an Egyptian origin.

Perhaps the most remarkable event connected with the Epidaurian serpent was the embassy sent from Rome in the year 462 A.U.C. under Quintus Ogulinus. The description of the advent of the divine serpent is one of the most animated passages in Ovid's Metamorphoses,§ and which, so far as the main facts go, is confirmed by Livy,‖ Valerius Maximus,¶ and Aurelius Victor.** That such an embassy was sent, and brought back a serpent, seems undoubted, as also that it was received with divine honours by the populace of Rome, and it may also be admitted that the plague was stayed after its arrival, but whether in consequence of it or not, is another question. The Romans thought it was, and Serpent Worship was established in Rome from that time forward. On the other hand, we learn from Pausanias'†† mention of it, that the Æsculapian serpent continued to be venerated in Greece till after the Christian era.

Another, and almost as interesting an example for our present purposes, occurred in Athens. When Minerva contended with Neptune for the city, she created the olive, which became sacred to her, and planted it on the Akropolis and handed over the care of it to the Serpent God Erechthonios. He is sometimes represented like the giants, as only half a serpent, the body of a man, the lower extremities as serpentine. Such, however, was not the usual or popular belief, inasmuch as we learn from Herodotus,‡‡ that when the Persians were approaching Athens the inhabitants, though warned by the oracle, refused to leave their homes till they learned that the great serpent, the guardian of the citadel, had refused its food, and left the place. When their Serpent God had deserted them, there was no longer any hope, and they fled.

There can be no doubt but that the ancient Tree and Serpent Temple stood where the Erechtheum now stands, and, being destroyed by the Persians, was rebuilt afterwards in its present form. The tree, I believe, occupied the Caryatid Portico, the serpent the lower cell adjoining, where also the well of Neptune seems to have been situated. The fane of the goddess occupied the higher level, and was approached by a different entrance.§§ Be all this as it may, the real point is that here we have in

* Pausanias, II. p. 137.
† Loc. cit. 175.
‡ Ælian, de Animal. XVI. 39.
§ Metamorph. XV. 5.
‖ Liv. X. 47.
¶ Val. Max. 1, 8, 2.
** Au. Victor, XXII. 1.
†† Loc. supra cit.
‡‡ Herod. VIII. 41.

§§ I am aware that in this distribution of the parts I differ from Beulé, who excavated this temple, and published the result of his researches. It would be out of place to attempt to give my reasons here, but my objections to his plan are not given without due consideration.

Athens a temple dedicated to Tree and Serpent Worship, and perhaps the only one specially so devoted which is now standing in Greece.

Besides, however, the prominent instances in which the snake figures in Greek mythology as the representative of the gods, or as delivering its oracles, or guarding sacred places or things, its influence occasionally crops up in places where we should least suspect it. Nothing, for example, can well be more curious than the story of Alexander's birth, as told by Plutarch.* That Olympias his mother should have kept tame snakes in the house is scarcely to be wondered at, as Illyria is a country where they abound, and where also their worship was prevalent. It is curious, however, that it should be thought worthy of record that one was found in her bed, and that Philip should have believed in the possibility of the serpent being the real father of Alexander the Great. The same view is taken by Lucian,† who seems to adopt without hesitation the idea that Alexander was born of a serpent. Even Cicero ‡ does not discountenance the story when he tells us that on the occasion of the illness of Ptolemy, one of Alexander's generals, from a poisoned wound, the serpent of Olympias appeared to him in a dream, having a root in his mouth. This Serpent, who, from the context we are led to infer, was the father of Alexander, then pointed out the place where the herb grew, and the wound cured by its application.

It is possible that the story may have arisen from some connexion with the Bacchic mysteries, into which Olympias was initiated, and in which serpents always played a prominent and important part, and we know that Alexander wished to connect his eastern conquest with that of the Indian Bacchus,§ but explain it as we will, the myth is curious as arising in so advanced a stage of Grecian enlightenment.

The traces of Tree Worship in Greece are even fuller and more defined than those of the Serpent *Cultus* just alluded to. In this instance we have fortunately an elaborate treatise on the subject by a thoroughly competent scholar,‖ to which the reader is referred, and the slightest possible notice will consequently suffice for our present purpose.

As each succeeding Buddha in the Indian mythology had a separate and different Bo Tree assigned to him, so each god of the classical Pantheon seems to have had some tree appropriated as his emblem or representative. Among the most familiar are the oak or beech of Jupiter,¶ the laurel of Apollo, the vine of Bacchus. The olive is the well-known tree of Minerva. The myrtle was sacred to Aphrodite. The apple or orange of the Hesperides belonged to Juno. The populus was the tree of Hercules,** and the plane tree was the "numen" of the Atridæ.

Of all these the oldest and most celebrated was the oak, or rather grove at Dodona, originally founded by the Pelasgi,†† it may be some sixteen centuries before the Christian era: it remained an oracle till the time of Constantine.‡‡ It thus certainly survived, even if its foundation did not precede, that of its great rival, the

* Plutarch, Vita Alex. II.

† Lucian, dial. Mort. XIII. 1. Pseudo Kallisthenes, I. 10.

‡ Cicero de Divinat., II. 66.

§ Arrian, V. 2 and 3. Quintus Curtius, VIII. 10. 12.

‖ Bötticher, Baumcultus der Hellenen, 8vo. 1856, p. 554, pl. 63.

¶ Pausanias, I. p. 40, VII. 643.

** Pliny, 12. 2.

†† Strabo, VII. p. 327.

‡‡ Aristides, I. p. 84, II. p. 12. Max. Tyr. 14. 1.

serpent oracle of the neighbouring Temple of Delphi. It was from the branches of this time-honoured tree that the sacred pigeons, combining the rustling of their wings with that of the leaves, made up those sounds which were interpreted as oracles throughout the whole period of Grecian history. It was not, however, only as a shelter for the sacred pigeons, or that the wind might rustle through their leaves and agitate the bells that hung among their branches, that the trees of the Dodonian grove were held to be sacred. Tradition ascribed to them the power of speaking for themselves, and even when cut down, as in the case of the ship Argo, a piece of the sacred oak inserted either in prow or keel, had the power of communicating to these adventurous navigators the will of Jove.*

It is not quite clear whether or not any structural temple, properly so called, ever was erected in the grove at Dodona. None certainly is described by Pausanias or any one else, and on the whole the context seems to bear out the conclusion that the grove was the *ἱερόν*, and that except altars and minor adjuncts it was not profaned by any works of human hands.

The laurel at Delphi was as celebrated as Dodona's oak. It was under its shade that Python the son of Earth sought refuge when wounded by the arrows of Apollo, and where his oracle existed before the Sun god conquered it.† The earliest temple here was constructed of laurel wood, afterwards of bronze, and only in later days of stone, when apparently the oracle and with it the site of the tree was included in the sanctuary.

The story of Daphne need hardly be alluded to.‡ It is so well known, and so is the continual use of the laurel throughout classical antiquity as a sacred emblem of Apollo, as a sign of victory, the indispensable accompaniment of every triumph, and also as a healing power almost as important as the serpent of Æsculapius.§

In the opening cantos of the Iliad there is a scene which may serve as well as any other to illustrate the feelings of the Greeks on this subject.‖ When the host was detained in Aulis, and Agamemnon was sacrificing under the shade of a sacred plane tree, a serpent creeps from under the altar, and, climbing the tree, devours deliberately, one after the other, the eight nestlings of a sparrow. The ninth one was the mother bird herself, thus prophesying the nine years they were to tarry before they conquered the wide-streeted Troy. To authenticate the wonder, the serpent was then metamorphosed by Jupiter into stone, and we learn afterwards, that the tree was considered as sacred, inasmuch as Pausanias saw the wood of it preserved in the Temple of Diana in the second century.¶ That nothing may be wanting to complete this as an illustration of their worship, it was while the Greeks were detained at Aulis that Agamemnon was—like Abraham—constrained to sacrifice his child, but as a goat was accepted for the one, so the Grecian hero was saved from a similar sorrow by the substitution of a deer by the goddess Diana. This looks like a period of transition, when at least the most objectionable features of the old faith were becoming obsolete, and might practically be set aside.

It would be easy to multiply these instances of Tree and Serpent Worship among the Greeks to almost any extent; but enough has probably been adduced to show how

* See Bötticher, Baumcultus, pp. 113, 164.

† Euripides, Iph. in Taur. 1245.

‡ At conjux quoniam mea non potes esse.
Arbor eris certe, dixit, mea.—Ovid, Meta. I. 558.

§ See Bötticher, pp. 338–393.

‖ Pausanias, IX. 748.

¶ Homer, Iliad II. 304, et seq.

important a part it played in the mythology of Greece during the whole period of her independent history. When to this we add the knowledge of the purely anthropic and ancestral character of her popular Pantheon, we cannot but feel how little title Greece has to that purely Aryan rank which her language would seem to assign to her. There must always have been a very large admixture of Turanian blood in the veins of the inhabitants of that country, varying, of course, in extent in the different states, but except, perhaps, in Sparta, nowhere entirely evanescent.

ITALY.

It does not appear, from anything that has yet been brought to light, that the Etruscans were either worshippers of Serpents or of Trees. It is true the evidence is not conclusive, and is at best merely negative. We have none of the scriptures of the people. We cannot read their inscriptions, and such temples and religious edifices as remain are all of late date, contemporary with the advanced Roman civilization, and when consequently they may have been weaned from their earlier superstitions. It may also be observed that Serpent and Tree Worship are exactly those forms which are least likely to leave permanent traces of their existence except through the traditions of the people in some form of writing. When the Tree or Grove is cut down all traces of it are soon obliterated, and natural decay alone is quite sufficient to cause its complete disappearance, and when the Serpent dies there is no longer a god or an image of one in the sanctuary.

These considerations must make us pause before giving any very decided opinion on the subject; for, reasoning *à priori*, the Etruscans were just such a people as one would suspect of being likely to indulge in such a form of faith.

Their *quasi* Turanian origin, their ancestral worship, the importance they attached to sepulchral rites, the very absence of temples of a permanent character, and many other circumstances, would lead us to expect to find this worship among them, but till it is found it is needless to insist on what at best are mere probabilities.

One, however, of the first religious acts of the Romans brings us back to an old line of memories. When Romulus, so says the tradition, had slain Aeron king of Cenina in single combat, he hung the "Spolia Opima" on an ancient oak on the Capitoline Hill, which the shepherds before that time had considered as sacred, and there marked out the boundaries of the Temple of Jupiter, which was the first and became afterwards the most sacred of Roman temples.*

On the other hand, almost the only tradition that seems to give a local and indigenous form to Serpent Worship is that connected with Lanuvium, a place sixteen miles south of Rome. Here we learn from Ælian there existed a large and dark grove, and near it a temple of the Argive Juno. In this place was a vast and deep cave, the abode of a great serpent. To this grove the virgins of Latium were taken annually to ascertain their chastity, which was indicated by the dragon.† If the serpent accepted the offering, not only was their purity considered as established, but a good and fertile season was sure to result from the success of the ordeal.‡ A similar oracle seems to have existed in Epirus, where a circular grove once stood surrounded by

* Livy, I. 10. † Ælian, Var. Hist. IX. 16. ‡ Propertius, Eleg. VIII. 4.

a wall in which the sacred serpents were kept, descended it is said from the great Python of Delphi, and here dedicated to Apollo. On the great festival of the year a virgin priestess entered the grove naked, holding in her hand the sacred food. If they took it readily, a fruitful harvest and a plentiful year were sure to follow. If they refused, it was considered as the gloomiest of auguries.* The one difference between the two oracles being that in the Eastern oracle the serpents were not called upon to decide as to the chastity of the priestess, but merely to prophesy as to the prospects of the year.

Except in the instance of Lanuvium the traces of this primitive religion became infinitely more scarce in Italy than they were found to be in Greece, but whether this arises from their non-existence, or merely because they were not recorded, is by no means clear. As mentioned on a previous page,† the actual worship of the serpent was introduced from Epidaurus to Rome 462 A.U.C., but the fact of such an embassy being sent on this occasion indicates a degree of faith on the part of the people, which could only have arisen from previous familiarity.

In the Augustan age, enlightenment was too far advanced for such a primitive form of faith to have any real hold on the public mind. Indeed, when such a treatise as that of Cicero De Natura Deorum became popular many much more advanced beliefs than that in serpents were trembling in the balance, but the poets still delighted in referring to those forms which time and mystery had long rendered venerable. Ovid's Metamorphoses are full of passages referring to the important part which the Serpent performed in all the traditions of Classic Mythology.

Every one is familiar with the circumstances of the two snakes sent by Minerva to destroy Laocoon ‡ for his attempt to undeceive the fated Trojans. Their task accomplished, they sought refuge behind the shield of Pallas in her temple in the town. Still more characteristic was the appearance of a serpent from the tomb, when Æneas was sacrificing to the manes of his father Anchises,§ and his hesitation as to whether the unexpected apparition should be considered as the *genius loci*, or an attendant on his deceased parent.

In the other poets there are numerous allusions to Serpents and Serpent Worship, which in themselves, taken separately, would not be of much importance, and which consequently it would be tedious to quote, though taken altogether, with the other information we possess, they do indicate a prevalence of reverence for the serpent in Rome greater than might be expected from so enlightened and so freethinking a community. There is one passage, however, in Perseus ‖ which it is impossible to pass over. It is that in which the satirist orders "two serpents to be painted "on the wall to indicate that the place is sacred." The form of this painting we learn from several examples at Pompeii and Herculaneum,¶ where two of somewhat conventional form, and in very conventional attitudes, approach an altar or some object which their presence seems intended to sanctify. There is every reason to suppose that such representations were much more common than the few remains we possess might at first sight lead us to suppose, and that the serpents were also

* Ælian, de Animal. XI. 2.

† *Vide ante*, p. 14.

‡ Virgil, Æneid, II. 200 and 227.

§ Ibid., V. 84, et seq.

‖ Pinge duos angues:
Pueri, sacer est locus.—Sat. I. 112.

¶ Antichità d'Ercolano, IV., p. 65. pl. xii.; Mazois, II. pl. 24, &c.

frequently represented as the *genii loci*,* and as mixed up with Mithraic or Tree Worship. The instances in which this occurs are so numerous that if collected together they would appear at first sight to make out a strong case, but notwithstanding all this the inhabitants of Imperial Rome cannot fairly be said to have been either a Tree or Serpent worshipping race. It is curious to observe, however, how some of the great men among the Romans still cherished the remnants of this superstition. Scipio Africanus † is reported to have believed that he had been nursed by a serpent, and Augustus allowed it to be understood that his mother Atia had received him from a serpent, remembering probably the story of Olympias, the mother of Alexander the Great.‡ The people of Rome, it is said, on one occasion showed more sympathy with the young Domitius (afterwards Nero) than with his half-brother Britannicus, because "serpents had once watched over his childhood."§

The Emperor Tiberius‖ kept a tame serpent for his amusement, but when he found it one morning eaten by ants he drew the augury that he must henceforward guard himself against an attack from the many-headed multitude. Hadrian, it is said, procured a large serpent from India, which he placed in the Temple of Jupiter Olympius at Athens,¶ which he had just rebuilt.

It is a difficult question to determine how far the representation of serpents on coins may be taken as indicating the existence of Serpent Worship in the cities to which they belong, or to what extent they should be considered as merely heraldic, like other animals or plants which were emblematic of other cities. If they might be enlisted, the coins of Tyre** would go far to confirm what we gather from other sources (*ante*, p. 10) of the prevalence of Serpent Worship there. The most remarkable series, however, of coins of this class are those known as Cistophoroi, belonging to certain cities of Asia Minor. On the obverse of these there is generally in the centre a bow case supported by two serpents standing erect, the one apparently male, the other female, and accompanied by emblems, the meaning of which is not easily determined. On the reverse they generally have a cista mistica, half open, and from it a serpent is issuing (Woodcut No. 1). Around this there is a wreath of vine leaves and grapes, indicating clearly a connexion with the Bacchic mysteries, in which such a cist was employed, and in which serpents always performed an important part.

No. 2.

ROMAN PROCONSULAR COIN OF TRALLES.

All these serpent coins belong to the Roman period, the earliest apparently being struck during the pro-consulship of Q. Tullius Cicero (brother of the orator) B.C. 91, and after being the coinage of Asia Minor for more than a century they fade into the imperial coinage of the Empire.†† Those which have been found up to the present time belong to the following ten cities (Pinder says eleven, but Parium is doubtful),

* Antichità d'Ercolano, vol. I. pl. xxxix.

† Gellius, Noct. Att. VI. 1.

‡ Suetonius in Aug. c. 94.

§ Tacitus, XI. 11.

‖ Suetonius, Vit. Tib. 72.

¶ Xiphilin, Rom. Hist. Script. III. 358.

** Maurice, Indian Ant. VI. p. 273.

†† The best account, so far as I know, of these coins is in a paper by M. Pinder, in the Transactions of the Akad. der Wissenschaften. Berlin, 1855. As what is said in the text is mainly based on this, it will not be necessary to refer to it again.

Pergamos, Thyatira, Smyrna, Ephesus, Sardes, Laodicea, Adramyttium, Tralles,* Apamea, and Nysa. As will be observed, this list comprises all the Seven Churches of Asia, with the exception of Philadelphia, and it is by no means clear that it, too, may not be eventually included. Is this coincidence accidental? If not absolutely, it certainly is nearly correct to assert, that no people adopted Buddhism except those among whom Serpent Worship can certainly be traced as pre-existing, and it appears probable that the worshippers of the serpent should in like manner be more open to the influence of Christianity than the refined and sceptical Greek or Roman.

This is not the place to attempt the investigation of such a subject, even if the materials existed for the purpose, but I may state, that my impression is, that these coins and other evidence† do prove the existence of a form of Serpent Worship in the cities of Asia Minor till after the Christian era. And, if I am not mistaken, the presence of such a form of faith may have influenced the early spread of Christianity in these cities to an extent not hitherto suspected.

Germany.

We look in vain through the classical authors for any trace of Serpent Worship among the Germans, nor indeed ought we to expect to find any among a people so essentially Aryan as they are, and always were; while, on the other hand, we have not in Germany, as we find in Greece, any traces of that underlying race of less intellectual Turanians who seem everywhere to have been the Serpent worshippers all the world over.

By whatever name they may have been known, these Ophite races seem, in Europe at least, never to have penetrated far inland from the shore of the sea. The deeply-indented coasts of Greece thus presented a singularly favourable locality for their settlement. They swarmed up the rivers of France, and the shores of such an inland sea as the Baltic was also well suited to their habits. They were adepts at draining lakes or embanking the estuaries of the rivers on which they settled. Fish seems to have been their principal food, and fishing consequently their chief occupation. What domestic animals they possessed they pastured on the alluvial plains which were kept clear of forests and fertilized by the floods. Such a people were, however, utterly incompetent to deal with the forests that covered the soil of Germany, and incapable of that steady organization of labour without which success in agriculture is impossible; especially under so rigorous a climate, and conditions so unfavourable as those which the surface of Germany must have presented to the earliest settlers there.

If, however, we find no traces of Serpent Worship among the purely Teutonic races, the evidences of Tree Worship are numerous and complete. Tacitus, in his Germania, alludes to it frequently. In one place he distinctly states that the Germans have no images, and decline to enclose their gods within walls, but consecrate groves and woods, within which they call on the name of God.‡ They called together the people of their own race in woods sanctified by the auguries of their forefathers or pristine awe,§

* Those of Tralles have also the Indian humped bull on the obverse (pl. 1, figs. 18 and 20), though what this may mean it is impossible at present to say.

† Herodotus, I. 78.

‡ Tacitus, Germ. 9.

§ Prisca formidine, Loc. cit. 39.

and sacred groves and trees are mentioned by name both by him and Cæsar.* The most frequent mention, however, of the sacred groves and trees of the Germans is to be found in the earlier Christian writers, who, when narrating the events that accompanied the conversion of the nation to Christianity, relate how these were cut down and destroyed, in order that the old superstitions might be eradicated. These have been collected and arranged by Grimm † with his usual industry and intelligence, so that it is hardly necessary here to go over the same ground again. The conclusion he arrives at (p. 60) is that "individual gods might have dwelt on hill-tops, or in "caves, or rivers, but the festal universal religion of the people had its abode in "*woods*, and nowhere has another temple yet been found."

The first care of the Christian missionaries, wherever they went, was to cut down the groves of the Pagans, and to desecrate their ancient places of worship, or to speak more correctly, to consecrate them by the erection of a chapel or church within their sacred precincts. They soon discovered that by the first course they only excited the wrath and enmity of the natives, by the latter they conciliated them, and drew them insensibly towards the purer faith; but they fail to tell us how long these quasi converts persisted in venerating in their hearts the god-like grove rather than the miserable stone and mortar house in which the priests told them their new god alone consented to dwell.

It would be well worth while, if anyone would take the trouble, to trace how long trees and groves continued to be objects of veneration after the Germans were converted to Christianity. One of the last and best known examples is that of the "Stock am Eisen" in Vienna, the sacred tree into which every apprentice, before setting out on his "Wanderjahre," drove a nail for luck. It now stands in the centre of that great capital, the last remaining vestige of the sacred grove round which the city has grown up, and in sight of the proud cathedral of the Christian, which has superseded and replaced its more venerable shade.‡

Sarmatia.

If a line were drawn from the shores of the Caspian Sea north of the Caucasus to the mouth of the Vistula or Dwina in the Baltic, it would be coincident with one of the oldest routes of communication between the east and the west, and one that probably was the road by which Serpent and Tree Worship were introduced into the north of Europe. It was the route by which Woden is said to have migrated westward in the first century before Christ, taking with him all that strange mythology which is connected with his name. It was on this route that Hercules met the serpent-maiden Echidna, and where she gave birth to the Eponymous hero of the Scythian nation.§ Here, too, resided the Amazons, the female warriors, whose institutions seem so mysteriously connected with Serpent Worship. At the far end of this route Procopius tells

---

* Loc. cit. 40. 43. Cæsar, Ann. 2. 12; 4. 73.

"The Khonds use neither temples nor images in their worship. They cannot comprehend, and regard as absurd the idea of building a house in honour of the deity, or the expectation that he will be peculiarly present in any place resembling a human habitation. Groves kept sacred from the axe, hoar rocks and hill tops, fountains and the banks of streams, are in their eyes the fittest places for worship."—Major Charteris MacPherson, Journal Royal Asiatic Society, vol. XIII. p. 235.

† Deutsche Mythologie, c. IV. pp. 57 to 77.

‡ The festival of the Christmas tree at the present day, so common throughout the whole of Germany, is almost undoubtedly a remnant of the Tree Worship of their ancestors.

§ Herodotus, IV. 9.

us that "in his day the barbarians worshipped forests and groves, and in their barbarous "simplicity placed trees among their gods."*

In Sarmatia, according to Erasmus Stella, "for some time they had no sacred rites; "at length they arrived at such a pitch of wickedness that they worshipped serpents "and trees." The Samogitæ, we are told, worshipped the serpent as a god, and if any adversity befell them, concluded that their domestic serpents had been negligently served. In Lithuania the people "believed vipers and serpents to be gods, and worshipped them with great veneration." Jerome of Prague, in the fifteenth century, according to Silvius, saw these wretched idolaters offer sacrifices to serpents. Every householder had a snake in the corner of his house, to which he gave food and offered sacrifice. Cromer † charges the Prussians with the same idolatry, and Masius ‡ mentions a royal town near Wilna where in his day (*adhuc*) serpents were worshipped by many of the inhabitants, and in Livonia it is characteristically added that the inhabitants were accustomed to sacrifice their most beautiful captives to their serpent gods. §

None of these indications are worth much in themselves, and the authorities on which they rest are not such as will bear the test of critical examination, but the general impression they leave is, that Serpent Worship must have prevailed in Eastern Europe to a great extent during the middle ages. It seems incredible that the authors named, and especially such a work as that of Olaus Magnus, should be so full of anecdotes of serpents and Serpent Worship in a country where nothing larger than a viper or adder naturally is found, if there were not some foundation for their belief.

Olaus Magnus,‖ quoting from Crantzius and Mechavita, states that the Poles worshipped their gods, Fire, Serpents, and Trees, in woods. This state of things, he says, lasted in Poland down to the year 1386, when the prince and his brethren were converted to Christianity; but he adds, that though nearly extinguished, these superstitions still linger (1555) in remote parts of Norway and Wermelandia. In addition to this, however, we have evidence which it seems impossible to doubt, that both Trees and Serpents were worshipped by the peasantry in Esthonia and Finland within the limits of the present century (see Appendix A), and even then with all the characteristics possessed by the old faith when we first become acquainted with it.¶

Scandinavia.

Among the problems that perplex the investigator of northern antiquities there are few that present so many difficulties as those which concern the advent of Woden, and the origin of the religion of which he was the chief. At the first glance he appears to have many affinities with the Buddha of the east. The name (Boden) is not dissimilar, the name of the fourth day of the week being Wodensday in the north, Budhhár in the east, and dies Mercurii in Latin, and the confusion that existed in the mind of the Romans between Mercury as the chief god of the Germans, and this Woden, shadow out a thread of tradition which might point to a solution. Woden,

* De Bello Gotico, II. 471, Bonn, 1833. † De Rebus Polon. III. 43. ‡ De Diis German. c. 29.

§ This paragraph is abridged from Deane's Serpent Worship, p. 245, et seq. I have not been able to verify the references.

‖ Lib. III. ch. 1.

¶ Der Ehsten abergläubische gebraüche, &c., von J. W. Boecler, beleuchtet von F. R. Kreutzwald. St. Petersburg, 1854.

too, came from the east just at the time when we know that active missionaries were spreading the doctrines of Buddhism on all sides external to the central kingdom of India, within whose limits it had been previously confined. There certainly also was at that time an amount of Buddhism current among the western nations whose presence it is difficult to account for except on the assumption of some such migration. The more closely, however, the question is examined the less hope does there appear to be that a solution may be reached in this direction.

There are not, perhaps, in the whole world two religions so diametrically and so essentially opposed to one another as Buddhism and Wodenism, nor two persons so different as the gentle Śákya Muni, who left a kingdom, family, and friends to devote fifty years of his blameless life to the attempt to alleviate the sufferings of mankind, and Odin, "the terrible and severe God, the Father of slaughter: he who giveth "victory and reviveth courage in the conflict: who nameth those that are to be "slain."*

The leading doctrinal characteristic of Buddhism in its early form is its atheism; the Scandinavian, on the other hand, had Woden, Thor, Freya, and a host of minor gods, rulers of men during their lifetime, and continuing the active personal interference with the affairs of men after their elevation. Among the practical characteristics of Buddhism there was, first, the remarkable extension of the Jewish Commandment, "Thou shalt do no murder" into "Thou shalt not kill," including in the prohibition everything that had life; while the greatest glory of the northern hero was the number of his enemies he had slain, and nothing escaped from his joyous bloodthirstiness. Another peculiarity of Buddhism was the negation of all worldly pleasures and enjoyments. It is hardly possible to conceive anything more incongruous than would have been the presence among the roistering mead-drinking warriors of the north, of a yellow-robed ascetic, sworn to celibacy, living on alms, and devoting his life to pious contemplation; his one hope and highest aspiration being, that after infinite transmigrations he might be so purified by suffering that he might eventually obtain absolute rest by annihilation and absorption into the original essence of all things. How different this from the northern Walhalla. "The heroes," says the Edda,† "who are received into the palace of "Odin have every day the pleasure of arming themselves, of passing in review, "of ranging themselves in order of battle, and of cutting one another to pieces; "but so soon as the time of repast approaches they return on horseback all safe "and sound to the hall of Odin, and fall to eating and drinking. Though the "number of them cannot be counted, the flesh of the boar, Sæhrimnir,‡ is sufficient "for them all; every day it is served up at table, and every day renewed entire. "Their beverage is ale and mead. One single goat, whose milk is mead, furnishes "enough of that liquor to intoxicate all the heroes. Odin alone drinks wine; "wine is for him both meat and drink. A crowd of virgins wait on the heroes "at table, and fill their cups as fast as they empty them."

This, certainly, is not Buddhism, at least as that religion is known to us by anything that has hitherto been published on the subject. How far the revelations

* Mallet, Northern Antiq. (Bohn's edition), p. 21.

† Mallet, Northern Antiq., p. 104.

‡ Mallet, Prose Edda, 429.

of the sculptures of the Sanchi Tope may induce us to change our opinions of the earlier form of that faith remains to be seen. There is, certainly, a much greater similarity between the Buddhism of the Topes and the Scandinavian mythology than between it and the Buddhism of the books; but still the gulf between the two is immense, and if any traces of the doctrines of the gentle ascetic ever existed in the bosoms of Odin or his followers, while dwelling near the roots of the Caucasus, all that can be said is, that they suffered fearful shipwreck among the rocks of the savage superstitions of the north, and sank, never again to appear on the surface of Scandinavian mythology. If the two religions came anywhere in contact it is at their base, for underlying both there existed a strange substratum of Tree and Serpent Worship; on this the two structures seem to have been raised, though they afterwards diverged into forms so strangely dissimilar.

As will be seen in a subsequent part of this work, recent discoveries have narrowed, to a certain extent, the gulf which separated them at the time of their greatest development, and it is by no means impossible that if we are able to go further back they may be found to approximate still more closely. We do not yet, however, see much prospect of reaching a point where the two may come in contact, except at the point where they both start from their foundations; but the inquiry is too new, and the facts yet gathered are far from being sufficient to enable us to speak with anything like certainty, except regarding the later forms of either of these faiths.

The myth of the Yggdrasil ash is told in considerable detail in the Prose Edda, though its meaning will hardly be understood till we are more familiar with the corresponding features in Indian mythology.

" It was under the ash, the chiefest and holiest seat of the gods, that they " assembled every day in council. The branches spread over the whole world, and " even reach to heaven above. It has three roots, one stood over Mimir's well, in " which wisdom and wit lie hidden; and one over Niflheim, a place where those " wicked people are sent who die from natural causes, and this root it is, that is " continually gnawed by the serpent Nidhögg, with whom in Hwergelmir there are so " many snakes that no tongue can recount them.* The third root of the ash is in " heaven, under it is the holy Urdar-fount; it is here the gods sit in judgment. Near " this sit the three Norns or fates, who fix the lifetime of all men. In its branches " sits an eagle who knows many things, and a squirrel, Ratatösk, runs up and down, " and seeks to cause strife between the Eagle and Nidhögg. Four harts run across " the branches of the tree and bite the buds." In addition to this is the great Midgard serpent Jörmungand, " who being of parentage of bad augury, was thrown " by All-Father (Odin) into the ocean, but the monster grew to such an enormous " size, that holding his tail in his mouth, he encircles the whole earth."†

Without continuing these quotations further at present, enough has perhaps been brought forward to show that Yggdrasil is in the first place a reminiscence of the trees

* Pliny refers to the connexion of the serpent with the ash, but in a different sense (XVI. 13). He says snakes will not rest in its shadow, but shun it at a distance, and adds, from " personal experience," that, " if a " serpent is so surrounded by a fence of ash leaves that he cannot escape except by passing through fire, he will " prefer the fire rather than pass through the leaves."

† Translation of Prose Edda, 410 et seq.

of fate and knowledge of the Garden of Eden, though wisdom lay in a well of water at the root of the northern tree, of which Odin drank and gained knowledge,* instead of eating its fruit, which, with an ash, was not a probable form of the myth. It is also probably enough to enable us to recognize in the eagle, the Garuḍa, and in the Nidhögg, the Nagas of eastern fable, though the squirrel does not there appear to have been necessary to keep alive the enmity that always existed between them. And in Ṭhor fishing for the Midgard serpent, and the part he is to play at the end of all things, we may without difficulty recognize a reflex of the churning of the ocean and the renewal of all things by Vishṇu through the instrumentality of the great serpent. As might be expected from the nature of the country and style of its historians, we have fewer accounts of the actual form of the worship than of its doctrinal importance. Still we are told† that in front of the great Temple at Upsala "there grew a huge tree of unknown kind, that spread with large boughs, and was "green both summer and winter," and near the same temple a sacred grove, every tree and every leaf of which was considered the most sacred thing in the world.‡ It was called Odin's Grove, and in it the most solemn sacrifices were performed, especially every ninth year, when nine human victims were sacrificed from among the captives if in time of war, or nine slaves if in time of peace.

The serpent is not mentioned as an actual object of worship in any written history; though no doubt the superstition prevailed with the others down to the time when the whole was abolished in the ninth century on the introduction of Christianity. Yet we are told that in the sixteenth century, "There are house serpents "which are accounted in the northern parts of Sweden as household gods; they are "fed with sheep and cows' milk, and to hurt them is a deadly sin." The same author tells us that "serpents rest deep under the roots of birch trees, the multitude "of them cause heat with their breath, and so keep the leaves green in winter."§ All this is foolish enough, but the thousand and one stories about serpents which crowd the pages of the good Archbishop of Upsala suffice to show that even in his day the superstition had not died out among the common people, and though serpents were no longer worshipped, the time when they were so was not yet forgotten.|| At the same time it seems tolerably clear that such a serpent mythology as existed in Sweden could never have sprung up naturally in so northern a climate, where all the snake tribe are so insignificant. It must have been imported from the East, though we have yet to learn by whom this was done, and at what exact time it was effected.

---

* Page 411.

† Olaus Magnus, III. 5.

‡ Mallet, p. 113.

§ Olaus Magnus, XXI. 47 and 48.

|| Castren, in his Travels in Lapland, gives some very curious details about the feelings of the Lapps with regard to Serpent and Tree Worship at the present day. According to their traditions, Snakes, like men, live in societies, each with a captain and subordinate officers; once a year each community meets in general assembly, and not only has each serpent the right to bring his own grievances forward, but the jurisdiction of the chief extends to men who have slain or offended any of his subjects.—*Reise Erinnerungen aus den Jahren* 1838–44, pp. 66–77. A good deal of information on this subject will be found in a Swedish work by Hylten-Cavallius, entitled Wärend och Wirdarne, p. 142, for the worship of Trees as at present existing, and pp. 329 to 332 for that of Serpents.

France.

We seem to know less of the primitive worship of the early inhabitants of Gaul than of that of almost any other country of Europe. This may arise partly because the Gauls were so far civilized before the classical authors became acquainted with them, that their old beliefs had lost much of their individuality and freshness, while they were not so far advanced or civilized at the time when Christianity blotted out the old religions, as to feel sufficient interest in them to care to record their forms. A good deal also is no doubt due to the fact that the subject has not been carefully investigated by any competent authority since the new school of criticism was introduced. The French antiquarians do not yet seem to have discovered the safe channel between the whirlpools of credulity and the dry sand banks of frigid scepticism.

Nearly all that we know of the religion of the ancient Gauls is gathered from the celebrated passage in Cæsar's Commentaries,* when he pauses from the narrative of his exploits to describe the civil and religious institutions of the people he had conquered. In this account there is absolutely no mention of either Tree or Serpent Worship; on the contrary, he tells us that their principal deity was Mercury, not probably the god known by that name in the Roman Pantheon, but it may be Woden or some such synonym. After him came Apollo, Mars, Jupiter, and Minerva. Rather a strange selection, and stranger classification if we are to accept them as the Roman gods whose names they bear; but most probably they were local deities who, to his apprehension, more closely resembled these gods than any other his readers might be acquainted with.

Cæsar's assertion that the Druids were the priests, and by inference the only priests of the Gauls, is considerably modified by the subsequent testimony of both Strabo† and Diodorus,‡ who divide the priests into three classes, the Bards, the Druids, and the Soothsayers. All these authors agree in describing the principal rite to consist in sacrifices, performed apparently in the open air, and by inference in groves. They also agree in stating that human victims were frequently immolated in what appears to have been considered the most solemn and acceptable of their sacred rites.

Notwithstanding the silence of the principal authorities, we are not without evidence as to Tree Worship having prevailed. Maximus Tyrius,§ for instance, distinctly asserts that the "Celts worship Jupiter, but under the form of a tall oak tree;" and Pliny ‖ describes in detail the veneration of the Druids for the oak, especially the mistletoe, which grew on the oak, the ceremony accompanying its removal being apparently in Pliny's eyes the most important of those connected with the worship. It is, however, more from Christian writers that we acquire a conviction that Tree Worship prevailed extensively among the Celts.

There is, for instance, the famous pear tree, that grew at Auxerre in the fourth century, which was hung with trophies of the chase, and venerated as god by the people to such an extent that its destruction by the Holy Amator was considered

* De Bello Gall. VI. 13, 20.

† Geographica, IV. 275.

‡ Hist. V. 31.

§ Diss. 8. ed. Reiske, I. 142.: Κέλτοι σεβοῦσι μὲν Δία, ἄγαλμα δὲ Διὸς Κελτικὸν ὑψηλὴ δρῦς.

‖ Hist. Nat. XVI. 95.

a triumph, not only worthy to be related at length in the life of Genarius,* but sung in indifferent Latin verse some centuries afterwards by Herricus.† From the Life of St. Amandus‡ we learn that groves and trees (*arbores et ligna pro diis colerent*) were worshipped in the north of France, near Beauvais (Belvacence), and the destruction of the tree, which was dedicated to the devil (*arborem quæ erat dæmoni dedicata*), is recorded as a most meritorious act.

The second Council of Arles§ denounced those who venerated trees, or fountains, or stones, and declared those guilty of sacrilege who neglected to destroy them. That of Tours‖ issued a similar decree, almost in the same words; and even as late as 1262 the Council of Nantes condemned those who worshipped stones in desert and woody places (*locis sylvestribus*). These instances might no doubt be multiplied to almost any extent if anyone would take the trouble to look for them, but, as before mentioned, the French archæologists have hardly turned their attention to the subject.¶

The traces of Serpent Worship in Gaul are so few and so evanescent that, in ordinary circumstances, an author would be justified in asserting that it did not exist among the Celts any more than it did among the Germans, and in passing by the subject altogether. Such a superstructure, however, has been raised on a passage in Pliny** that it is impossible to treat it thus. Among the many marvels and puerilities of his Natural History, there is none more absurd than that of the egg (*anguinum*) produced by the breath of a number of serpents, who meet together for the purpose of producing it, apparently on midsummer eve. It is projected by them into the air, and must be caught in a blanket before it falls, and the fortunate possessor must be on horseback, and gallop off with it; for if the snakes catch him before he crosses running water, a worse fate than Tam o' Shanter's will befall him! This fable is reported on the authority of the Druids, and it is added that this *anguinum* is considered a charm by them. It is, I believe, the only passage in any classical author that connects the Druids with serpents, or by implication would lead us to suspect that some superstition regarding serpents may have existed in Gaul.

If the records of the early provincial Christian councils in France were examined, it is possible that some denunciation of Serpent Worship may be found. If General Penhouët†† is to be trusted, there are frequent traditions of the destruction of serpents by the early Christian missionaries, and these may fairly be construed as meaning Serpent Worshippers, if such passages exist; but till they are abstracted and published, no argument can be based on them.

There is still one argument which has occasionally been hinted at in the previous pages, which may be considered as tending to show that Serpent Worship may have prevailed among the Celts. They certainly indulged in human sacrifices, and where this custom prevails, we generally find Serpent Worship accompanying it. The converse also is generally true. The worshippers of the serpent were those who, so far as we know, were most addicted to the sacrifice of men. If this proposition could be

* Act. Sanctor. Bolland, 31 Julii, p. 203.

† Quoted by Grimm, Deutsche Myth. (2d ed.), p. 69.

‡ Acta Benedict. sec. 2, p. 714.

§ Arles Concil. II. can. 23.

‖ Concil. Tur. II. can. 16.

¶ On Tree Worship in Gaul, see D. Monnier, Traditions Populaires comparées. Paris, 1854. p. 716 ff.

** Hist. Nat. XXIX. 3.

†† The Rev. Bathurst Deane, Worship of the Serpent, p. 283, et seq.

established absolutely, it would be a sufficient proof of the prevalenee of Serpent Worship in Gaul, but the premises are as yet mueh too far from being established to enable us to draw any such definite conclusion from them. They may eventually be brought to do so. At present it must suffice to indicate the form of the argument without attempting to base any theory on so slender a foundation.

Ou the whole, therefore, we are probably justified iu assuming that Tree Worship did exist among the Celts as among the Germans till their conversion to Christianity; but, ou the other hand, there seems to be no sufficient evidence to show that they were worshippers of the serpent, and if the Druids were priests of the Celts, whieh there seems no reason for denying, there is nothing to counect them with that faith, though no doubt they may not only have tolerated but indulged in local superstitions, as many Christians do at the present day.

At the same time reeent researches have brought to light eircumstances whieh would lead us to believe that there existed iu Franee an earlier pre-Celtic race allied to the Esthonians aud Finns. They may have been Serpent Worshippers, but they seem to have beeu obliterated by the Celts in very early pre-Christian times, and their fossil remains have uot yet been examiued to a suffieient extent to enable any positive opinion to be formed on the subjeet.

Great Britain.

If we have reason to eomplain that the French archæologists have not turned sufficient attention to their pre-historic antiquities, the same reproach cannot certainly be applied to those of this eountry. From the days of Aubrey and Stukeley to the present day volume after volume has issued from the press, and the transactious of learned societies are full of papers on the subject. Every barrow has been explored, every antiquity measured and described, and it must be added every etymology has been enlisted, aud every scrap of evidence gathered together and amplified, till a fabric has been raised of such marvellous magnitude that it is startling to find on what slight foundation it rests, and how soon it would topple over if the breath of reason could only be brought to bear upon it. In the meanwhile, however, every upright stone has beeome a Druidical remain, and every circle or line of stones an Ophite temple. There was a time, aecording to our autiquaries, when the Druids ruled absolutely in this land, and when, under their auspices, Serpent Worship was as essentially the religiou of the people as Christianity is now. The belief that this is so has becomo from reiteration so engrained, that modern science will probably have a harder task to extirpate it, thau the Romans had to abolish the real Druids, or the early Christian missionaries had to induce the people to forsake the worship of the serpent in countries where it prevailed in reality.

Fortunately the eontroversy lies in a very narrow compass. There are, I believe, only two very short paragraphs in any classical authors which mention Druids in connexiou with Britain, and not one that mentions Serpent Worship, and no English author prior, at all events, to the 13th eentury alludes to either the one or the other.*

* I make this absolute statement with considerable confidence, not only because no paragraph of the sort has been quoted by any of the advocates of this faith, but because there is a very full and careful index to the "Monumenta Historica Britannica," and the word Druid does not occur in it.

Of the two classical passages, that in Tacitus applies strictly to the Isle of Mona (Anglesea), and will be referred to hereafter. The other is that in Cæsar's Commentaries,* and is so important that it must be quoted at length, and in its own language. After describing the Institution of the Druids in Gaul, he goes on to say: "Disciplina (Druidum) in Britannia reperta, et inde in Galliam translata esse existimatur, et nunc qui diligentius eam rem cognoscere volunt, plerumque illo discendi causa proficiscuntur." Had this slight allusion not slipped from Cæsar's pen, there would have been absolutely no evidence of the existence of Druids in England; and after all it hangs on the value to be assigned to the word "existimatur," it is thought or believed! Neither Cæsar or any other Roman ever said he saw a Druid in this country; they never mention their temples or sacred places, and no one ever assisted at their rites. Still, with this paragraph before us, and with the knowledge that the majority of the inhabitants were Celts, it cannot be denied but that Druids may have existed in England, but even then their connexion with Serpent Worship rests wholly on that very apocryphal passage in Pliny (vide *ante*), in which he asserts that the Druids used the *anguinum* as a charm.

The other paragraph is more to the point.† In the year 61 A.D., Paulinus Suetonius was called away to suppress a revolt in the Island of Mona. He there met the army of the natives on the shore, and saw that the women and Druidesses were rushing about with dishevelled locks, and torches in their hands, urging the men to the contest.‡ When the rebellion was suppressed, the sacred groves in which their human sacrifices had been performed were cut down, and we are led to infer Druidism suppressed. Tacitus then goes on to narrate with infinitely more detail the far more important revolt of Boadicea, but, strange to say, in that great national uprising there is absolutely no mention of Druids, either in his narrative or in that of Dion Cassius.§ No groves were cut down, no rites abolished, when it was suppressed; and if any legitimate inference can be drawn from such silence, no Druids existed in the more civilized parts of England.

From whatever point of view the subject is looked at, it seems almost impossible to avoid the conclusion that there were two races in England,—an older and less civilized people, who,‖ in the time of the Romans, had already been driven by the Celts into the fastnesses of the Welsh hills, and who may have been Serpent Worshippers and sacrificers of human victims, and that the uncritical Romans confounded the two. They seem rather to have dwelt on the picturesqueness of the naked blue-painted savage as a contrast with those races they were familiar with, as a Catlin revels in the manners and virtues of the Red Indian in contrast to the vices and effeminacy of his more civilized oppressor.

Be this as it may, it is principally from Welsh Triads, so-called, and the Welsh bards, that we depend for our knowledge of the Druids and their doings, and Serpent Worship in this country. If we knew when the works of the Welsh bards were

* De Bello Gall. VI. 13.

† Tacitus, Ann. XIV. 29.

‡ If I wanted an illustration of this scene, I do not know where I could find a better than on the walls of the Caves at Ajanta. The original copy of the picture was unfortunately burnt in the fire at the Crystal Palace in 1866; but it is engraved in Mrs. Spier's Life in India, p. 302.

§ Dion Cassius in Xiphilinus' Abridgment, LXII. 1 & 4.

‖ Norris's Cornish Drama, II. 401.

reduced to the form in which we now find them, and if we could depend on the translations we have, some light might no doubt be thrown on our subject.* It is, however, an unfortunate peculiarity of the Celtic mind that when they attempt to elucidate the history of their country from their annals, they adopt a species of logic totally distinct from that followed by the Saxon, so that it becomes impossible to use the information they offer. Still it does not seem reasonable to doubt but that remnants of the Druidical religion, and perhaps also of Serpent Worship, may have lingered in the Welsh hills long after they had disappeared from the plains. Where we do find tradition attaching them to any of the monuments of the plain, it is through Welsh agency and almost within sight of the hills, as at Stanton Drew in Somersetshire,† that the serpent is introduced.

Beyond this, though we do occasionally find traditions of the serpent, they are few and far between, and of uncertain origin; one, for instance, is related by Mathew Paris, of St. Albans.‡ Writing in 1260 (?) he relates that the Saxon Abbot Aldred filled up a great hole which once was the abode of an immense dragon, in a place which was still called the Wurmenhert. This appears to have been surrounded by a circular vallum, which we infer still existed in the 13th century, though no trace of it now remains. The circular enclosure and the crypt may be considered as certain, they so exactly resemble the Irish Raths; but the dragon is, I fear, too far off to be depended upon, though it is one of the most authentic traditions we possess.

If this is so, it may be asked, what is the evidence on which the Druidical origin of such monuments as Stonehenge and Avebury have been assumed? The answer fortunately is simple—absolutely none. It never was pretended that any direct testimony existed, and the negative evidence is perfectly complete. No ancient author, no one, in fact, anterior to the invention of printing, ever refers to any stones or stone temples, circular or in any other form, as connected with the worship of the Druids or the Celts. On the other hand, every tradition that exists, whatever their value may be, points to the Arthurian age as that to which they owe their origin.

If it is further asked, what evidence there is to connect these temples with Serpent Worship, exactly the same answer must be given—not one tittle has yet been adduced. The one direction in which it seems probable some such connexion may be established, is from their similarity to the Indian examples, which it is the object of this volume to describe; but whether these will be sufficient for this purpose can only be decided when the argument is fully elaborated. Meanwhile are we correct in calling them temples at all? The one peculiarity of Celtic worship that seems best established, is the love of trees—their fondness of groves for their sacred rites. Is it probable that they would chose the downs of Wiltshire, especially such a spot as that where Stonehenge stands, for the site of their greatest temple—a spot where no tree ever grew or could grow? That they might erect a tomb or cenotaph among the graves of their forefathers seems probable enough; and if Avebury was a battle

* Skene's translation of the four most ancient Welsh poems, which has just been published, has gone far to set this question at rest. It cannot be said that the word Druid does not occur in them, but if we were not looking for it, it is hardly in such a manner as would attract attention, and the part they play is most insignificant, besides it is by no means clear to what age or authority such references really belong.

† Archæologia, XXV. p. 198.

‡ Vitæ Abbatum, p. 40.

field, that would account for the locality where it is found, but it seems difficult to suggest a reason for their being where they are on any other hypothesis.

This, however, is not the place to examine the evidence on which the age or purposes of these monuments is to be determined. It is, however, impossible to pass over the subject entirely in silence, as reference will occasionally have to be made to them in the following pages; while unfortunately nine people out of ten in this country at the present day believe that Stonehenge and Avebury were built by the Druids; that they were Dracontia or Serpent Temples; and every one can point out the altar stones on which the human victims were sacrificed, and in fact knows all about their religion and rites, and it may be added believes in their primæval antiquity. Till these erroneous impressions are dispelled, the subject we have in hand can hardly be rendered intelligible.

A far more promising field for the investigation of Serpent Worship in Britain occurs in Scotland, on the east coast, north of the Forth. In that country, now known as Pictland, there exists even at the present day a great number of Megalithic monuments, many of which are covered with sculptures of a class totally distinct from those found anywhere else, and which have hitherto baffled the ingenuity of antiquaries. Among them the serpent appears frequently and so prominently that it is impossible to doubt that he was considered as an object of veneration by those who erected those monuments, while on the other hand Serpent Worship could hardly have originated in the north of Scotland, where the snakes are so few and contemptible. Mr. Stuart* enumerates twenty-three representations of the serpent on these stones, thirteen times accompanied by emblems, ten times without them. In some instances, such as the Newton stone, the serpent is evidently the object for which the stone was set up, and he is accompanied by the broken sceptre, which may either be a hieroglyphic for God or King, or may only mean holy or great, or some such adjective, but it certainly implies distinction, if not consecration.

The age of these sculptured stones is known with tolerable certainty, inasmuch as the greater number of them have either the Cross itself or Christian emblems engraved upon them, and these must therefore be subsequent to the age of St. Columba, who arrived in Scotland apparently in 563, and died in 597. Many of those also which have only Pagan emblems are so nearly identical with the Christian stones that they must be about the same age. Some, however, are ruder and simpler, and the series fades back into the plain unsculptured Menhir, of which many exist in the same district. There seems, indeed, to be no essential break either, so far as design or purpose† is concerned, between the rude unchiselled blocks of Carnac and Avebury

---

* Sculptured Stones of Scotland, vol. II. p. lxxiv.

† From his position as Archbishop of Upsala—in one of the last countries in Europe converted to Christianity—and writing in 1555, no one was in a better position to know the truth about these stone monuments than Olaus Magnus, and his testimony is clear and distinct. "Habent hæc saxa in plerisque locis erecta, longitudine x., vel xv., xx., xxx., et amplius, et latitudine iv. vel vi. pedum mirabili situ. Sed mirabiliori ordine ac mirabilissimo charactere ob plurimas rationes collocata sunt. Literato rectoque et longo ordine videlicet pugilorum certamina—quadrato turmas bellantium et spherico familiarum designantia sepulturas. ch. xxix.—Or again, Quos humi recondere placuit honorabiles statuas lapidum excelsorum, prout hodie cernuntur mira compagine immensa saxa, in modum altissimæ latissimæ januæ sursum transversumque viribus gigantum erecta, &c. ch. xxx." There are other passages in the same author bearing directly on the subject, but too long to quote. They, however, all seem to describe so correctly, not only the form, but the uses of such monuments as

and such elaborate Christian obelisks or Swenos stone at Forres, or the group that once surmounted the mound at St. Vigeans.*

We shall probably not err far if we regard these traces of Serpent Worship as indicating the presence in the north-east of Scotland of the head of that column of migration, or of propagandism, which, under the myth of Wodenism, we endeavoured in a previous chapter to trace from the Caucasus to Scandinavia. The Edda seems sufficient to prove that a form of Serpent Worship did certainly prevail in the latter country in the early centuries of the Christian era; and nothing seems more probable or more in accordance with Pictish traditions,† than that it should have passed thence into Scotland, and should have left its traces everywhere between the Orkneys and the Firths.‡ There is no evidence, however, of Serpent Worship, in this form at least, having passed south of the Forth. The traces of it that may exist in England or Ireland—if any—most probably belong to an earlier pre-historic people, and may have been introduced by another and more southern route.

Africa.

We tread on surer ground, when leaving Serpent Worship in its most attenuated form, and in the uncongenial climate of its furthest extension to the north and west, and turn to Africa, where it always was at home, and where it now flourishes in all its pristine vigour. Serpents are, and always must have been, so numerous and important in Africa, that it is there, if not in Mesopotamia, that we should, *à priori*, expect their worship to flourish, and it is by no means impossible that it was so. We know so little, however, of what happened in Africa in ancient times—except in Egypt—that it is difficult to speak with any confidence on the subject, and the institutions of Egypt were so abnormal and so exclusively their own, that we cannot reason from them to any general conclusions. Perhaps when the subject is carefully looked into, more may be ascertained than is now known, but our present purpose is with the worship as it exists at the present day, or did in recent times.

One of the best known examples of modern Serpent Worship exists in Upper Egypt, at a place called Sheikh Haredi, from a tomb of a Mahomedan saint of that name, which exists on the spot. The account given of the place by Norden,§ who visited it in 1738, with a mere change of names, is an exact counterpart of what might have been found in Pausanias or any ancient author describing the grove of Esculapius,

---

Avebury and Stonehenge, that in so far as the testimony of this author is concerned, it may be considered as conclusive. Perhaps I may be allowed to add that though I only became aware of the existence of these passages a few months ago, they are entirely in accordance with the conclusions I had long ago arrived at from an examination of the monuments themselves.

* All these will be found described in Stuart's "Sculptured Stones," above referred to, and also in Colonel Forbes Leslie's "Early Races of Scotland." Edin. 1866.

† Skene's Chronicles of the Picts and Scots, p. xcv. et seq.

‡ There are some traditions in Northumberland, such as that of the Laidley Wurm of Spindleston Heugh; and there was a Wurm hill at Lambton, and at other places in the neighbourhood (Walter White, "Northumberland and the Border, p. 249, et seq.). All this would perfectly accord with the theory that it was the result of a Scandinavian course of immigration which reached these two points on the coast.

§ Travels in the East, ii. 40.

at Epidaurus. When any one was so unwell as to require his services, an ambassadress was sent in the person of a spotless virgin—as at Lanuvium—and if his godship pleased he came out of his cave, hung himself around her neck, and allowed himself to be carried in procession to the sick man's bedside. Here he stayed, as Norden irreverently suggests, a length of time proportionate to the gifts offered to his priests, and then returned alone to his dwelling. Dr. Pococke's episcopal dignity seems to have been so offended by the monstrosity of the superstition, that he abuses the serpent and his attendants, but he confirms in every particular Norden's account. He was told it had been there since the time of Mahomet; that they sacrificed to it sheep and lambs. They added that when a number of women visit him, which they do once a year, he comes out and twines himself about the neck of the most beautiful.*

From Wilkinson† we learn that the worship still continues, but has fallen somewhat into disrepute of late.

It does not seem to be a matter of much doubt but that the Serpent was extensively worshipped in Abyssinia before the introduction of Christianity in the fourth century. All the lists of their kings which have been brought home by Bruce, Rüppell, and others, commence with "the Serpent" and his progeny, though we are not told when he reigned nor where. We are further told that when Ábreha and Átzbeha founded Axum 340 A.D., "that one portion of the people of Ethiopia then worshipped the Serpent, the rest followed the Law of Moses. Abuna Abba Salâmâ then introduced Christianity, and the inhabitants were baptized," &c.‡

It is by no means clear whether the great dragon who is said to have lived at Axum § was a god or merely a serpent, more probably the former, as he was burst asunder by the prayers of nine Christian saints. Be all this as it may, we have the direct testimony of Bruce ‖ that the Shangalla, in that neighbourhood, "worship "various trees, serpents, the moon, planets, and stars in certain positions;" and more instances might no doubt be found if looked for. It is, however, on the west coast that the worship flourishes in all its pristine vigour.

Although no one has resided long enough on the Guinea coast with learning and leisure sufficient to write anything like an exhaustive treatise on the religions of that country, we have what is nearly of equal value for our purposes in a series of narratives of Portuguese, Dutch, French, and English travellers, extending over more than two hundred years. Those anterior to 1746 have been digested by Astley ¶ into a continuous narrative and description; and in 1760 President de Brosses,** of the French Academy, wrote a lucid account of what was then known on the subject, and from that time various travellers have added to our knowledge; but the best and fullest are the narratives of M. Répin,†† a surgeon in the French navy; but

* Pococke in Pinkerton's Voyages, xv. p. 269, et seq.

† Handbook of Egypt, 301.

‡ Dillmann in Zeitschrift der Morgenländischen Gesellschaft, vol. VII. p. 338, et seq.

§ Ludolf. Comment. iii. 284 ?

‖ Travels, ii. 554.

¶ Astley's Collection of Voyages, 4 vols. quarto, London, 1846.

** De Brosses, du Culte des Dieux Fetisches, &c. 12mo. Paris, 1760.

†† Le Tour du Monde, 1863, p. 9, et seq.

we have also that of Capt. Burton and Commodore Wilmot,* who went on an official mission to Dahomey in 1863. The one point on which we desire more information is as to the extent of this form of faith, and as to the ethnological relations of the people who practise it. We are told, for instance, that when the Dahomans invaded Whidah in 1726, they killed the sacred snakes, and otherwise outraged the religious feelings of the Whidans.† Both countries are now united under one rule, and apparently with one religion. Was it otherwise 140 years ago? and can the distinction now be traced? These and such like questions are well worthy of more attention than they have hitherto received, for if we are ever to understand the ancient peculiarities of this faith, it must be by a thorough study of the best living examples.

Hitherto we have been only gathering together, as it were, the fossil remains of an extinct religion, whereas in Africa not only does Serpent Worship flourish at the present day, but it exists in conjunction with all those peculiarities of which only traces can be found elsewhere. Ancestral worship, accompanied by human sacrifices on the most lavish scale, is the leading characteristic of the Dahoman religion, and with it we have the institution of a female warrior class, which we have hitherto only known through the beautiful Amazonian fictions of the Greeks or the legends of the Hindoos, as to the Strî-râjya, but in Dahomey the institution exists to this day in all its hideous savagery.

The three gods worshipped in Whidah, or to speak more correctly, the three classes of gods, are Serpents, Trees, and the Ocean;‡ the same trinity as was established in the Erechtheum, in the Akropolis of Athens, more than three thousand years ago. Of these, the serpent called Danh gbwe, or the earthly serpent, is the first. "It is esteemed the supreme bliss and general good. It has 1,000 Danh-si, or "snake wives, married and single votaries, and its influence cannot be meddled with "by the two others, which are subject to it."§

The ancestor of the present race of serpent gods is said to have deserted from the Ardrah people ages ago, in consequence of their wickedness, on the eve of a battle, and to have been received by the Whidah people with the highest honours.‖ He is reported to be still alive, as all these gods are immortal, though it need hardly be added, no European has seen him, but his descendants seem to be among the most beautiful, and certainly are among the most harmless of their kind.

Des Marchais gives a full description of the worship addressed to this god, and a picture of a procession, in which the king, the king's wives, and all the nobles took part,¶ bearing presents and offerings to the serpent god. Prayers are addressed to him on every occasion, and answers are returned by the snakes in conversation with the high priest. The one thing we seem to miss is the Esculapian character. It may be that this is included in his characteristic of an omniscient and all-powerful god, but it does not seem to be especially mentioned.

---

* Mission to the King of Dahomey, 2 vols. 8vo. Murray, 1864.

† Capt. Snellgrove's Narrative in Astley, iii. 489.

‡ Bosman in Astley.

§ Burton, vol. II. p. 139.

‖ Des Marchais' (1725) Voyages, ii. p. 135, et seq.

¶ A copy of this plate is given in Astley, vol. III. plate 7.

Women, when touched by the serpent, are said to become "possessed." They are seized with hysteria, and often bereft of reason. When so affected they are secluded in hospitals prepared for their reception, and generally afterwards are considered as priestesses,—Fetish women,—though returned to civil life. The bulk of the priestesses are girls devoted either before their birth or at a very early age to the service of the god. They are brought up in the temple, taught singing, dancing, and various accomplishments, exactly as the nautch girls are in the temples of Southern India, and when of age are married to the god. On this occasion they are marked with the image of the god by pricking the skin with needles and rubbing in indigo, or some blue dye, which is indelible. This seal is said to be set upon them by the god himself,* and, as in Greece, no one dare to divulge his mysteries.

Besides this earthly serpent, there is another, the heavenly one, commonly called Danh. It is the rainbow, and makes the Popo beads, and confers wealth on man. Its emblem is a coiled and horned snake of clay, in a pot or calabash.†

The second god in the Dahoman Pantheon is represented by lofty and beautiful trees. They are prayed to and presented with offerings in times of sickness, and especially of fever. The most revered of these is the cotton tree (Bombax), whose wives equal those of the snake, and the Loco, the well-known poison tree of the West African coast. The latter numbers few Loco-si or wives, but, on the other hand, has its own fetish pottery, which may be bought in every market.‡

The youngest brother of the triad is Hu, the ocean. The Huno, or ocean priest, is now considered the highest of all, a fetish king at Whidah, where he has 500 wives. The offerings to this god are rice, corn, oil, beans, and also cloth, cowries, and other valuables; but at times the king sends as an ocean sacrifice, from the capital, a man carried in a hammock, with the dress, the stool, and umbrella of a noble. A canoe takes him out to the sea, and he is thrown to the sharks.

The human sacrifices or "customs," as they are usually called, of Dahomey, are one of the most remarkable religious observances of the world. They have been frequently described, but by no one so fully or intelligently as by Captain Burton, in his volumes we have just been quoting from.§ They are divided into greater and lesser customs. At the former not less than 500 or 600 victims are sacrificed; at the latter, at which Captain Burton and his companions assisted, 30 or 40 seem to suffice. The idea seems to be that when the king leaves this world it is necessary his wife, his servants, and his domestic animals should accompany him, and they are all slaughtered accordingly. The lesser customs are an annual act of ancestral worship in honour of the departed king, and also to keep up his stock, though in the land of the immortal this seems unnecessary. Besides that, whenever a battle is fought or any great event happens, a messenger is despatched to propitiate the

* From Suetonius we learn that when Atia, the mother of Augustus, was touched by the serpent in the temple of Apollo, she was marked with a stain (macula) like a painted serpent, so that she did not afterwards dare to appear in the public baths.—Sueton. in Aug. c. 94.

† Burton, ii. 148.

‡ Burton, ii. p. 140, l. 141.

§ Burton. As almost the whole work is devoted to this subject, it is needless to specify pages.

late king by keeping him "*au fait*" in the news of his late kingdom. It is said the present king would not be unwilling to do away with, or at least to modify, some of the most revolting features of this great slaughter, but that his subjects would regard such an act as a neglect of his most sacred duties, and he might lose his throne as a punishment for such impiety.*

None of the works above referred to make it clear what the negro's ideas of immortality are, probably because none such exist. That they have an idea of a future state, and that they consider this world as merely one of transition, is evident. All pass on to the next and better world, but with the same wants, feelings, and desires that they possessed while sojourning here, and apparently with the same distinction of rank. The last king, however, is the one especially honoured, and the reigning monarch, when he dies, expects the chief worship to be paid to him, and no doubt he is the one who takes the greatest interest in sublunar affairs. They never rise apparently to the rank of gods, but if they do not die they are at least very soon forgotten.†

When contemplating this, to us, strange religious development, the question inevitably arises, How far are we to consider this Dahoman worship as a living fragment of the oldest religion of the world, or how far may it have grown up in more modern times?

The traditions of the country are, as might be expected, far too vague to be of any avail in such an enquiry, and we are left to draw our conclusions from such information as we can gather elsewhere. We know from the Egyptian monuments that neither the physical features nor the social status of the negro have altered in the slightest degree during the last 4,000 years. If the type was then fixed which has since remained unaltered, why not his religion also? There seems no *à priori* difficulty. No other people in the whole world seem so unchanged and unchangeable. Movements and mixtures of races have taken place everywhere else. Christianity has swept Serpent Worship out of what were the limits of the Roman world, and Mahomedanism has done the same over the greater part of Northern Africa. Neither influence has yet penetrated to the Gold Coast, and there apparently the negro holds "his old faith and his old feelings fast" in spite of the progress of the rest of the world. It may be very horrible, but so far as we at present know it is the oldest of human faiths, and is now practised with more completeness in Dahomey than anywhere else, at least at the present day.

America.

There are few things in connexion with the ancient mythology of America more certain than that there existed in that country before its discovery by Columbus extreme veneration for the serpent. Whether or not this should be designated "worship" is not so clear. The total absence of any native literature renders it extremely difficult to realise the exact interpretation to be put on any observed phenomena, and we

* Burton, ii. 176.

† Among the Zulus the snake is held in great respect, and is not willingly killed; as their dead ancestors are supposed to reappear in the form of snakes.—Colenso, on the Pentateuch, p. VI. p. 142.

gather very little trustworthy information from the early Christian missionaries or historians. They were either too ignorant or too prejudiced to take a dispassionate view of what they saw, and were too much inclined to see the serpent of Eve, or the deluge of Noah, in the vague traditions of the natives; though, to account for these, they were obliged to make St. Thomas missionary to Mexico—before it was founded—as well as first Bishop of Madras. The consequence is, that we are dependent either on a very imperfect examination of the Sculptures, or on very vague oral traditions, for our knowledge of the subject; and it need hardly be added, that with only such data it is extremely difficult to arrive at any satisfactory conclusion. At the same time, however, it must be admitted that if a systematic examination of such data as exist were undertaken, with special reference to Tree and Serpent Worship, a great deal might yet be effected; but as no one has yet attempted the investigation, the subject must for the present be left in its original obscurity.

The principal deity of the Aztec Pantheon seems Tezcatlipoca, or Tonacatlecoatl, literally the Sun Serpent. According to Sahagun, in his character of God of Hosts, he was addressed by the Mexican high priest: "We entreat that those who die in "war may be received by thee, our father the sun, and our brother the earth, for "thou alone reignest."*

The name of the primitive goddess, the wife of Tezcatlipoca, was Cihuacohuatl, or Tonacacihua, the female serpent or the female sun. She, according to the Mexicans, gave to the light at a single birth two children, one male the other female, to whom they refer the origin of mankind.†

A still more remarkable myth is that of Quetzal-coatl, literally the feathered serpent. He is by some represented as born of a pure virgin in the province of Tollan; by others as a stranger coming from a "far countrie," some time between the sixth and ninth century of our era. Be this as it may, he was the great lawgiver and civilizer of the inhabitants of Anahuac. He taught them religion, gave them laws, instructed them in agriculture and the use of metals, and the various arts of life. He is generally represented as an old man, with a white flowing beard and venerable aspect. He was, in fact, the Lycurgus and the Bacchus of Central America, and having finished his mission he withdrew, like the former, it is said, by sea, promising to return. So implicitly was this believed by his subjects, that when the Spaniards appeared on the coast they were joyfully hailed as the returning god and his companions. Alas! they came only to destroy them and their institutions.

If all the evidences bearing on this legend were thoroughly sifted by some one competent to the task, I feel confident they would result in an historical residuum; and if so, it would throw great light on one of the most perplexing problems connected with the civilization of the New World.

As we shall see presently, Serpent Worship was the faith of a great and prosperous kingdom in Cambodia at the time just indicated as the age of the Mexican prophet; and it is more than probable that the worship prevailed in China and the islands to the eastward at that time. Is it possible that it may have crossed the Pacific, and

---

* Squier's Serpent Symbol in America, p. 162.

† Gama, Descripcion Historica y Cronologica de las pedras de Mexico, 1832, p. 39.

landed on the western coast of America, and, finally, bloomed in Anahuac? If such a solution were possible, it would explain many similarities between the religion and arts of the Old World and the New, which are now extremely puzzling, for want of some such evidence of intercommunication.

On the other hand, if we may trust the antiquaries of the United States, there are great serpent mounds formed of earth, 1,000 feet long and more,* which would seem to prove that before the present race of Red Indians inhabited the states Ohio and Iowa, a race of Serpent Worshippers occupied their places, and they have been the ancestors of the Toltecs. When, however, we remember with what curious credulity Stukeley manufactured a Dracontium out of Avebury, and Bathurst Deane saw a serpent seven miles long in the groups of Menhirs at Carnac, we must pause before we feel sure that these American mounds do really represent serpents at all. This point cannot be settled without much more accurate surveys and more cautious observers than have yet turned their attention to the subject.

If it should turn out that these are really representations of the great serpent, and that this worship is indigenous in the New World, we are thrown back on the doctrine that human nature is alike everywhere, and that man in like circumstances and with a like degree of civilization does always the same things, and elaborates the same beliefs. It may be so, but I confess it appears to me that at present the evidence preponderates the other way. It should be mentioned, however, that in America the snake that is worshipped is always the indigenous rattlesnake. Whether as separate images or as adorning the walls of the temples of Yucatan, this characteristic seems invariable, and in so far would favour the local origin of the faith. The greatest difficulty of the investigation arises from almost absolute destruction of all the monuments of the capital by its barbarous conquerors, and the consequent paucity of real reliable data on which to found our conclusions.

It seems, however, impossible to read the numerous evidences which Müller† has collected together with so much industry not to feel convinced that Serpent Worship did prevail all over the continent. In Peru apparently with qualities similar to those of the Serpents in the Old World.‡ But in Mexico, and among the North American Indians, occasionally with attributes of terror which were never ascribed to him on this side of the Atlantic. Quetzalcoatl is always an exception to this inference; and on the whole it seems more reasonable to suppose that these characteristics are to be ascribed more to the horror of the Christian narrators than to the feelings of the worshippers. We have no native accounts, and depend consequently wholly on those who looked on the worship from an outside and antagonistic point of view.

If, however, we may trust Bernal Diaz, he tells us that living rattlesnakes were kept in the great temple at Mexico as sacred and petted objects. They were kept in a cabin of diversified form, in which a quantity of feathers had been strewed, and there they laid their eggs and nursed their snakelings. They were fed with the bodies of the sacrificed, and with dogs' meat.§ The same author tells us that on

* Smithsonian Contributions to Knowledge, vol. I. See also Squier's Serpent Symbol, p. 137 to 141.

† Amerikanische Urreligionen. Basel, 1855.

‡ Müller, p. 366.

§ Bernal Diaz, translated by Lockhart, i, 233.

Cortes' march to Mexico they arrived at a place called Terraguca, which the Spaniards called the Town of Serpents, on account of the enormous figures of these reptiles which they found in the temples, and which the natives worshipped as gods.* But though it is impossible to read any of the narratives of the conquerors without being struck with the frequency with which sacred Serpents and Serpent Worship are spoken of, it is always as a thing accursed, and to be avoided; never as an object worthy of attention, or to be inquired into, and their narratives consequently throw very little light on the subject. The Sculptures would do more; but it will require a long and patient investigation by some one competent person on the spot before their evidence can be considered as available; at present we know very little of what they may contain.

It need hardly be remarked that human sacrifices were found accompanying Serpent Worship in America almost to as great an extent as in Dahomey. Even here, however, it is probable we must make a distinction which may be of some importance. In Africa the sacrificial rites seem to be purely ancestral. In America they were made to propitiate gods, not apparently the ancestors of the reigning family, nor nearer to them in time than Quetzalcoatl. The principal object seems always to have been augury to obtain from the gods an indication of their will, which does not seem to have been the case in Dahomey. It was also no doubt considered that the sacrifice itself was agreeable to the deity, and it was expected that the oracle, which was the declaration of his will, would be favourable in proportion to the number of the victims.

It is by no means improbable that when looked for, Tree Worship will also be found to have prevailed extensively in the New World. Mr. Tylor mentions two instances that came under his notice.† The first was a venerable deciduous cypress, with a stem sixty feet in circumference near its root, and with a fountain gushing up within the hollow of the trunk itself. It was hung all over with votive offerings, besides hundreds of locks of hair, teeth, and bits of ribbon. The other was treated in the same manner, and had the valuable property for whoever touched it, that all feeling of weariness left him. Müller also finds traces of Tree Worship all over the continent of America, and generally in juxtaposition, if not in actual connexion, with that of the Serpent.‡ But here again we must pause for further information before attempting to generalize.

* p. 125. See also pp. 3. 7.

† Anahuac, 215, 265.

‡ Amerikanische Urreligionen, 494. See also 107, 124, 264, *et seq.*

PART II.—EASTERN ASIA.

Persia.

The Eastern branch of our subject has been even less investigated by European scholars than those divisions noticed in the previous pages. This has arisen partly from a less degree of familiarity with Eastern tradition, but more probably because until the very recent discoveries in Cambodia and at Amravati no very tangible data existed on which any satisfactory conclusions could be based. The subject is now, however, assuming a very different aspect, and before long it may be hoped that great light will be thrown on the Tree and Serpent Worship of the ancient world, from a study of those forms of that faith which we now know existed at one time in India.

With Persia the case is slightly different. We have no material remains of Snake Worship in that country, and very little native history. The Zend-Avesta is the work from which we might hope most, not only from its antiquity, but because of its doctrinal character. It is, however, of very little use for our present purposes, inasmuch as it, like the Vedas, embodies the religious belief only of the Aryan, or as they are called here, the Iranian branch of the Persian people, and it need hardly be repeated here that they are not, and never were, serpent worshippers anywhere. If, indeed, there is one point which comes out more clearly than another in the course of this investigation, it is that Serpent Worship is essentially that of a Turanian, or at least of a non-Aryan people. In the present state of the enquiry it would be too bold a generalization to assert that all Turanian races were Serpent Worshippers; and still less can it be affirmed that all who looked on the Serpent as a God belonged to that family of mankind. It is safe, however, to assume that the whole tendency of the facts hitherto brought to light, lies in that direction; and it seems probable that eventually the worship of the Serpent may become a valuable ethnographic test of the presence of Turanian blood in the veins of any people among whom it is found to prevail.

At the time when the Greeks became acquainted with Persia, the whole country, under the influence of the Achæmenian kings, had been brought to acknowledge Zoroasterism with its elemental Fire Worship as their principal form of faith. This religion in its purity,—if we know it in that state,—was the faith which the Iranians brought with them from their original seats when they separated from the Indian Aryans, and was practically their common faith both in India and in Persia. In the latter country, however, in the time of the Achæmenidæ, it was strangely mixed up with Magism, a religion of much more Semitic, or even, it may be suspected, Turanian form, and the two were at that time so blended, that in the accounts of the Greeks at least it is impossible to separate the one from the other.

At the time when the Greeks first make us practically acquainted with Persia, Tree and Serpent Worship had ceased to be regarded as the religion of any important body in the state, though the probability is that it may have been followed to a considerable extent by large classes of people in that vast empire. As, however, the Persians despised, and the Greeks did not observe the Ophites, we are left almost entirely at the mercy of the Mahomedan historians and poets of the eleventh and following centuries for such faint glimmerings of truth as can be picked up, and anyone who has ever opened one of their books will know what blind guides they are in such an investigation. It is doubtful whether even the critical skill of European scholars will ever sift a substratum of tangible history out of the fables of Firdausi or Mirkhond. At present the task has hardly been attempted, and when it has, with only a small modicum of success.

By far the most important and most interesting person in ancient Persian history, for our present purposes at least, is Zohák. According to all accounts he came from Arabia, and took his title, Bívar-asp, from his body guard of 10,000 horsemen by whom he was always accompanied.* His genealogy from Tází or Táj, the eponymous of the Arabs, is given both in the Bundehesch and the Mojmil.† His father is represented as a simple possessor of flocks and herds, but he is said to have conquered Central Asia, and to have fixed his residence at Babel.‡ His reign, or rather that of his dynasty, is said to have lasted 1,000 years, when he was overthrown by Feridún, with the assistance of Gavah the blacksmith, by whom the original line of Jemshid was then restored.

Feridún has been identified almost without doubt with Thraêtaona of the Zend-Avesta, celebrated as the slayer of the three-headed Serpent Dahâka, who was the creation of the evil power Angra Mainyus,§ or more popularly Ahriman.

Zohák is represented by all the Mahomedan historians as having two snakes growing at his back, one from each shoulder, and they add that it was necessary to appease these monsters by sacrificing daily two young men in order that their cravings might be satisfied with their brains.‖ All this has hitherto been mysterious enough, but as we shall presently see, all women of the Nága race had one serpent between their shoulders, and all men—in India—one with three, five, or seven heads; the two of Zohák seem an earlier form, being the exact duplication of those of the females, and it is also probable that the *three* heads of the Zend-Avesta¶ include the human head between the two snakes. We shall be in a better position to judge of this presently, but whatever explanation we adopt, it seems only to be an earlier form of a myth with which we are now becoming familiar in India. The human sacrifices are only what we find so universally accompanying Serpent Worship all the world over.

The most startling novelty with regard to Zohák is the assertion that he came from Arabia, where we have no reason to suppose that Serpent Worship then pre-

---

* Justi Bundehesch, 1868, Glossary s. v. béwarásp. Handbuch der Zendsprache, 1866, Glossary s. v. Dahâka.

† Windischmann, Zoroastrische Studien, pp. 30, 37, c. 39.

‡ Is it possible that this is the Arab dynasty which, according to Berosus, ruled in Babylon in the 13th century B.C.? Rawlinson's Ancient Monarchies, vol. I. p. 193.

§ Windischmann, quoting from the Yaçna, IX. 8, p. 29. *See also* Westergaard in Weber's Indische Studien. vol. III. p. 416.

‖ Mojmil (156); Windischmann, 37; Sháh Námeh, Atkinson's translation, p. 14.

¶ Tribus oribus præditum, tribus capitibus. Masaudi, III. p. 252, and the Mahomedans, on the contrary, always speak of "Two Serpents borne on the shoulders of Dahák."

vailed. Perhaps it only means right bank of the lower Euphrates, which to a man writing in Afghanistan, or the north-east of Persia, might be so described; the original seat of the empire being Babylon would bear that interpretation. Moses of Chorene * would try to persuade us that Zohák was identical with Astyages the Mede, but as his assertion seems to rest more on a verbal coincidence than on historical evidence, too much reliance must not be placed upon it. The Serpent dynasty most probably reigned in Media rather than in Persia proper, but they must have been extinct before the time of Cyrus, though all this requires more careful examination than it has yet met with.

One remnant of the race of Zohák seems to have survived in Cabul, and it would be especially interesting to us, if we knew more about it, as it seems the connecting link between the Persian and Indian Serpent Worship. According to the Mojmil, "When " Táj, the primogenitor of the Arabs, was settled in Babel, one of his sons married " a daughter of Feridún and settled in Cabul, and his son was Rustem's maternal " grandfather."† We find further particulars of the family in the Sháh Námeh. When Zál the son of Sám went to Cabul he found Mihráb, a descendant of Zohák, on the throne, and having fallen in love with his daughter, Rudabeh, he was forbidden by the Mubids to marry her, because the chief of Cabul was of the family of Zohák, the Serpent King. The father too from this circumstance dreaded the resentment of Manuchehr if he allowed the union, and not without reason, for the king ordered Sám to destroy Kábul by fire and sword, and especially the house of Mihráb, then ruler of the serpent race, and all his adherents were to be put to death.‡ Fortunately for the lovers the difficulty was got over, and the result was the birth of Rustem, the most wonderful hero of Eastern romance. The point of interest to us, however, is, that it is probably to the preservation of this race of Serpent worshippers that we owe that remarkable development of Buddhism, which distinguished the valley of the Cabul river between the decline of the Greco-Bactrian kingdom and the rise of the Mahomedan power in that quarter.

The last material trace of Serpent Worship that is found in Persia occurs in a bas-relief at Nakshi-Rustem, near Persepolis. It represents Ormuzd bestowing the circlet of royalty on Ardishir Babegán the first king of the Sassanian line (A.D. 226). Beneath the feet of the horse on which the god (?) is seated, lies Ardevan, the last of the Parthians, and round his head are twisted two writhing snakes,§ not such as probably adorned the shoulders of Zohák, but still sufficiently important to mark that the sculptor intended to represent the Parthian as of the hated race of Zohák, the follower of the accursed Ahriman, whom Ormuzd tramples under foot while bestowing the emblem of royalty on the Zoroastrian, Fire-Worshipping Sassanian.

The more closely it is looked at the more probable does it appear that not only in this instance, but throughout the whole ancient history of Persia, the so-called dualism is much more an ethnographical expression than the result of any theological

* History of Armenia, Postscript to Book I. "Les descendans d'Astyages établis en Arménie portoient encore le nom de Vischabazouni, ce qui signifie Race de dragon. Cette dénomination leur venait du nom du roi des Mèdes."—St. Martin, I. 285.

† Windischmann, 37.

‡ Atkinson's translation of Shah Nameh, p. 77 et seq.

§ Ker Porter, vol. I. plate xxiii.; Flandin et Coste, Voyage en Perse, plate clxxxii.

elaboration. It was the opposition of Turan to Iran, of Zohak to Zoroaster, of Ormuzd to Ahriman—an Aryan race, with their pure elemental worship, intruding into a country occupied by a serpent-worshipping people of Turanian origin, but instead of totally abolishing and ignoring the religion of the conquered, forcing it into an unnatural combination with their own. All this, however, was carried out in such a manner as to represent their own, as the source of all that is good and elevated, and that of the subject race as the origin of all that is evil and accursed.

The answer to the question whether Tree Worship did or did not prevail in Ancient Persia will mainly depend on the signification scholars may eventually agree to assign to the Homa or Soma worship, which forms so important a ceremonial observance both in the Vedas and the Zend-Avesta. If the Soma plant always was the Asclepias acida or Sarcostema viminalis, which is now used by the Brahmans for that purpose, it cannot be called Tree Worship in the sense in which the term is used throughout this essay. The Asclepias is a creeping shrub, almost without leaves, and only remarkable for a milky juice, to which the most important virtues are ascribed. It is now used as freshly expressed,* but in former times was fermented so as to produce intoxication.

On the other hand, Windischmann, who had probably rendered himself more familiar with the spirit of the Zend-Avesta than any other scholar, thus expresses himself on the subject. "Homa is the first of the trees planted by Ahura-Mazda " in the fountain of life. He who drinks of its juice never dies. According to the " Bundehesh, the Gogard or Gaokerena tree bears the Homa, which gives health and " generative power, and imparts life at the resurrection. The Homa plant does not " decay, bears no fruit, resembles the vine, is knotty, and has leaves like jessamin, " yellow and white."†

In another place he says, "From this it appears that the White Homa or the " Tree Gokard is the Tree of Life which grew in Paradise."

In Persian mythology the Homa was also personified as a god, and converses with Ahura-Mazda with regard to the origin of all things, as if he were co-equal in knowledge with the great god of the Persians himself. Whatever form, however, it may have taken, our author adds, the Soma was unquestionably the greatest and holiest offering of ancient Indian or Iranian worship.‡

It would require a much more intimate knowledge of the subject than can be obtained from such translations as have been made, or such books as have been published, to speak at all definitely regarding the Homa. From such data as are available it would appear that the Homa had its origin in the same myth as the Trees of Life and Knowledge which grew in Paradise, and that it passed through a stage of Bacchic mystery, though whether the vine or some other plant was then the Homa is by no means clear; and at last it sank into the present innocent Soma form, which, however, can hardly be regarded as anything but a reminiscence of its former greatness and importance.

---

* Haug Essays, p. 247 ff. Wilson, Introduction to the Rig-Veda-Sanhitâ, vol. I. p. xxxvi. et seq.

† Ueber den Somacultus der Arier. p. 131.

‡ Windischmann, Zoroastrische Studien, pp. 89, 167, 251.

We shall have frequent occasion to speak of the Bodhidruma or Tree of Knowledge of the Buddhists, in the sequel. It is the principal object of worship at Sanchi, and among the most important at Amravati. It will only be possible to ascertain what connexion may have existed between it and the Gaokerena of the Persians, or the Homa, when some competent scholar, familiar with both Zend and Sanskrit, looks through the original authorities with special reference to this inquiry.

Though sufficiently absurd, the following legend from the Sháh Námeh is curious. Sikander, after the conquest of India, went to Mekka, and thence to a country where there were two trees, one male, one female. The first spoke during the day, the latter at night. Whoever had a wish went there to have his desires accomplished. Sikander longed for length of days. When he came under the tree a horrible sound arose and rung in his ears; and on his asking what it meant, the attendant priest replied that fourteen years of his life still remained. Again he asked, "Shall I see "Rúm and my mother and children before I die?" The answer was, "Thou wilt "die at Karshán."*

The oldest known authority for this legend is the Pseudo-Kallisthenes, who wrote apparently about the year 200 A.D.† As he relates it, there were two trees, one of the Sun, which spoke in the Indian language, and one of the Moon which spoke Greek.‡ In the Mediæval fables, the "leafless tree" was introduced between these two. This tree is mentioned by Marco Polo,§ and under the name of the "Arbre Sec" was one of the favourite myths of the Byzantine and of early Christian travellers, though it is even now by no means clear where it grew (my impression is that it was in Seistan, though others place it in Khorassan), nor what exact meaning the Mediævalists attached to the fable.

Unfortunately the classical authors afford us little or no assistance in regard to Tree Worship in the countries westward of India, except the incidental remark of Quintus Curtius, in speaking of the inhabitants on the banks of the Indus, "Arbores maxime colunt,"‖ there is no passage bearing, so far as I know, directly on the subject.

The Chinese travellers are hardly more communicative; but Hiouen-Thsang does mention a great Pipal tree of Peshawar,¶ under whose shade the four preceding Buddhas had reposed, and under it the last had predicted the appearance of the great Kaniskha, who in consequence had erected alongside of it, about the Christian era, the largest and tallest of all the Stupas of which we have any record. This tree seems to have existed and been reverenced down to the time of Baber (in 1504), who mentions it as the great tree of Bekram.** The Gûrh Katri he describes as close to it was probably the remains of the Monastery of Kaniskha. Even its site cannot now be ascertained.

CASHMERE.

Although from its position on the map, Cashmere might fairly be considered as an integral part of India, still its circlet of mountains has been sufficient to keep it distinct and separate, and we consequently find there vestiges of the old faith better

* Atkinson, Translation, p. 507.
† Zacher, Pseudo-Kallisthenes. Halle, 1867, p. 102.
‡ Loc. p. 161.
§ Marsden, p. 109.
‖ Hist. Alex. VIII. 9.
¶ Histoire de la Vie de Hiouen Thsang, I. p. 83.
** Leyden's translation of Memoirs of Baber, 157, 264.

preserved than in most places on the plains. Another circumstance which has tended also in the same direction is that the Aryans on entering India do not seem to have turned aside to conquer or at least permanently to occupy the valley. If they entered India by crossing the Indus at or near Attock,—and there seems no good reason for doubting that this was so,—this seems so strange that we feel almost inclined to believe that Cashmere was really then in the state described in the earliest legends, a great lake, or at least a valley so filled with water and so swampy as to be unfit for human habitation. Though this may not be quite true we are no doubt justified in assuming that 4,000 or 5,000 years ago a much larger portion of the valley was under water than is the case now, and the real snakes may then have been relatively more important than their Naga successors afterwards became.

Be this as it may, Cashmere has always been considered, in historical times, as one of the principal centres of Serpent Worship in India, and hitherto it has been principally from her legends that what little was known of the Nagas has been gathered.

Cashmere is also fortunate in possessing in the Râja Tarangiṇî something more like a connected history than almost any other country of India, and from its pages, with the incidental notices by classical, Chinese, and Mahomedan authors, we are enabled to form a tolerably distinct view of the subject.

Although from the context there is a strong presumption that Snake Worship prevailed in the valley from a very early period, still we have no direct testimony to the fact till the century before the Christian era, when the King Dâmodara having, it is said, offended some Brahman was converted into a snake,* and still, it is said, haunts the spot. He was succeeded by three Tartar princes, known from history and from their coins to have been Buddhists, and to have reigned about the Christian era. In the reign of their successor Abhimanyu we are told that "in consequence "of the disuse of the prescribed institutes, and the abolition of every form of sacrifice, "and a departure from the lessons of the Nîla Purâṇa, the Nagas were particularly "incensed, and visited the offences of the people with severe and unseasonable storms "of rain and snow, and those especially perished who had adopted the Bauddha "heresy."† Gonerda III., who succeeded this king, prosecuted the reform which that prince had commenced.

The ancient ritual, according to the Nîla precepts,‡ was restored, and the worship of the Nagas and the offering of sacrifices re-established.§ During the following centuries we have several legends of Nagas, but the faith of the kings is seldom mentioned, and seems to have oscillated between Snake Worship, Buddhism, and Hinduism, but as our historian belonged to the latter faith his testimony is not always quite to be depended upon. When Hiouen Thsang entered the valley in 632,

---

* Wilson's Abstract of the Râja Tarangiṇî in Vol. XV. Asiatic Researches, p. 22. All the future references to this work are derived from the same source, which seems better and more trustworthy than the translation by Troyer. The volume and the page will, therefore, only be quoted.

† A. S. XV. p. 24.

‡ A. S. XV. p. 25.

§ The Nîla Purâṇa has not hitherto been seen by any European, but I trust to being able to add an abstract of its contents in an Appendix to this work. At my request Mr. J. Muir, the well-known Sanscrit scholar, wrote out to Sir D. Macleod, the Chief Commissioner in the Punjab, and he procured two copies from Cashmere, which are now in the hands of Professor Cowell, who has kindly undertaken to make the required analysis.

in the reign of Báláditya the last king of the Gonerdiya race, he found the Buddhist religion still very prevalent in the valley, though he admits that the king only interested himself in the hereties and in the temples of their gods, and despised the faith of Buddha.* He repeats the usual story of the valley having been a lake, but adds, "50 years after the Nirvâna (B.C. 493?) a disciple of Ânanda converted the Naga "Raja, he quitted his tank, built 500 monasteries, and invited sages and saints to "come and dwell in them."†

It is not, however, only in the valley that our Chinese traveller repeats the Hindu legends about serpents and their power, but at every stage of his journey from Cabul to Cashmere, he everywhere finds some spot where a dragon king or Naga Raja resided, and played an important part in the legendary history of the land. These legends, as might be expected, were found in the seventh century very much altered from their more primitive forms, but they are interesting, in the first place, as showing how essentially the north-west corner of India was at one time the seat of Serpent Worship, and also, in what manner it was eventually—except perhaps in Cashmere—amalgamated with Buddhism.

Among these legends one of the most pertinent to our present purpose is that of a member of the family of Śâkya—that of Buddha—who when travelling in Udayana—the Kamboja of the Hindus, lying northward from Peshawar—fell in love with a serpent king's daughter. He was eventually married to her, and by the advice and with the assistance of his father-in-law, killed the king of the country and obtained the sovereignty. Though his wife had obtained and was confirmed in the possession of a human body, a nine-headed snake occasionally appeared at the back of her neck, which on a certain occasion her husband cut off at a single blow while she was asleep. The result was blindness, of which she was afterwards cured by Śâkya-muni himself, and her son Uttarasena was present at the distribution of his relics at Kuśinagara, where the great ascetic obtained Nirvâṇa.‡

An almost equally curious legend is told of a Buddhist priest (Bhikshu) who became a serpent, because he had killed the tree Elâpatra, and resided in a beautiful lake or spring near Takshaśilâ (Taxila). In our traveller's day when the people of the country wanted fine weather or rain, they went to the spring accompanied by a priest (Śramaṇa) "and snapping their fingers, invoke the dragon, and immediately "obtain their wishes."§ In these legends the chief characteristic of the Serpents throughout the East in all ages seems to have been their power over the wind and rain, which they exert for either good or evil as their disposition prompts.‖

A curious confirmation of the prevalence of Nagas in the north-west of India is obtained from the Buddhist account of the proceedings consequent on the Third

* Hiouen-Thsang, II. 180. † Voyage de Hiouen-Thsang, I. 168. ‡ Hiouen-Thsang, II. 141.

§ Hiouen-Thsang, II. 152. General Cunningham visited this spring at Hassan Abdul in 1863, and found it still reverenced. Other legends are told at pp. 49, 99, 133, &c.

‖ This power over the weather, which is one of the leading characteristics of Nagas, has led to their being confounded with the Vedic Ahi. In their origin and purpose I believe the two to have been perfectly distinct, but in the process of time the one legend borrowed from the other till the two have become so mixed up together that it will now be extremely difficult to separate them again. My own impression is that the Vedic myth is an adaptation of a local superstition; borrowed in fact from the serpent-worshipping aborigines among whom the Aryans were settled.

Convocation held B.C. 253. Missionaries were then sent to all the neighbouring countries. Among others Majjhantiko was dispatched to Kashmîra and Gandhâra.* A Naga king of that country, named Aravâlo, endowed with supernatural powers, by causing a furious deluge to descend was submerging all the ripened crops in Kashmîra and Gandhâra. The Nagas and their king tried every means to terrify the missionary, but were subdued by his calmness and address; "whereupon the Théro "propounded his doctrines, and the Naga king attained the salvation and state of "piety in that faith." In like manner "in the Himawanta (Himalaya) regions, 84,000 "Nagas were converted, and the Naga king placing the Théro on a gem-set throne "respectfully stood by fanning him. On that day the inhabitants of Kashmîra and "Gandhâra, who had come with offerings to appease the wrath of the Naga king, "bowing down to the Théro (instead of the Naga king) stood reverentially by his "side," &c. These extracts from the Mahawanso,† depict faithfully the Buddhist belief on the subject two centuries before Hiouen-Thsang's time, though not from personal observation. The account is further interesting, because these in the north-west were the only Nagas to whom missionaries were sent by Aśoka. Either it was that the others had been converted before, or that Cashmere and the mountain countries east and west of it, were the most prominent seats of the faith.

These accounts by native authorities are fully confirmed by such scanty notices as we glean from classical authorities; Onesicritus tells us that two ambassadors sent to the king of Cashmere by Alexander, brought back news that the king of the country cherished two large serpents of fabulous dimensions.‡ Maximinius of Tyre tells us, that when Alexander entered India, Taxilus (King of Taxila) showed him a serpent of enormous size which he nourished with great care and revered as the image of the god whom the Greek writers, from the similitude of his attributes, called Dionysus or Bacchus.§

The latest authority we have, is that of Abulfazl, who tells us that in the reign of Akbar (1556—1605) there were in Cashmere 45 places dedicated to the worship of Śiva, 64 to Vishṇu, 3 to Brahmâ, and 22 to Durgâ, but there were 700 places in the valley where there were carved images of snakes which the inhabitants worshipped.‖

All this is fully confirmed by the architecture of the valley; with very few exceptions, all the ancient temples of Cashmere seem to have been devoted to Serpent Worship. They stand in square courts which were capable of being flooded and were crossed by light bridges of stone, some of which still remain. Even at the present day some of these temples are unapproachable without wading, in consequence of the water which surrounds them, and all might be rendered so by a slight repair to their waterworks. There are, of course, no images in the sanctuaries which long prevented antiquaries from perceiving the form of faith to which they were dedicated. But where the deity is a living god and mortal, when he and his worshippers pay the debt of nature, they leave no material trace to recall the memory of their past existence.

---

* In this wide sense Gandhâra seems to include all the countries westward of the Indus as far as Candahar. Relics of this missionary, as we shall presently see, were deposited in No. 3 Tope at Sanchi.

† Turnour, Translation, p. 72 and 73.

‡ Strabo, XV. 698.

§ Maxim. Tyr. Diss. XIII. ed. Lip. 140.

‖ Ayeen Akbaree, Gladwin's Translation, p. 137.

Cambodia.

There is another country on the other side of the Bay of Bengal the study of whose antiquities is nearly as important to the elucidation of Serpent Worship in India, as those of Cashmere, though in a totally different sense. In the last-named country we look for the "incunabula" of the faith, in Cambodia for its fullest known development. The ruined cities of Cambodia have, however, been only so recently discovered, and are yet so little known, that it is extremely difficult to feel sure on many points connected with their history or purposes.* Whatever doubt may, however, exist on other points, it seems certain that the great Temple of Nakhon Vat was wholly dedicated to Serpent Worship. Every angle of every roof is adorned with a grim seven-headed serpent, with a magnificent crest of what is apparently intended for feathers, and every cornice of every entablature is adorned with a continuous row of these seven-headed deities, but without crests. The former may be counted by hundreds, the latter by thousands. But it is not only these; every balustrade, every ridge, almost every feature of the building bears the same impress. The arrangements too of the temple are such as are suitable for Serpent Worship, and that only. There is no image in the sanctuary, and no worship represented in the bas-reliefs. All the courts are tanks to contain water, and everything recalls the temples of Cashmere, but with ten-fold magnificence. Neither in India, nor so far as is known is there any other temple, displaying the same amount of patient labour devoted to the elaboration of appropriate ornament over so extended a surface as in this newly-discovered temple. It is 600 feet square at base, and rises to a height of 180 feet in the centre, while every part is covered with carvings in stone, generally beautiful in design, and always admirably adapted to their situation, and to tell the story they were meant to convey. The startling thing to us is, that simultaneously with the erection of the great cathedrals of York, Amiens, or Cologne, a larger and more magnificent temple than either of them was being erected in another part of the globe, in a style and dedicated to a religion of which the western builders knew nothing. What seems equally strange is that all memory of the people, and all knowledge of their buildings, should have so completely passed away that till within the last ten years no one in Europe suspected their existence.

We shall not know whether the other temples in the city of Nakhon Thom are equally dedicated to Serpent Worship till some one visits them who has some previous knowledge of the subject. They are so completely overgrown with jungle that photography will hardly help us in this instance. They were more extensive, and seem to have been as elaborately ornamented as the one temple of which we

* The temples were first discovered by M. Mouhot, a French naturalist, in 1858–60, but he did not pretend to any knowledge of their history. They were afterwards visited by Dr. Bastian, who has written voluminously regarding them, but either it is that he knows nothing about them, or for some reason he is afraid to commit himself to any statements regarding them. The greatest amount of information has been obtained from the photographs of Mr. J. Thomson, and his personal communications. From these sources a tolerably connected account is condensed in my History of Architecture (II. p. 713, et seq.), to which the reader is referred. Since it was published, Messrs. Edmiston and Douglas, of Edinburgh, have published a selection of Mr. Thomson's photographs, with explanatory text taken principally, with my consent and collaboration, from my work above referred to.

have some knowledge, but they seem rather to have been dedicated to some bastard form of Buddhism than to the worship of the Serpent in the form in which it is found at Nakhon Vat.

The question that principally interests us at this stage, is to ascertain how this marvellous development of Serpent Worship arose in Cambodia, and at what time.

The first impulse would be to assume that it was indigenous, but this certainly does not seem to be the case. The architecture of the temple is, if anything, elassical —Roman Doric. The ornaments—bassi-relievi—are all subjects borrowed from the Râmâyana or Mahâbhârata, and fade gradually into the myths of the Hindu religion. The people are Indian. The natives, wherever they appear, are represented as an abject race, and are very cruelly treated by the superior race who were the builders of the temple, and the carvers of the bas-reliefs.

Another theory, which at first sight seemed plausible, was that the worship had reached Cambodia from the north. We know from Hiouen-Thsang that Serpent Worship was to be found in Koutche in the north of Thibet,* we know that the Strî Râjya, or Amazon kingdom, was in Thibet,† and we have so many traces of Serpent Worship all along the north of the Himalaya, Hindu Kush, and Caucasus, that it looks like a Scythian or northern form of faith, and may have leaked through the mountain ranges into both Cashmere and Cambodia, radiating from a common northern centre.

When more closely looked into, this theory seems as untenable as the last. The communication between Thibet and Cambodia is barred by ranges of mountains, which have hitherto proved practically impassable either as trade routes or for military operations. The southern country could only be reached through China, and Serpent Worship could hardly have passed through that country without leaving more traces of its passage, or bringing with it more evidences of Chinese civilization, than appears to be the case. We know so little, however, of the local superstitions of China that we must pause before expressing any decided opinion on this subject.

The only remaining hypothesis that suggests itself is that they came from India direct by sea. When we turn to their own traditions for any confirmation of this, the answer is distinct, "Our ancestors came from Myang Rom, or Romavisei, not far from Takçasila" (Taxila).‡ Startling as this may at first sight appear, there are many circumstances which not only take away from its strangeness, but seem to render it probable. In the first place Taxila, as just pointed out, was one of the great centres of Serpent Worship. The country they claim to have migrated from is, by the ancient Sanskrit authorities, called Kamboja.§ Their capital they call Inthapattapuri (Indraprastha), and that of Siam was Ayuthia (Ayodhyâ), the two capitals of the Mahâbhârata and Râmâyaṇa, and almost all the other principal towns throughout the country bear Sanskrit names. If Halifax, Boston, and New York, are evidence of an English people having settled in America, the names of the Cambodian cities are equally conclusive in this respect.

---

* Mémoires, I. 4.

† Asiatic Researches, XV. 48.

‡ Bastian, Völker des Östlichen Asien, I. p. 393.

§ Wilford, A.R., VI. 516., VIII. 336; Muir, orig. Sanscrit Texts, II. 368. ff. &c.

Another argument which seems as important as any other, is the similarity of the style of architecture in the two countries. This is not only traceable in the arrangement of their temples, but in the details. The Cashmere pillars are curiously like those of the Grecian Doric order,* those of Cambodia are even more classical, but resemble Roman Doric. Nothing similar to either has yet been discovered between the two points, but there is an amount of classical influence apparent in the sculpture at Amravati which seems to supply a connecting link.

The improbability of such a migration is considerably lessened by the knowledge that an Indian colony did reach Java, by sea of course; did introduce there their own faith, and built those wonderful temples of Brambanan and Borobuddor, which in many respects resemble, though they do not rival, those of Cambodia. All this has been rendered more probable within the last year by the discovery of Serpent Worship existing to the extent it does at Amravati, near the mouth of the Kistnah, the very country whence navigators set sail who were about to cross the bay of Bengal going to the Gold Coast,† which we may almost certainly fix at Ligor, and this seems to point out the route which the Cambodians took on their migration.‡

Every day since my attention was turned to the sculptures at Amravati, fresh evidence of the prevalence of Serpent Worship in Central India has come to light, and it seems now tolerably clear, either that serpent races passed down the valley of the Indus, across Central India by the valley of the Godavery, and thence by sea to Cambodia; or that they passed from Tashsaśilâ direct by land to Amravati, and thence to the Golden Chersonese. If a straight line is drawn on the map between these two first-named places it passes over Sanchi and other spots where Snake Worship once prevailed, and on the whole this route seems to be the one the emigrants would most probably have taken; but we are only yet on the threshold of the inquiry, and must wait for further information before deciding.

The time when this migration took place is not so easily fixed, but it appears to have first commenced in the fourth century, (after 318,) to have been continued in the fifth and sixth, and probably reached its height in the era of the religious disturbances and persecutions in India in the tenth and eleventh centuries. Cambodia was conquered by the Siamese between the years 1351–74, the capital destroyed, and depopulation set in. From that time Serpent Worship seems to have declined rapidly from its position of splendour and supremacy, and to have been succeeded by Buddhism, which is now the faith of all the civilized Indo-Chinese provinces.

The Cambodian legends which refer to the colonization of the country and the building of the city of Inthapattapuri, are all extremely similar to those related by Hiouen-Thsang, when speaking of the country whence they came, as noticed above. In all the dragon king's daughter is the principal personage, and from her the royal race claim to be descended. In the Cambodian legend it is related that the banished prince, Phra Thong, was driven, after a long sea voyage, on an island where grew a wonderful Talok tree, "Grewia inæqualis." He ascends its branches to look about him, but the tree grows faster than the celebrated beanstalk of Jack, and he

* Essay on the Arian order of Architecture as exhibited in the Temples of Kashmir, by Captain A. Cunningham, J.A.S.B., September 1848.

† Ptolemy, VII. 1.

‡ Jour. Asiat. Soc. Beng. XVII. 86.

fears he shall never see his mother earth again. In descending, however, he finds himself in a wonderful grotto in the hollow of the tree, where he meets with the dragon king's daughter, and marries her. The father consents to their union, and builds the city of Nakhon Thom for their residence, where he comes frequently to visit his beloved daughter; but the people complain of his presence, and his ungrateful children frighten him away by placing an image of the four-faced Brahma over the gate of the city.*

Another form of the legend is, that king Pathumma Surivong, while reposing under the wonderful tree, saw the dragon king's daughter bathing with her companions in a neighbouring lake, fell in love and married her, and went to the underground abode of his father-in-law, where he spent a fortnight. According to this legend he behaved much better to the old Serpent than Prince Phra Thong.

According to a third form, Indra had come down from heaven, but had neglected to bring any female attendants with him; feeling the loneliness of his situation, took up with the dragon king's daughter, who bore to him Ketumalea, the father of Pathumma Surivong, who seems really to have been the founder of the city.†

We have a date twice repeated, 957–8 A.D., for the accession of the last-named king, and if the names above quoted were really or closely connected with one another, as the legends would lead us to suppose, the migration and all the subsequent events down to the founding of the city really took place in the tenth century. If we were to draw our conclusions from the legends alone, this view must probably be adopted; but the context, and the indications from Indian experience, incline me to extend the time between the first migration and the building of the city to four or five centuries; but it is at present little more than guess work, in so far as the earlier dates are concerned. The circumstance that interests us most is the important part played in these legends by Nang Nakh, the Serpent King's daughter, and the description of her father and his kingdom. Foolish and legendary as all this may appear at first sight, it assumes considerable importance when we find it resulting in some of the most wonderful temples which the world ever saw, and in the most remarkable development of pure Serpent Worship anywhere to be found.

CHINA.

It is extremely difficult to ascertain anything that is at all satisfactory regarding the worship of the Serpent in China. No scholar, so far as I know, has investigated the subject, nor has any traveller devoted special attention to such indications of it as may exist in the country. We are consequently left to such stray passages as are scattered here and there in the various authors who treat of Chinese subjects, and

* The Serpent King was, it appears, a Sabbatharian, at least he devoted every seventh day to prayer. Bastian, I. 397. See also Trans. R.A.S., vol. II. p. 94, where Col. Low reports, "Every seventh day the mighty "Raja Naga issues forth from his palace, and having ascended a high mountain, pours forth his soul in ardent "devotion."

† All these legends are taken from Bastian's Völker des Östlichen Asien, pages 393 to 439. They are so mixed up together and with extraneous matter that it is impossible to quote separate pages, even if it were worth while.

without knowing exactly what reliance to place on the information so afforded. It is nevertheless impossible to observe the very important part the Dragon plays in the imagery and decoration of Chinese temples, on the dress and ornaments of the kings, or on the standards of the army, without feeling that some important symbolism is concealed beneath its almost universal employment. It is true that in modern times the dragon has been invested with wings, and teeth, and claws, and transformed into a monster more horrible than any nightmare that ever disturbed the sleep of a mediæval herald; still it is difficult to avoid the conviction that, if we could trace him far enough back, we should find that he was developed out of something much more nearly resembling "a beast of the field."

To take one instance among many, Kæmpfer* relates that two heaven-sent Serpents watched over the first washing of Confucius, for which a spring burst forth from the floor of the cave in which he was born. It would be interesting, for many reasons, to know when this tradition arose, and whether it is really Chinese or imported from India. Confucius was nearly contemporary with Buddha, and at a slightly subsequent time† was teaching doctrines so similar to those of the Indian philosopher, that now that they have got mixed up together in China, it is extremely difficult to discriminate what belongs to each. The connexion between Buddhism and Serpent Worship will be sufficiently apparent in the following pages. It would be curious if the same parentage could be traced for the Chinese philosophy.

The following is another example. "Father Martin, one of the Jesuits who "obtained a settlement in China, says that the Chinese delight in mountains and "high places, because there lives the dragon, upon whom their good fortune depends. "They call him the father of happiness. To this dragon they erect temples, shaded "with groves."‡ This is exactly what we would expect; but when we meet with such a passage as this we are forced to ask, If this be so, why has not everybody seen it, and why have others not told us the same story?

The most satisfactory evidence I have obtained regarding Serpent Worship in China is from a Chinese work, entitled "The Great Cloud Wheel Rain asking Sutra." It is an Imperial work, printed in its present form under the auspices of Keen Lung, A.D. 1783, and forms part of a great collection of Buddhist standard works. It is supposed to be spoken by Buddha in the "beautifully adorned Great Cloud Circle "Hall of the Nâga-Râja Nanda Upananda, and consists of a succession of Dhâraṇis "imparted by Buddha to the dragons for the sake of those who in their worship "desired rain."§

The most curious part of the book is the plates. These represent, first, a Naga temple, which very much resembles—though the likeness is, of course, accidental—the tabernacle of the Jews. The shrine is a tent, standing in a rectangular enclosure,

---

* Japan, 426. See also Life of Confucius, Chinese Classics, vol. I. p. 59.

† Confucius was 8 years old when Buddha died.

‡ The Rev. Bathurst Deane, quoting Cambray, Mémoires Celtiques, p. 163.

§ The work in question was lent to me by the Rev. S. Beal, a thoroughly competent Chinese scholar, who furnished the above particulars. His opinion is, that the work even in its present form is older than the 13th century, though the woodcuts may be more modern. See also J. R. A. S. XX. 170.

surrounded by canvas screens. The furniture consists of an altar and four lighted candles. Seven tables, or stands, are laden with cakes (shewbread), and as many with fruits; and seven lamps take the place of the seven-branched candlestick. There are four woodcuts representing the deities worshipped in the temple. One of these is reproduced in fac-simile in the annexed woodcut. It is a form of the Serpent God which was invented in India in the twelfth or thirteenth century, and with which we shall presently become familiar.* A human head and body, ending in a serpentine form from the waist downwards, but with the much more characteristic accompaniment of a degenerate serpent hood. In the first figure in this Chinese work, the Nâga has three serpents rising behind its head; in the second, five; in the third—that in the woodcut—seven; and the last, nine serpents. The lower extremities of the first and second are spotted like serpents. This one and the fourth have scales more like those of a fish. In India between the third century B.C. and the thirteenth A.D., we find serpent hoods ranging from three to seven heads, but never the human body terminating in a serpent downward, till after the last quoted date.

No. 3.

NÂGA, FROM CHINESE SUTRA.

Although all this may have been derived from India, and in its present form probably was so, still it is interesting to find it practised in China so long after it has been forgotten there. At the same time, however, as hinted in speaking of Cambodia (p. 49), it is by no means clear that both India and China may not have borrowed their Serpent Worship from some common centre in Thibet. We are not yet, however, in a position to say whether it penetrated to China by the southern route it afterwards certainly took, or whether it may not have reached it by the north, or from a common centre in Tartary.

OCEANIA.

It has long been known that Serpent Worship prevailed to a considerable extent in some at least of the islands in the Pacific, but the notices of it that I have met with are singularly vague and unsatisfactory. No one with the requisite local knowledge has yet thought it worth while to collect and arrange the facts, so as to render them available as historical data; and till this is done, it is impossible to employ usefully even such information as we possess.

My own impression is that, wherever we find human sacrifices prevailing, or what—if we dare put such words together—we ought rather to designate as religious

* Vide infra, page 67.

cannibalism, there Serpent Worship will be found also. In the Feejee islands it certainly exists. Degei, one of their principal gods, is supposed to be enshrined or to exist in the form of a serpent, lying coiled up in a cave of Navata, a mountain on the coast of Viti Levu. Some traditions represent him with the head and part of the body of a serpent, the rest of him being of stone, emblematic of his everlasting and unchangeable nature.*

The savages of Australia, it is said, believe in the existence of a gigantic serpent, who created the world by a blow of his tail, and who is the cause of earthquakes. Nothing will induce them, however, to reveal to the white man the rites with which they worship the serpent, but which are reported to include human sacrifices and cannibalism.†

Traces of Serpent Worship are found at Suku and Kedal, and other places in Java, but there apparently not connected with Buddhism,‡ but as a local superstition of the natives; and other instances might be quoted, if it were worth while, or they could be depended upon. So little, however, is this the case, that the subject would hardly have been worth mentioning at all, were it not that one of the most interesting problems connected with the subject is the supposed connexion between the Serpent Worship of the Old World and that of Central America. Is it possible it could have migrated viâ the Feejee Islands and the Marquesas? There does not seem to be any other route which presents greater probabilities, if we are prepared to concede the previous question that America did borrow her Serpent Worship from the East; but as yet this is far from being settled.

Ceylon.

We must wait for further information before we can speak with anything like certainty, either regarding the extent to which Serpent Worship prevails in Ceylon, or with reference to any material evidences which may attest its existence in former days. Except Mr. Upham's,§ no work that I am aware of treats of the subject, and no drawings except his have been published which afford any information regarding it. Though far from being exhaustive, Mr. Upham's work is sufficient to show how imperfect the conversion of the natives to Buddhism has been, and to what an extent the worship of the Nâga still prevails. In Ceylon, however, it seems now to be mixed up with Demon Worship and the worst superstitions of the Hindu Pantheon to such an extent as to be barely recognizable, and it will require considerable labour to resolve all these superstitions into their component parts.

In addition to this, I have seen native drawings of mythological subjects, which show a greater admixture of Serpent Worship than would be found in similar representations on the continent of India; and I have also had access to original drawings by Europeans in which the three or seven-headed Naga is found adorning

* Seemann, Mission to Viti, p. 290.
† Manuscript information.
‡ Sir S. Raffles, Java, vol. ii. p. 47. Crawfurd's Dictionary of the Eastern Archipelago, sub vocibus.
§ History and Doctrine of Buddhism in Ceylon, by Ed. Upham. London, 1829.

almost every sacred spot in the country.* The difficulty is to judge from such imperfect materials of what is really old and what may have been added, and till the photographer reaches Ceylon this uncertainty must probably prevail in so far as people in Europe are concerned; but any competent antiquary on the spot could very easily tell us all we wish to know.

On the other hand, the testimony of the Buddhist scriptures seems to be as distinct as such evidence can be expected to be, that Ceylon was inhabited by a Naga race of serpent worshippers when converted to Buddhism, the legends say in the sixth, but more probably in the third, century, B.C. Whether Gorresio, the translator of the Râmâyaṇa, is correct in asserting that the Râkshasas whom Râma encountered in that island were Nagas or not, is a question that must be left to Sanskrit scholars to decide. It does not appear that the passages are so understood by the modern Hindus. Snakes never appear as Râma's opponents in any of the thousand and one representations of that famous war; but Gorresio may be correct nevertheless, and it would be interesting to know.†

The three Ceylonese historical works which have been translated—the Mahâwanso, the Ratnâcari, and Râjâvali—all commence with an account, more or less detailed, of the conversion of the Nagas of Ceylon by Buddha himself.

The account in the Mahâwanso is to the following effect‡:—In the fifth year of his Buddhahood, the vanquisher of the five deadly sins perceiving that a conflict was in hand between the Nagas Mahodaro and Chûlodaro for possession of a gem-set throne, out of compassion to the Nagas visited Nâgadwîpo.§

At that time this Mahodaro was a Naga king of a Naga kingdom, 500 yojanas in extent, bounded by the ocean. His sister had been given in marriage to a Naga king of the Kanawaddhamâno mountain, and her son claimed the throne by inheritance, &c. "To them the vanquisher preached a sermon of reconciliation. Both "parties rejoicing thereat, made an offering of the gem-set throne to the divine sage. "The divine teacher alighting on the earth, seated himself on the throne, and was "served by the Naga kings with celestial food and beverage. The lord of the universe "procured for 80 koṭis of Nagas, dwelling on land and in the water, the salvation "of the faith, and the state of piety" (p. 6).

The maternal uncle of Mahodaro, the Naga king of Kalyâṇî, who was preparing to join in the war is also converted, and at parting Buddha promises to return, meanwhile bestowing on the Naga king the gem-set throne, and having planted the Râjâyatana tree, at parting addressed them thus, "Oh, Naga kings! worship this my "sanctified tree; unto you, my beloved, it will be a comfort and a consolation."

The same story is told, with slight and unimportant variations, in the other

* Mr. Nicholl, the artist who made the drawings from which all the architectural subjects in Sir J. Emerson Tennent's work were engraved, recently showed me his original sketches. Everywhere at Anurâdhapura, Pollonarua, Dambool, &c. the Naga appears prominent. The engraver, not knowing what it was, has converted it into a head-dress, which it requires a very practised eye to recognize as a seven-headed snake.

† When so good a Sanskrit scholar as Muir doubts, it would be presumptuous in me to advance an opinion. See Sanskrit Texts, II. 436.

‡ Mahawanso translated by the Hon. G. Turnour, p 4.

§ The translation limits the term Nâgadwipo to the northern portion of Ceylon, but on what grounds does not appear. The context seems to imply the whole island.

two histories, and from that time forward the Mahawanso teems with Naga legends; they seem, however, all to refer to the continent of India rather than Ceylon, and will be alluded to when necessary hereafter. The conversion of the island seems to have been complete in the time of Asoka, B.C. 250,* and as the earliest of the scriptures we have were not reduced to writing in their present form before the fifth century after Christ, we must not expect from Buddhist authorities any admission of a faith adverse to Buddhism existing in the island at that date.

This, however, is just one of those cases in which the monuments are so useful to supplement the "litera scripta." If they were examined we should see how far the conversion was radical, and to what extent the people still adhered to their old faith. My impression is, that after more than 2000 years, their conversion is still far from being complete. Whenever any competent person will look below the surface, I am very much mistaken if the old Serpent Worship is not found still practised by the aboriginal races in all remote parts of the island; but it is useless speculating when real information can be so easily obtained.

Whatever may be the result of the investigation into the Serpent Worship of Ceylon, there is no doubt whatever about the prevalence and importance of Tree Worship in that island. The legend of the planting of the Râjâyatana Tree by Buddha has already been alluded to, but the history of the transference of a branch of the Bo Tree from Buddh-gyâ to Anurâdhapura is as authentic and as important as any event recorded in the Ceylonese annals. Sent by Aśoka (250 B.C.) it was received with the utmost reverence by Devanampiyatisso, and planted in a most conspicuous spot in the centre of his capital.† There it has been reverenced as the chief and most important "numen" of Ceylon for more than 2000 years, and it, or its lineal descendant sprung at least from the old root, is there worshipped at this hour. The city is in ruins; its great dagobas have fallen to decay; its monasteries have disappeared; but the great Bo Tree still flourishes according to the legend, "Ever green, never "growing or decreasing, but living on for ever for the delight and worship of "mankind." Annually thousands repair to the sacred precincts within which it stands to do it honour, and to offer up those prayers for health and prosperity which are more likely to be answered if uttered in its presence. There is probably no older idol in the world, certainly none more venerated.‡

India.

In every essential respect the religious history of India is extremely similar to that of Persia, but with one curious accidental difference, which influenced to a considerable extent their outward aspect and ultimate fate. From the accession of the Achæmenidæ till the old religions were practically swept away by the Mahomedan invasion, all the countries of Central Asia were united under one sceptre, and subject

* Throughout this work the year 250, as a date easily remembered, is assumed as that of Asoka. It is probable that the true date of his accession is 270, and as he reigned 35 years, his death took place in 235 B.C.; 250 B.C. is therefore a fair mean, and has the merit of involving no hypothesis as to the chronology of the period.

† Mahawanso, chap. xviii.

‡ Sir Emerson Tennent, Col. Forbes Leslie, Chapman, and indeed everyone who has written about Ceylon, mention the fact. The drawings of it also are numerous.

to one code of laws. The consequence is, that the Turanian, the Semitic, and the Aryan races, which successively occupied those countries known as Persia in its widest sense, all became more or less amalgamated into a homogeneous people, and their religions were also fused into one great whole. The Aryan religion of Ormuzd was united in bonds of most unholy matrimony with the Turanian form of Ahriman, and the Magian religion acted as a flux to unite the two, at least to such an extent as probably to defy all the efforts of modern analysis to separate them again into their original elements.

The case of India was widely different. No native tradition represents India as ever united under one rule. When the Greeks visited it they found it divided into 122 different nations,* and the number probably was never less, it may have been more, till towards the end of the seventeenth century, when the Moguls under Aurangzebe nearly succeeded in rendering their sway paramount in India; but just as the house of cards was about to be completed, it fell to pieces from the inherent want of cohesion in the parts.

This circumstance renders the history of the religions of India very much more perplexed and more difficult to follow; but once the subject is mastered the Indian form becomes not only more instructive, but also very much more interesting to the student of comparative mythology.

No Semitic element apparently ever existed among the populations of India, but from the earliest historical times we find two well defined and perfectly distinct races. One, the Aryan, or Sanskrit-speaking race, who entered India, it is generally supposed, across the Upper Indus, and eventually spread themselves throughout the whole of the valley of the Ganges, and the countries between the Vindhya and the Himalaya mountains. The other a Turanian race, known as the Dravidians, and speaking Tamul, or languages closely allied to it, entered India probably earlier than the Aryans, but across the Lower Indus, and now occupy the whole of the southern part of the peninsula nearly up to the Vindhya mountains.†

There seems to be no difference of opinion among Indian ethnologists with regard to these two great divisions of the people, but it is not quite so clear whether there was not a third occupying the countries north of the Vindhyas and between them and the Himalayas, of which they were dispossessed by the Aryans. The language of the superior race has so completely taken possession of every department of literature at the earliest period to which our knowledge extends, that we have no written record of the existence of this aboriginal people; and the blood of all has in modern times been so mixed by migration and colonization, that it seems impossible to dig back to the roots through the jumble of languages and races that now exists in the valley.

The mode in which the question presents itself as bearing on the present inquiry is this:—It may safely be asserted that no Aryan race, while existing in anything like purity, was ever converted to Buddhism, or could permanently adopt its doctrines. If we take, for instance, the three leading features of that faith, atheism, metempsychosis,

* Arrian, Indica, VII.

† Comparative Grammar of the Drávidian or South Indian family of Languages, by the Rev. R. Caldwell, B.A. London, 1856.

and absence of caste, they are essentially Turanian, and found everywhere among people of that race, but are distinctly opposed to the feelings of the Aryans wherever they are found. It is quite true that the Indian Aryans may, during their 2,000 years residence, have become so mixed with the native tribes, and so impure, that some of their families may have temporarily adopted the new faith. Even this, however, seems hardly probable, when we consider how they cling at the present day to their old sacred books, and how many germs of the old faith still survive even in the filth and corruption of doctrine in which they are now immersed.

On the other hand, it does not appear that the Dravidian races ever were essentially, or to any great extent, serpent worshippers, or ever were converted to Buddhism. It may be too bold a generalization, in the present state of our knowledge, to assert that no race ever permanently adopted Buddhism who had not previously been serpent worshippers—but, if not quite true, it is nearly so; and though Serpent Worship can be detected south of the Kistnah, it is not, nor does it ever appear to have been, the national faith. In like manner, though there were Buddhists in Drâviḍa-deśa, there are no traces of Buddhist buildings or establishments now to be found south of Amravati.

If this should eventually prove to be the correct view of the case, it becomes necessary to assume the existence in the valley of the Ganges of a people differing from Dravidians and more closely allied to the Thibetans, the Burmese, and other Indo-Chinese races. Some kind of Buddhism probably existed beyond the Himalayas before Śâkya-muni's time. It still flourishes there, and seems indelible in all these lands. In India it did attain great prevalence and power during a thousand years, but it does not seem to have existed before the time of Śâkya-muni; and it is now so completely washed out, that there probably does not exist a single Buddhist, certainly not a Buddhist establishment, between the Himalayas and Cape Cormorin.*

Assuming this view of the matter to be correct, we shall of course look in vain, in the Vedas or any of the earlier writings in Sanskrit, for any trace of Serpent Worship. Not only was it repugnant to their own feelings, but they so utterly despised the Dasyus—or by whatever other name they chose to designate the aborigines—that they would not even condescend to notice their superstitions.†

The traditions from which the Râmâyaṇa was compiled also represent a state of Aryan society so comparatively pure, that, except in cases above alluded to (p. 55), there is probably no mention of Nagas there. But the heros of the Mahâbhârata were much less pure a race. Their origin, their polyandry, and other peculiarities, all point to the Himalayas; and from this work, consequently, we may expect some light on Serpent Worship. The poem, however, was compiled—in its present form at least—by Brahmans long after the events it describes; and although many ancient fragments are encrusted in its more modern form, little even of its narrative can be accepted as true history.

---

* In a recent statistical report on the population of Bombay, I see "Boodists" enumerated among the sects. Who are they?

† M. Vivien de St. Martin, in his "Géographie du Veda," pp. 103—4, states that the Aryans ascribed to the Dasyus the power of controlling the elements, and of granting or withholding rain at their pleasure. If this were so, it was not to the people themselves, but to their Serpent God, that this power should have been ascribed by the writers of the hymns of the Vedas. I confess, however, that my reading of the work in Wilson's translation does not bear out this attribution.

MAHÂBHÂRATA.

One of the most remarkable coincidences connected with the subject of Serpent Worship arises from the fact that this great epic poem, which may practically be considered as one of the books of the Hindu Bible, opens, like the Pentateuch, with a curse on the Serpent. What is even more curious is that in both instances the same "equivoque" as to the name exists: read carelessly or in a translation, the curse in the Mahâbhârata is on the reptile, not on its worshippers, just as happens in the Bible, where, however, the conciseness of the narrative does not enable us to rectify the meaning from the context. In the Hindu epic, however, the story of the great sacrifice for the destruction of the Serpents is so mixed up with historical and human action that it is evident at once that the ambiguity* about the name is only seized upon by the Hindu poets as an excuse for introducing the supernatural into an ordinary human transaction, and to enable them to give rein to that exuberance of fancy which is the curse of their poetic effusions. It is not of course to be expected that anything like real history can ever be elaborated out of such a mass of fables, but if any competent Sanskrit scholars were to apply themselves to the task, they might at least recover as reasonable a narrative as it is now possible to frame out of such materials as are available for the history of Greece before the fall of Troy.

Passing over the first canto, which is a general introduction to the whole poem, the next three (ślokas 657 to 2197), are wholly occupied by the affairs of the Naga race, commencing with the marriage of the two sisters Kadrû and Vinatâ with the Rishi Kasyapa, and the strange desires of the two with regard to their progeny. These led to Kadrû, the eldest, being the mother of 1,000 Nagas, who were the progenitors of the whole serpent race. The names of her principal descendants are then given,† some of which have already been quoted, others will frequently be referred to in the sequel; such, for instance, as Śesha, Vâṣouki, Airâvata, Takshaka, Karkotaka, Kâliya, Aila or Elâpatra, Nîla and Anîla, Nahusha, and others. Her sister, on the other hand, became the mother of Garuḍa, who, in consequence of the trick played by Kadrû on her sister, became the all-powerful enemy of the Naga race, and hence also the mother's curse, from which such fatal consequences flowed.

When divested, however, of its poetic garb, and all its mythological rubbish, the story of the Mahâbhârata, in so far at least as Serpent Worship is concerned, does not seem difficult to understand, and may be succinctly narrated.

The Lunar race, to which the heros of the great war belonged, were a second great horde of the Aryan race, who seem to have entered India across the Upper Indus at least 1,000 years after the purer so-called Solar race. The first seat to which we can trace them back seems to be Takt-i-Bahai, north of Peshawar.‡ Thence, passing

---

* In the Âdi Parva the word used for serpent is almost invariably "Nâga." In the Vana Parva, where Bhîma gets into trouble with Nahusha in the form of a real serpent or boa, it is as usually "Sarpa."

† Âdi Parva 1551, et seq.

‡ Bellew, Report on the Yusufzais, p. 136. Some very curious sculptures have recently been discovered at this place, but they are all long subsequent to the age of Bhârata, and betray a Bactrian; or at least a Western influence, which give them a character very different from anything found in India. They are all Buddhistic;, but with a strong infusion of Græco-Bactrian feeling.

through the Punjâb, we find them settled at Hâstinapura, between the Jumna and Ganges, about the thirteenth century B.C., when the real action of the poem commences.

The first transaction in which the Nagas appear, is the burning of the forest of Khâṇḍava.* Simply, it seems, that when the family at Hâstinapura became too numerous, it was determined to found a second capital, and for this purpose the spot where Delhi now stands was cleared by burning the forest which then occupied its site, and dislodging the Nagas who occupied the spot. The Nagas were protected by the Buddhist deity Indra. But, attacked by the Vedic god Agni, the Brahman poet represents them as all perishing except their king Takshaka.

Subsequent to this the relations between the Pâṇḍus and the Nagas seem to have been of the most friendly description. Arjuna, in his first banishment, marries first Ulûpî,† the daughter of a Naga king at the foot of the Himalayas, near Hurdwar; and shortly afterwards he formed a still more important connexion, by marrying Chitrângadâ, daughter of Chitravâhana, the Naga king of Manipur, by whom he had a son, Bhabra-vâhana, who played so strange a part in a subsequent episode, when his father, in the performance of the Aśwamedha, or horse sacrifice, again visited Manipur.‡ From these and other minor particulars it would seem that the author of the Mahâbhârata wished to represent the Aryans of that day as cultivating friendly relations with the aborigines. The real quarrel took place some time after the great war was ended, and in this manner:—Parîkshit, the grandson of Arjuna, had succeeded to the throne; and one day, while hunting in the forest, incensed at the contumacious silence of a hermit,§ insulted him by hanging the dead body of a snake round his neck. His son and disciple cursed the king for the insult to his father, and invoked the aid of Takshaka, the king of serpents, to avenge it. The consequence was, that on the eighth day from that time Parîkshit was bitten‖ by Takshaka, who is always represented as king of Takshaśilâ.¶ It was to avenge this assassination of his father, that Janamejaya undertook the great sacrifice for the destruction of the Nagas.** Thousands—myriads—had already perished, when the slaughter was stayed at the intervention of Astîka, a Brahman, though at the same time the nephew of Vâsuki, the serpent king of the eastern Nagas.†† It is probable the remnant either, like Astîka, became converts, or at least promised submission to the dominion of the Aryans. We consequently hear no more of them for three or four centuries, till at last, about the year 691 B.C., we find a Naga dynasty on the throne of Magadhá;‡‡ and it was under Ajâtaśatru, the sixth king of this race, in the year 623, that Buddha was born, and the great regeneration of the subject races was inaugurated.

---

* Âdi Parva, Fauche's translation, 8050, et seq.

† Loc. 7788.

‡ Wheeler's History of India, vol. I., p. 404. Professor Goldstücker informs me that the version of the Aśwamedha adopted by Mr. Wheeler is not really a part of the original Mahâbhârata, but the facts are the same in both versions. (*See* Westminster Review, April 1868.)

§ Âdi Parva, 1696, et seq.

‖ Idem, 1801.

¶ Idem, 678, 830, et seq.

** Idem, 2073, et seq.

†† Idem, 1025, et seq.

‡‡ Wilson's Vishnu Purâna, p. 467. Lassen's Ind. Alt. I. (2d ed.) App. p. xxxviii. et seq.

If we knew more of the local ethnology of India, all this narrative might probably be authenticated to an extent which it is now impossible to attempt. It is curious to observe that in Manipur, the scene of Arjuna's marriage with Chitrângadâ, and his slaughter by her son, that at the present day the peculiar god of the Royal family is a species of snake, called Pa-kung-ba, from which the family claims descent. When it appears, it is coaxed on to a cushion by the priestess in attendance, who then performs certain ceremonies to please it. This snake appears sometimes, they say, of great size; when he does so, it is indicative of his being displeased with something. So long as he remains of a diminutive form, it is a sign he is in good humour.*

In the immediate neighbourhood of Manipur there are numerous tribes of aboriginal people, still called Nagas. From their name and locality it might be supposed they must be serpent worshippers; but no one has yet observed that form of faith among them. The subject must, therefore, be remitted for further inquiries.

The locality of Janamejaya's sacrifice is said in the Mahâbhârata to have been the Kurukshetra, the famous battle-field of the Pâṇḍus and Kurus, north-west of Delhi, but another and more probable site is still pointed out at Agrahaut, in Orissa.† There, within the precincts of a very old and remote, but now ruined, temple, may be seen numerous small models of temples, said to have been there placed by Janamejaya, to represent those princes who could not be present on the occasion. They are probably not so old; but it is strange to find the traditions of the Mahâbhârata still clinging to these spots, and Serpent Worship still prevailing there. At least, not far from this—at Sumbulpore—in 1766, Mr. Motte and another‡ went to visit a great snake that had been worshipped there since the world began! They saw him emerge from his cave, which he does every seventh day,§ and accept the offering of a goat which his worshippers had provided. After devouring it, he took a bath in a canal that surrounded his dwelling place; and from the mark he left in the mud at the edge, Mr. Motte estimated his diameter to have been about two feet. He does not even guess his length, but it must have been considerable. When Major Kittoe visited Sumbulpore in 1836 he was still alive,‖ and probably is so still; and I have no doubt but that numerous other deities of the same sort could easily be found if only looked for; but attention has never hitherto been directed to the subject.

RISE OF BUDDHISM.

As has been frequently suggested in other works,¶ the great characteristic of the ancient as well as of the modern history of India is the constant recurrence of one typical phenomenon which controlled the destiny of the nation in all ages to which our knowledge extends. From the earliest dawn of tradition to the present

---

* Account of the Valley of Munipur, by Major Macculloch: Records of Government of India, No. XXVII. 1859.

† Asiatic Researches, XV. 257.

‡ Asiatic Register, vol. I. p. 82.

§ Vide ante, note, p. 51. Is it possible that the period of creation in Genesis being limited to seven days is a part of the primæval Ophite faith?

‖ J. A. S. B. vol. VIII. p. 478.

¶ History of Architecture, by the Author, vol. II., p. 446, et seqq. &c.

day the great underlying stratum of the population of India seems to have been of Turanian race, very unwarlike, and incapable of any rise in civilization, except through admixture of blood. These consequently easily fell a prey to the hardier and more warlike races bred in the countries now known as Bokhara and Afghanistan, and the result has been that at periods of from five to ten centuries horde after horde has crossed the Indus, and settled in the fertile plains of India. For awhile these retained their freshness and vigour, but by degrees, partly from the enervating effects of the climate, but more from intermixture with the aboriginal races, they sunk to the lower level of the indigenous inhabitants, and in their turn became a prey to the next horde that followed the steps of their forefathers across the Indus.

For our present purpose it is not necessary to inquire when the first great immigration of the Aryans or Dravidians took place, or when they first settled in the north and south of India respectively. It is sufficient that we are able to state that the less pure horde of the Aryans known as the Lunar race probably reached the Ganges about the thirteenth or fourteenth century B.C. From that time till the third or fourth century, or for more than one thousand years, no horde of any race, so far as we know, crossed the Indus. This may, in a great measure, be owing to the existence of the powerful empires of Assyria and Persia on the other side of the river, which may have kept the barbarians in check, or to local causes we cannot now detect. Be that as it may, the fact that interests us here is, that during this long period the blood of the Aryans had become so mixed and so impure that the Veda was no longer possible as a rule of faith, and when Śâkya-muni attempted to revive the religion of the aboriginal Turanians his call was responded to in a manner which led to the most important consequences, in a religious point of view, not only in India, but to all the Turanian families of mankind.

So far as we can now see, Buddhism was little more than a revival of the coarser superstitions of the aboriginal races, purified and refined by the application of Aryan morality, and elevated by doctrines borrowed from the intellectual superiority of the Aryan races. Buddha himself was undoubtedly of purely Aryan race, being the descendant of a junior branch of the Solar kings of Ayodhyâ. Burmese traditions represent his son Rahula as assuming the garb of a priest;* but the Hindus, with more probability, record his succeeding to the throne of his grandfather, and we gather from them, that the dynasty retained its Brahminical faith till its extinction shortly afterwards.† The dissemination of the Buddhist religion is wholly due to the accident of its having been adopted by the low caste kings of Magadhá, and to its having been elevated by one of them to the rank of the religion of the State.

As a part of the reform which he introduced, ancestral worship was abolished, and the sepulchral tumulus became the depository of relics of saints, Serpent Worship was repressed, and its sister faith of Tree Worship elevated to the first rank.‡ Absolute negation of sensual enjoyment, which to the Turanian in all ages

* Bigandet, Life and Legend of Guadama, p. 229. † Wilson's Vishnu Purana, p. 463.

‡ When in 1866 I wrote the second volume of my History of Architecture, I, after hazarding the assertion "that before the Aryans reached India, the inhabitants of the valley of the Ganges seem to have been Tree and Serpent Worshippers," then added, in speaking of the Buddhist reform (p. 448): "Serpent Worship was utterly rejected, but Tree Worship was adopted as an important part of the new faith." When in the following

is as the breath of life, was elevated into a crucial test of faith, and asceticism became ultimately the one path to salvation. There is every reason to believe that human sacrifices were common in ancient India. War was the normal state of its kingdoms, and persecution is too essentially a characteristic of the Aryan races not to have flourished there. On the other hand, the Buddhist expanded the Jewish commandment "Thou shalt do no murder" into "Thou shalt not kill," and extended it to the meanest of created beings. No war was ever waged by Buddhists, as such, and toleration of the faith of others was one of the most marked characteristics of the new religion. No faith was ever so essentially propagated by persuasion as that of Buddha, and though the Buddhists were too frequently persecuted even to destruction, there is no instance on record of any attempt to spread their faith by force in any quarter of the globe.

The Turanian of course had no caste, so that institution was put aside only to be revived when a second upheaval of local superstition under Aryan influence on the decay of Buddhism brought Śivaism and Vishnuism to the surface, together with all the monstrosities of the modern Hindu pantheon.

Although doubts have been expressed as to the exact date of Buddha's birth to the extent of about 60 years, the usual chronology,* which is that adopted throughout this work, represents him as born at Kapilavastu, a small principality on the north of the Ganges, in the year 623 B.C., and he died at Kuśinagara, not far from the place of his birth, 543 B.C., in the eighth or eighteenth year† of the reign of Ajâtaśatru, the sixth king of the Naga dynasty of Magadha, who was then the lord paramount of Northern India.

The name of Śiśunâga is applied by the Brahmans to the first king of this dynasty; the Buddhists give it to the tenth, and add the following legend:—On a certain occasion one of the chief of the courtezans bore a child to one of the Lichchhawi Rajas, but the child proving an abortion was put into a basket, and at night thrown on a dungheap. A certain Nâgarâja, the tutelar of the city, observing it, encircled it with its folds, and sheltered it with its hood. The people who congregated there made a noise, "Śu, Śu," to frighten the snake, and on examining the basket found the abortion matured into a male child with every mark of greatness on it. In consequence of this incident he received the name Śiśunâga, and in time ascended the throne of Magadha.‡ The second convocation was held 100 years after the death of Buddha, during the reign of his son Kálásoka, and we gather, though somewhat indistinctly, that his successors, including the nine Nandas, till

---

spring I discovered the Amravati sculptures in the coach house at Fife House, I hastened to add as an erratum on the last page a recantation or at least modification of this assertion. Further investigations now incline me to go back to my old faith. The serpent, I believe, was rejected by Buddha and his earlier followers, but cropped up again among other mediæval corruptions, and, as we shall presently see, became an important element in Buddhist mythology.

* I have myself no doubts as to the correctness of the usually received date, and propose as soon as this work is published to submit my reasons for this belief to the Royal Asiatic Society. Meanwhile the conclusions I have arrived at in my chronological researches will be found in the table at the end of this volume. The reasoning on which they are founded must be reserved for the journal of that society, but the results have meanwhile been adopted as data throughout this work.

† Turnour, Mahawanso, XLVII., LII.

‡ Turnour's Introduction to the Mahawanso, XXXVII. See also Bigandet, Life of Gaudama, p. 362, et seq.

the accession of the celebrated Chandragupta (B.C. 325), were Nagas or serpent worshippers pure and simple.* They certainly were considered as of very low caste and hated by the Brahmans, and were not loved by the Buddhists.

With the Mauryan kings Buddhism seems to have entered on a new phase; at least in Aśoka's inscriptions we have no trace of the worship of either Buddha himself, nor of Trees nor Serpents. Pure abstract morality seems to have been the form it then took or was intended to take.† But in the Mahâwanso, one of the great events of Aśoka's reign, is the despatch of a branch of the Bo Tree of Buddh Gyâ to Ceylon,‡ showing that form of faith to be then prevalent; and in the Caves of Orissa, which probably are anterior to the Christian era, we find both Tree and Serpent Worship prevailing. There are, however, few periods of Indian history during which such scanty materials exist for settling any point, either historical or mythological, as during the two centuries and a half before the Christian era. We know nothing that happened during that period, and we hardly see where light is to come from to illumine those dark ages.

Immediately preceding the Christian era a great revolution took place in Buddhism under the influence of Nâgârjuna,§ one of the most important names connected with the history of the religion. Although we cannot fix the date of this patriarch with absolute certainty, we can within very narrow limits. The quotation from the Thibetan Târanâtha in Vassilief's work‖ places him between 14 years B.C. and 28 A.D., both dates reconcileable with a not very long life. But we have another means of ascertaining it even more satisfactorily. Nâgârjuna was the ruling spirit in the great council or convocation held under Kanishka, the Tartar king of Cashmere and Northern India. In a tope erected by this king at Maṇikyâla a number of Roman consular coins were found around the principal deposit. These date from 73 to 33 B.C.,¶ and as we cannot suppose they were deposited there till some time after the year in which they were coined, the building of the tope by Kanishka must be placed within the thirty years that preceded the Christian era.

At that time the Buddhists were divided into eighteen sects, grouped into four great divisions,** a circumstance from which we may infer that Buddhism was torn by internal dissensions, and might have perished without the impulse given by this fresh importation of Tartar blood from the north. At the same time also we learn that Milinda, king of Eastern Panjâb, had silenced the Buddhist priests in argument, and driven them from the country across the Himalaya to Rakshita Tal and Manasarovara.†† At this critical juncture the youthful Nâgârjuna appeared. He was then a monk in the celebrated monastery of Nâlanda in Behar‡‡—the Monte

* Mahá Padma and Nanda, the only two of their names we know with certainty, are both names of serpents. Their coins I believe to be those depicted, J. A. S. B., vol. VII., pl. LX,, No. 1 to 9. On all these the serpent is the principal symbol.

† J. A. S. B., VII. p. 219; J. R. A. S., XII. 153.

‡ Vide ante, p. 56.

§ His name is singularly suggestive, being compounded of "Nâga," a serpent, and a tree, "Arjuna," under which he was born. Vassilief, &c. Bouddhisme, 213.

‖ Le Bouddhisme, 201.

¶ Cunningham, Bhilsa Topes, 130.

** Asiatic Researches. XX. 92, 297.

†† Cunningham, Bhilsa Topes, 130.

‡‡ This monastery took its name and probably owed its original sanctity to a dragon or Nâga called Nâlanda, who resided in a pool close by. General Cunningham saw in 1861–62 the tank in which he resided. Report to Government for those years, p. 12.

Cassino of Iudia,—and proelaimed himself the restorer of the old faith. Aeeording to this prophet the words uttered by Śâkya Muni during his life-time had been heard and noted down by the Nagas, who had kept them to themselves in their own abode, till sueh time as mankind should beeome worthy to receive them. Nâgârjuna gave out that he had reeeived these doeuments from the Nagas and was commissioned to proelaim them to the world.* This gave rise to an eutirely new sehool of Buddhism known as Mahâyâna, or as M. Julien translates it†, the "Grand Véhieule," as opposed to Hînayâna or the "Petit Véhieule;" the distinetion betweeu the two being iu almost every respeet identieal with that whieh exists between Evangelieal and Mediæval Christianity.

This is another of those eurious historieal eoineidenees that exist between Christianity and Buddhism, aud there are few so startling. In the first three eenturies after the death of its founder, Buddhism was a struggling seet, sometimes petted, sometimes perseeuted, but in spite of all we are told, in subsequent legeuds, never spread to any great extent among the people. Three hundred years after Buddha, Aśoka did for Buddhism exaetly what Constantiue did for Christianity. He adopted it, made it the religion of the state, and with all the zeal of a eouvert, used every exertion to assist iu its propagation. Six hundred years after Buddha, Nâgârjuna and Kanishka did for the eastern faith what St. Beuediet and Gregory the Great did for the western, they ereated a ehurch with a Hierarchy aud Doctrine. We must go on further still for four eenturies more, to Buddhaghosa (A.D. 410) and to Hildebrand, before we find our Mediæval ehurehes quite eomplete, and the priesthood quite segregated from the laity, and the system perfeeted in all its parts. Iu the sixteenth eentury after Christ eame the reformatiou, and with it the restoration of Evangelieal Christiauity. Iu the sixteenth eentury after Buddha eame a reformatiou, but it was one of extermination of the faith, in so far as India was eoneerned. Śankara Âehârya was the Indiau Luther, but his aim was widely different. Whatever may have been the abuses and eorruptions that had erept into Buddhism in the eighth and teuth eenturies of our era, they were replaced by a faith mueh less pure, and far fuller of idolatrous absurdities than that whieh it superseded. What the westeru reformers aimed at, was to restore the Christian Hînayâna. In the east this was not thought of, hence the different fate of the two faiths. In Europe Christianity was invigorated by the struggle, in India Buddhism perished altogether.

The eonsequeuee of all this is, that we are now very mueh in the position of a foreign investigator who might have entered some great eonventual establishment in Europe in the fourteenth or fifteenth eentury to study Christianity. Worse than even this; it is as if the monasteries of the middle ages had lasted for four or five centuries longer without any reform or light from without, and that theu an attempt should have been made to aseertain within their walls what primitive Christianity originally may have been. The explorer would have found lives and legends of saints in abundanee; miraeles aud divine eommunieations without eud; ponderous tomes of seholastic divinity, and a marvellously falsified history. Instead of the Bible, he would have beeu referred to that mass of beautiful but purely legendary fietions whieh, in the eourse of eenturies, had attaehed themselves to the uame of the Virgin

* Vassilief, Bouddhisme, 119.

† Voyages de Hiouen-Thsang, *passim*.

Mary, and to all the members of the Holy family. All this, too, he would have found mixed up with stories from the Old Testament, and from the lives of Mediæval saints in most marvellous confusion. If among all these works he chanced to light on the Bible, it certainly would not be pointed out to him as the one true Life of Christ, or as the basis of the Christian faith. We would, no doubt, appreciate the Gospels of Buddhism if we found them; but all that has yet been disinterred from the monasteries of Thibet, or the libraries of China or Ceylon, is subsequent to Buddhaghosa; more than one thousand years after the death of the founder of the religion, and long after the Naga revelation had superseded the original faith. We are thus precisely in the position of the student of Christianity who had only the library of some Mediæval monastery at his command. In so far as books are concerned, we depend almost wholly for our knowledge of the Life of Buddha on the Lalita Vistara,* and other works of the same age aud class. The Lalita Vistara, however, was reduced to its present form in the fourteenth century of Buddha, and is the exact counterpart in purpose and authenticity to the Legenda Aurea, and similar works of the Christian middle ages. It is true all these Buddhist books profess to be founded on earlier works, and no doubt this to some extent is true; but as these earlier works have not yet been discovered, we are left very much to our own powers of critical discrimination to say what is original and what may have been added to suit the tastes and feelings of an age long subsequent to the events.†

Looking at what has been done within the last twenty years, it is not impossible that we may recover even the original Sûtras, the Vinaya and the Abhidharma, as they are said to have been compiled by Upâli, Ânanda, and Kâśyapa immediately on the death of Śâkya Muni,‡ or at all events we may hope that the keen criticism of modern scholars may be able, at least to some extent, to separate the wheat from the chaff, and restore to us a tolerably correct picture of primitive Buddhism as it existed before the Christian era. Notwithstanding all the difficulties of the task, considerable progress has already been achieved in this direction. Burnouf's contributions are invaluable,§ while the works of Barthélemy St. Hilaire,‖ of Bigandet,¶ and Vassilief,** are most useful résumés of what is known. The Germans also and our own scholars have collected a mass of materials, and discussed and dissected a number of problems which will clear the way for a correct understanding of many questions whenever a serious attempt is made to combine the whole into a consecutive history.

In the meanwhile it is of the utmost importance that everything should be gathered together and published that can throw any light on Buddhism anterior to the time when the books we now possess were reduced to their present form. The

* Translated from the Thibetan by Foucaux. Paris, 4to., 1847.

† If anyone would wish perfectly to realize the position of Buddhist scholars at the present day, let him read carefully any one of the many versions of "Lhystoire du Noble et Vaillant roy Alexandre le Grand," as compiled in the middle ages, and compare it with the narrative of the life of the same monarch as related by classical authors. Having done this, he will appreciate the difficulty in which Oriental scholars are now placed as regards the early history of Buddhism in the life of the founder of that religion.

‡ J. A. S. B., vol. I. p. 6; Asiatic Researches, XX. 42, &c.

§ Introduction à l'Histoire du Buddhism Indien. Lotus de la boune loi, &c.

‖ Le Bouddha et sa Religion. Paris, 1860.

¶ The Life or Legend of Gaudama. Rangoon, 1866.

** Le Bouddhisme, ses Dogmes, son Histoire, et sa Littérature, traduit du Russe par La Comme. Paris, 1865.

only written documents which certainly belong to the earlier epoch are the edicts of Aśoka, engraved on the lâṭs at Delhi, Allahabad, and elsewhere; and on rocks at five or six places in India, extending from the shores of the Bay of Bengal to Guzerat, and to the Himalayas and Peshawar on the north. Except that at Bhabra,* these are neither doctrinal nor historical. They are dry moral precepts, and so unlike the Buddhism "quæ nunc est," that, but for collateral secondary evidence, it might very well be doubted whether they belonged to that religion at all, or it might be disputed, as was done by the late Professor Wilson, whether they were written by Aśoka. The Bhabra inscription and further investigations have set these questions at rest. But the picture these inscriptions afford us of Buddhism 250 B.C. is a wonderful contrast to what we find in the Lalita Vistara of Thibet,† as compiled in the eighth or ninth century of our era, or any other written records of the religion which we possess.

Next in importance to these inscriptions are the sculptures of the two Topes, illustrated in this work. The gateways at Sanchi were erected, as nearly as can be ascertained, in the first half of the first century of our era, and, therefore, nearly contemporary with Nâgârjuna. They are not pure, but they are purer than anything else of their kind now known to exist. Buddha never appears in them as an object of worship. The Dagoba, the Chakra or wheel, the Tree, and other such emblems are reverenced. The Serpent does appear but rarely, and we have very little of the absurd supernatural fables which afterwards form the stock of the legends. At Amravati, three centuries afterwards, we find a state of affairs much more in accordance with modern notions. Buddha is worshipped, but the Naga is his co-equal. The Dagoba, the Tree, the Chakra, are all reverenced; and almost all the legends of modern times may probably be traced in its sculptures, though in a purer form than in the books. The first may be taken as the nearest approach we possess to an illustrated Bible of the Hînayâna period, five hundred years before the oldest Buddhist book we possess; and Amravati as a pictorial illustration of the Mahâyâna three centuries after its promulgation, and just before Fa-Hian‡ visited the country and gave us the earliest description we have of the faith by any outsider, since at least the very meagre and unsatisfactory accounts of the Greeks.

In the frescoes that cover the walls of the Caves at Ajanta is found a third picture, three centuries later than the sculptures at Amravati, this time representing the state of Buddhist belief just before its decline. Owing to the unfortunate fire at the Crystal Palace these are not now available for purposes of illustration, but they may become so hereafter. Even, however, if we possessed drawings or photographs of them, they could never be so important for the history of the faith as the sculptures of the two Topes of Sanchi and Amravati, which represent it before the existence, in their present form, of any of the books we now possess. Our regret, however, at the loss of these copies, is very much lessened, in so far as our present purposes are concerned, by the knowledge that there were no traces of Serpent Worship in the paintings. The only representations of the Naga found at Ajanta are among

* J. R. A. S., XVI. p. 367.

† These inscriptions will be found reprinted, in so far as it is necessary for present purposes, in Appendix B.

‡ Foĕ-Kouĕ-Ki, translated by Rémusat, &c., 4to., Paris, 1836.

the sculptured decorations of the doorways or in detached bas-reliefs outside the caves,* where they may be considered as accessory or subordinate to the principal form of worship. For a history of Buddhism, the paintings are of great interest; as illustrating either Tree or Serpent Worship, they are comparatively unimportant.

The same remark applies to the frescoes in the Caves at Baugh, and generally to the western Caves. The tendency of the migration from Takshsaśilâ seems to have been southward, and towards the East, and never to have descended the Ghauts or penetrated into the Concan. On the other hand, the most recent example I am acquainted with of any great Naga sculptures belonging to the classical age of Indian art, is the well-known bas-relief at Mahavellipore,† on the eastern shore, about forty miles south of Madras, and executed apparently in the thirteenth century. This is carved on two great masses of granite rock, and extends about 90 feet north and south, by 30 or 35 feet in height. On the northern or right-hand portion, a group of elephants, beautifully executed, is advancing towards the centre, and above them some thirty figures, interspersed with lions and other animals, are all turning in the same direction. On the left-hand rock the lower part was evidently intended to contain the representations of the rest of the animal kingdom, but is only commenced. The upper portion has a number of human figures, equal to that of the other half of the bas-reliefs, and all equally turning towards the centre. The artist has utilized the edge of the northern rock, so as to give his principal figures a higher relief than could be obtained in the flat portions, and also to heighten their effect by having a shadow behind them. But unfortunately from this cause they were so exposed that the upper portion has been broken away. When Mr. Babington drew them, in 1827, only the lower part of the great Naga was remaining, but his wife below him was quite perfect, and presents us with a form not found either at Sanchi, Amravati, or Ajanta. The Nagas here, both male and female, are represented as Serpents at full length, but human from the waist upwards. They still, however, generally have the Snake hood of three or five heads canopying their own; in the same manner as in the Chinese woodcut, No. 3, introduced on page 53, where this more modern form of the Naga has been adopted.

No. 4.

SIVA WITH NAGAS FROM HULLABEED, ABOUT 1300 A.D.
[*From a Photograph.*]

This form is found among the sculptures at Hullabeed and in the Caves at Iwullee, both certainly of the thirteenth or beginning of the fourteenth century, and the form continues down to modern times; but this example at Mahavellipore is, so far as I

* I possess some hundreds of *sculptured* representations of the Naga. I never saw or heard of a *painted* Naga anywhere.

† This bas-relief was described by Bishop Heber and Mrs. Graham. A notice of it by Mr. Goldingham appeared in the Asiatic Researches, vol. v. A view of it was published by Daniell; but the best is that by Messrs. Babington and Hulston, in the Transactions of the Royal Asiatic Society, vol. ii. plates I. and II. I have two photographs of it by Dr. Hunter, of Madras, lying before me.

know, among the earliest examples of the form.* In other respects the grouping there of the figures around the Naga is so similar to what we find at Sanchi, that it is at first sight difficult to believe that twelve or thirteen centuries had elapsed between the execution of the two sets of sculptures. Such, however, appears undoubtedly to have been the case; and this great southern bas-relief worthily closes a series of Takshae sculptures, which for the present we must be content to commence with Sanchi, though there is little doubt but that earlier examples will hereafter be found;† but whether that is the case or not, many intermediate illustrations will certainly be discovered when looked for, and so enable us to complete as curious a picture as anywhere exists of the latest form of the primæval worship of the world.

Hindu Religion.

It might have sufficed for our present purposes to have stopped when we had brought the history of Serpent Worship in India to the point when the Buddhist scriptures were rescued from the keeping of the Nagas and revealed to mankind. As this happens to be also the time when the Gateways were added to the tope at Sanchi, we might have left the sculptures to tell their own tale, and continue the history of Naga worship from that point. It will add, however, very much to the clearness of what follows if we anticipate still further, and describe briefly what took place afterwards.

Speaking broadly, the modern religions of India may be divided into two great groups or classes, that of Śiva and that of Vishṇu. It is extremely difficult to offer even a plausible conjecture as to the origin of the former, or to guess when it first came into vogue. It has been attempted to identify Śiva with the Rudra of the Vedas, and it may be so, but it is certainly a local, not an Aryan form of faith, and seems originally to belong rather to the south than to the north of India. It may have existed there as a native local superstition for any length of time, but it only rose to eminence on the decline of Buddhism. Its principal teacher if not its founder, in its present form, seems to have been Śankara Âchârya, who may have lived in the eighth or ninth century.‡

There does not seem to be a trace of Tree Worship mixed up with it, nor any real connexion with Serpent Worship. It is true Śiva is occasionally represented holding a cobra or other venomous snake in his hand; serpents are also sometimes twisted round his neck or entwined with his hair; but in all these instances the serpent is a weapon, an implement of terror, not an object of worship. As the

---

* When I published, in 1845, my description of the Rock Temples of India, I fixed the date of the excavation of Mahavellipore within the limits of the thirteenth century (pp. 58, 59). I have since seen no reason to alter this description.

† There are, I believe, older Naga sculptures in Cuttack, but whether this is so or not, it is interesting to find the three principal seats of Naga worship at three nearly equidistant points on the shores of the Bay of Bengal, Cuttack, Amravati, and Mahavellipore; exactly opposite to Cambodia, which as above explained was its principal seat in modern times. Sanchi seems to have been a sort of half-way house between these places and the North, for all their traditions point to Takshaśilâ as the original seat whence this form of faith was disseminated, and the Yavanas as the people by whom it was propagated.

‡ Asiatic Researches, XVII. 139.

destroyer everything that can add to the terrible was represented with him. In his hands the serpent is as a sword or trident, and, as his chaplet of skulls, merely meant to overawe and impress the beholder. It never is many-headed, and never seems the guardian god. It is only the earthly serpent taught to do the will of its master.

Occasionally the serpent does appear in a more religious aspect in connexion with this form of faith. He is sometimes represented as entwined round the Lingam, and in some southern temples two serpents are sometimes seen erect with their heads above the Lingam, on either side as if worshipping it. In all these instances, however, the serpent is subordinate. It seems nothing more than we would expect to find in a country where Serpent Worship was at one time so prevalent that the apostles of the new faith should represent the older as doing homage to the new god. In so far as the materials available enable an opinion to be formed, the amount and nature of the Serpent Worship we find mixed up with Śivaism is just what we might expect when a new form of faith superseded an old one. Much of the more ancient worship passes into the new, partly because the priests desire to conciliate the votaries of the old, partly in order to exhibit the triumph of the new god, but more perhaps because nothing is so difficult to kill as an old superstition, and the more unreasonable it is the harder it dies.

When we turn to the Vaishṇava group of religions, we find a very different state of things. This religion is descended from a group of faiths in which the Serpent always played an important part. The eldest branch of the family was the Naga worship, pure and simple; out of that arose Buddhism, as frequently hinted above, and on its decline two faiths—at first very similar* to one another—rose from its ashes, the Jaina and the Vaishṇava. The first named was the purest and most direct descendant of Buddhism, retaining more of its doctrinal purity, and less of the local element, and consequently less Serpent Worship than the other. Still the Naga is almost always to be found in Jaina temples, and placed where it evidently was intended as an object of worship, but subordinate to the saint to whom the temple was dedicated.

The Vaishṇava faith, on the other hand, arose contemporaneously with the Śivite, on the ruins of Buddhism, but with much less of the appearance of being a local indigenous superstition; on the contrary, it bears many marks of being a foreign introduction, as if imported at some remote period by some of the immigrant races, and after rotting and fermenting for ages in the fertile soil of India, at last found the means of coming to the surface between the eighth and the tenth centuries. Garuḍa, Vishṇu's Vâhana, the enemy of the Nagas, is almost certainly the hawk-headed deity of Assyria; and in all the avatars of Vishṇu we find more traces of western superstition than in anything Śivite; but what interests us most here is, that the Naga appears everywhere in Vaishṇava tradition. There is no more common representation of Vishṇu than reposing on the Śesha, as the seven-headed snake is called by the Brahmans, contemplating the creation of the world. It was by his assistance that the ocean was churned and Amrita produced. He everywhere

* Asiatic Researches, IX. 270., and XVII. 285.

spreads his protecting hood over the god, or his avatars, and in all instances it is the seven-headed heavenly Naga, not the earthly cobra of Śiva.*

The worship of the Tulsi plant, which is one of the commonest forms of Vaishṇava adoration, is another of those indications which point to a common origin for the two religions. It would of course be absurd to designate as Tree Worship the adoration of such a plant as Sweet Basil, but the descent from the "Ficus religiosa" to "Ocymum Sanctum" is just such a change as might be expected to take place when a dogma is transferred from an older and higher faith to one of a less elevated character. Both symbolize the worship of the vegetable kingdom, and are a part of that curious association of men with animals and plants which is so marked a characteristic of both the Buddhist and Vaishṇava forms of faith.

The strongest evidence; however, of the connexion between the worship of Vishṇu and that of Buddha is found in the fact, that the Hindus, even to the present day, recognize Buddha as the ninth avatar of Vishṇu. From a historical point of view they are no doubt correct in this; all the eight preceding avatars refer to events that certainly preceded the time of Śakya-muni, and when we understand them they may point to a long chain of tradition out of which Buddhism arose, and into which Buddhism fell, which, when philosophically examined, may throw a flood of light on the origin of Buddhism and of Indian religions generally.†

At present it must suffice to point out that the group to which Buddhism belongs comprises Tree and Serpent Worship as the base, combined with the association of men with animals, especially monkeys, either in consequence of the doctrine of metempsychosis, or as the origin of that belief. These grew into Buddhism, and then bifurcated into the Jainism and Vishnuism of modern times.

It is extremely difficult in the present state of our knowledge, to say to what particular section of the Indian population this group of religions belongs. We know that they were anti-Aryan, yet they do not appear to belong to the Dravidian group. The peculiar deity of the latter I fancy must have been Śiva, and his worship is antagonistic in every essential to those religions composing this family. We must pause till we know more of the ethnology of India before we can decide this question in anything like a satisfactory manner.

Meanwhile, however, the similarity of this family of religions points to an identity of race which can hardly be mistaken. For the present, Scythian is a term that might

---

* Nothing is more common than to connect the worship of the Lingam with the impurities with which the Hindu religion is only too justly reproached. This, however, is a mistake. The worship of Śiva is too severe, too stern, for the softer emotions of love, and all his temples are quite free from any allusion to it. The contrary is the case with the Vaishṇavas, who abhor the Lingam. Love pervades all their myths, and their temples are full of sexual feelings generally expressed in the grossest terms. The existence of any such representation in a temple at once fixes it as originally dedicated to the worship of Vishṇu, or some of his Avatars.

† The 10th or coming Avatar of Vishṇu is Kalki, or the Horse, of which we shall have several opportunities of speaking when we come to describe the sculptures of the Amravati Tope, where the horse frequently appears as an important character, but with a rôle not easily understood. The Chakra or Wheel, which occupies the principal place among Buddhist emblems both at Sanchi and Amravati, afterwards becomes one of the principal emblems of Vishṇu. But perhaps the most striking coincidence is to be found at Puri. The Temple there occupies the site where the tooth relic of Buddha was long enshrined, and the worship of Vishṇu under the name of Jaganath, as there practised, is little else than very corrupt Buddhism.

possibly be applied with advantage. It is sufficiently vague, but perhaps it would be wiser to wait for more definite knowledge before applying any terms.*

The subject is only mentioned here because it will recur again and again in the following pages, and unless these generalizations are borne in mind, the sequel will hardly be intelligible. The sculptures at Sanchi and Amravati may not suffice to settle these questions, but if I am not mistaken they throw as much or more light upon them than any other documents that have yet been brought to light.

Modern Worship of Trees and Serpents in India.

Few probably have read the preceding pages without it occurring to them to ask the question, Does Serpent Worship exist in India at the present day, and if so, to what extent? If the inquiry were addressed to even our best-informed Indian authorities, the reply would probably be negative. We have actually possessed India now for more than a century. The Asiatic Society was established in 1784. Since then, with the branch societies in Madras and Bombay, and the Asiatic Societies of England, France, and Germany, some hundreds of volumes have been published, containing some thousands of papers. As not one of these is devoted to Serpent Worship, or even describes it as existing, it may well be argued that it cannot possibly now be found there.

To this line of argument the answer is plain. None of these thousand and one papers are devoted to the ancient worship of the Serpent, nor do any of them contain anything beyond the haziest allusions to the Naga or his previous influence. Yet, if I mistake not, before this work is concluded, it will appear that the Serpent did play an important part in the mythology of India, and that his worship not only prevailed, but considerably influenced forms of faith where we would least suspect his presence.

The truth of the matter seems to be that attention has not hitherto been specially directed to the subject, and till this is the case, the most obvious evidences might be passed by without being noticed.

As an instance of this, I may perhaps be allowed to quote against myself what occurred at Ajanta. I spent a considerable time in exploring these caves, but my mind was full of architecture. I measured everything, drew every detail, and familiarized myself with every architectural affinity. But neither then nor subsequently† did I note the presence of any Nagas. Now that my attention is turned to it, I find in drawings and photographs twelve or fifteen sculptured representations of the seven-headed Naga, and there may be many more. I now also recollect seeing Nagas in all the Jaina temples at Abu, at Sadree, and elsewhere, but I then passed them over. Now I cannot take up a photograph of any temple belonging to the group of religions which include the Buddhist, Jaina, or Vaishṇava faiths, without seeing snakes everywhere, but in places where neither I nor anyone else detected them before.

---

* It would take a volume to discuss, and an unlimited number of references to establish these conclusions. At present I will only refer to two inscriptions; that at Buddh Gyâ, Asiatic Researches, vol. I. p. 284, and that of Belgola, vol. XVII. p. 270.

† I have twice published on the subject of these caves; first, on the Rock-cut temples of India, folio, 1845, and subsequently, a volume on the same subject in 1864, illustrated by photographs by Major Gill.

The same I believe to be the case with the living worship. In Forbes' Oriental Memoirs,* in Bishop Heber's Travels, and in fifty other places, allusions are made to the feelings of respect and reverence paid by the natives of India to snakes, and no one can reside long in the country without perceiving it; yet, except in Miss Frere's charming little volume, entitled "Old Deccan Days," I hardly know a book in which snakes, and especially seven-headed snakes,† play an important part, or which reflects the feelings of the natives regarding them. The stories of serpents there related are only an accidental selection out of thousands of similar legends, all which might easily be localized or traced to their source, and many of which will no doubt be investigated so soon as attention is really directed to the subject.‡

Two instances of Serpent Worship, at Munnipore and Sumbulpore, have already been mentioned (page 61). Two others are still more remarkable. In the great temple at Madura the three principal images in the Tosak Khâna are a golden (?) image of Hanumân, another of Garuḍa, the Vâhana of Vishṇu, but the terrible enemy of the snakes. Between these two stands an image of the seven-headed Naga, richly jewelled, and under a splendid canopy. In the great temple at Seringham, likewise, the principal images are two golden statues of the seven-headed Naga, larger apparently than that at Madura, and even more richly jewelled;§ and I have no doubt that many other such might be found, but they have not yet been looked for.

In the meanwhile the following two paragraphs, introduced incidentally in two works published in London during the present season, may serve to indicate the class of illustrations which will no doubt be found everywhere when looked for. "At "the Nág Kûán or Serpent Well, in the city of Benares," says Mr. Sherring, "the "Nág or Serpent is worshipped. In a niche in the wall of one of the stairs is "a figure representing three Serpents (query, a three-headed Serpent), and on the "floor is an emblem of Mahâdeva in stone, and a snake crawling up it. The well

* Vol. II. pp. 329, 384, &c.

† In the narrator's narrative (p. xxvii.), the following singularly naïve and interesting passage occurs:—"All "the cobras in my grandmother's stories were seven-headed. This puzzled us children, and we would say to "her, 'Granny, are there any seven-headed cobras now, for all the cobras we see that the conjurors bring "'round have only one head each.' To which she used to answer, 'No, of course there are no seven-headed "'cobras now. That world is gone, but you see each cobra has a hood of skin, that is the remains of another "'head.' Although we often looked for seven-headed cobras we never could find any of them." Had they not been converted to Christianity they might have believed in them, even if they had not seen them.

‡ No one at all familiar with the subject, who reads these tales, can fail to be struck with the similarity that exists between them and many of those collected by the brothers Grimm and others from German and Scandinavian sources, and also with some of the more ancient Grecian myths. The usual mode of accounting for this identity, which can hardly be accidental, is to assume that the tales were originally invented by Aryan nurses beside the cradles of the race in Balkh and Bokhara, and that they were carried east and west by their Alumni when they set out on their travels some 4,000 or 5,000 years ago. The results of my reading have led me to conclusions widely different from this fashionable hypothesis. My belief is that all the serpents and dragons, all the dwarfs and magicians of these tales, all the fairy mythology, in fact, of the east and west, belongs to the Turanian races. These, as I have frequently had occasion to mention, underlie the Aryan races everywhere in Europe as in Asia, and occasionally crop up here and there through the upper crust, often when least expected. So far as I understand the idiosyncrasy of the two races, nothing can be more antagonistic to the tastes and feelings of the Aryans than these wild imaginings; while few things, on the contrary, could be more congenial to the comparatively infantile intellect of the Turanian race.

§ Both these groups were photographed by Captain Tripe, and published by him for Government with other views of the temples in which they are found. I had hoped to have obtained more information regarding them before publishing, but have been unsuccessful.

" is visited for religious purposes only once a year, namely, on the 24th and 25th " days of the month of Sáwan, when immense numbers of persons come to it from " all parts of the city. The women come on the first day, the men on the second; " they offer sacrifices both to the well and to Nágeśwar, or the Serpent God." *

The other relates to Tree Worship. " In Beerbhoom once a year the whole " capital repairs to a shrine in the jungle, and makes simple offerings to a ghost " who dwells in a Bela Tree." " The shrine consists of three trees—a Bela Tree " on the left, in which the ghost resides, and which is marked at the foot with " blood; in the middle is a Kachmula Tree; and on the right a Saura Tree." " In " spite of the trees being at the most 70 years old, the common people claim the " greatest antiquity for the shrine, and tradition says that the three trees that now " mark the spot neither grow thicker nor increase in height, but remain the same " for ever." †

There is no doubt whatever with regard to the worship of Trees in modern times, and numerous instances might be adduced if necessary. The Bo Tree at Buddh Gyâ is worshipped now as it was in the days of Aśoka,‡ and the Tree at Anurâdhapura is, as mentioned above, the principal object of worship in Ceylon at the present day. And all over India there are numerous examples which we may hope some day to see registered.§

Since this work was commenced I have made every effort to obtain from India information regarding the present existence of Serpent Worship, but though not so successful as I could have wished, I have been able to obtain several documents on the subject of considerable interest. One of these is by Dr. C. E. Balfour, of Secunderabad, whose long study of native manners and customs especially qualify him to speak on the subject. The other is from Colonel Meadows Taylor, so well known for his various literary works connected with India, and who likewise is especially competent, by long residence and intimate knowledge of the natives, to speak regarding their forms of worship. Both these documents, with several others of more or less importance, will be found printed in the Appendix. They are satisfactory as far as they go; but we shall never know exactly what we are to believe regarding the present position of Serpent Worship, till some qualified persons make a special study of it on the spot.

From these documents, as well as from such information as I have been able to gather from other sources that were available, my impression is that successive immigrations of non-worshipping races have nearly obliterated the religion of the Serpent from the valleys of the Ganges and Indus. I believe it still exists in Cashmere

---

* The Sacred City of the Hindus, by the Rev. M. A. Sherring. London, 1868, p. 89.

† Annals of Rural Bengal, by W. W. Hunter, B.C.S. London, 1868, p. 131.

‡ Buchanan Hamilton, in Martin's Eastern India, I. p. 76.

§ The following instance of Tree Worship which I myself witnessed is amusing, even if not instructive. While residing in Jessore I observed at one time considerable crowds passing near the factory I then had charge of. As it might be merely an ordinary fair they were going to attend, I took no notice; but as the crowd grew daily larger, and assumed a more religious character, I inquired, and was told that a God had appeared in a Tree at a place about six miles off.

Next morning I rode over, and found a large space cleared in a village I knew well, in the centre of which stood an old decayed Date tree, hung with garlands and offerings. Around it houses were erected for the attendant Brahmins, and a great deal of business was going on in offerings and Pûjâ. On my inquiring how the God manifested

and Nepaul, and in the hills generally, but not in the plains. Though I have no proof of it, I cannot help suspecting its existence also in the hills north of Sylhet. I feel nearly certain it will be found throughout the valleys of the Nerbudda and Tapty, and among the hill tribes perhaps as far East as Burdwan. It probably is also more or less prevalent all along the western Ghauts down as far as Travancore, and sporadically over the whole of the Madras Presidency. Its existence in any particular spot now must not be taken as a proof either of its presence or absence at an earlier period. Its presence may show either that a Serpent-worshipping tribe have not been disturbed or may have migrated to that spot, and its absence may equally be taken to prove either that it never existed there, or that it has been obliterated by other forms. All this will require much care and study before it can be satisfactorily mapped out; but the subject is one of great interest, as bearing on one of the oldest forms of faith that the world knows, and would amply repay any pains that might be bestowed on its investigation.

NOTE.

The annexed woodcut—which ought to have been inserted on page 42—is interesting, not only as showing the Tree and Serpent in juxtaposition, and honoured on a Babylonian cylinder, but because the Tree is of a form with which we are familiar* on the earliest types of Indian coinage, as will be explained hereafter.

No. 5.

CYLINDER, WITH TREE AND SERPENT. From Lajard.

The cylinder from which the representation is taken is in the collection of Mr. Steuart, and is engraved in Lajard's Culte de Mithra, Plate VI., Fig. 4., but without any indication by which its age could be determined. My impression is, that many of these cylinders, and this among the number, are more modern than is generally supposed, and may come down to Achæmenian times. In itself this representation is perhaps not of much importance, but it may be well to quote it, in order that those who are familiar with similar objects may turn their attention to them as sources from which information may be obtained regarding Tree or Serpent Worship. This is certainly not a solitary example.

---

his presence, I was informed that soon after the sun rose in the morning the Tree raised its head to welcome him, and bowed it down again when he departed. As this was a miracle easily tested, I returned at noon and found it was so!

After a little study and investigation, the mystery did not seem difficult of explanation. The Tree had originally grown across the principal pathway through the village, but at last hung so low, that in order to enable people to pass under it, it had been turned aside and fastened parallel to the road. In the operation the bundle of fibres which composed the root had become twisted like the strands of a rope. When the morning sun struck on the upper surface of these, they contracted in drying, and hence a tendency to untwist, which raised the head of the Tree. With the evening dews they relaxed, and the head of the Tree declined, thus proving to the man of science, as to the credulous Hindu, that it was due to the direct action of the Sun God.

* J. A. S. B., vol. VII., Plate XXXII.

No. 6.

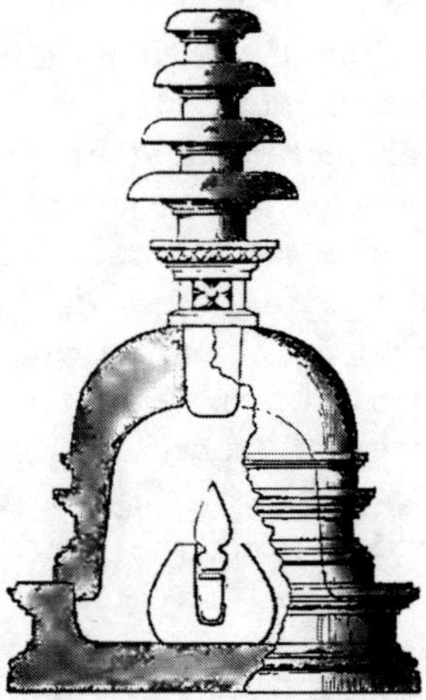

RELIC CASKET, FROM MANIKYALA,
In the possession of General Cunningham.
No. 6.

THE TOPE AT SANCHI.

CHAPTER I.

INTRODUCTORY.

BEFORE proceeding to describe the two buildings which form the subject of the present work, it may be convenient to point out, as briefly as possible, the general characteristics of Buddhist architecture, and to indicate the relations of these two monuments to the other members of the group to which they belong.

In the first place, it cannot be too strongly insisted upon, or too often repeated, that stone architecture in India commences with the age of Aśoka (B.C. 250). Not only have we as yet discovered no remains whatever of stone buildings anterior to his reign, but all the earliest Caves either in Behar or in the western Ghâts show architecture in the first stage of transition from wood to stone. One half, indeed, of the essential architectural structures of the Caves at Bhâjâ and Kârlee, and of the earliest at Ajanta, is wooden, and the wood still remains in some of them to the present day. Though some of these Caves are earlier than the Christian era, none are so old as the time of Aśoka.*

Whether looked at from an archæological, an architectural, or an ethnographic point of view, this wooden origin of Indian Buddhist architecture is one of the most interesting facts connected with the subject. To the archæologist it affords an assurance that in this instance, at least, we have got to the beginning of things, and that all beyond the first imitation of wood can only be rude masses of stone that in themselves tell no tales, and can only be dated from evidence external to themselves.

The architect, in studying this art, feels that for once he is assisting at the birth of a new style, and that during the five or six centuries, to which this work refers (B.C. 250 to A.D. 360), he is gradually watching the growth of an original form of art, which was uninfluenced by any external or foreign element, but left to its own innate powers of development.†

The steps by which the rail at Sanchi was elaborated into that at Amravati will be pointed out in the sequel, in so far as they are at present ascertained;

---

* For particulars I must refer the reader to my History of Architecture, II., p. 456, et seq.

† The nearest approach to anything like this in the west, is to be found in Lycia. Its early tombs are as wooden as the Caves of India, but they fell almost immediately under the influence of Greek art, and became Ionic before they had time to develope themselves into a native Lycian style.

and it forms as interesting an example of the natural development of style as anything in the history of architecture. There may, it is true, be some difference of opinion as to the beauty of the Amravati example, but there can be none as to its originality; and even those who may be inclined to dispute the taste displayed in its design, must admit that it is singularly appropriate to the purposes to which it is applied, and in richness of ornament one of the most elaborate pieces of architecture to be found in any part of the world.

It is perhaps, however, in an ethnographic point of view that this wooden origin of Buddhist architecture is most interesting. As I have frequently had occasion to point out in another work,* the Aryan races are not builders. They always had too firm a conviction of the immortality of the soul, and consequently of the existence of a future state, ever to care much for a brick or stone immortality in this world; and no material art satisfied the cravings of their higher intellectual powers. The Turanians, on the contrary, never rose to a distinct idea of an external God, nor of a future state, but supplied the place of the latter by metempsychosis and final annihilation, while their intellectual status never enabled them to create such a literature as would satisfy that hankering after immortality which is inherent in the human breast. It consequently happens that all the literature of India belongs to the Aryan or Sanscrit speaking races, and all the buildings to the Turanians or those speaking Dravidian or cognate tongues. The result of this distinction, in so far as the present subject is concerned, is this: so long as the Aryans retained their purity of blood and supremacy of power, no permanent buildings were erected in India. On the other hand, if there is one fact with reference to Buddhism more clear than another, it is that it is the religion of a Turanian race. It was not a reform on the Vedic religion of the Aryans, but simply that when they had lost their purity, Sâkya Muni called on the subject races to rise, and moulded their feelings and their superstitions into that form of faith we now know as Buddhism. It was when these Turanians first came into power that permanent architecture was thought of in India; and as they grew in strength, and their influence extended, so did their architecture acquire consistency, and spread over the length and breadth of the land. They had no literature, or next to none; at least we have not yet found one Buddhist book that was reduced to its present shape till nearly 1,000 years after the death of the founder of the religion;† but we have buildings everywhere, and it is this circumstance that renders their architecture so valuable in an historical point of view, and so interesting as an expression of a great ethnographic fact.

Stated in its broadest term, the distinction is this,—all the literature of India is Aryan, all the architecture Turanian; and the latter did not come into existence till the former race had lost their purity and power, or, in other words, till the Turanian religion, known as Buddhism, rose to the surface, and its followers usurped the place hitherto occupied by the Aryans and their Vedas.

Without attempting too minute a classification, the Buddhist buildings erected in India since Aśoka's time may be arranged in three principal groups:—

---

* History of Architecture, Introduction, et passim.

† Max Müller, Chips from a German Workshop, I. p. 196.

1st. Topes or Stûpas, with their surrounding rails and lâṭs; two of the oldest known examples of these, which happen also to be among the richest and most elaborately ornamented, form the subject of the present work.

2nd. Chaityas. Both in form and purpose these are almost absolutely identical with the early Churches of the Christians, though several of those cut in the rock were most probably excavated before the Christian era.

3rd. Vihâras, or Monasteries, forming in the earliest times the residences of the monks or priests who were attached to the service of the Topes or Chaityas, but afterwards the independent abode of monastic communities, who had chapels or places set apart for devotional purposes within the walls of their monasteries.

Taking the last first, we are almost wholly dependent on rock examples for our knowledge of the arrangement and mode of adornment of Indian monasteries. Of these, probably not less than 800 to 1,000 examples are still known to remain in India, of all ages, and extending from a century or two before the Christian era to the tenth or eleventh century afterwards. They also are of all sizes, from the simple cell of a single anchorite to a great hall 80 feet square and more, and sometimes surrounded by sixteen or twenty cells for the accommodation of the monks. The difficulties of lighting naturally limited the extent of each individual example in the rock, but they are generally found in groups of twenty or thirty Vihâras, affording, when taken together, accommodation for a large religious community.

The ruins of a very large Vihâra have been recently excavated at Sârnâth, near Benares.* It had, however, been destroyed by fire, and nothing but the foundation of the walls now remains. A still larger one was cut through by the railway works near Sultangunge in Bhagulpore, and destroyed of course; but here also nothing but the foundations remained, sufficient to show the plan, but nothing more. In 1861–2 General Cunningham found the remains of the great Nâlanda Vihâra to extend 1,600 feet in one direction by 400 in another, and no doubt excavations might bring some interesting particulars to light regarding this most celebrated of Indian monasteries, but too much must not be hoped for.† It was built of wood and brick, and for more than 1,000 years it has been used as the quarry of the fertile district in which it stood.

At Sanchi there are the remains of several Vihâras. One of the best preserved is represented in the Photographic Plate, No. XXIII. Its date is comparatively modern, probably ranging from the eighth to the tenth century, and its dimensions are so small—about 100 feet across—that it would hardly be worth notice were it not that it happens to be the best preserved specimen of a Buddhist structural Vihâra known to exist in India. It will be described further on.

As might be expected, the Chaitya Caves are much fewer in number than the Vihâras; not more than twenty have been described; and it is hardly probable that more than thirty exist. As before hinted, they are almost exact counterparts of the choirs of Christian churches, consisting of a central nave, at the inner end of which stands the Dagoba or Stone Altar, either containing or simulated to contain a relic. Round this and along either side runs an aisle, which is entered by one

---

* J. A. S. B., Volume for 1844, p. 473.

† General Cunningham's Report to Government for 1861–62, p. 11.

of three doors, which open outwardly under a gallery corresponding to the rood-loft of Christian churches. The central aisle was covered with a roof, supported by wooden ribs, like the hull of a ship turned upside down—semicircular internally, but of an ogee shape outside. In all the earlier Caves the ribs were put up in wood, and at Karlee remain to this day as they were put up 1800 years ago, but in later Caves their form was repeated in stone, and afterwards merged into a purely lithic ornament.

The only example of a structural Chaitya yet brought to light is a small one at Sanchi, which will be described when speaking of Plate XXII. Like the Vihâra it is small, and so much ruined that it is not easy to feel sure how it was originally finished, but as a unique example it is well worthy of attention.

We should not, perhaps, be justified in asserting that the Stûpas* or Topes were at all times the most important monuments of the Buddhist. They have become so now, but that may be owing to their form and the solidity of their construction, which has prevented their decay, while the more complex structures of the Vihâras and Chaityas, and the frailer materials of which they were composed, have caused their disappearance. Judging from the glowing descriptions given by the Chinese travellers of the Sanghârâmas (Halls of Assembly) which they visited, and the monasteries in which they were entertained, it would appear that they considered them at least as important.

The Tope is, however, a solid circular pyramid† of brick or stone, and from its form, and under similar circumstances, might have lasted as long as those of Egypt. Those, however,—especially in the valley of the Ganges,—have long been used as quarries by the inhabitants of these thickly-peopled plains, and have consequently disappeared. With very few exceptions, it is only in remote or in thinly-peopled districts that any examples are now to be found.

It scarcely admits of a doubt but that the Tope is the lineal and direct descendant of the funereal Tumulus which, from the very earliest age to which our knowledge extends, the Turanian races—and probably some others—raised over the graves of their dead. Such Tumuli exist all over the north of Asia; they are found in Asia Minor and in Greece. They crowd the cemeteries of Etruria. They are far from being uncommon in Germany, and in the western parts of France. We all know what numbers of them dot the downs of Wiltshire and Devon, wherever an open country enabled a pastoral people to despasture their flocks without the necessity of clearing away the forest; and they are frequent in Scandinavia, and over the whole of the north of Europe.

It is doubtful whether any sepulchral Tumuli exist in India. If these were of earth, the probability is they would be washed away by the overflowing rivers or by the tropical rains, but they do exist in Afghanistan, grouped around the Topes.‡ There are two peculiarities which distinguish the Tope of India from the Tumuli of other countries. The first is, that being of brick or stone the material enabled them to assume a rounded or domical form, while the earthen Tumulus was as generally

* From the Sanscrit, *Stûpa*, a mound or heap.

† Clemens of Alexandria, Stromat. I. 15.

‡ Masson, in Wilson's Ariana Antiqua, 61, et seqq.

straight lined. The circular form seems to have been adopted to assimilate them with the roofs of their other sacred and domestic buildings, which we learn from the sculptures were always curvilinear in outline. The second peculiarity is, that, instead of being the last resting place of a body, they had become depositories of relics only. Precisely the same change took place in the Middle Ages, when the stone coffin became an altar, and the place of the deposit of relics and other treasures, instead of containing a body. In India, where the practice of burning the dead seems always to have prevailed, this probably took place from the first. It may, however, be considered as an argument in favour of the foreign (Scythian ?) nature of Buddhism in India, that the Tope should have been domical from the first instead of straight-lined, and should always have been a relic-shrine, never apparently a tomb.

In addition to its primary and general use as a relic-shrine, the Tope in India was also very commonly used as a memorial tower to mark a sacred spot.* Of the 84,000 Stûpas which Aśoka is traditionally said to have erected, we gather from the Chinese travellers that one half at least were erected to mark spots where Buddha or some Bôdhisatwa had performed some miracle, or done something worthy of being recalled to the attention of the faithful.† When Messrs. Masson and Honigberger opened the Topes in Afghanistan, they found about one half contained relics; the remainder were "blind Topes," and contained nothing.‡ The same probably will be found to be the case, though to a less degree, in other countries. Where the Tumulus was a grave in reality, the chances are that not one in a hundred would be a memorial tower, though these last would probably be the largest and most important.

No. 7

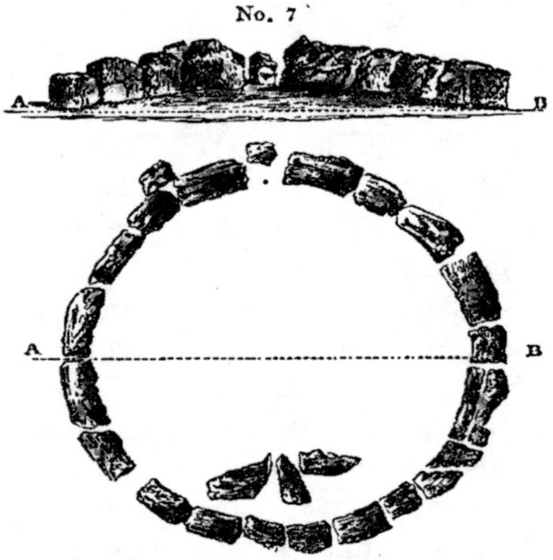

SEPULCHRAL CIRCLE AT AMRAVATI.
From a Drawing in the Mackenzie Collection.

The rails which surround the Indian Topes are sometimes as important as the Tumuli themselves. In the case of Sanchi, and especially at Amravati, they are certainly more so. Like the Topes, their origin is sepulchral. The circles of rude stones found all over Europe certainly are so in most cases. They may sometimes enclose holy spots, and may possibly have in some instances been places of assembly, though this is improbable. Their application to the purposes of ancestral worship is, however, not only probable, but appropriate. Sometimes a circle of stones encloses a sepulchral mound, as at New Grange in Ireland,§

* Properly speaking, the Tumulus containing a relic ought always to be designated "Dagoba," a word derived from "Dhâtu," a relic, and "Garbha," literally the womb, but here used as the receptacle or enclosing shrine. The memorial tower ought, on the contrary, always to be called "Stûpa," from the Sanskrit word Stûpa, a cairn or heap. The difficulty in applying these terms is, that there are no external signs by which the two can be distinguished, and till the contents of all are ascertained, any attempt at precision might only lead to errors.

† If anyone had the patience to classify them, this probably would be the result, at least so it appears in reading the travels of Fahian and Hiouen Thsang.

‡ Wilson's Ariana Antiqua, p. 68, et seqq.

§ Archæologia, 1770, and frequently since described.

and very frequently in Scandinavia* and Algeria.† In India rude stone circles are of frequent occurrence. In the neighbourhood of Amravati alone there are some hundreds of them (Woodcut, No. 7), and all are sepulchral; but, like the Topes when adopted by the Buddhists, they were sublimated into a symbol instead of a reality.

Another circumstance of interest connected with the rail at Sanchi is, that it is only the first step from the wooden form. Its construction and general appearance will be easily understood from the annexed diagram (Woodcut, No. 8) and the photographs. From these it will be perceived that there is nothing lithic in its character. The three intermediate rails must, during construction, have been held in their places by some means not now apparent. The next pillar was pushed laterally to receive their ends in the mortices prepared for them, and the top rail was then fitted on to a tenon on the top of the post (as at Stonehenge), so as to hold the post upright and in its place. All this is good carpentry, but it is very clumsy masonry.

No. 8.

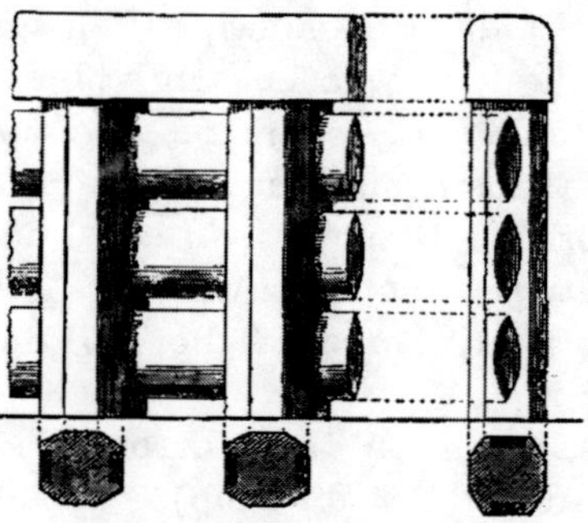

GREAT RAIL AT SANCHI.
From a Drawing by Colonel Maisey.

In Ceylon the top and intermediate rails were omitted. One or three rows of upright stone posts were arranged round the Dagobas,‡ as in the Thûparâmaya (Woodcut, No. 9), but not joined together. In theory these look much more like the rows of detached rude stone pillars of northern climes. In practice, however, they too look as if they had just passed through the wooden stage. Their form is so slender, and their ornaments so essentially wooden, that they can hardly have assumed their present shape directly from a rude stone obelisk. My own impression is that they were used as the supports of tapistry, which on festal occasions was hung between them. When Fa-hian visited Ceylon (A.D. 405), he was present when the Tooth relic was carried to Mehentele, which, like the procession of Jagannâth, was the great annual festivity of the place. On these occasions both sides of the roads were hung with paintings of the 500 different manifestations of Buddha, "painted in different colours, and executed with such care as to appear living."§ This is so exactly doing on canvas what we, about the same time, find

No. 9.

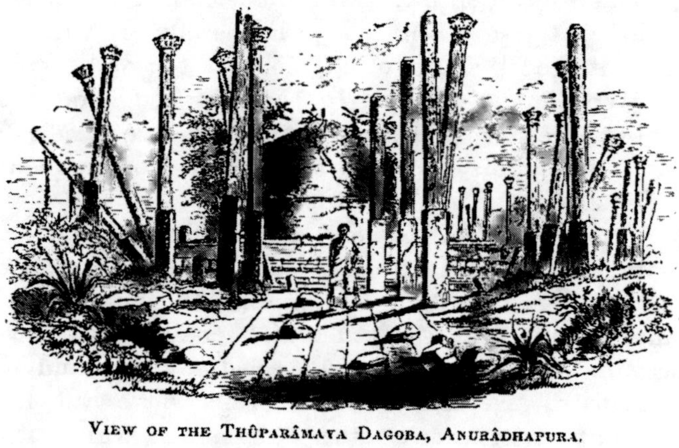

VIEW OF THE THÛPARÂMAYA DAGOBA, ANURÂDHAPURA.

* Olaus Magnus, I. 29, and subsequently in every work on Sweden.

† Journal de la Société Archæologique de Constantine.

‡ Transactions Royal Asiatic Society, III. pl. 17, 18, 20, &c.; History of Architecture, II. Woodcut, 1007.

§ Foě-Kouě-Ki, p. 335.

done on stone at Amravati, that it seems hardly doubtful but that the one is the counterpart of the other, and for the Ceylonese form these tall thin pillars seem peeuliarly appropriate.

The Buddhist rail, in the form in whieh it is found surrounding the great Tope at Sanehi, is espeeially interesting to Indian antiquaries, inasmuch as it was eopied everywhere at that age, and became the favourite arehitectural ornament of the age. At Bhâjâ and Kârlee, in the early Caves at Ajanta and at Kenheri, all the string courses and friezes are mere eopies of this rail. Like the wooden triglyph of the Dorie order, it was repeated through eenturies in stone. It oecurs on the eentral Dagoba at Amravati, but not on the rails or any of the surrounding buildings. We do not find it, however, in any of the Caves of Ellora or Elephanta; indeed its use seems to have died out about the fourth or fifth century, but meanwhile its greater or less prevalenee is no bad test of the real or eomparative age of the building in whieh it is found.

No. 10.

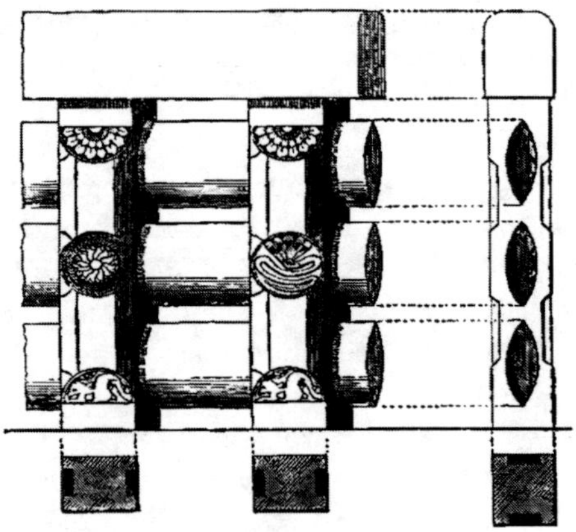

Rail of Second Tope at Sanchi.
From a Drawing by Colonel Maisey.

The next step in the elaboration of these rails is found on that surrounding the second Tope at Sanehi (B 2 on Map). This Tope is relatively much taller in form than the great Tope, whieh is an almost eertain sign of a more modern age, though it still may be anterior to the Christian era, and its rail earlier than the gates attaehed to the old rail of the great Tope. The innovation in this instance eonsisted in plaeing a eentre dise on the pillar, ranging with the eentral rail, and two half dises at top and bottom* (Woodeut, No. 10). In the instanee here given, too, the Serpent appears with the five heads, but whether this is a solitary instanee or frequently repeated, we are not informed.

At Muttra, General Cunningham found fragments of a rail on which this form was repeated, with the addition of groups of seulpture, on what appeared to have been the angle columns. The rail which enelosed the great Bo Tree at Buddh-Gya was square in plan, measuring 131 feet by 90, and was ornamented as riehly as that at Muttra. Neither of these rails have yet been published, nor have we any representation of many other fragments which exist in various other parts of India. This is to be regretted, as the next step is a very long one, and it must have taken some eenturies of elaboration before even the riehest of those mentioned beeame so highly ornamented as that at Amravati. At Amravati all the three rails have eireular dises eovered with a lotus or water leaf ornament externally, and with figures seulptured on their internal faces. The top rail also is adorned with a frieze of figures internally, and on the outer faee with a procession of men bearing a roll sueh as is used in Buddhist processions in Burmah

* The probability seems to be that when the rail was in wood, nails with large heads or metal plates were used to keep the structure in form, as is still sometimes done in framed doors or gateways, and that these afterwards became ornaments, and were used architecturally, as we find it here and elsewhere.

at the present day. The whole rail, in fact, which is 14 feet in height, is covered with sculptured ornaments, and as it was at least 600 feet in length, it may perhaps be considered as the richest and most elaborate piece of screen work in the world.

The only connecting link which has been discovered between these two forms is in the Western Caves. In front of the great Cave at Kenheri, for instance, there is a low parapet wall, so weather-worn that it is difficult to make out its details. The annexed careful drawing (Woodcut, No. 11)—which, however, is fully confirmed by photographs—shows it to possess most of the essential features of the Amravati rail. Each of the three intermediate rails has a disc, and the octagon pillars have a central circle and two half-circles. There is a waving line at top, and an animal frieze below.

No. 11.

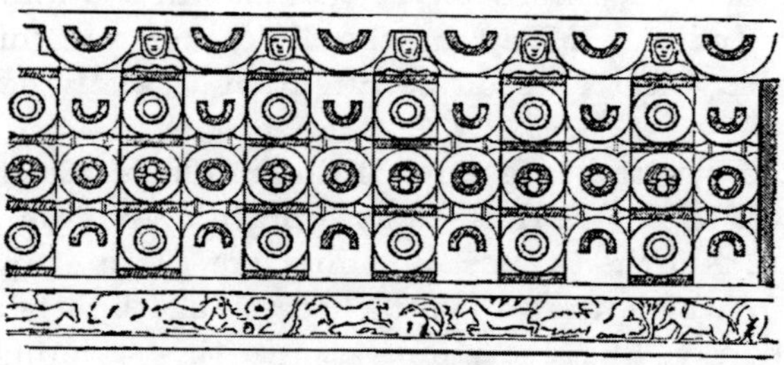

DWARF RAIL IN FRONT OF KENHERI CAVE.
From a Drawing by E. W. West, Esq.

Another rail similarly situated in front of the great Cave at Nassick, containing the Gotamiputra inscriptions (Woodcut, No. 12), shows an advance in this case, and possesses all the features of the external face of the Amravati rail, excepting of course the sculptures, which the scale, and probably the material would not admit of. Its animal frieze can only be indicated, it is so completely weather-worn. So far as I can make out, this Nassick rail is about the same age as that at Amravati; that at Kenheri may be either a little older or a little more modern. It is so weather-worn that it is difficult to determine which. My present impression is, that the Nassick rail belongs to the fourth, the other to the beginning of the fifth century of our era. They are both examples of the completed design, and certainly long subsequent to anything found at Sanchi or at Gya or Muttra.

No. 12.

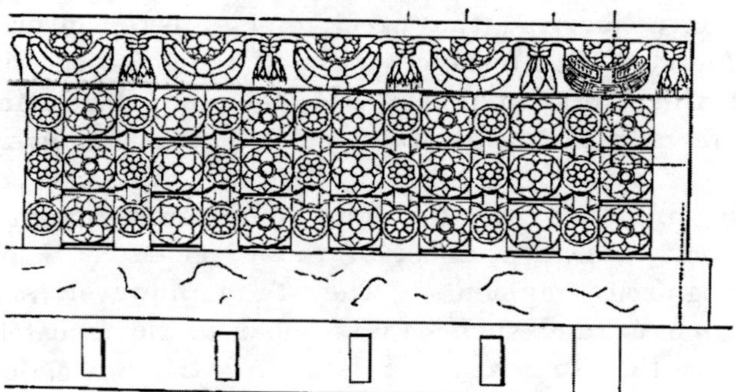

RAIL IN FRONT OF NASSICK CAVE.
From a Drawing by E. W. West, Esq.

So far as is at present known, the Amravati rail, besides being the richest of detached examples, was the last of its race. After the fourth or fifth century the rail became attached to the Tope in the form of a range of pilasters, and the procession path, instead of being behind the rail, as at Sanchi, was on a terrace above the range of pilasters as at Manikyala.* In the Topes in Afghanistan it frequently

* History of Architecture, Woodcuts, 978, 979.

degenerated into a mere ornamental band at some height from the ground, and gradually lost all trace of its origiual significance.

When thoroughly investigated there are few architectural arrangements that will afford a more curious illustration of architectural development than these Buddhist rails. Already we can trace them from the rude circular sepulchral enclosure to such plain unadorned erections as those at Sanchi or Stonehenge, and thence to those of Buddh Gya; from that we can go on to that at Amravati, and till they lose themselves in the north of India. Many of the links are yet missing, though they will no doubt be easily supplied so soon as attention is really directed to the investigation.

Another interesting feature connected with these rails is the gateways attached to them. These are frequently represented in the sculptures at Amravati and the paintings at Ajanta, but the only examples known to exist standing are those at Sanchi. They are more modern than the rail to which they are attached, being slightly subsequent to the Christian era; but still betray, like everything else in this style of architecture, their wooden origin. Such a form could never have been invented in stone; and the reason they are not more frequently found, is probably that they were generally executed in wood, even when attached to stone rails. The Chinese Païloo is undoubtedly the lineal descendant of these gates; but even that is very generally at the present day constructed either wholly or partially in wood. It must, indeed, have required considerable courage to attempt such a construction in stone,* and the wonder is rather that several should have survived the wreck of eighteen centuries, rather than that so few should be found. The form of those at Sanchi and their sculptures form the first division of this work, and need not, therefore, be further enlarged on here; and as they are the only examples of their kind, no classification is possible.

The lâts or Stambhas form another group of early Buddhist monuments that must not be passed over. Four or five out of a larger number of those erected by Aśoka still exist, either standing or in recognized fragments. They form, however, such excellent rollers for the British road maker, and such capital sugar or rice mills for the native zemindar, that the wonder is that so many are left. All those of Aśoka are similar to one another,—circular stone shafts of a single block, 30 or 40 feet in length, and surmounted by a capital with the falling leaf or bell-shaped form found at Persepolis. This form of the capital, together with the Grecian or rather Assyrian honeysuckle ornament with which it is generally associated, are two of the most valuable ethnographic indications which the architecture of this age affords. As we have every reason to suppose that the real architecture of Aśoka's time remained essentially wooden in all its forms, it is curious to observe him copying the details of the architecture of the countries of his allies, Antiochus or Antigonus, in his first attempts at a more permanent style in stone. So far as we now know, the use of these foreign forms were confined to lâts and detached objects, and

---

* Henry of Huntingdon's description of the Trilithon at Stonehenge is curiously applicable here:—" Ubi lapides miræ magnitudinis in modum portarum elevati sunt, ita ut portæ portis superpositæ videantur."—Monument. Hist., p. 694.

were not employed in buildings, properly so called, till more than two centuries after their introduction, and then very much modified from their original forms. The object for which Aśoka's pillars were erected was, that certain edicts might be engraved upon them, which he desired to enforce on his people. Those at Pathari and Erun were erected by the Guptas in the fifth century, and mark the change that had taken place in Buddhist feeling. His own personal greatness and glorification was the object of the king who erected the more modern examples, and no longer a disinterested desire for the religious welfare of his people, which seems to have been Aśoka's only motive. Intermediate between these two periods we have numerous examples. Some cut in the rock, as at Karlee and Kenheri; but generally they are found attached to Topes. Two certainly at one time adorned each of the four entrances of the rail at both Sanchi and Amravati, and several of these still remain; most of them, however, are prostrate, though some are standing.

The capitals of those of Aśoka were generally surmounted by a single lion or elephant* or other animal. At Sanchi and Karlee we have four lions seated back to back on their capitals, and at the former place sometimes a single figure of a man standing. My impression is, that wherever four animals are found surmounting a column, they were not intended as the final ornament, but as the support of a wheel—probably in metal—or some other Buddhist emblem. In other instances we have four men, and these overshadowed by the seven-headed serpent. At Amravati they seem more generally to have been crowned by miniature Dagobas, but sometimes also by men, and by other emblems.† As all these will be more particularly described in the sequel, when this occurs in the Plates, it is not necessary to dwell more on their peculiarities in this place.

---

* History of Architecture, Woodcuts, 969 and 970.

† From some photographs recently received from Nepal, it appears that the practice still prevails there. The statues of their kings stand or are seated on the capitals of tall pillars, sometimes with metal umbrellas over their heads, and in one instance at least the king is shaded by the Serpent hood. This in the nineteenth century!

CHAPTER II.

TOPES AT SANCHI.—(Plates I. and II.)

THE Topes at Sanchi, which it is proposed to illustrate in the following pages, form part of a great group of these monuments situated between the towns of Bhilsa and Bhopal, in Central India. They extend over a district seventeen miles east and west, and about ten miles north and south, in five or six different groups, and number altogether between forty and fifty tumuli of various dimensions. The smallest of them are no doubt mere burying places of local chiefs, erected over their ashes, and contain no objects of interest. Others are Dagobas, or relic shrines, in the correct sense of the word; while the great Tope itself (A, Plate I.) is a Chaitya or Stûpa,* erected apparently to commemorate some event in Buddhist history, or to mark some sacred spot.†

The great Tope at Sanchi (Plate II.) consists, first, of a basement 121 feet in diameter and 14 feet in height. On the top of this is a terrace or procession path, 5 feet 6 inches wide, within which the dome or tumulus itself rises in the form of a truncated hemisphere to a height of 39 feet. This was originally coated with chunan to a thickness of about four inches, but whether ornamented with painting or moulded plaster ornaments cannot be ascertained, owing to the very fragmentary state in which the coating now exists. On the top of the dome was a level platform, measuring 34 feet across. This was surrounded by a circular railing of stones, some of the pillars of which are still found among the ruins. Within this was a square Tee or simulated relic box, consisting of sixteen square pillars with rails, and measuring 11 feet 6 inches each way. Within this again was a circular support for the umbrella which invariably crowned these monuments. When Captain Fell visited this monument in 1819,‡ all this was *in situ* and nearly perfect; but shortly afterwards some bungling amateurs dug into the monument, and so completely ruined it, that the form of its superstructure can now only with difficulty be made out.

The most remarkable feature, however, connected with this monument is the rail which surrounds it at a distance of 9 feet 6 inches from the base, except on the south, where the double flight of steps leading to the berm or procession path reduces the width to 6 feet 4 inches. As before mentioned, it is 11 feet in height, and consisted apparently of 100 pillars, exclusive of the gateways. Each of these was apparently the gift of an individual, and even the rails between them seem to have been presented

---

* Vide ante, page 79.

† The whole of these Topes were carefully opened and examined by General A. Cunningham and Lieut.-Colonel Maisey in 1851, and the results published by the first-named officer, in his work on the Bhilsa Topes, by Smith, Elder, & Co. in 1854.

‡ J. A. S. B., vol. III. p. 490, et seqq. General Taylor, of the Bengal Cavalry, who was probably the first British officer that visited the monument, confirms the account given by Captain Fell. He discovered the Tope when encamped near it, during the campaign of 1818. Three of its gates were then standing, and a great part of the Tee still *in situ.*

by different persons. General Cunningham collected 176 short inscriptions from this rail,* all by different individuals, and each recording that the member on which it was engraved was the gift of some pious person, male or female, but all unfortunately unknown to fame. Not one, at least, has yet been satisfactorily identified.

There is absolutely no sculpture on the rail, but fortunately four gateways were added to it about the Christian era, and these are covered with sculptured decorations of the most elaborate kind. Two of these are still standing, and the fragments of the other two are to be seen lying on the ground. The most perfect is the northern entrance, the rear elevation of which forms the frontispiece to this volume. The total height to the top of the central ornament is 33 feet 6 inches. The height to the under side of the lowest rail is 18 feet 6 inches in the centre, and the width of the opening between the two pillars is 7 feet clear. The greatest width is across the lowest rail, and measures within a fraction of 20 feet. The whole, as will be seen from the frontispiece and the photographs, is of a singularly wooden form, and is jointed and morticed together more like a piece of carpentry than a structure of stone.†

Number 2. Tope (B, in Plate I.) is very much smaller than that just described, being only 39 feet in diameter. It springs from a basement 6 feet in height, supporting a terrace or berm 5 feet 4 inches wide. Its section is that of a hemisphere stilted to the extent of 3½ feet. Its proportional of height, therefore, is 29 feet to 39, or as 3 to 4 nearly; that of the great Tope was only as 1 to 2, showing an advance, which is an almost certain indication of a more modern age.‡ The rail is 7 feet 6 inches in height, and elliptical in plan, in order to allow a clear space of 8 feet as well in front of the ramp as round the other parts of the building. The enclosure thus measures 69 feet by 74½ feet. As before explained, the rail is to some extent ornamented (Woodcut, No. 10), but has no gateways of the same imposing character as those of the great Tope. The angle pillars are, however, ornamented as well as the intermediate rails, and afford some indications of great value. (See Plates XLII. and XLIII., which will be noticed hereafter.)

As before mentioned, the great Tope seems to have been a "monumental tower." Nothing was found in it. This one, on the contrary, contained four steatite boxes, in which were placed relics "of Kâśyapa Gotra, missionary to the whole of the Himawanta," and of Madhyama, both these names being mentioned in the Mahawanso as missionaries sent by Aśoka to the Himalaya country,§ thus confirming to the fullest possible extent the inscriptions on the box. Another contained relics of Mogaliputra, who was the head of the Buddhist church at the third convocation (B.C. 241), and altogether the Tope possessed memorials of ten of the principal personages of the Buddhist community during the reign of Asoka. The three named above were well known before the Tope was opened, the other seven were less famous, but their connection can now be traced.‖

---

* Cunningham, Bhilsa Topes, 235, et seq.

† All the above dimensions are taken from Colonel Maisey's MS. notes.

‡ Cunningham, Bhilsa Topes, p. 177.

§ Mahawanso, p. 74.

‖ These particulars are taken from General Cunningham's work, pages 285, et seqq. He and Colonel Maisey seem to have divided the "find" between them. Colonel Maisey's share is now on exhibition at South Kensington Museum; General Cunningham's is in his own house, Clarendon Road, Kensington.

There is another Tope at Sanchi, which is illustrated to some extent in this work. It stands near to the great Tope, and on the same platform (D 3, in plan, Plate I.) At first sight it appears only as a formless cairn of stones, but on examination it was found to consist of a dome 40 feet in diameter, standing on a base measuring 52 feet across and 6 feet high. The dome was originally crowned by a pedestal or Tee 4½ feet square, supporting a Chatta about 3½ feet diameter. Some fragments of the Rail are scattered about, but the principal ornament is the fragment of one of the Gateways, which is still standing (Plate XXI.,) and though only about half the dimensions of those of the great Tope, is quite equal to them in elegance of design or richness of ornament.

The great interest of this Tope, or rather Dagoba, is that it was found to contain relics of Śáriputra and Mahá Mogalána, two of the principal disciples and followers of Buddha himself.* These were probably the most precious possessions of the fraternity at Sanchi.

As the other Topes at or about Sanchi are not illustrated in this work, it would be tedious and unnecessary to dwell on them here. They are all described and delineated in General Cunningham's work, to which the reader is referred for details. Some of them are of great value for the elucidation of the history of Buddhist art, but none equal either in elaboration or in interest to the three just enumerated.

History.

Although there are no data which enable us to ascertain positively the dates of the Sanchi Topes, there are certain indications which fix them within certain limits with a reasonable amount of certainty. One of the most distinct of these is in an inscription on a representation of a Tope on the Southern Gateway (Plate XVII.) now fallen and lying on the ground. It is to the effect that the beam on which it was found was "the gift of Ânanda, the son of Vasishṭa, in the reign of Sri Śâtakarṇi."† Unfortunately for our argument, there are several kings of the Ândhra dynasty who bore this name. The first reigned A.D. 10 to 28, according to my calculation; the second 64 to 120 A.D., and his long and prosperous reign would seem to afford a presumption that it was during his lifetime that these Gateways were erected. General Cunningham and Colonel Maisey both arrived at the conclusion that it was during the reign of the first that they were added to the Rail,‡ and they may be correct, but a second question arises on this point. The Gateways are not all of the same age. There is a considerable difference in style, and Colonel Maisey thinks the Gateway bearing this inscription is the oldest. On the whole I am inclined to agree with his reasoning on the point, though the data available are not sufficient to justify a positive opinion being expressed regarding it. I feel, however, little doubt but that the four Gateways of the great Tope, and the Gateway of No. 3, were all erected within the limits of the first century after Christ, and I think the probability is that the South Gateway belonged to the first thirty years of it;

* All these particulars are taken from Cunningham, Bhilsa Topes, p. 295, et seqq.

† Cunningham, Bhilsa Topes, p. 264.

‡ Bhilsa Topes, p. 265.

in other words, was being carved while Christ was preaching at Jerusalem. The presumption is confirmed to the fullest possible extent by the style of architecture and of the sculpture, though it is difficult to make this argument available with those who are not intimately acquainted with the Caves of Karlee, Ajanta, and other contemporaneous examples.

The inscriptions on the Rails, though so numerous, do not contain a single historical name that can be recognized with certainty; but the style of the characters in which they are written is very similar to that used in the inscriptions of Aśoka, and never employed,—so far as is at present known,—after the Christian era.

For the Tope itself we have neither inscription nor architectural mouldings, and our Chinese travellers fail us here, as neither of them visited Sanchi, nor did any other mediæval writer, and no tradition exists among the Brahminical or Mahomedan inhabitants of the country as to the origin or date of this memorial of a long-forgotten faith.

In this difficulty the Mahawanso helps us a little.* It relates that when Aśoka was sent by his father to be governor of Ujjéni he tarried some time at Chaityagiri, or, as it is called elsewhere, Wessanagara,† the modern Besnagar, close to Sanchi. He there married Devî, the daughter of the chief, and by her had twin sons, Ujjenio and Mahindo, and afterwards a daughter, Sanghamitâ. The two last named afterwards entered the priesthood, and played a most important part in the conversion of Ceylon to Buddhism. Afterwards "when Mahindo visited his royal mother at Chaitiyagiri," before setting out for Ceylon, she established the thero in the superb Chaitya Vihâra, which had been erected by herself.‡ In all this it is true there is no mention of the Chaitya itself, and it may have existed before Aśoka's time, but there is absolutely no proof of this, and till some one stone monument is discovered in India with an ascertained date anterior to 250 B.C., we must be content to commence our history there. On the other hand, the capital of the pillar (Plate XXXIX. Fig. 1.) and the lions which surmount it are so similar to the works we know to be Aśoka's elsewhere, that we may safely assume they belong to his age. There is also a mutilated inscription, on which General Cunningham reads doubtfully his monumental title of Devânaupriya.§ If this is really his, it settles the question that the Tope was erected by him, though for what purpose he has not attempted to explain.

Without going further into the evidence, which is not necessary in this place, it may fairly be assumed that the great Tope is one of the 84,000 which Asoka is traditionally said to have erected. If so, it is the only one of them all still remaining in India, and the oldest stone building in the country.‖

The Rail may have been commenced immediately afterwards by the faithful of the congregation, and completed in 50 or 100 years. The Gateways were probably added to the then existing Rail at the time when the languishing religion of Buddha

---

* Mahawanso, p. 76.

† Turnour, Pali Annals, J. A. S. B., VII., p. 930.

‡ Mahawanso, p. 76.

§ Bhilsa Topes, p. 259.

‖ General Cunningham's dates are, for the Gates, 19 to 37 A.D.; for the Rail, 250 B.C.; and for the Tope itself, 500 B.C. (page 270, et seq.) With regard to the two first I agree with him, but I think he exaggerates the age of the Tope, without assigning any valid reason for so doing. Assuming the Tope to have been erected by Aśoka, which I see no reason for doubting, this would hardly interfere with his date for the Rail.

was restored to its pristine position by the eloquence of Nâgârjuna, backed by the political influence of the Turushka Kanishka. Everything about them seems to indicate such a revival. If I might be allowed to state what I cannot prove, I would suggest that they must have been completed before the death of Śâlivâhana, 78 A.D.

The superb Vihâra erected by the lovely Devî was, I am afraid, entirely of wood, and no trace of it consequently now remains.

The age of the second Tope seems intermediate between these dates. Its taller form shows it to be more modern than the great one, and the more ornate character of its Rail is a strong indication in the same direction. On the other hand, the character of its sculptures and the form of the letters in its inscription show that it is older than the Gateways of the large Tope, if we might guess, say by 100 to 150 years. It cannot well be more, for the ten persons whose relics it contains were all alive in the reign of Aśoka; and men do not become saints, and little bits of bone or beads that belonged to them do not become valuable, till their corporeal form is forgotten. Had they been buried here, it would have been otherwise; but we must allow a hundred years to have passed since their death before these relics were enclosed in steatite boxes and a Dagoba built over them. As a mean date I would be inclined to place No. 2 Tope at from 100 to 150 years B.C.

The third Tope is so ruined—as mentioned above—that there is nothing in its architecture that would enable us to fix its date. The Gateway may be of the same age as those of the great Tope, or slightly more modern; but even if this were ascertained it would not enable us to determine the age of the Tope itself. It may have been added afterwards, as those of the great Tope certainly were. The fact of its containing relics of the companions of Buddha is equally useless for the purpose of fixing its date. They may have been brought here at any time. If, however, I am correct in a suggestion I will make in describing Plate XXXVIII., it may go some way towards settling this question. My impression is, that the scenes there depicted have reference to the acquirement or recovery of these very relics; and if this is so, the erection of this Tope is probably about contemporary with that of the greater one. If it should turn out as I believe that Aśoka is the hero of the sculptures of the historical scenes in the Gateways of the great Tope, the probability is that, after erecting it to commemorate some miracle or event, he sought further to sanctify the place by adding a relic shrine. According to this hypothesis, he conquered or recovered these relics from their original possessors, and erected this smaller Tope as a chapel for their reception. The Gateway, in that case, is at least two centuries more modern than the building to which it is attached.

There are six or seven other small Topes on the same platform as the great Tope (Plate I.) They are all, however, now merely formless heaps of loose stones, and none of them yielded any results to their explorers.

Ethnography.

It would add very much to the clearness of what follows, if, before proceeding to describe the individual bas-reliefs, it were possible to determine even approximately the races of the people represented in the sculptures at Sanchi, as well as to what epoch of history the events depicted should be ascribed.

Even on the most cursory glance, there is no difficulty in discriminating between the two principal races who take the most prominent part in all the events depicted. There is a third, probably a fourth, race represented, but as they occur only once, there are no sufficient means of comparison to determine who they may be, and it will therefore be sufficient to allude to them when describing Plates XXVIII. and XXX.

Of the other two there can be little difficulty in recognizing one as "Hindus," meaning by that term the civilized race who, at the time when the Gateways were erected, occupied the valley of the Ganges, and who, from their capitals of Ayodhyâ and Indraprastha or Pâṭaliputra (Palibothra), had been the dominant class in India for at least 2,000 years before the time to which we are now referring. Originally these people were no doubt pure immigrant Aryans; but before Śâkya Muni preached his reform, their blood had become so mixed with that of the aboriginal and inferior races as to render the success of that new gospel possible. They still, however, retained the civilization and the pre-eminence which the original intellectual superiority of the Aryans had imparted to them.

In the sculptures they are easily recognized by their costume. This consists of the dhoti, wrapped round the loins in precisely the same manner as it is at the present day; sometimes they have also a chudder over their shoulders; and all wear the turban. This last seems to be mingled with the hair, and twisted into the most fantastic shapes, more resembling the form now seen in Burmah than those usual in Bengal; but still it is fundamentally always a long strip of cloth wound round the head in what was no doubt then considered an elegant and fashionable form.

The costume of the women is more difficult to describe, though this is principally in consequence of its scantiness. Both at Sanchi and Amravati the women always wear enormous bangles about the ancles and wrists, and generally strings of beads round the neck, but their body clothing generally is limited to a bead belt round the body below the waist. From this belt slips of cloth are sometimes suspended, more generally at the sides or behind than in front, and sometimes also a cloth, worn something like the dhoti of the male sex, is also added, but when that is the case it is represented in the sculptures generally as absolutely transparent.

The most remarkable part of the female costume is the head dress, which is as voluminous as the body dress is scant. It is represented, Figs. 1., 2., and 3., Plate III., and seems to consist of two long plaits of hair mixed with beads, and a thick roll of cloth, so as to form a sort of tippet, almost covering the whole of the back of the wearer.

It is, however, not only in the Topes that this absence of dress is so conspicuous. In all the sculptures at Karlee, or Ellora, or Mahavellipore, or in the paintings in Ajanta, the same peculiarity is observable. Everywhere, indeed, before the Mahomedan conquest, nudity in India conveyed no sense of indecency. The wife and mother of Buddha are at times represented in this manner. The queen on her throne, the female disciples of Buddha, listening to his exhortations, and on every public occasion on which women take part in what is going on, the costume is the same.* It is equally remarkable that in those days these unveiled females seem to have taken part in every public transaction and show, and to have mixed with the men as freely as women do in Europe at the present day.†

All this is the more remarkable, as in Buddhist books modesty of dress in women is frequently insisted upon. . In the Dulva, for instance, a story is told of the King of Kalinga presenting to the King of Kośala (probably Oude) a piece of muslin, which afterwards fell into the hands of a lewd priestess. She, it is said, wore it in public, while it was so thin that she, notwithstanding this, appeared naked, to the great scandal of all who witnessed the exhibition.‡ The probability is, that the story and the book that contains it are of very much more modern date than our sculptures. It certainly is in direct conflict with their evidence.

The other race above alluded to is very easily distinguished from that just described, both in appearance and in their social status. The costume of the men consists of a kilt, literally a kilt, not a cloth wrapped round the loins, but so far as can be judged from the sculptures, needle made, and fastened by a buckle or string. They also wear a cloak or tippet, which seems to be equally shaped and sewn, a thing apparently utterly unknown in India till the fashion of shaped garments was introduced by the Mahomedans.§ Their head dress is also very peculiar; either it is that their hair was twisted into a long rope or plait like a Chinaman's, and then bound round the head in a conical form, or a piece of cloth or rope was similarly twisted. Their most marked peculiarity, however, is that they all wear beards, whereas no single individual of the other race either at Sanchi or Amravati has a trace of a beard or of even a moustache. This is the more remarkable, as Nearchus tells us that the Indians daub their beards with various colours, so that some are white, others black, some red, some purple, and others green! || Curtius tells us they never shave.¶ Diodorus assures us that they nourish their beards during their whole lives, and received this custom from Bacchus, whom they call the bearded deity; and Strabo tells us they suffer their beards to grow without cutting, and dye them various

* When we first visited Japan in 1860, the females were seen "tubbing" in the public streets in the open light of day. Whatever it may be now, nudity conveyed no idea of indecency to the Japanese ten years ago.

† In India there are some tribes where the females still go nearly naked. The Putooas, for instance, described by Mr. Samuells, J. A. S. B., XXV. p. 295, have no other dress than a string tied round their waists, from which every morning they suspend a fresh bunch of leaves in front and another behind; literally the costume of our first parents in Paradise. In the south of India some of the females, of the races on the west coast especially, wear nothing above the waist, in curious contrast to the countries where the Mahomedans have held sway, where the women are now generally secluded, or, if appearing in public, are completely veiled.

‡ Asiatic Researches, XX. p. 85.

§ Buchanan Hamilton, in Martin's Eastern India, II. 699.

|| Arrian, Indica, XVI.

¶ Q. Curtius, VIII. 9. 22.

** Diodorus, IV. 5.

colours by way of ornament;* and Solinus gives the same testimony. It is true all these authorities may have copied from one another, and that they may only refer to one people on the banks of the Indus, but the shaven condition of all the Hindus on our monuments and the universal prevalence of beards with the other race are very remarkable.†

The costume of the women differs from those of the Hindus even more than that of the men. They wear a petticoat striped like that of the other sex, and apparently gathered in at the knees, so as to form a neat and modest dress, and a cloak or tippet similar to that of the men is thrown generally over one shoulder so as to leave one breast bare, but sometimes both are covered. On their heads they wear a neat and elegant turban (Plate III., Figs. 4. and 5.). They wear no bangles nor ornaments of any kind.

Who then are these people? From their dwelling in the woods and the peculiarity of their costume both General Cunningham‡ and Colonel Maisey are inclined to regard them as priests or ascetics, though the latter remarks, "they are nowhere "seen worshipping Topes, trees, wheels, or the disc and crescent symbols. In one "compartment they may be seen worshipping the serpent in a fire temple,"§ &c. It is curious that in their only appearance at Amravati (Plate LXX.) they are equally worshipping the serpent, but never mixed with those paying respect to the other objects of adoration.

After a careful study of all the bas-reliefs bearing on this subject, it does not appear to me doubtful that the sculptors at Sanchi meant to represent this people as the aboriginal inhabitants of the country of Malwa, to whom the Hindus came either as conquerors or as missionaries. The Topes were erected of course and Gateways sculptured by the latter race, and they represent the other as always inferior and engaged in servile employments, but they do not represent them as converted to Buddhism. As just mentioned, they nowhere join in worship with the superior race, and the only act of adoration in which they are engaged either here or at Amravati is the adoration of the five-headed Naga. This is the more remarkable, as we shall see hereafter, that both at Sanchi and Amravati the Naga is the tutelary deity and emblem of the other, or at least of another race.

The circumstances which apparently induced General Cunningham and Colonel Maisey to regard them as priests, was that their costume resembled that of ascetics in Burmah and other Buddhist countries at the present day. This hardly, however, seems a sufficient reason for the purpose. From their appearing so frequently on Buddhist monuments, we may certainly assume that they were converted eventually to Buddhism, and being a tribe dwelling in woods their priests may have become forest ascetics as contradistinguished from the monastic orders of the more civilized race. If this were so they may have retained the form of dress, and it may have become the fashionable costume of ascetics in future ages. One such certainly

* Strabo, XV. 1024.

† Only two instances of bearded men occur at Amravati. Both of them appear to be the same people as those so frequently represented at Sanchi.

‡ Bhilsa Topes, pp. 204. 208. 210, et passim.

§ M. S., 20.

appears at Amravati (Plate LXXXVI.), but at Sanchi they seem most unmistakeably to be represented as a tribe, not as a priesthood.

It would be extremely convenient if there were any local name which we could use in speaking of this people. To call them, however, either Gonds or Khonds, Bhils, Meenas, or by any other name, would be begging the question, and putting forward an hypothesis for which no grounds have yet been obtained. In the following pages I propose to call them Dasyus, not because there is any local or traditional authority for such a name, but because in the Vedas and the heroic poems such a term seems to be applied to the aboriginal people of India as contradistinguished from the Aryans.* It is here used for non-Aryan as distinguished from Aryan, and involves no theory and interferes with no name appropriated to any known tribe, and as such may be conveniently employed till some better is suggested.

If I were asked to give them a distinctive name I would unhesitatingly suggest Takshaka, or, to adopt Colonel Tod's spelling, Takshac, as the most appropriate, his description of that race seeming to apply in almost every particular to this people. They were essentially Serpent worshippers, "Naga and Takshac being synonymous "appellations in Sanscrit for the Snake, and the Takshac is the celebrated Nagvansa "of the early heroic history of India."† They were also essentially the artificers and architects of India,‡ and lastly, they are known to have possessed Assergurh § in this neighbourhood in the Middle Ages, and may have been settled there from time immemorial. Their original seat was Taxila, which was also the metropolis of Serpent Worship, and the spot whence it spread all over India.‖ On the whole, however, it is probably better to avoid affixing any definitive name to them in the present stage of the inquiry.¶

Sculptures.

Although anyone may, by a careful study of the drawings and photographs, learn to discriminate between the different races of men represented in the sculptures, the task becomes very much more difficult when we attempt to ascertain what particular event each bas-relief represents, or to give a name to each individual scene. About one-half of the bas-reliefs at Sanchi, however, represent religious acts, such as the worship of the Dagoba or of Trees. Once or twice the Wheel is the object of adoration, and once the Serpent. In all these cases there is no doubt or difficulty. There are also half-a-dozen scenes that can be identified with more or less certainty as representing events in the life of Śâkya Muni, and a considerable number of representations of scenes in domestic life, regarding which it will probably be impossible ever to feel sure that we know who the actors in them are. Nor is it of

---

* I make this statement on the authority of Muir's Sanskrit Texts, vol. I., 2nd edition, passim. See also Vivien de St. Martin, Géographie du Véda, p. 98, et seqq.

† Tod's Annals of Rajasthan, I., p. 104.

‡ Ibid., p. 671.

§ Ibid., p. 105.

‖ Cunningham's Report, 1863-64, p. 5.

¶ Another element of identification is to be found in their beards. The Greeks, who practically only knew the Indians of the North West (Taxila), represent the Indians as bearded. These people are the only ones in our sculptures with hair on their faces.

much importance here. Eating, drinking, and making love are occupations so common among mankind, that it matters little who the parties are who are so engaged in the Sanchi sculptures. But besides all these, there are several important bas-reliefs representing historical events, which it would be very interesting to identify if it were practicable. Generally the lowest architrave in each of the Gateways is so occupied, sometimes both in front and back, as in the Northern Gate, and the two lowest in front of the Eastern, and two historical scenes are represented in Plate XXXVIII., one from the Western, the other from the Southern Gateway, both of which have fallen.

The two latter represent the siege of a city in order to recover and to obtain possession of some relics, and the triumphal return of the army with the precious deposit; and, as will be afterwards explained, it is probable that the caskets contain the identical relics that were enshrined in No. 3 Tope, and are now in this country. Be that as it may, the question is, who is the hero of the fight? and who brought home the relics to Sanchi? Assuming the sculpture to have been executed about the Christian era, does it represent a transaction in the reign of Aśoka more than two hundred years earlier, or did the king who erected the gates order these bas-reliefs to be executed to commemorate some great exploit of his own? If the king had engraved his own name on the gate, the latter would have been the probable solution, but the inscription states that the sculpture is the "gift of Ânanda, the son of Vasishṭha, in the reign of Śrî Sâtakarṇi." On the whole, therefore, considering that it is a religious monument, and the general self-denying character of Buddhism, it is more probable that the events represented had passed into the domain of religious history before they were sculptured on the Gateways, and that they were actions sanctified by time.

Unfortunately the other inscriptions, though so numerous, afford us no assistance in this inquiry. It is probably correct to assert that there is not one single inscription, either at Sanchi or Amravati, which has any reference to the subject about or upon which it is engraved. They all record gifts, and gifts only, and it would be as reasonable to look for an explanation of the Resurrection or the Last Supper from the inscription of a memorial window in modern times as to try and find out from those on the Topes what the sculptures represent.*

We are thus left pretty much to conjecture; but we shall probably not err far if we consider Aśoka as the hero in all, or nearly all, the purely historical bas-reliefs. Not only was Aśoka the great apostle of Buddhism before the Christian era, but, as before mentioned, he was especially connected personally with Sanchi. He resided here during the life of his father, when he was only governor of Ujjain, and before his conversion to Buddhism. He married the daughter of the Seṭṭhî, or Shreshṭî, of the place, and she at least continued to reside here after her children

* Another circumstance of a mechanical and it is hoped temporary nature adds to our difficulties here. When Colonel Maisey was at Sanchi he was unable to procure wood either in sufficient quantities or of sufficient lengths to get up near enough to draw the historical bas-reliefs. We are forced, therefore, to depend on Lieutenant Waterhouse's photographs, which are on too small a scale to be distinct, and on Colonel Maisey's verbal descriptions for our information. Both are excellent in their way, but till they are photographed to a larger scale, or drawn, they cannot be compared with the others in such a manner as to detect minute differences, on which the whole question frequently hinges.

had grown up, and had not only been converted, but had assumed the priesthood in the Buddhist hierarchy. It was probably, therefore, through the influence of Aśoka that the inhabitants of Malwa first heard of Buddhism, and if so, there is no one so likely to have become a popular local hero, nor any one whose acts would more probably be represented on the religious edifices of the place.

To this may be added, that the bas-reliefs, in so far as they can be made out, do represent just such an advent of the Hindus, and the conversion of the natives of the country to Buddhism, as is involved in this hypothesis. It serves at least to explain all we now know of them, and may, therefore, be usefully employed till at least some other is started from information not at present available.

It may seem premature, before describing the sculptures, to attempt anything like a criticism of their merits. It may, however, add to the intelligibility of what follows to point out how extremely different these are to the usual sculptures brought home from India, or represented in Hindu drawings. Neither at Sanchi nor at Amravati are there any of those many-armed or many-headed divinities who form the staple of the modern Hindu Pantheon. There are none of those monstrous combinations of men with heads of elephants or lions or boars. All the men and women represented are human beings, acting as men and women have acted in all times, and the success or failure of the representation may consequently be judged of by the same rules as are applicable to sculptures in any other place or country. Notwithstanding this, the mode of treatment is so original and so local, that it is difficult to assign it any exact position in comparison with the arts of the Western World. It certainly, as a sculptural art, is superior to that of Egypt, but as far inferior to the art as practised in Greece. The sculptures at Amravati are perhaps as near in scale of excellence to the contemporary art of the Roman empire under Constantine, as to any other that could be named; or, rather, they should be compared with the sculptures of the early Italian renaissance, as it culminated in the hands of Ghiberti, and before the true limits between the provinces of sculpture and painting were properly understood.

The case is somewhat different as regards the sculptures at Sanchi. These are ruder, but more vigorous. If they want the elegance of design at Amravati, they make up for it by a distinctness and raciness of expression which is wanting in these more refined compositions. The truth seems to be that the Sanchi sculptures, like everything else there, betray the influence of the freedom derived from wood carving, which, there can be little doubt, immediately preceded these examples, and formed the school in which they were produced.

There can now be very little if any doubt but that this school of Indian art owes its origin to the influence of the Greek kingdom of Bactria. Of late years considerable collections have been made of Buddhist sculptures from ruined Topes in the neighbourhood of Peshawer.* These are in many respects extremely similar to those at Sanchi, but more closely allied to the classical type. In many of the

* I speak confidently of these sculptures, as I have photographs of a considerable number, and specimens of others exist in this country. Unfortunately, no means exist as yet of conveying a knowledge of them to the public.

Punjab examples the costumes and mode of treatment is almost purely western, but we are always able to trace the steps by which the Grecian design becomes Indianized, and changed into the type we find at Sanchi and Amravati.

Perhaps, however, the crowning point of interest in these sculptures is, that they complete our knowledge of the history of stone art in India. Hitherto we have been groping our way backwards with uncertain steps, never knowing at what conclusions we might ultimately arrive. As far back as the tenth or eleventh centuries we had abundant examples of structural buildings, and we found that each was perfect in the direct ratio of the age. The history of art in India, so far as we could trace it, was written in decay, and finding each example more perfect than the one that followed it, there was reasonable hope that some day we should find something that would stand comparison with the arts of the Western World.

Beyond the tenth century we were left for guidance almost wholly to the rock-cut examples. These, however, owing to the coarseness of the material out of which they were excavated, and the difficulties inherent in Cave art, could not be depended upon as trustworthy indications of the state of refinement of the arts in their age. In so far, however, as architecture is concerned, we learned from them that stone was first thought of as a building material about the age of Aśoka, certainly after the time of Alexander, and the commencement of the first intimate intercourse between the Western and the Eastern World.*

The knowledge that we have now gained of the early history of the art of sculpture in India, from the study of the examples at Sanchi and Amravati, enables us to point with equal certainty to Bactria as the fountain head from which it was introduced. We can thence follow it through the time when, from being a rude and imitative art, it rose to its highest degree of refinement in the fourth or fifth century of our era, at which time it had also become essentially localized. From that point our history is easy, though somewhat discouraging, from its downward tendency towards the present state of art in India. We are now also able to trace the Yavanas step by step, as they penetrated over the Upper Indus, and spread their influence and their arts across the continent of India to the very shores of the Bay of Bengal, at Cuttack, and Amravati. With almost equal certainty we can follow them as they crossed the bay, and settled themselves in Cambodia and Java. But the people who did all this were not Greeks themselves, and did not carry with them the Pantheon of Greece or Rome, or the tenets of Christianity. They were a people of Turanian race, and the form of worship they took with them and introduced everywhere was that of Trees and Serpents, fading afterwards into a modified form of Buddhism.

* See History of Architecture, by the Author, II. 455, et seqq.

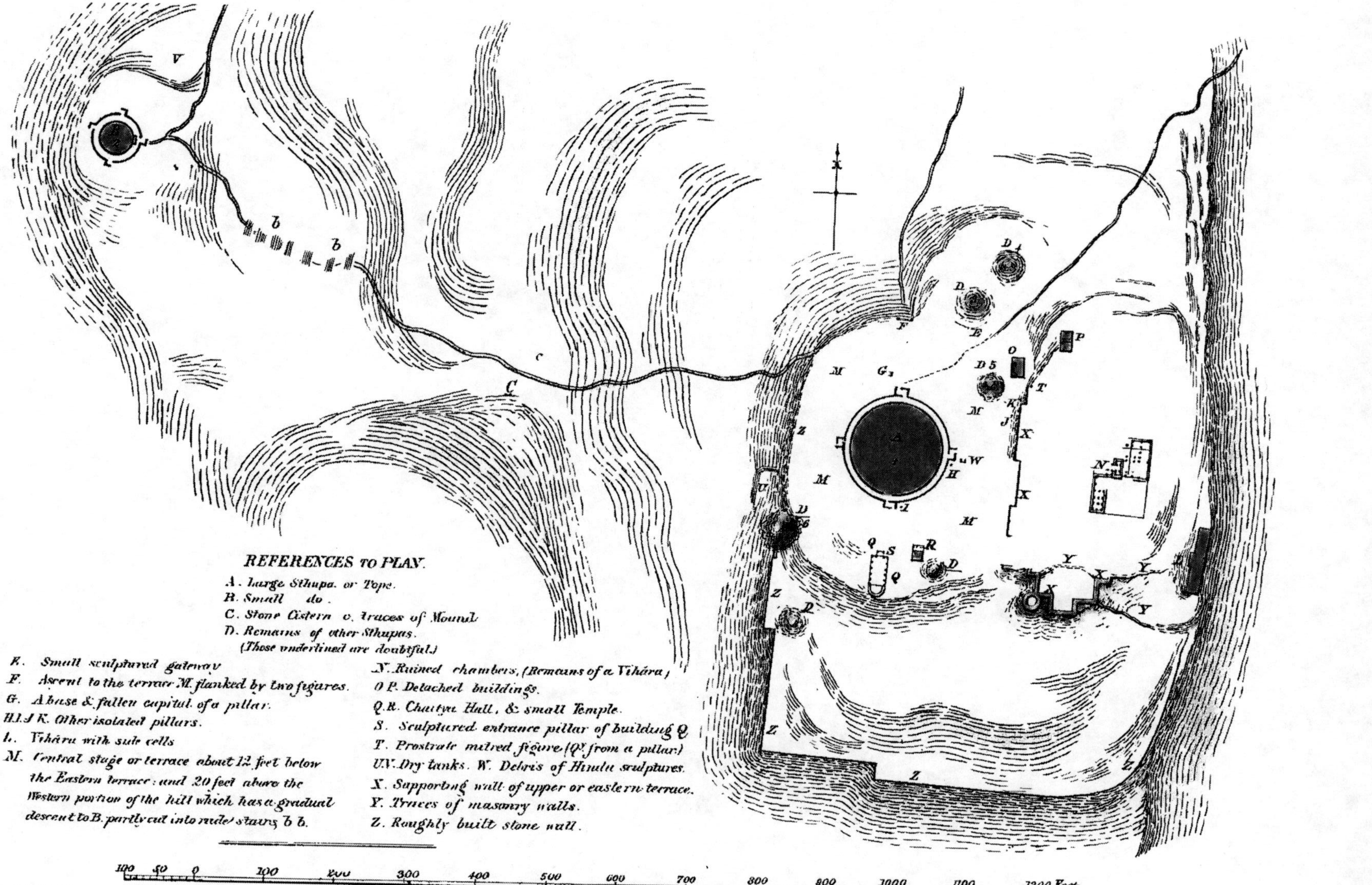

COL. MAISEY DEL

W. BRIGGS, LITH.

SANCHI.

PLATE II.

FIG. I.

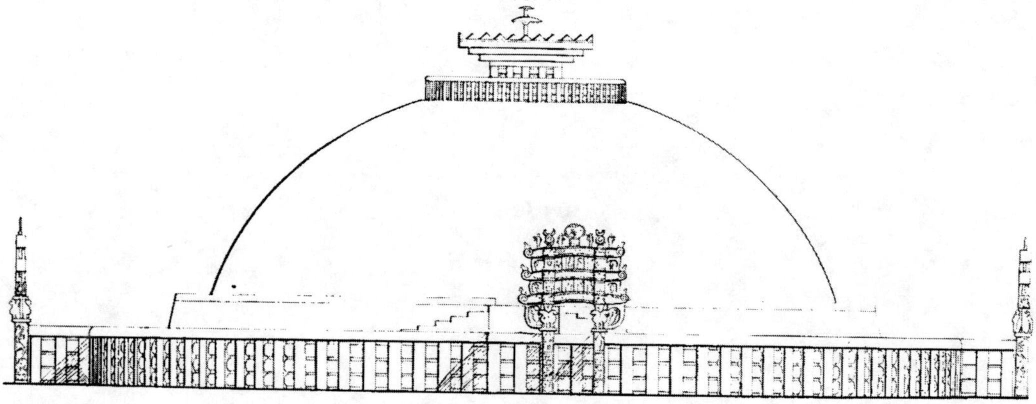

FIG. 2.

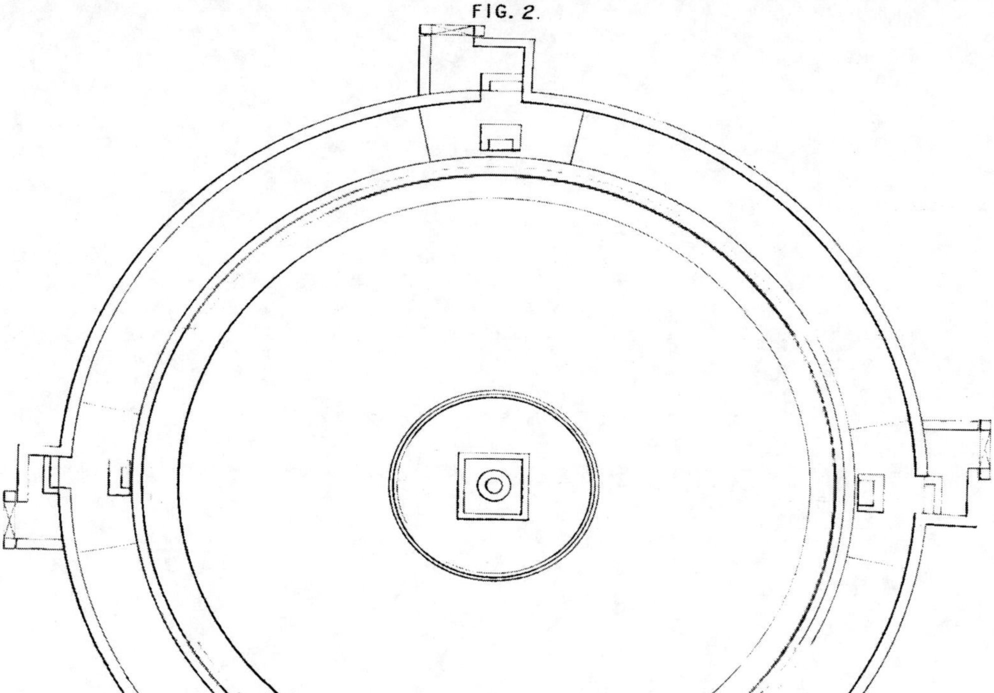

PLAN AND ELEVATION OF TOPE.

SANCHI. PLATE III.

FIG. 1.

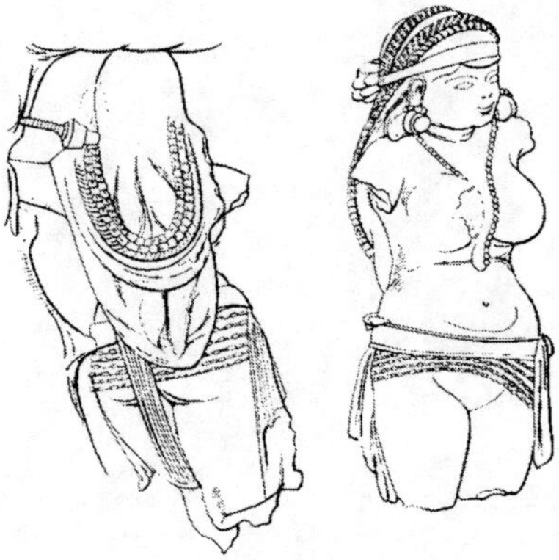

FIG. 2.

FIG. 3.

FIG. 4.

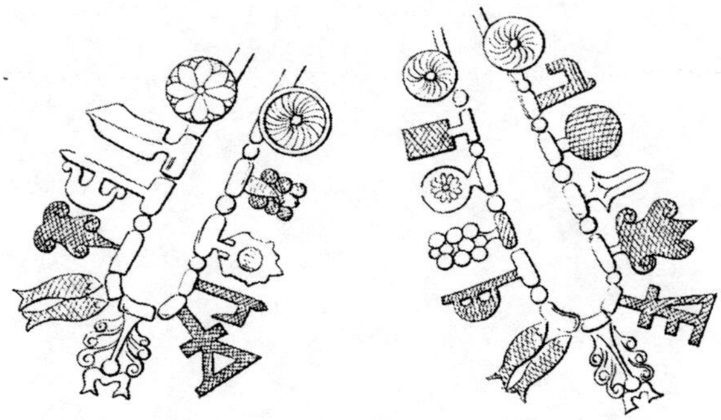

FIG. 5.

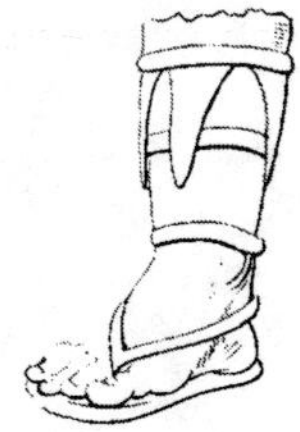

FIG. 7.

FIG. 6.

FIG. 8.

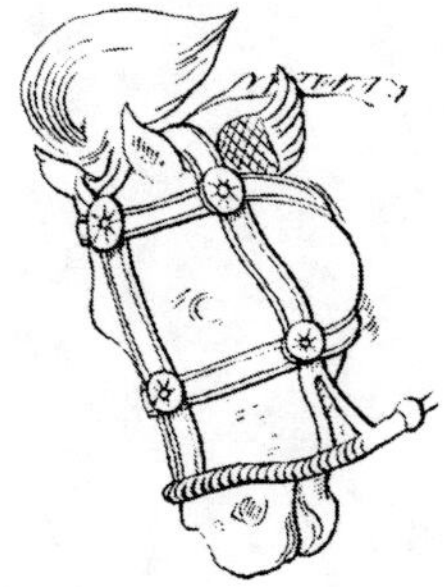

DETAILS FROM SCULPTURES.

SANCHI.

NORTHERN VIEW OF TOPE.

SANCHI.

PLATE V.

EASTERN VIEW OF TOPE.

DESCRIPTION OF THE PLATES.

SANCHI TOPE.

FRONTISPIECE AND PLATES I. TO V.

THE frontispiece to the work is an elevation drawn to scale of the Northern Gateway of the great Tope, as seen from the inside. A photograph of the same subject will be found on Plate VII., and a comparison between the two is not only useful but interesting at starting, as it proves, in addition to their artistic merits, how exquisitely truthful Colonel Maisey's rendering is of these complicated subjects. Although reduced in scale to bring it within the size of the page, the drawing adds considerably to our knowledge of the bas-reliefs as reflected in the photograph. The elevation is also useful as showing the relative dimensions of the Gateway as compared with those of the Rail to which it was added.

Plates I., II., and III. have already been partially described. The first shows the relative position of all the monuments in the immediate neighbourhood of the great Tope at Sanchi, and includes all those which are referred to in the following pages. The other groups of Topes at Sonári, Satdhára, Bhojpur, and Andher, are described in detail by General Cunningham, in his work on the Bhilsa Topes; but as I possess no photographs or information regarding them beyond what is found in his work, they will not again be referred to in these pages. They are principally interesting in consequence of the relics which were found in the chambers in their interior, which throw considerable light on the history of Topes in general, and the purposes for which they were erected. They are, however, all smaller than those at Sanchi, and very inferior in richness of decoration, so that they add very little to our knowledge of the architecture of the Topes, or the mode in which they were ornamented. They are, besides this, in so ruinous a condition that photography would hardly be available for their illustration, and they possess no sculptured bas-reliefs of any description.

Plate II. contains a plan and elevation of the great Tope restored by Lieutenant-Colonel Maisey, from the fragments found by him on the spot. The details of their restoration and the measurements have already been given at page 87, and need not therefore be repeated here.

Plate III. contains various details in costume, &c., some of which have been referred to already, others will be noticed in the sequel.

Plates IV. and V. are complementary to Plate II., and represent the great Tope as photographed by Lieutenant Waterhouse from two slightly varied points of view. The first shows the North Gateway, nearly in front on the right hand, and a side view of the East Gateway on the left. In the foreground, but too much out of focus to enable its details to be distinguished, stand the ruins of the Gateway of the small Tope (No. 3), shown more in detail in Plate XXI., with which it will be described further on.

Plate V. represents the Tope with the Eastern Gateway, nearly in front, and the North Gate is seen sideways on the right hand. Between the two is seen the Rail, which is nearly perfect throughout this quadrant, and enables us to judge of its relative importance as compared with the Tope itself. The berm or platform from which the dome springs, is also distinctly visible in both these photographs.

In neither view is it possible to distinguish any remains of the stucco which once covered the whole of the dome. Fragments of it are still found lying about, sufficient to show that its thickness was about four inches; but there is nothing to enable us to determine whether it was painted, or whether it was covered with ornaments in relief, as there is every reason to believe was the case at Amravati. From such representations of Topes as are found among the sculptures at Sanchi, the inference would rather seem to be that the surface was plain, but that on great festival occasions it was adorned with wreaths and garlands hung on pegs, and it may also have been adorned with tapestries or painted cloths, but so far as can now be seen, not by any permanent decorations.

The Tee and its enclosures have been thrown down, though some fragments of them are still seen lying on the surface of the mound,—quite sufficient, apparently, to justify its restoration, as shown in Plate II. Even, however, if no fragments remained, there could be no doubt but that a Tee once adorned the summit of the monument, and that it must have been very similar to the one here represented. It is probably quite correct to assert that no Dagoba ever was erected without this indispensable adjunct, and from the numerous representations we have of it, both at Sanchi and Amravati, and in other places, we can have little doubt as to its general appearance. Its dimensions are given by the diameter of the platform on the top, irrespective of other evidence.

FRONT VIEW OF NORTHERN GATEWAY.

REAR VIEW OF NORTHERN GATEWAY.

PLATES VI. AND VII.

FRONT AND BACK VIEWS OF THE NORTHERN GATEWAY.

IN describing the photographs, it will not be necessary to allude to the various sculptures on the pillars of the standing Gateways, as they have all been drawn by Colonel Maisey, and lithographs from his drawings will be described in their proper places further on. Owing, however, to the difficulties of getting up to them, none of the horizontal architraves above the Elephant capitals were drawn by him, with the exception of the central piece of the back of the lower architrave of the Northern Gateway (Plate XXXII.). We are thus left almost wholly to the photographs and Colonel Maisey's manuscript notes for our knowledge of these, which is to be regretted, as some of them appear at least as interesting as any that are drawn.*

On the right hand projection of the lower architrave, in front, "is a conical-" roofed hut, with figures and animals."† The face of the stone is so weather-worn, that it is unfortunately impossible from the photographs to add anything to this very meagre description. The hut, however, looks very like a Serpent temple.

"On the left-hand projection, huts, with numerous male and female figures, some " praying and others carrying various implements," whether Dasyus or Hindus is not stated. So far as can be made out, they seem to belong to the latter class.

"The central compartment has on its right the gateway and buildings of a " walled city, like those in other sculptures. Inside are numerous spectators and " some figures apparently doing homage to two sacred elephants or to their riders. " Near the outside of the gate stands a male personage wearing the Dhotî and large " Turban" (Hindu) "attended by several figures in respectful attitudes. The Chaori " and Chatta which accompany him mark him either as a king or a saint. There " are also a number of women with covered jars or vases."

"Next appears a four-horsed chariot of a different shape from those seen else-" where (see Plate III.). It contains a man dressed as above, and attended by " Chatta and Chaori bearers (women) and two children with tufts or plumes in their " heads. On the left another stage of the ceremony is apparently represented. The " same chariot is seen unharnessed, the yoke held up by a woman. The two children " still occupy it, but the king, or whoever he may be, is standing near the pole with " his arm stretched over the yoke, and is apparently conferring some grant or gift " to the priest or ascetic (Dasyu) before him, into whose hand he is pouring water, " an ancient mode of sealing a gift. The costume of this last figure is what is

---

* I presume the same difficulty which prevented Colonel Maisey from delineating them, prevented General Cunningham from making out these subjects sufficiently to enable him to describe them. No mention of them is made in his work on the Bhilsa Topes.

† As all the quotations between inverted commas in these descriptions are from Colonel Maisey's manuscript notes, this one reference will serve for all.

"usually seen in the only class that can be identified with priests, ascetics, and "saints." (Vide ante, p. 93.) "Above this group, and facing towards the city, "is another empty chariot, which a man, dressed as the preceding, is about to "harness; the four horses are seen in front."

Colonel Maisey then goes on to state that he considers this to represent a religious procession, and the dedication of the chariot to the Sun. As before stated, I am more inclined to regard it as a meeting between Aśoka or some Hindu Prince with the Dasyu Chief of the place, either on the occasion of a treaty of peace or to obtain a cession of land for the service or building of the Dagoba, or it may be his conversion to Buddhism. If the Prince is Aśoka, it is probable that the children in the chariot may be Mahendra and Sanghamittâ, and not impossible that the Dasyu Chief may be their maternal grandfather; but such speculations must wait for more intimate knowledge of the subject than we now possess.

On the back of the architrave the same subject is apparently continued, and fortunately we have a drawing of the central portion (Plate XXXII.), in describing which its subject will be more easily made out than from the present photograph.

On the left hand projection, behind the Hindu Raja, we have a walled city with figures. On the right hand projection, two Hindus, accompanied by two females and three very small children, watching two animals in a pond. Was there a Zoological Garden at Wessanagara?

The upper architraves of the Northern Gateway are more easily described and understood. The second or central one in front is wholly devoted to Tree Worship. Seven Trees of different species stand on or behind altars. They are all surmounted by Chattas and adorned with wreaths, and between each are persons in attitudes of adoration. The bas-relief in the rear of this architrave is a little more complicated. In the centre is a King or Prince seated on a high-backed throne, before whom are women and boys (?) dancing and singing. Beyond these, to the left, a Hindu Chief, with his wife and child, worship a Tree, over which float winged figures bearing offerings. To the right of the throne are "grotesque giants with pointed ears, like "the classic fawns, playing musical instruments, dancing, and drinking. Had this "sculpture occurred in a Hindu temple, it would have been called the Court of "Indra, and as Indra was one of the deities most anciently acknowledged by the "Buddhists, it may possibly be so in this instance,"—a suggestion in which I entirely concur.

The top lintel in front is devoted to mixed Dagoba and Tree Worship; there being five Dagobas and two Trees, each with all the accompaniments of honour, terrestrial and celestial, which marks the respect shown to these objects in the sculptures of Sanchi. On the rear space of this architrave, Elephants and their young are represented as bringing lotus flowers and garlands to do honour to the sacred Tree.

On the blocks that divide these bassi-relievi over the pillars, we have in front men riding on cows or oxen—a very common practice at Sanchi; boys on bridled winged lions, and winged deer; on the rear, men mounted on kneeling horses; boys on deer, and at the top winged deer again.

The other subjects and emblems will be more easily described and better understood when we come to describe the lithographs further on.

FRONT VIEW OF EASTERN GATEWAY.

REAR VIEW OF EASTERN GATEWAY.

PLATES VIII. AND IX.

EASTERN GATEWAY.

THE Eastern Gateway, for reasons hinted at above, but which will be more intelligible when the whole are described, appears to be more modern than the Northern, though it is difficult to put this difference of age into years. It has also this further peculiarity, that its sculptures are much more mythological and much less historical than those of the Gateway just described.

As lithographic representations of the sculptures of the pillars will be found in the following Plates, it will be convenient to reserve them for future description. At present, as in the case of the Northern Gateway, we shall only deal with the horizontal architraves above the Elephant capitals.

The lowest of these in front is wholly occupied by one composition, representing the worship of the Tree, with its usual accompaniments. In the centre stands a tree behind an altar, under which is the Trisul emblem,—to be described hereafter,—and above it float heavenly winged figures. "On the left is a procession of musicians, " and men carrying bunches of flowers, standards, and long poles capped with discs " and emblems. To the right of the tree are two worshippers, together with a " number of female musicians, and a kneeling caparisoned elephant, over which a " woman waves a Chaori. Upon the hind leg of the elephant stands a man shaded " by a Chatta, in the undress seen in Plate XVII., which seems to be a kind of " devotional costume.* A child holds his girdle, and a woman seems to be addressing " him. On the extreme right a personage of rank in a chariot, accompanied by " a second chariot, and a number of armed men."

So far as I can make out, this appears to me to be the same scene as that represented in Plate LIX. Fig. 2. of the Amravati sculptures. If I am correct in my conjecture regarding that bas-relief, the figure standing on the foot of the elephant would be Ŝâkya Muni himself, and the woman and child his wife Gopî and his son Rahula.† It is impossible, however, to speak with confidence without a more detailed representation than the photograph affords.

The rear of this architrave is occupied wholly by a number of elephants worshipping the Dagoba.

The second or middle architrave in front is occupied principally, like the one below it, with Tree Worship. "In the centre stands a sacred tree, surmounted by numerous

---

* I have copied this literally from Colonel Maisey's manuscript, though, as far as I can make out from the photographs, the man standing on the elephant's foot is a Hindu, not a Dasyu, as Colonel Maisey states.

† If the principal figure is Buddha, it would reconcile the apparent discrepancy between Colonel Maisey's description and the appearance of the photograph; the garb on an ascetic might easily at that height be mistaken for that of a Dasyu.

" figures, some shaded by Chattas. On the left of the tree are the buildings and " walls of a city, which are crowded with spectators. On the right a number of " praying figures, and the footmarks of Buddha shaded by a Chatta." Both to right and left of the central tree are richly-caparisoned horses, not mounted, but led by the hand; over two of them at least are Chattas, and they seem to be objects of almost as much respect as the tree itself, or the footprints of Buddha. This worship of the horse we shall have frequent opportunities of observing in future, but more frequently at Amravati than at Sanchi.

The rear of this architrave is one of the most curious at Sanchi. It represents all the beasts of the field doing homage to the sacred tree. We have long been familiar with the animals worshipped by the Egyptians, and by other nations who have followed their example to a certain extent; but we must go to India to meet with that elevation of the brute creation which consisted in associating them with men in acts of devotion. In this instance we can recognize " lions, deer, sheep, buffaloes " or oxen, camels, rams, and large eagles." But the most remarkable among this strange congregation is the five-headed Naga himself! He is easily recognized, and there can be no doubt as to the intention of the sculptor; but it does seem strange that the god who everywhere else is worshipped should here be represented as worshipping, and not a human or celestial god, but the Tree. It is evident we are here still far removed from the supremacy which the Serpent afterwards assumed at Amravati.

The top lintel of the Gateway in front is identical in subject with that of the Northern Gateway. Five Dagobas and two Trees occupy the centre, with the projections. Both Dagobas and Trees are hung with garlands; each is surmounted by a Chatta, and adored by winged figures floating above, and human worshippers standing between them.

The rear of the lintel, like the intermediate front Rail of the Northern Gate, is occupied by seven sacred trees, each of a different species, but all similarly honored.

The only other remarkable peculiarity on this Gateway that it is worth mentioning here, is that the intermediate block behind is occupied by men mounted on two-humped Bactrian camels. We would *now* consider this a proof positive that they came from Central Asia, as this animal is not now known in India, but we do not know when the single-humped camel was first introduced into India, nor whether or not the two-humped was the usual beast of burthen in those days.

The emblem that crowns this Gateway, and other details, will, as in the case of the Northern Gateway, be more easily understood when the subsequent Plates have been described.* It will be convenient, therefore, to pass them over for the present.

---

* When in 1847 I published my work entitled " Picturesque Illustrations of Indian Architecture," I engraved a view of this Gateway as the frontispiece from a drawing in the possession of the Royal Asiatic Society. I never learnt by whom that drawing was made, but, from some circumstances, I fancy it must have been taken about 1830. At that time both the Trisul ornaments on the top were standing and the pedestal for the Wheel in the centre, besides many other details which have since disappeared. The Gateways have suffered more during the forty years that have elapsed since they were discovered by the English than they did during the previous eighteen centuries!

PILLARS OF NORTHERN GATEWAY.

PILLARS OF NORTHERN GATEWAY.

PILLARS OF NORTHERN GATEWAY.

PILLARS OF EASTERN GATEWAY.

PILLARS OF EASTERN GATEWAY.

PILLARS OF EASTERN GATEWAY.

PLATES X. TO XV.

THESE six photographs represent from varions points of view the three external faces of the npright pillars of the Northern and Eastern Gateways, which are still standing. It will not be necessary to describe their sculptures in detail in this place, as all these bas-reliefs have been drawn by Colonel Maisey, and lithographs from his drawings will be found in the Plates of this work. As these are much more distinct than the photographs, it will be more convenient to describe them in detail when referring to the snbsequent plates. The photographs are nevertheless extremely interesting, not only as anthenticating the lithographs, but also as showing the position of each bas-relief with reference to the others; and it may be possible hereafter to trace some connexion between them. In Colonel Maisey's volume they are arranged consecutively as they stand on the pillars, but I fail to catch any trace of a story running through them, and have conseqnently arranged them in this work according to their snbjects. It is most important, however, that others should have the means of knowing how they are placed on the monument itself, and for this purpose the photographs are indispensable. With a little familiarity, the subjects as lithographed are easily recognized in the photographs, and each is referred to specially in the descriptions which will be given hereafter.

The bas-reliefs exist only on two faces of the pillars. On the inner side, or that turned towards the Dagoba, the lower part is completely concealed by the pre-existing Rail, so that there is only room for one square piece of sculpture in each. In both Gateways this consists of a representation of a Dagoba on the right-hand pillar, and a sacred Tree on the left (Photographs VII. and IX.), these two being the principal objects of worship at Sanchi, and therefore selected when only two could be represented.

The outer faces of the four pillars are covered with architectural ornaments which are not represented in the lithographs, being sufficiently clear in the photographs. On the Eastern Gateway this consists in a rich ornamentation of lotus flowers, interwoven with a scroll ornament; not in snch good taste as snch ornaments are generally found to be in monuments of this class in India.

On the Northern Gateway the ornament on the right-hand pillar (Photograph XI.) is in much better taste, and of its class is as good and elegant as anything to be fonnd either at Sanchi or Amravati. It does not seem to have any particular meaning, bnt the same detail is fonnd on the intermediate props between the architraves in front of both Gateways.

The ornament on the left-hand pillar of the Northern Gateway (Plate X.) is the only one which seems to have any symbolical meaning. The central part consists of a floral ornament somewhat similar to that on the companion pillar, but narrower, and on each side of it are eight hooks or pegs, from which depend wreaths or garlands. From the second peg two necklaces of emblems are suspended, which are represented on a larger scale in Plate III. Fig. 4. Some of these will be easily recognized; others will be referred to in the sequel. At the bottom of the pillar are the sacred impressions of the feet of Buddha, and at the top an ornament which, in order to avoid theory, I have ventured to style the Trisul or Trident ornament. It is one of the most common features both here and at Amravati. It crowns both these Gateways (Plates IV. to IX.). It is seen on the standards and arms of the soldiers everywhere. It is found on all or nearly all the old Buddhist coins, and generally may be said to be one of the most favourite emblems of the age. Yet it must be remarked it is never worshipped, as the Wheel emblem is, nor as the Tree or Dagoba are. As an object of worship, it is certainly inferior to these; as an ornament, it occurs more frequently and nearly as prominently.

Although so common, it is not very easy to explain what the meaning always may be which the early Buddhists attached to it. The key to the mystery may, however, probably be found in the annexed diagram from one of the notes by Rémusat on the travels of Fa Hian.*

This emblem is also found in China and Thibet, inscribed with Sanscrit letters, which serve further to designate the parts. Thus the lowest marked "a" means the earth; the circle "va" represents water; the triangle "ra" fire; the crescent "ka" stands for the wind; and the cone marked "kha" for ether. General Cunningham,† by a different process, makes out that it is compounded of the old Pali letters, meaning the same thing; though in this case it is not quite clear whether the emblem was derived from the letters, or the letters from the emblem.‡ But this is of little consequence, as by any of these processes we arrive at the same conclusion that the Trisul ornament represents the five elements or the material universe.

No. 13.

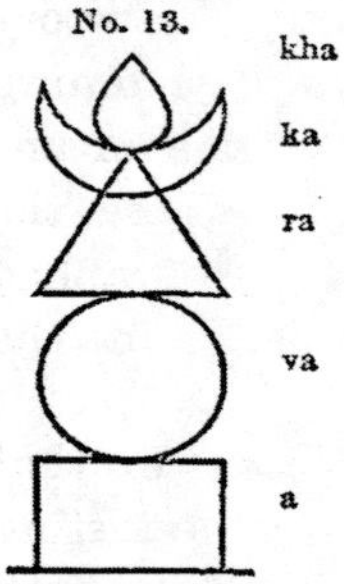

When, however, it is placed on the top of a pillar, as is done in this case, and very frequently at Amravati, and connected with the feet of Buddha on the base, it is not so clear what the combination means; but without wishing to put it forward for more than it is worth, I would suggest that the two together may stand for Buddha, or the first person of the Triad—Buddha, Dharma, Sangha—the two latter being represented by the Wheel and the Tree. It must be recollected we are now speaking of times before Buddha was represented by images to be worshipped. If the first person of the Triad was represented on the monuments at all, it must have been by some emblem. So far as can at present be perceived, there was no other which can be appropriated to him.§

* Foë-Koue-Ki, p. 92.

† Bhilsa Topes, 355.

‡ General Cunningham then goes on to state that he considers this emblem the representation of Dharma, the second person in the Buddhist Triad. Here I cannot follow his reasoning. If any, the Wheel represents the Law.

§ In the Foë-Koue-Ki there is a curious story (chap. xx.) of a king—Prasenajit—"who having a strong "desire to see Buddha, who was then absent in heaven, caused a head of an ox to be sculptured in sandal wood, "in such a manner as to represent the image of Foë, and placed it where he had sat." In this form the legend is quite unintelligible; but may not this emblem have been called "the Ox-head emblem" from its similarity to that animal's head, and hence the confusion of ideas?

RUINS OF SOUTHERN GATEWAY.

SANCHI.

PLATE XVII.

RUINS OF SOUTHERN GATEWAY.

SANCHI.

PLATE XVIII.

RUINS OF SOUTHERN GATEWAY.

PLATES XVI., XVII., AND XVIII.

SOUTHERN GATEWAY.

THIS Gateway is entirely prostrate, and was apparently lying on the ground as it is now when Captain Fell visited Sanchi in 1819.

Colonel Maisey is inclined to consider it as the oldest of the four Gateways. "The "pillars," he says, "are different in style from the others, and the buildings and "costumes struck me as having served as the models for those of the other gates, "which, though evidently the work of superior artists, have not so original an "appearance." It is difficult to form a positive opinion on such an argument as this without seeing the sculptures themselves, but it is probable Colonel Maisey may be right. But, on the other hand, there is so much more of Serpent Worship in the sculptures, and they show a certain character of finish that would rather seem to place them, as sometimes I felt inclined to do, as the third. Though with the materials at my command, I am unable to offer a decided opinion on the subject, I think the sequence in which they were erected is tolerably clear. The North and East Gateways, with their elephant capitals, certainly come next to one another, and of the two the Eastern is certainly the most modern, and it is therefore probable that they are either the first or the last pair. There is a reason, however, which seems to me even more cogent than that assigned by Colonel Maisey why the Southern Gateway should be oldest. On looking at the plan, Plate II., it will be perceived that it is opposite the flight of steps that leads to the terrace from which the dome springs. This must, therefore, always have been the principal entrance, and when only one Gateway existed it seems most improbable that it should be anywhere else. It is as unlikely that they should adopt such an ill-balanced arrangement as to add the Western Gateway next, but more probable that the Northern one should have been erected as a pendant to the Southern, and also because it faced one of the principal ascents to the terrace. If this is so the Eastern followed next, and the Western was the last added. Its dwarf capitals being exceptional, also favours this idea.

In an artistic point of view, the question is not very important, as all four probably were erected within the limit of 100 years; but as this is the Gateway that bears the Sâtakarṇi inscription,* and is consequently the one on which the age of the whole mainly hinges, it is important that its relative position in the series should be correctly determined, if it is possible to do so.

One of the pillars of this Gateway, with its lion capital, is seen photographed in Plate XVI. A lithograph of the principal bas-relief in front of one of the pillars—

* This inscription is seen on a Dagoba in the centre of the architrave in the foreground of Plate XVII.

the only one accessible as it lies on the ground—will be found in Plate XXX., and its lion capital is represented in Plate XXXIX. The principal historical bas-relief, representing a siege, is lithographed in Plate XXXVIII. Fig. 2. Each of these will be described in its proper place further on, and will suffice to convey a tolerable idea of the sculpture of this Gateway.

The fragments represented in the foreground of Plate XVI. seem to be among the sharpest and clearest of the whole series. Those to the right hand and further off are portions of Fig. 1. Plate XXXVIII., but we have unfortunately no drawing of the bas-relief in front of it—part apparently of the intermediate architrave. On it are seen a group of men and women among trees, the two men with five-headed snakes, and the five women with single snakes. The continuation of the bas-relief will be observed in Plate XVII. behind the principal one, where two more men and several female figures will be observed with the same Naga accompaniments. In the centre of the architrave is a Dagoba with flying figures worshipping, and beyond, the right-hand portion is filled with sacred trees.

In front of this all across the picture (Plate XVII.) is the upper architrave, divided as usual between Tree and Dagoba Worship, three Dagobas and four Trees occupying the central portion. On the projection on either end is the sacred horse, caparisoned, and with the royal Chatta borne over him. On the blocks over the pillars are men riding on oxen, bearing offerings in their uplifted hands.

In addition to these sculptures, another is described by Colonel Maisey, but unfortunately neither drawn nor photographed. "It represents the worship or perhaps " consecration of a Chatta-shaded Tope of two terraces with hovering Kinnaras. " On the Tope is an inscription.* To the left are numerous male and female figures, " standing as on the folds of snakes, whose heads canopy their heads. The costume " is Indian (Hindu). The group seems to represent some person of distinction, " attended by male and female followers, some of whom worship the Tope, while " others bring offerings, &c. On the right a procession approaches, consisting of some " person of rank, shaded by a Chatta, in a two-horsed chariot, preceded by musi- " cians and horsemen, one of whom carries the curious spouted teapot-looking utensil " which occurs so frequently in the sculptures. Three elephants, with standard bearers, " bring up the rear." This curious bas-relief, Colonel Maisey says he was deterred from drawing, in consequence of its being much corroded by exposure, and refers to a native drawing published in the J. A. S. B., vol. III., p. 481, which, however, is so incorrect that but for his testimony it would be impossible to recognize it as representing the subject he describes.

* Cunningham, Bhilsa Topes, p. 266 (Ins. 191).

SANCHI. PLATE XIX.

RUINS OF WESTERN GATEWAY.

SANCHI.

PLATE XX.

RUINS OF WESTERN GATEWAY.

[illegible]

PLATES XIX., XX., AND XXI.

Western Gateway and Gate of small Tope.

The Western Gateway fell only a few years ago, in consequence apparently of the clumsy digging into the Tope of some nameless amateurs, who overwhelmed it with the rubbish they threw down from the Tope itself. Only one of the pillars is now standing, but the other, though on the ground, is accessible, and all their sculptures have been drawn, and will be found among the lithographs in this work, and will be described further on as they occur.

The architraves are occupied apparently with the same class of subjects as those represented on the other Gateways, with only such variation as the taste or skill of the sculptor might suggest. There are also as usual two historical scenes. One of these, representing the triumphal return of the army bringing back the relics, is engraved on Plate XXXVIII. The other seems either the commencement or a continuation of the same subject. All this is in perfect accordance with the sequence just pointed out; and the triumph is thus the concluding historical scene on the Gateway last erected. If this is so, however, it assumes a preconcerted design for the whole of the sculptures, which would bring them more nearly together than I would feel inclined to do from the other indications available.

There are no inscriptions or any marks on the Gateway of No. 3 Tope, represented on Plate XXI., which could assist us in ascertaining its age; and as Colonel Maisey has not drawn any of the more important sculptures, we are left almost wholly to the photographs for what knowledge we may gather regarding it. The fact of the Tope, containing relics of the two principal disciples of Buddha—Śâriputra and Mahâ Mogalâna—is, as before mentioned, no test of its age. These may have been preserved in some chapel or shrine connected with the great Tope from the time of Aśoka till the Christian era, and been accessible to the public, as relics frequently were in early times, and this Tope may have been erected to contain them when the fashion of concealing them came into vogue. Even, however, if it was as old as the great Tope, its age is no test of the age of its Gateways. The style of their decorations is therefore the only evidence we have, and so far as can be judged from the photographs—we have only one drawing of this Gateway, Plate XLII., Fig. 3.—there is no difference between the sculptures of the Gateway and those of the great Tope. A careful examination on the spot might reveal peculiarities which we cannot see in our illustrations.

I have placed it in juxtaposition with the Western Gateway, because the one possesses the same dwarf capitals as the other does, and in so far as this feature is concerned this would indicate that it was of the same age. Lion capitals we know are as old as the time of Aśoka, and this might readily suggest their employment, as was done in the Southern Gateway, as already pointed out. Elephants are also found surmounting the capitals of pillars as early as Aśoka's time;* so that these two forms had long been familiar to the architects of the Sanchi Tope. The dwarf capital, however, is new, so far as we now know, and is so ugly that we cannot help wondering at its introduction after the other beautiful forms, but its symbolism may have been more attractive to the eye of the devotee than its want of grace is repulsive to our artistic taste, so we must not judge too hastily.

The sculpture on the front of the only lintel still "in situ" is of considerable interest for our purposes, and is thus described by Colonel Maisey:—"The front "face of the lintel is curious; the volutes are formed of snakes, and the portion "over the pillars are men slaying monsters half elephant half snake." (This does not occur elsewhere, so far as I know.) "The centre portion has several groups "apparently on the banks of a river. On the extreme right and left are snake-"canopied men seated with one arm encircling the neck of a woman. In the centre "is a pavilion, on the roof of which are six spectators, and under it a male per-"sonage seated on a throne. Like the figures right and left, he is attended by "several women, one of whom is seated, and talking to him. Kinnara (flying "figures) hover near the pavilion, marking it and the person under it as sacred. "Between the groups are rocks, among which various figures may be detected."

The photograph is unfortunately on too small a scale to enable us to add anything to this description. This is to be regretted, as the serpent volutes are a curious architectural fact, and as these spirals occur on all the Gateways it would be very interesting if we could trace back the form to a Serpent origin. It may, however, be only a caprice in the present instance. The monster, half elephant half serpent, is also new, but cannot be distinguished in the photograph.

The groups in the foreground of the photograph (Plate XXI.) seem to represent the same objects as are found in the other Gateways, but seem better done, and the whole seems so much more to resemble what is found at Amravati, that on this ground alone I would feel inclined to place it as the most modern of the Sanchi Gateways. It certainly is the most essentially Ophite of the group.

If the ruins of the Tope itself were searched, it is probable that some of the pillars of the Rail might be recovered. If this were the case, their ornamentation would prove a surer test of age than the Gateways. As it is only at Sanchi that these Gateways are found, we have no means of ascertaining their relative age by comparison.

---

* History of Architecture, vol. II. p. 459.

PLATE XXII.

SANCHI.

CHAITYA HALL.

RUINS OF VIHARA.

PLATES XXII. AND XXIII.

CHAITYA AND VIHARA.

As before mentioned (p. 80), these (marked Q in Plate I.) are the only remains of a structural Chaitya hall that have yet been discovered standing in India. But, judging from its style, it must be considerably more modern than any of the buildings just described. As will be seen from the plan, it consists of a nave with six pillars on each side, and measuring internally 29 feet north and south, by 19 feet 4 inches. Beyond this is a choir 27 feet by 19 feet, surrounded by a wall 4 feet thick, though at present only about 2 feet high; but the photograph reveals to us the fact that the last pillar was evidently built into a wall to its whole height. "In the "centre," Colonel Maisey says, "of the curved end is a mass of débris "which seems to have been the remains of a Chaitya, or relic shrine, "such as is seen in the Buddhist Caves." "Round the exterior of the "circular part," he adds, "are traces of masonry at some distance."

No. 14.

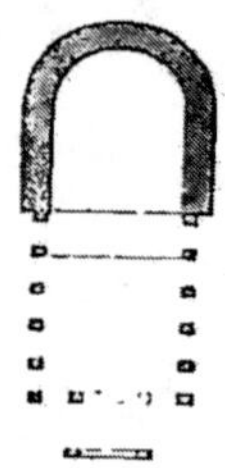

PLAN OF CHAITYA HALL.
Scale, 30 ft. to 1 in.

There can be no doubt but that this is just such a hall as we meet so frequently at Karlee, Ajanta, and elsewhere. It must originally have had a wooden roof, of a form it would not be difficult to restore, and it was surrounded by an aisle, but whether entirely free, or supported by wooden pillars, is not quite clear. The fact of its internal pillars being of stone and of the slender masonic shape shown in the photograph, proves it to be much more modern than the Cave at Karlee or the oldest at Ajanta, which it is nearly certain date from about or before the Christian era. These, though in the rock, retain in every feature their original wooden constructive form. Here, where wooden pillars would have been admissible, stone takes their place. This could hardly have happened before the fourth or fifth century. It may be even more modern than that date.

It would be extremely interesting, if it could be ascertained by excavations what the width and form of the outer aisle were in this example, as enabling us to understand what is now obscure in those cut in the rock. In all those the ornamental pillars extend on each side of the nave, as here, to nearly where the Dagoba stands—as we would express it, to the entrance of the choir. The apse is in all the older rock-cut examples surrounded by plain octagonal shafts without base or capitals, but why this should be so has hitherto always been a mystery. If, however, it was the custom, as in this instance, to enclose the choir by a solid wall in a structural Chaitya, it is evident that such a form could not be adopted in the rock, as in this case the circumambient aisle would thus have been absolutely dark. In structural examples the aisle could easily have been lighted from the exterior; indeed, it probably was an open colonnade. The plain pillars in the rock may thus have been intended to reproduce the solid wall of the structural example. Possibly that part was ornamented with frescoes in structural Chaityas, and may have been hung with tapestries on state and festival occasions in those excavated in the rock.

VIHARA.

The photograph—Plate XXIII.—represents in like manner almost the only standing remain of one of the Vihâras or Monasteries which, when Buddhism was flourishing, were to be found in every part of India. From its plan (marked L in Plate I.) and details it is, however, evidently much more modern than even the Chaitya hall last described. The central cell is a feature not found in the Caves before the sixth or seventh century, and this one has so Hindu-like an aspect that it is impossible not to suspect that it may be much more modern. There were apparently only three cells on each side, one 12 feet by 8, the other two 8 feet square. These open into a verandah, at one end of which is a figure of Buddha seated crossed-legged and similar to another which occupies the central sanctuary. Colonel Maisey's drawing of the last of these is reproduced in Plate XLI. Its style would tend to the impression that it at least belongs to the latest date of Buddhist art in India. Four statues of Buddha very similar in style and design to this stand within the Rail of the great Tope opposite to each of the four entrances. They are all, however, evidently so modern that they have no connexion whatever with the original design, and may have been added as late as the ninth or tenth centuries of our era.

No. 15.

VIHARA AT SANCHI.
Scale, 50 feet to 1 inch.

The great Vihâra (marked N in Plate I.) seems to have been situated exactly opposite to the eastern entrance of the great Tope, but it is now so completely ruined that its plan can hardly be made out, and no details of architecture are standing from which its character or age could be determined. The spot, however, is interesting, as this probably is the site of the Mahâ Chaitya, erected by Aśoka's Queen, and in which Mahindo resided (B.C. 250) before proceeding on his mission to Ceylon.*

* Vide ante, p. 90.

SANCHI.

PLATE XXIV.

FIG. 1.

FIG. 2.

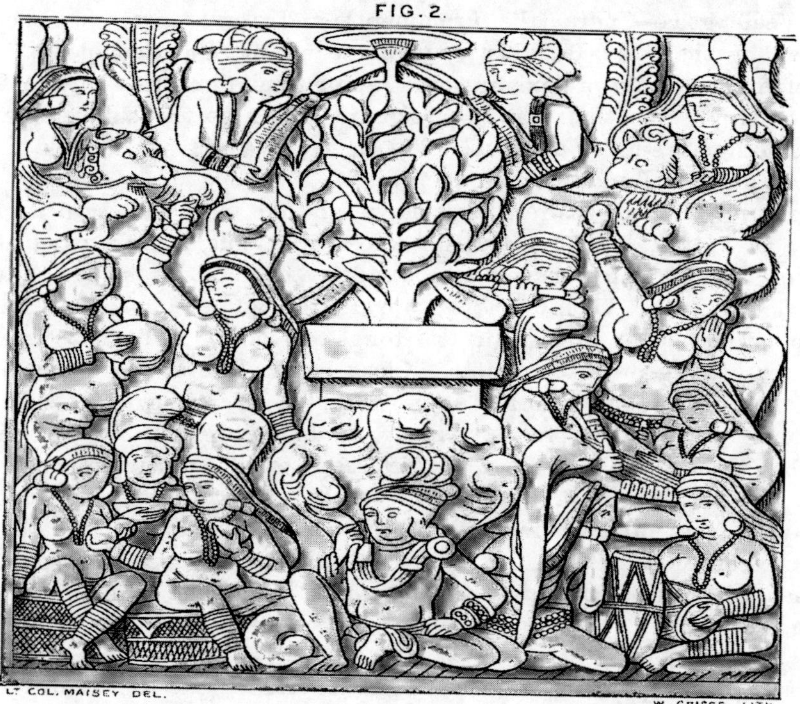

Lt. COL. MAISEY DEL. W. GRIGGS, LITH.

NAGA SCULPTURES.

PLATE XXIV.

The subjects of the two bas-reliefs, lithographed from Colonel Maisey's drawings in Plate XXIV., may be taken as the typical form in which the Naga is generally represented both at Sanchi and Amravati. The upper one is found in the centre of the inner face of the left-hand pillar of the Eastern Gateway (Plates XIV. and XV.) The lower one is found in the corresponding position on the left-hand pillar of the Western Gateway (Plate XIX.), but whether this correspondence of position is accidental or has any meaning is by no means certain. It is worth remarking, however, as such coincidences may eventually lead to some theory of decoration being discovered.

The upper bas-relief represents those people I have ventured to call Dasyus, worshipping the five-headed Naga, who appears in a small hexagonal temple, raising his head over what appears to be an altar. In front of him stands a pot of fire, but whether this is to be considered as a fire altar or not must be left for future consideration; but what is still more remarkable is that fire is certainly issuing from the openings in the roof of the temple. I am of course aware that it has been frequently suggested that the Serpent is the emblem of the Sun, and that Fire is the natural representative of the Solar Deity; but all this is indistinct everywhere, and it does not appear to have any local reality in India. On the other hand, we know that two of the principal Vedic gods—Indra (the firmament) and Agni (fire)—were adopted into their pantheon by the early Buddhists, and it seems more reasonable to connect this appearance of fire with the pre-existing worship of Agni than with any far-fetched allusion to solar worship. We shall have occasion to return to this subject presently, as fire occurs in another bas-relief at Sanchi, but never at Amravati, nor, so far as I know, in any more modern Buddhist monument.

In the foreground of the bas-relief we have an old man seated in a circular leaf-thatched hut. A scarf is bound round his knees and loins, a very usual attitude in India at all times. His upper garment is hung up behind him in the hut, and in front is a bearded man of his own tribe, apparently addressing him. Near the last is another pot of fire, with three pairs of tongs or ladles, and what appears to be a bundle of sticks to keep up the flame. Close beside him are an elephant, two buffaloes, sheep, and deer; but whether it is intended that they too should be worshipping, or merely represent property, must be left uncertain for the present. On the left of the picture two boys and a girl seem to be amusing themselves at play, but, which is remarkable, they are as decently clad as their elders, and in strange contrast with the superior race in the lower picture of the Plate. The whole scene is represented as passing in a forest. Above are trees and rocks, with monkeys and peacocks; below, a reedy marsh opening into a lake with lotus flowers, and occupied by geese.

The lower bas-relief represents a very different scene. In the centre of the upper part is the sacred tree, behind its altar, with its Chatta and garlands, occupying the same position the serpent did in the other. Two Garuḍas or Devas,* or flying figures, present garlands, and two female figures, riding on griffons of strongly marked Assyrian aspect, approach it on either side.

In the centre of the lower part of the picture sits the Raja or chief male personage on the Naga, whose five-headed hood shelters him. On his right sit three ladies on stools, eating and drinking, and each with her tutelary snake behind her. Above those a female Chaori bearer and a woman with a bottle—let us hope of water; but they, too, have snakes behind them. On the other side are two women playing on drums,† two on harps, one on a flute, and a fifth dancing, but all likewise with snakes, and all in the costume which I have ventured to designate as that of the Hindus.

The worship of the Naga by the bearded Dasyus, as represented in the upper bas-relief, does not occur again at Sanchi, and it occurs only once at Amravati. There, however, the five-headed snake very frequently occurs in front of the Dagoba, and in a position where it is intended it shall be worshipped not only by Dasyus, but by all the world.

The Hindu male or Chief canopied by the Naga, as shown in the lower, occurs at least ten times ‡ at Sanchi, and must have occurred several hundred times at Amravati.

What are we to infer from this? Is it that the Naga is the god of the aboriginal Dasyus, whom the intruding Hindus adopted so far as to represent him shielding and honouring them? The Hindus, it must be recollected, were the builders of the Topes and the carvers of the sculptures, and there is no instance at Sanchi of a Hindu doing honour to the snake. The snake there always honours them. Or is it that the race I have called Hindus were the real Naga people, and they taught the Dasyus to do honour to their god? These questions will recur continually to every one reading the following pages, and it is premature to attempt to decide them now; but I may state that my impression is, that Snake Worship was an old and prevalent form of aboriginal faith all over India before the Aryan immigration, and that the Aryans adopted it in proportion as they became mixed with the aborigines and their blood became less and less pure. It is not mentioned in the Vedas, hardly hinted at in the Râmâyaṇa, occupies a considerable space in the Mahâbhârata, appears timidly at Sanchi in the first century of our era, and is triumphant at Amravati in the fourth, and might have become the dominant faith of India had it not been elbowed from its place of power by Vishnuism and Sivaism, which took its place when it fell together with the religion of Buddha, to which it had allied itself so closely.

---

* Both General Cunningham and Colonel Maisey call these figures Kinnaras. If I am rightly informed, however, that term is properly applied only to a flying figure with a horse's head. Garuda is probably the correct name to apply to them. Care, however, must be taken not to confound these Buddhist figures with the Garuḍa of the Mahâbhârata, the celebrated son of Vinatâ, and the dreaded enemy of all the Naga race. Perhaps Devas would be the most correct denomination. These are the first of the Buddhist hierarchy, and at least in one instance are represented as acting as here shown. "When Bosat was about to arrive at that place —the Bo-tree at Buddh Gya—all the Dévas of the world of forms first hung on the Tree silken banners and streamers."—See J. R. A. S., XX., p. 157.

† If anyone will observe the way the snake attaches itself to the back of the left-hand drummer girl, they will understand how the *two* snakes grew out of the shoulders of Zohak. Some such representation of him must have existed in the time of Firdusi: hence the fable.

‡ I speak of those only I have been able to detect in the photographs; neither General Cunningham nor Colonel Maisey were sufficiently aware of their importance to count them.

SANCHI. PLATE XXV.

FIG. 1

FIG. 2

FIG. 3.

LT. COL. MAISEY DEL. W. GRIGGS, LITH.

TREE WORSHIP.

PLATE XXV.

WHATEVER doubt may exist as to the extent to which the Hindus intend at Sanchi to honour the Serpent, or to represent the Serpent as honouring them, there is none whatever as to the reverence they everywhere are represented as paying to Trees. These alternate with the Dagobas on the architraves as the two principal objects of worship, but taking also the representations on the pillars into account, the Tree is certainly the chief divinity of the place.

That represented as the principal subject (Fig. 3.) of this Plate, may be considered as a typical example. It occurs in front of the left-hand pillar of the Eastern Gateway (Plates XIV. and XV.), next to the Fire Temple, with the Naga of the last Plate, and their juxtaposition may have some meaning, all the figures in the Naga bas-relief being Dasyus, all those in the Tree picture being Hindus. The tree itself is the Pipal (*Ficus religiosa*), the true Bo-tree of the present Buddha. A temple has been built around it, and it is represented as growing out of its windows. In front is an altar, on which is the Trisul emblem, and it is difficult to understand what its presence here can mean, unless it is "Buddha," or "Sacred to Buddha." Above the tree is the ennobling Chatta, and on either hand Garuḍas or Devas bearing offerings. Below, on each hand, two male worshippers in the costume of the Hindus.*

Fig. 1. of this Plate is one of several subjects to which it is difficult to attach any distinct meaning or story. In the centre is a tree of a different species from any we have yet met with; and two men in Hindu costume, one on either hand, seem to be offering worship to it. In addition to this, however, there are two small shrines or temples, each with what appears to be an altar in front. That in the centre above has no worshippers. The one on the left below is encircled apparently with a wall of rude stones; that on the right by the usual Rail. Men in Hindu costume seem to be offering prayers to both these temples—are they tombs?—and between them a child is seated cross-legged, in the attitude we usually associate with Buddha. This bas-relief is in front of the left-hand pillar of the Northern Gateway (Plate XXXI.), a little higher than Fig. 2., which is the lowest of three bas-reliefs which ornament the inner face of this pillar.

The tree in Fig. 2. is of a different species from that represented in Fig. 3., though it occurs in both the upper corners of Fig. 1. There, it does not appear as a sacred tree at all. In this bas-relief it stands behind an altar, and has garlands pendent from its branches, but no ennobling Chatta surmounts it. Notwithstanding this, one male and eleven female figures are certainly worshipping it, and one woman presenting an offering.

It would be interesting if the species of this tree could be determined, as

* The inscription, according to Cunningham, p. 263, reads, "The pillar gift of Nâgapriya Achavada, the Śreshṭhî or Chief of the weavers."

according to Buddhist tradition each of the twenty-four successive Buddhas of the present "Kappo" had a different Bo-tree.* Their names, in Pali, are all recorded, and could no doubt be identified with known trees, and many of them with those represented in these sculptures. This is evidently a flowering tree (Champa?), and occurs more frequently than any other, except the "Religiosa," which we know to be the Bo-tree of the present Buddha.†

The women in the bas-relief all wear the enormous chignon which ladies in these days seem to have considered a sufficient substitute for all other dress. In this instance, however, their costume is not quite so open to this objection as is usually the case either here or at Amravati.

---

* Turner's Mahawanso, p. XXXII.

† I have been unfortunate in not being able to procure from any competent Indian botanist the assistance requisite to enable me to determine the species of the various trees represented in these bas-reliefs. There is difficulty attending it, no doubt, as the representations are to a considerable extent conventionalized; but still artists who could draw animals so well, that in no instance can a mistake be made as to which is intended, could also draw trees so as to enable them to be identified. The subject, however, is neither pressing nor very important, and can be done hereafter. There are, I think, only six or seven species altogether, and there can be very little doubt as to one or two of these. Ward, in his Hindu Mythology (3d edition, vol. I. 263), enumerates the following trees as considered sacred and worshipped by the followers of Vishṇu :—the Pipal and the Banyan, *Ficus religiosa* and *Indica;* the Vukoolu, *Mimusops elengi;* the Huritukee, *Terminalia citrina;* the Amalakee, *Phillanthus emblica;* and the Nimbu, *Melia azodaracta.* Except the Banyan, all these will, I believe, be found in our bassi-relievi.

FIG. 1.

FIG. 2.

Lt. COL. MAISEY DEL. W. GRIGGS, LITH.

TREE WORSHIP.

PLATE XXVI.

The two bas-reliefs represented in Plate XXVI. occur the one over the other on the inner face of the right-hand pillar of the Northern Gateway; Fig. 2. is, however, on the pillar above instead of below Fig. 1. (Plates X. and XII.) Both are representations of Tree Worship, but the lower one is remarkable because the two principal devotees are monkeys. Two men in Indian costume stand behind them, with their hands in the attitude of prayer, and beside them two females with offerings in their hands. In front of the altar, behind which the Tree stands, are two other Hindu females, with a child between them, kneeling in deep devotion. Of the two monkeys one is making an offering to the Tree, the other is in ecstasies.

In describing the back of the Eastern Gate, we have already seen all the beasts of the field (not monkeys) hastening to do honour to the Sacred Tree, but here we have monkeys mixed with men, or rather preferred to them; as the men stand back, while the monkeys present their offerings, they are really the principal worshippers. All this may have arisen partly from the tenderness for animal life and kindness to all created beings that Buddhism always inculcated; partly from the doctrine of metempsychosis, which was always an essential part of the faith; but something may in this instance be due to local tradition. It was in the forest of Daṇḍaka, certainly not far from Sanchi, that Râma met with Hanumân, the godlike monkey, who played so important a part in the subsequent records of the Râmâyaṇa. If monkeys could fight in Hindu tradition side by side with men, why in Buddhist forms should they not pray with them?

The Sacred Tree, in this instance, appears to be the *Ficus religiosa*, but two other trees are represented, which occur frequently in the bas-reliefs. The one with the large fruit appears intended for a species of Jack (*Artocarpus integrifolius*), the other a flowering tree, which has not yet been identified.

The upper bas-relief (Fig. 1.) represents a Hindu Raja, known to be so by his Chatta, with four female and two male attendants, doing honour to the Tree, to which two of the females, more fully clad than usual, are presenting wreaths. Above, two Garuḍas, bearing offerings, are seen full length. This is one of the few instances in these bas-reliefs in which these figures are seen complete, so that all their features may be distinguished. Their feet, wings, and tails are those of birds; their heads and bodies are those of human beings, but always, as far as can be made out, males, which may be an objection to the name of Harpy, which would seem a name that might be appropriate. These in classical representations were always apparently females, and of an odious nature. Here they are always represented as heavenly messengers, and bringing offerings. As Garuḍas are always represented as the fifth in rank among the eight heavenly beings* in the Buddhist pantheon, that name is probably the one the Buddhists would themselves employ.

* In the Lalita-Vistara (Foucaux), p. 250, et passim, they are enumerated as les Dieux ou Devas, les Nâgas, les Yakchas, les Gaṅdharbas, les Assouras, les Garuḍas, les Kinnaras, et les Mahôragas.

Above the tree on the right is another figure very common in these sculptures, but seldom seen so completely as in this instance,—a winged lion figure, on which a man rides, bearing an offering. There are abundance of winged lions on the Assyrian sculptures, but they are never represented as flying. At Sanchi they are always in the air, and always carrying human figures bringing offerings to the Tree or shrine. The representations at Sanchi are, of course, very much more modern than those in Assyria, but it is not clear that the Indian form may not be of an original stock as old or older than the Assyrian.

PLATE XXVII.

SANCHI.

FIG. 1

FIG. 2

FIG. 3.

L^T COL. MAISEY DEL.

W. GRIGGS, LITH. INDIA MUSEUM

TREE WORSHIP.

PLATE XXVII.

On Plate XXVII. are engraved three forms of Tree Worship, which have been reduced to a smaller scale than usual, as they do not present any great features of novelty, but are interesting as indicating some of its forms. Fig. 1. represents eighteen men in Hindu costume, some sitting, some standing, doing homage to a Pipal tree surmounted by a Chatta and attended by Garuḍas. It is from the inner face of the right-hand pillar of the Western Gateway (Plate XIX.).

Fig. 2. is immediately above it on the same Gateway, and presents a somewhat more varied form of the worship. Below are three men, one standing in a gateway, in front of an altar, but this group does not seem to have any connexion with that above. In the middle of the picture are three men, three women, and a child, who also seem bent on doing honour to the tree. Above these, on the left hand, are five women, apparently of inferior rank, and on the right hand a lion, an elephant, a boar, an ox, a horse, and a sheep. Among them is a round, very jolly human face, with large ears, and evidently intended to represent a giant or ogre, or some of those semi-human beings so common in Eastern story. The interesting part of the bas-relief is that these animals evidently rank with the females opposite, and join with the men in doing honour to the Holy Tree.

The third bas-relief on this Plate is one which it is extremely difficult to make out, not that there is anything new in the form or in the objects worshipped, but that owing to the imperfect knowledge of perspective possessed by the artist, it is extremely puzzling to suggest what the stone work between the two trees is intended to represent. It looks at first sight like a stair with a rail on either hand, but it does not lead to any terrace or building, and the object for which it was designed, or why the two similar trees should be planted at each end, is by no means clear.

In other respects the sculpture presents no novelty—men, women, and children, with drums and musical instruments, are assembled to do honour to the Trees. The upper one seems to be a Pipal, evidently the same as that in Fig. 2. The lower bears some fruit or flower, but so does that in Fig. 1., which from the form of its leaves is intended to be a Pipal (*Ficus religiosa*). In the centre picture a Plantain tree is plainly distinguishable, and above that the tree I have ventured to suggest may be a Jack, with the flowering tree that occurs in several of the previous bas-reliefs.

This sculpture is from the outward face of the right-hand pillar of the Northern Gateway at the top (Plate XII.).

Taken together, these three figures fairly represent the most popular form of worship at Sanchi. It will be observed that no Dasyus appear in them. Indeed there is no instance at Sanchi in which those people are associated with the Hindus in worshipping either Trees or anything else. Their worship of the Serpent or Fire or any other object is solitary and apart. It is difficult to understand why this should be so, as the Hindus seem never to hesitate to associate the beasts of the field with them in their worship, and if so why not their fellow men? This is the more remarkable as in other bas-reliefs these Dasyus are treated as equals, and many of the sculptures are wholly devoted to them and their pursuits, and this by the Hindus, who, we must presume, were the people who erected the monument and carved its sculptures.

The preceding—with one other example on the next Plate XXVIII. Fig. 2.—exhaust the illustrations of Tree Worship, in so far as they have been drawn by Colonel Maisey from bas-reliefs exclusively devoted to the subject on the pillars of the Sanchi Gateways. These Plates are far, however, from conveying an adequate idea of the extreme frequency of such illustrations, though they may represent nearly all the forms in which it is found. Taken altogether, the Tree is, generally speaking, the most usual and the most important object of worship represented in the sculptures at Sanchi Tope. Next after this comes the Dagoba, but neither so important nor so frequent. It may be suggested that this is owing to the great Tope being there itself to be worshipped, and that its mimic representation was therefore not needed. A careful study, however, of the sculptures renders this explanation hardly tenable. It can scarcely be doubted but the sculptures are intended to represent the creed, and the whole creed, of the people who erected the Gateways, and the relative importance of each part of the faith. It is probable, therefore, that the frequency or prominence of any object sculptured in these Gateways may fairly be assumed as representing its relative importance.

SANCHI. **PLATE XXVIII.**

FIG. 1

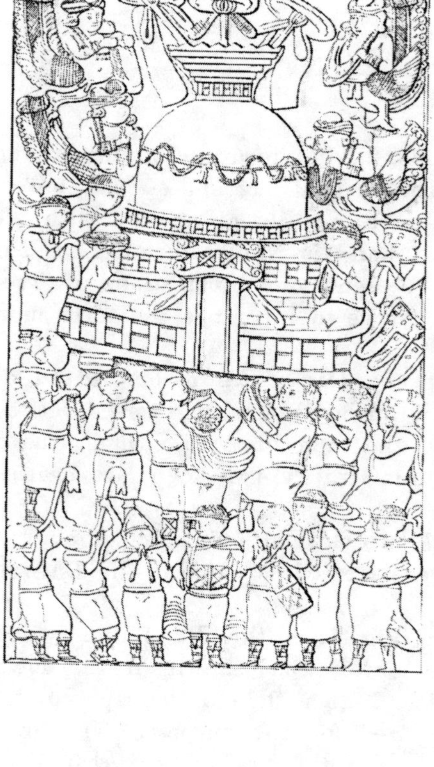

FIG. 2

FIG. 3

Lt COL. MAISEY DEL. W. GRIGGS, LITH.

TREE AND DAGOBA WORSHIP.

PLATE XXVIII.

Of the three subjects in this Plate, the one (No. 2.) in the upper corner on the right hand is wholly devoted to Tree Worship. The central portion of the lowest bas-relief (Fig. 3.) is devoted to the same form of faith, but in conjunction with the worship of the Dagoba. The upper one on the left hand is wholly devoted to the last form. The two first named conclude, for the present, our illustrations of Tree Worship at Sanchi, and the pictures in this Plate serve to introduce the form next in importance.

In Fig. 2. twenty-one men, with two Garuḍas or Devas, are assembled to do honour to the Tree, which in this instance is the flowering tree with reversed leaves, frequently alluded to above. The head-dresses of the men are more than usually exaggerated in this bas-relief, and so are the drums which two men are beating with clubs.

In the lower bas-relief (Fig. 3.) two men and two Garuḍas are doing honour to the Tree, in this instance the *Ficus religiosa,* and here treated as equal to the Dagoba, and alternating with it throughout.*

With the one exception of that represented in Fig. 1. of this Plate, the typical form of all the Dagobas in the sculptures at Sanchi is that shown in the lower figure (No. 3.). The dome is represented as a little higher than a hemisphere, and adorned by a wreath of flowers hung on pegs prepared for the purpose. The lower part is surrounded by a Rail, apparently detached, as in the case of the great Tope, and the summit is always surmounted by a Tee of the usual form. Above this is an umbrella, sometimes with flags, and almost always with two or more wreaths dependent from its angles. Garuḍas almost invariably hover around it, and offer garlands or baskets containing some objects it is impossible to distinguish.

When we come to describe the representations of Topes at Amravati, it will be seen what immense progress had been made in decorating these objects during the three centuries that followed the erection of the Sanchi Gateways. If, however, we compare the Sanchi Dagobas with those found in the Caves of Karlee, or the earliest at Ajanta, it will be seen that they are nearly identical. As it has always been assumed, though on perfectly independent grounds, that these Cave Dagobas dated from about the Christian era, this is another confirmation of the date above assumed for the Sanchi portals.

The exceptional Dagoba represented in Fig. 1. of the Plate is the upper bas-relief on the inside of the right-hand pillar of the Northern Gateway (Plate X.). It is very much taller than any of the others, and is surrounded by three Rails. The upper one of these, possibly the two upper, are attached. It may be merely ornamental

* The upper (Fig. 2.) is from the right-hand pillar of the Northern Gateway at top (Plate XI.). The lower (Fig. 3.) is from one of the beams or architraves of the same gate.

like those in the Topes in Afghanistan. The lower is certainly detached, and two figures are standing within it with offerings in their hands. This lower enclosure is entered by a gateway, apparently of wood, but evidently the prototype of the Sanchi portals. The Tee is surmounted by three umbrellas, with their dependent garlands, and on each side are two Garuḍas bringing offerings.

The most interesting point with reference to this bas-relief is, that the people who are represented in the foreground are neither the Dasyns nor the Hindus, who appear in all the other sculptures, bnt an entirely different race, and who are seen at Sanchi only in this bas-relief. They are all shaven, generally have their heads bare, and the hair bound by a small fillet. Their hair also is peculiar, being short and curly, like a negro's, or as that of Buddha is represented to be in more modern times. Their costume is a tunic with sleeves, fitting tightly to the neck, and reaching below the knees,* being unlike the kilt aud cloak of the Dasyns or the dhoti of the Hindu, and their boots or sandals (Fig. 5. Plate III.) are also qnite different from any seen elsewhere. Their musical instruments are also new to us. The donble pipe replaces the fife. The drum is differently formed, and the trumpets are of a kind seen nowhere else in the sculptures. Their banner alone, with its "stars and stripes," or rather stars and Union Jack combined, is like what we shall afterwards meet, but this may be local and peculiar to Sanchi.

Who are the people here represented? Their costume would indicate the inhabitants of a northern, or at least a colder climate. Their woolly hair points to a southern, unless it may be that some people with close curly hair did at this time inhabit Afghanistan or some of the countries near it. It has ever been one of the puzzles of Buddhism that the founder of the religion should always have been represented in sculpture with woolly hair like that of a negro. That the Prince Siddhârtha had flowing locks is certain, but how and when the change took place is the difficulty. If we could tell who the people here represented are, it wonld solve the problem. They probably were the first that made statues of Buddha, and they endowed him with their erisp locks. The impression left on my mind is, that they are inhabitants of the Cabul valley, not only from their costume and the tallness of their Tope, but because of their general resemblance to some sculpture found at Taḳ i Bahaï, north of Peshawar. They have no women with them, which is unfortunate, as their costume might afford some useful indications, bnt the circumstance of their absence shows that they were strangers. Some further light will be thrown on the subject before we are done; at present it had perhaps better be left nndetermined.

---

* Arrian (XVI.), quoting apparently from Nearchus, deseribes the Hindus as wearing tunics (κίθων) of eotton reaching to the knees. The kiton cannot, according to the usual interpretation of the word, be applied either to the kilt of the Dasyus or the dhoti of the Hindus, but might be applied properly to this garment. The context, however, makes it more likely that a kilt was meant, because he adds, "They also wear veils, which cover their heads and a greater part of their shoulders." If they wore the sleeved tunic represented in this sculpture, such a garment would be superfluous.

FIG. I.

FIG. 2.

LT COL. MAISEY DEL. W. GRIGGS. LITH.

FIRE TEMPLE, AND WHEEL WORSHIP.

PLATE XXIX.

THE wheel represented in the lower picture of this Plate is among the most common emblems both at Sanchi and Amravati. It crowned the centre of all the four Gateways, though only a fragment of it occurs now on the Northern one (Plate VI.). My impression is that all the pillars surmounted by lions in front of the Caves, as at Karlee, supported originally a wheel in metal,* and probably some of the Stambhas or pillars in front of the Gateways, both here and at Amravati, were crowned by this emblem. After the Tree and the Dagoba, it ranks third among the objects to be worshipped. In the Lalita-Vistara it is described as one of the seven precious things indispensable to a Chakravarti Raja. "The King," it goes on to say, "whose fore-"head has received the royal consecration, having thrown his mantle over one "shoulder, and placed his right knee on the ground, with his right hand pushes "the divine wheel, saying, 'Turn, venerable and divine treasure of the wheel, with "'the Law, bnt not without the Law.'"† The expression that at Benares Buddha begnn to turn the wheel of the Law, and afterwards that he did so at various other places, is one of the most common phrases in Buddhist scripture; and both from these expressions and the relative positions it occupies in the scriptures, it hardly appears doubtful but that the wheel represents Dharma, the second member of the Buddhist Triad. Of this, however, we shall be better able to form an opinion when the Amravati sculptures have been described. In the meanwhile, to avoid all theory, it will be convenient simply to describe it as the Chakra or the Wheel, leaving its meaning to be determined hereafter.

In this instance, as generally at Sanchi, it has thirty-two spokes. It was surmounted by a Chatta with garlands, and ministered to by Garuḍas. It stands on an altar, on each side of which is a deer in act of adoration, but whether the rest of the herd on the right hand are to be considered as worshippers or not, is more difficult to determine. Their presence here seems to be an allusion to one of the eight signs which distinguish the incarnation of Buddha. Of these the seventh is "Turning the wheel of the Law in the park of deer."‡ This deer park is especially famous in Buddhist legends. It was visited and carefully described by Hiouen Thsang.§ Among other things he mentions, "In the centre of the chapel (Chaitya) is a statue of "Buddha in copper, of the exact dimensions of Tathâgata, whom it represents "turning the wheel of the Law." The place is now known as Sarnath, north of Benares, and a celebrated Dagoba now standing there is the best known Buddhist monument in India. In Bnddhist times it was always known as the Mṛigadâva or Deer park, and renowned as the place where Sâkya Muni first and principally taught. The presence of the deer here, and the flowering trees and shrubs, seem

* Foĕ-Kouĕ-Ki, XX. 171.

† Lalita-Vistara, translated by Foucaux, III. 15.

‡ J. R. A. S., XX. p. 140.

§ Voyage, I. p. 132.

almost certainly intcnded to indicate this spot, and the wheel is either meant to represcnt the one that Buddha turned, or is at least symbolical of his preaching.

The eight men who are represcnted as worshipping scem all of equal rank, and as many more werc probably ranged ou the other side. They arc all dressed as IIindus, and all have their hands joincd in the attitude of prayer.

The upper figure in this Plate is one of several at Sanchi, of which it is very difficult to suggest a plausible interpretation. In the foreground ten Hindus in two rows appear to bc worshipping the façade of a rock-cut Chaitya Cave. This may bc intelligiblc enough, but on the right hand two human-headed rams, and on the left arc seen two monsters apparcntly joincd togethcr, half lion half dog, and abovc these flame issuing from the rock, occupies thc whole of the upper part of the picture.

The mousters in the uppcr part of this picture are, so far as I know, uniquc, but no doubt possess somc mystic meaning which somc one familiar with the Tantras may be able to explain. The most curious part, howevcr, is the fire and flamcs which seem issuing from the rock. Hithcrto wc have only met with fire in conjunction with the Dasyus and with Serpent Worship, as in Plate XXIV., but the people herc represeuted are all Hindus, and no trace of the Serpeut is visiblc. Besides the flame looks more likc a uatural phenomcnon than an artificial fire, but certainly is not an accidcnt, but from the conduct of the pcople in the foreground a thing to be worshipped.

I must lcave it to some one else to suggest a mcaning for this reprcsentation, as I have not myself met with anything that would tend to solve the mystery.

This bas-relief occurs on the top of the inuer face of thc lcft-hand pillar of thc Northeru Gatcway, Plate XI.

FIG. 1

FIG. 2

LT. COL. MAISEY DEL.

W. GRIGGS, LITH. INDIA MUS.

PILLAR SOUTHERN GATEWAY.

PLATE XXX.

This Plate represents in two parts one face of one of the fallen pillars of the Southern Gateway (Plate XIV.). The right-hand figure is the upper half, that on the left the lower part of the same pillars. As already stated, Colonel Maisey considers this as the oldest of the four Gateways. "It appears," he says, "to have been the "only gateway for a long period; its pillars are different in style from the others, "and the buildings and costumes represented in the sculptures struck me as having "served as models for those of the other gates, which, though evidently the work "of superior artists, have not so original an appearance." This conjecture is further confirmed by the architectural details, and for the reasons given above (page 89) I am inclined to agree entirely with this determination The abaeus is round, and surmounted by a Lion capital (Plate XXXIX. Fig. 2.). Immediately in front of it lies a lât, probably as old as the time of Aśoka (Plate XXXIX. Fig. 1.), with the peculiarities which occur in Tirhoot* and elsewhere of the age of the same king. Taking into consideration the certain pre-existence of this lion-capped pillar, it is extremely probable that when first attempting in stone a gateway of the sort, they should copy a stone form with which they were familiar. It may also be added that the mode by which the circle of the abacus is extended to the square of the pillar is weak and wooden, and would hardly be attempted after the square capitals of the other Gateways had been invented, but is just such a form as inexperience might suggest.

The sculptures in the upper part represent first the sacred Tree, with two umbrellas and garlands above, and on each side are objects which appear to be intended as representations of flags. The tree itself is the Pipal or *Ficus religiosa.* Below this is a building with pillars alternately plain and octagonal, and with pot bases very similar to those found in the Cave at Karlee.† On the altar in this building stands the "Trisul" emblem three times repeated. If I am correct in my belief that it represents Buddha in the Buddhist religion, it here is simply the emblem of the triune divinity of the Buddhist faith.‡

The lower part of the pillar is occupied by two has-reliefs of a more domestic character. In the upper one of these a Hindu Raja is attended by six females, two of whom support him with their arms. Let us hope he is not tipsy! but the next female carries a vessel which may contain wine, or some intoxicating drink, and she has a cup in her hand. The seated figure on the right holds apparently a cake. On the left one female bears the Chatta of State, the other is seated with her back turned to the spectators. The expression of the king's face is certainly that of a man in liquor.

* History of Architecture, II. 459.

† Ibid., 487.

‡ General Cunningham suggests (Bhilsa Topes, p. 359,) that this afterwards became the emblem of Juggernath, with his brother and sister. In this suggestion I entirely agree, but the transformation took place at a period long subsequent to that we are now engaged upon. The more I look at it the more do I become convinced that Vishṇuism is only very corrupt Buddhism.

The lowest bas-relief is more complicated and difficult of explanation. In the centre, on a tray, rests something which is certainly the principal object in the scene, but what is by no means clear. It may be a relic. Whatever it is, we know by the Chatta held over it, and the Chaori-bearer behind, that it is what is here honoured. In front a man's head lies on the ground, severed from its body. On the right are six Hindus, in attitudes of adoration, and on the left a female singer, by no means remarkable for her personal charms, is singing to the accompaniment of a drum. Four or five men in front seem to be charmed with her performance. Behind her, between the pillars, is a figure with a singularly calm and pleasing expression of countenance, and with a head-dress we have not before met with. Owing to the position in which this figure is placed, it is difficult to determine whether it represents a male or a female, and where all are shaven there is no sign on the face. From the necklace of pearls round the neck, it probably was intended for the Queen.

On one of the architraves of this Gateway (Plate XXXVIII.) we have a siege of a town, apparently to rescue a relic that had been carried off. Does this scene represent the rejoicing consequent on its recovery, and its safe deposit at Sanchi? And is that head in the foreground the head of the robber? The inscription is, unfortunately, only a fragment and unintelligible;* but even if made out, would only tell us probably who presented the sculpture to the Tope.†

The architecture of the palace or pavilion in which the lower scene takes place is so well made out on the bas-relief, that it would not be difficult to restore it. It is of course wholly of wood, but of a very ornamental character.

---

* Cunningham, Bhilsa Topes, p. 264.

† Is it possible that the explanation of this bas-relief is to be found in the following extract from the Vishṇu Purana (Wilson's translation, page 471): "Devabhúti the last Śunga prince being addicted to immoral "practices, his minister, the Kánwa, named Vasudeva, will murder him and usurp his kingdom." This event happened about the year 78 B.C., and is therefore not an unlikely one to be recorded in the Sanchi Gateways.

As this Devabhúti was the king who at least commenced the great Cave at Karlee, the finest and among the earliest of Chaitya Caves in India (J. B B. R. A. S., V. 153), we should be sorry to learn that he was addicted to drinking!

SANCHI.

PLATE XX

FIG 1

FIG 2.

BOAT SCENES.

PLATE XXXI.

THE objects represented in the upper part of the pillar figured in the last Plate close for the present our series of ritualistic illustrations drawn from the Sanchi Tope. With the lower part of that pillar we enter upon a series of historical and legendary subjects, much more difficult of explanation. Whatever meaning we may attach to a Dagoba, a Tree, a Wheel, or other emblem, it is easy to see that it was an object of worship, and it is a matter of comparative indifference who the worshippers may have been. With the historical scenes the case is different. We long to know who the actors are, when they lived, and the significance of the action the sculptor is bent on portraying. In the present state of our knowledge we can do little more than guess at this, but eventually it is probable more definite information may be obtained. Meanwhile, however, some of them are particularly interesting in an ethnographic point of view, or as illustrating the manners and customs of the age in which they were portrayed.

These remarks apply especially to the two boat scenes depicted in Plate XXXI. We have not an idea to what particular events either of them refer; but it would be difficult to bring into stronger contrast the two races whose acts are the subjects of the Sanchi sculptures. In the upper one we have the refined and elegant pleasure-boat of the Hindus; in the lower the rude canoe of the Dasyus. In the upper a festal water procession; in the other the matter-of-fact arrival or departure of some old chief.

Boats not unlike the upper one in design may still be seen opposite the Ghâts at Benares on festal occasions, or on the lakes at Oudypore,* or wherever a Hindu palace has a lake attached to it; but in so far as I have seen, not with a winged lion's head like this. On the present occasion the boat bears a relic casket, over which the royal umbrella is raised, and beside which the Chaori bearer stands. The scene is in a fresh-water lake, in which the lotus and other such plants abound, and around the boat are numerous figures with garlands in their hands, swimming and disporting themselves, supported on mussucks or inflated skins. It is not easy to make out whether those in the water are males or females; from their bangles and armlets, most probably the latter. There can be no doubt that the whole represents the triumphal procession of the relics across a lake or river, probably on some annual festival, but what lake or river we do not know, or what the relics may have been. If it were a periodical festival, this is of little consequence. If it represents some one great occasion, it would be delightful to know, but for this we must at least wait.

The lower picture, in strange contrast to the above, represents the rude canoe of the Dasyus, made up of rough planks, rudely sewn together by hemp or string.

* Tod's Rajasthan, vol. I. 373.

In the centre sits an old bearded Dasyu. Two other men are in the boat with him, one paddling, the other either steering or poling.

In the foreground are four of his tribe, with their hands joined in the attitude of respect or adoration. They are either welcoming the arrival of a venerated sage, or bidding him God speed on his departure,—which, or on what occasion, there seems nothing to indicate at present.*

This scene, too, takes place in a river or fresh-water lake, as may be gathered from the plants that grow in it, and the geese that swim about. One of these seems to run a great risk of choking itself with a fish it is trying to swallow, and another of being devoured by a crocodile, who is opening his jaws to seize him.

On the right, at the lower corner, is a sacred tree hung with garlands, and standing on or behind an altar; but the Dasyus do not seem to be paying any respect to it. Above it is a tree of another species, in which some monkeys are disporting themselves. Above this and on the other side are four other trees, all of different species, and conventionally portrayed, but with so much individual character that they might be easily identified. It is hardly necessary to attempt this here, as they do not seem to have any significance beyond representing a forest on the shores of the lake, though this seems an indispensable accompaniment to all scenes in which the Dasyus appear.

The upper scene belongs to the Southern Gateway, and is seen near the bottom of the fallen pillar (Plate XIX.). The lower is on the front of the Eastern Gateway, on the left-hand pillar in the centre (Plate XV.).

---

* Both General Cunningham and Colonel Maisey are inclined to give a much more elevated interpretation to the bas-relief than that I have ventured to suggest. The former considers it as representing Sâkyas Nirvâṇa (Bhilsa Topes, p. 204.), and Colonel Maisey thinks the whole is of Mithraic origin. I am sorry to differ from such authorities, but the scene seems to me as prosaic and realistic as any in the whole series.

PLATE XXXII.

SANCHI.

FIG, 1.

FIG, 2.

W. GRIGGS, LITH. INDIA

PLATE XXXII.

THE lower figure in this Plate has already been alluded to in speaking of the bas-reliefs on the back of the Northern Gateway (Plate VII.). It is here shown more in detail, and is the most complete picture of Dasyu life and manners which the Sanchi Tope affords, and is so interesting as to make us regret extremely that we have only a verbal description of the sculptures on the front of the same beam, eked out by a somewhat indistinct photograph. The subjects on the two sides of this architrave are evidently parts of the same action, and are among the most important historical bas-reliefs at Sanchi.

There appears to be nothing in this picture which it seems possible to interpret as having a religious significance. The man on the right, with the pot of fire before him, seems cooking his dinner, and his wife assisting him. There are the usual tongs and the pile of bits of wood or metal, to which it is difficult to attach a meaning if they are not firewood. There is no anvil and no hammer to lead us to suppose he was working metal, which at first sight seems probable.

In the background is a girl bearing a bundle on her head; a boy is practising shooting with a bow; a man and woman are making love; children are feeding tame deer, and playing. In the foreground two Dasyus are pouring water on the hands of two others of the same tribe. In front of the same architrave, it will be recollected, the principal ceremony is the king pouring water on the hand of a Dasyu chief,—as before mentioned, in confirmation of a grant or oath. Every one at all familiar with Hindu mythology will recollect when Vishṇu, in his fifth Avatar, descended upon earth to check the power of the great Bali, he asked for as much earth as he could compass in three steps; and when this was granted, he required that the king should confirm his grant by pouring water on his hand. This done, he stepped over earth, sea, and skies, and so deprived him of the sovereignty of the universe. In all Hindu sculptures the pouring of water on the dwarf's hand is the incident principally insisted upon.

On the left of the bas-relief the Hindu Raja, or rather two Rajas, are approaching, preceded, as we shall frequently have occasion to point out in the sequel, by drums and fifes and a boy bearing a spouted vessel like a teapot. The two children, also, who figure on the front of the architrave, reappear here.

From the lions and other wild animals who appear in the background, it is evident the scene is laid in the forest; but no object of worship appears anywhere, and no indication of a religious character. For the present we can do little more than describe it as a visit from the Hindu Raja to the Dasyu chief.

The upper bas-relief is from the inner face of the left-hand pillar of the Eastern Gateway (Plate XIV.). It is immediately below that representing the same people worshipping the five-headed Naga (Plate XXIV.), and may therefore have some connexion with it, though it is not easy to say to what extent this may be the case. In itself it represents a family of Dasyus following their usual avocations.

On the right two men are splitting wood with hatchets; and what is most remarkable is, that the heads of their axes are tied on to the shafts as if they were of stone. Yet in the same bas-relief we have the tongs or ladles, which certainly are of metal; and we can hardly understand a people who could make metal pincers using stone hatchets. On the left is a youth carrying a bundle of sticks, and in front of him another with two baskets slung as a bangy, as is so usual at the present day.

The principal interest of the picture rests, however, with the three old men in the foreground. The one in the centre is pouring something into his fire-pot. The one below him is blowing his fire with a fan, and he on the extreme left is apparently cooking something in the flame, but what it may be, it is almost impossible to guess. There are, of course, the usual tongs and slips of wood (?), and all the usual accompaniments as are found on all Dasyu bas-reliefs. One thing is further worth remarking in this, which is, that two at least of the men have their long hair tied up in a knot on the top of their heads, and not the conical head-dress or mode of dressing the hair usual in other Dasyu scenes.

In the centre of the background of this bas-relief is what at first sight seems a Dagoba in a square enclosure. It can hardly, however, be meant for this, as it has no Tee, and a Dagoba without a Tee is more absurd than a Christian steeple without a belfry, or a Mahomedan minaret without a gallery. Its mode of construction, too, is most peculiar. It looks as if it were made of ropes wound round an internal framework, and the two eye-like openings are just such as would result from pulling the ropes apart to make a window. It may possibly be a forest chapel, but if so it is strange that it should be introduced in the centre of the picture, and the people in the foreground paying no attention to it. Wherever a sacred object is introduced in the other sculptures, all present are turned towards it, and all are reverencing the sacred emblem, whatever it may be. Besides all this, the square enclosure is not, so far as is now known, a Dagoba form. Looking at all the circumstances of the case, my own impression is that it represents the tomb of some Dasyu chief, and is introduced merely to indicate the spot where the scene in the foreground is being enacted. It seems nearly certain that the rails that surround the Dagobas are refined copies of the rude stone circles which enclosed the graves of the common people, but we have as yet found no form out of which the Dagoba itself could have arisen. It is not copied from an earthen tumulus, as in that case it would have been a straight-lined cone; still less did it arise from a dome of construction, as all are, and always were, solid. Nowhere, indeed, has anything been found to suggest a type. But if this is a tomb of the aborigines, the mystery is solved. We have the prototypes both of the Rails and of the Dagoba itself; and both are in the form we now find them—exactly what we know Buddhism to have been—a refinement—a sublimation, if the expression may be used, of the faith and practice of a pre-existing Turanian civilization.

SANCHI. PLATE XXXIII.

LT COL MAISEY DEL. W. GRIGGS, LITH

BUDDHIST BAS RELIEF.

PLATE XXXIII.

THE bas-relief represented on this Plate is one of the most extensive as well as one of the most important of the Sanchi series. It occupies nearly the whole of the inner face of the right-hand pillar of the Eastern Gateway (Plate XIII.). There is only the warder below, and a small subject of Tree Worship above. It is more than usually interesting, also, from its being the only subject at Sanchi which can be ascribed with absolute certainty to Buddhism, as we now know it. There are others which may doubtfully be assumed to portray events in the life of Śâkya Muni, but this one certainly is meant as a short biography of the Prince.

The relief is divided into four parts. In the upper we have Mâyâ, the wife of Śuddhodana asleep on the terrace of the palace, dreaming that a white elephant appeared to her, and entered her womb. This dream being interpreted by the Brahmins learned in the Rig-Veda, was considered as announcing the incarnation of him who was to be in future the deliverer of mankind from pain and sorrow.* It is, in fact, the form which the Annunciation took in Buddhist legends. It does not, so far as our illustrations go, appear again at Sanchi, but it occurs frequently, as we shall presently see, at Amravati, and is repeated in almost every Buddhist book which alludes to the birth of the great ascetic.

In the lowest compartments of the bas-relief we have the accomplishment of this prophecy. The Prince Siddhârtha, at the age of twenty-nine, at the foot of the Bodhi-druma, or tree of knowledge, at Buddh Gya, in presence of his five disciples, lays aside his robes of state, and prepares to assume the garb of an ascetic, and commence that mission which he accomplished only after fifty-one years of self negation and of missionary labour.†

Of the two intermediate scenes, the upper occurs within the city of Kapilavastu, his father's capital, and does not appear to have any special meaning. Two men on horseback meet two others on elephants, and behind the latter are two loose horses attended apparently by a groom. In the centre is the standard, with the usual Trisul emblem. All this seems to represent a night scene in the city, with the guards going their rounds.

In the central compartment, the Prince Siddhârtha in his chariot issues from the city gate attended by bowmen and elephants. In front of the chariot walks a boy with a curly head, but with no apparent occupation. Before him march seven other

---

* Lalita-Vistara, p. 61. et seq.

† If this is a correct description of the bas-relief, the legend in the first century of the Christian era differed from that related in the XVIIth and XIXth chapters of the Lalita-Vistara in the eighth or ninth century. According to that authority, Śâkya Muni, after leaving his home, prepared himself for his mission by six years of the austerest penance—so severe that his five disciples could not support it, and left him. When nearly at death's door he recovers, eats what the village maidens bring him, bathes in the river Nairanjanâ, and then attains Buddhahood while seated under the Bodhi-druma, or tree of knowledge at Buddh Gya.

boys, two playing on fifes* and two on drums; two blow into a musical instrument formed of a shell, which is found frequently repeated in these bas-reliefs, though never at Amravati, and one has a smaller class of drum or tambourine.

The city walls and the windows of the houses are crowded with men and women looking at the procession, and all in the costume we have called "Hindu." This extends even to drummer boys, whose curly locks give them an aspect so unlike what is usually met with in India. Was it an artificial fashion, or were they foreigners? These questions have been before alluded to, for if we could answer them we might be able to say whence Buddha acquired the curly hair with which he is always represented in modern times. Except in the bas-relief (Plate XXVII. Fig. 1.), men are seldom so represented in the Sanchi sculptures, and then only persons in the condition of servants, who sometimes have curly heads, but boys are generally represented with hair in this form. There is no representation of Buddha at Sanchi after he had assumed the garb of an ascetic, but at Amravati, in the most modern sculptures, there are several, and in all these he has the short curly locks he always afterwards retained. I cannot help an impression that he acquired the peculiarity in Afghanistan, though still at a loss to account for the presence of a woolly-haired race in that province.

The trees here are of the usual character, except one above the Bo-tree, which looks like a vine. The architecture is identical with what is found in all these sculptures at Sanchi, and is no doubt a faithful representation of the style of the period.

---

* The fifes we have met with before, and shall frequently have occasion to notice them again in the sequel. Yet, so far as we can learn, the "flauto traverso," or flute breathed into at the side without a mouth-piece, was not known in Europe before the thirteenth century. Is it an Indian invention?

SANCHI. PLATE XXXIV.

FIG. 1

FIG. 2

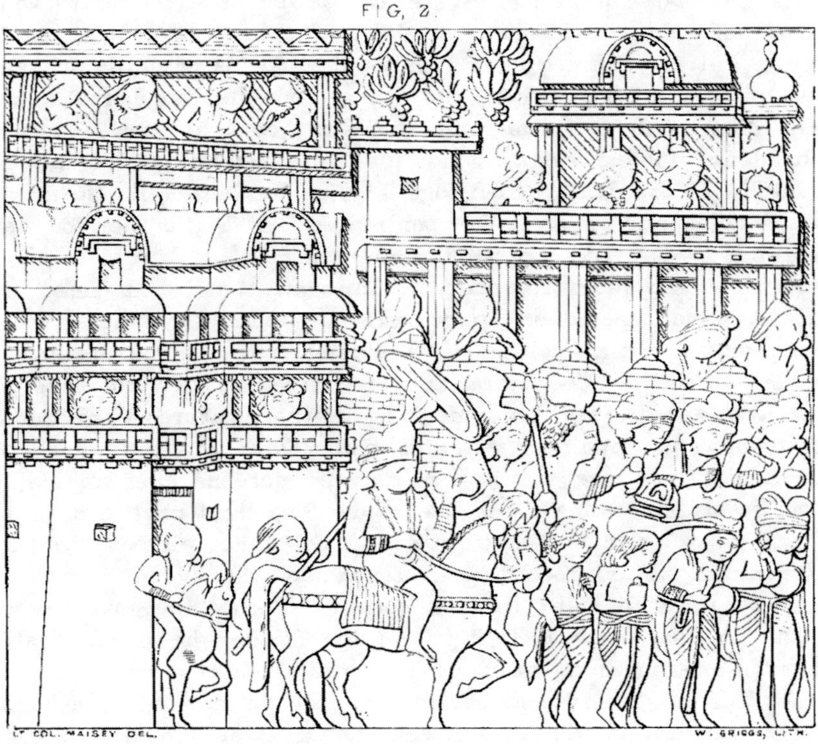

LT COL. MAISEY DEL. W. GRIGGS, LITH.

PROCESSIONS.

PLATE XXXIV.

THE two processional scenes represented in this Plate are both from the left-hand pillar of the Northern Gateway, one in front, the other on the inside (Plates XI. and XII.). There is nothing at first sight to distinguish these scenes from those on the last slab, but they are interesting as showing varieties of costume and of instruments which were not so distinctly depicted in the preceding Plates. The architecture of the palace is also here very clearly expressed. It is of wood, but so detailed that there would be little difficulty in restoring the building from its representation. The little square tower or pavilion, with its triangular battlements, which is introduced in the lower picture of the Plate, as well as in the last, though not exactly similar, is probably intended to identify the two as part of the same palace. The peacock which is seen in both may be introduced for the same purpose. Eating and drinking is going on at a great rate in the palace, and outside one boy bears the large spouted vessel like a teapot, but which probably contained some more exciting beverage than tea. The curly heads are here carefully distinguished from those with flowing hair. This is particularly remarkable in the case of the two boys in front of the Raja on horseback, in the lower bas-relief, but even there is nothing the least negroid in the faces. So far as features are concerned, they seem of the same type, but the distinction as regards the hair is carefully marked.

In the two pictures of this Plate, the Prince, whether on horseback or in his chariot, is easily distinguished by the umbrella borne over his head, but in both he bears in his hand an emblem we have not met with before, nor do we meet with it again. It consists of two balls joined together like a dumb-bell. So far as I know it is not found on coins, nor on any other sculptures, and I am, therefore, quite at a loss to suggest what it may be intended to represent.

These processions are more frequent at Amravati than even here, and as all are nearly of the same type, one cannot help suspecting that they were intended to represent the most popular legend in Buddhist mythological history. In the fourteenth chapter of the Lalita-Vistara, and elsewhere, we are told that whilst the Prince Siddhârtha was in the full enjoyment of all the pleasures of his rank, and of the most perfect domestic happiness with his wife, Gopâ Devî, he one day, while driving in his chariot from the city to his pleasure gardens, met an old, decrepid, grey-haired man, feebly stumbling along the road. The sight made a deep impression on the Prince, and he reflected that even his rank could not protect him from decay. Some time afterwards, while proceeding in the same manner, he met a poor man, squalid with disease; and a third time, a corpse. Both these gave rise to similar reflections on the ills that flesh is heir to. A fourth time he met a healthy, well-clad, and contented-looking man, wearing the robes of persons dedicated to religion; and, satisfied that this was the true career for man, he determined to sacrifice station, wife, family, everything, and devote himself henceforward to the redemption of mankind from the ills they had heretofore been subject to.

These four, which are called the "predictive signs," are singular favourites with the Buddhist legendary artists, and one cannot help suspecting that allusion to them is intended here; but if so, it is the play of Hamlet with the *rôle* of the Prince omitted. In no instance can the man suffering from age, disease, or death be detected. The initiated may, perhaps, recognize the scene by some mark, but neither at Sanchi nor Amravati is it distinguishable to the unassisted vision of the profane.

These two bas-reliefs are also interesting in showing very distinctly the mode in which the horses were harnessed to the chariot, and the form of the bridles by which they were guided. Arrian tells us that "the Indians have neither saddles "nor bridles, like those which the Greeks and Celts make use of, but instead of "bridles they bind a piece of raw bullock's hide round the lower part of the horse's "jaws, to the inner part of which the common people fix spikes of brass or iron, "not very sharp, but the richer ones have them of ivory. Within the horse's mouth "is a piece of iron like a dart to which the reins are fastened."* If this was the mode employed by the Indians in Alexander's time, they seem to have benefited by their intercourse with the west before the Sanchi sculptures were executed. If any one will compare the head stalls of the bridles represented in the Plate, with Figs. 6., 7., and 8. of Plate III., they will see how perfect the head gear of these horses had become; but the sculptures still leave it uncertain whether the horse was controlled by a bit in his mouth or by pressure on front of his face above his nostrils. An examination of the sculptures themselves might settle this point, though neither our drawings nor our photographs suffice for this purpose.

---

* Arrian, Indica, chap. XVI.

SANCHI.

PLATE XXXV.

FIG. I.

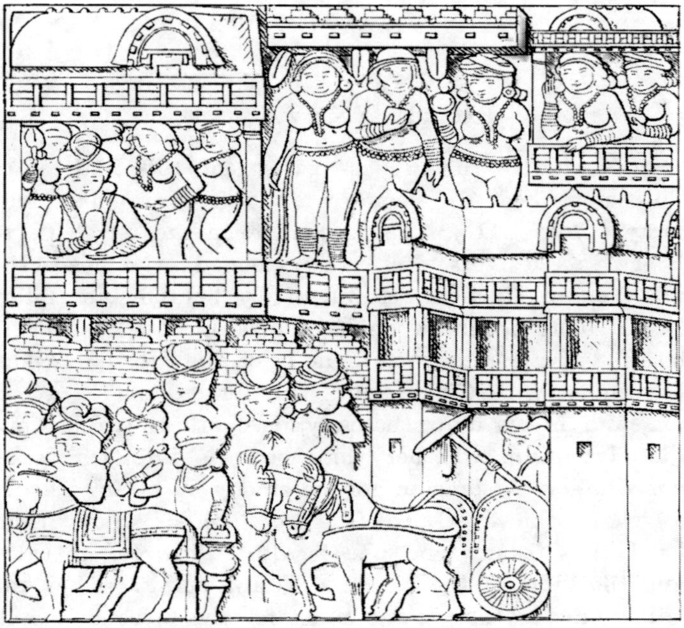

FIG. 2.

Lt. COL. MAISEY DEL.   W. GRIGGS, LITH.

SACRED HORSE AND DOMESTIC SCENE.

PLATE XXXV.

THE procession represented in the upper picture of this Plate is of a different character from those just described. It occurs in the front of the right-hand pillar of the Northern Gateway (Plate XII.). The second form the top. In this bas-relief the principal object is the sacred Horse richly caparisoned, who heads the procession, and towards whom all eyes are turned. Immediately behind him follows the man with the spouted pot, and behind him a chief in his chariot, bearing the umbrella of state, not over himself, but apparently in honour of the Horse. Above him sits a young chief, with two women with Chaoris, but no Chatta, and in a balcony on his left three more women, and in an upper balcony, two others looking out.

It is not easy to determine whether this scene is intended to represent the beginning of an Aśvamedha or of some minor ceremony in which the Horse bore a principal part. The whole, however, looks more like a scene from the Mâhâbhârata than from the Lalita-Vistara, and one is almost tempted to call the man in the chariot Arjuna, and the king in the balcony Yudhishṭhira. They may, however, be intended for very different personages, and must for the present go without names.

When speaking of the sculptures at Amravati, we shall have frequent occasion to revert to this subject, for the Horse there plays a more important part than he does at Sanchi, so much so as to open a wide door of speculation as to the connexion of this worship with that of the Sun god of the Scythians, in the still more mysterious worship of Poseidon by the Greeks. We learn from Herodotus* and others how important Horse worship and Horse sacrifices were considered by the Scythians, and cognate tribes, while we must not forget that both he (vide supra, p. 21) and Diodorus† represent the Scythians as born from a woman who was a serpent from the waist downwards. They were essentially a Nâga race, and their worship of the horse and their Amazonian tendencies all point to similarities between them and the people depicted in these sculptures, which must lead to the most curious ethnographical developments, so soon as they are properly investigated.

I refrain from entering on the subject here, for in the first place it is hardly germane to the main object of the work, but more because to treat of the worship of the Horse, and the importance of the sacrifices in which he was a principal object, would require an investigation nearly as intricate as that of Serpent Worship, and almost as large a work to explain its historical and ethnographical peculiarities. Next after the Serpent the Horse was probably the most important object in that old prehistoric animal-worshipping religion which prevailed among the Turanian races of mankind. After him came the Bull, known in Egypt as Apis, and now in India as Nandi. To complete this work, after the Tree and the Serpent, ought to come the Horse and the Bull. The two last must, however, be left for future

---

* I. 216, IV. 61, 72, &c.

† II. 43.

explorers in the regions of mythology. The Bull, because he does not occur in our sculptures, and the Horse, because, though he appears frequently, it is not with such prominence that it is necessary to do more than notice his presence.

It is much more difficult to fix anything like a definite meaning to the scene represented in the lower figure of the Plate. It no doubt tells a tale sufficiently familiar to those who first looked on the picture, but whether we shall now be able to recover the legend is more than doubtful. There seems no one character in the group sufficiently prominent to give him a name, and no action sufficiently defined to hang a legend upon.

In the upper left-hand corner four women are engaged in occupations sufficiently familiar to all who have visited the East; one is winnowing the grain, which a second pounds in a mortar, and a third rolls out into chitpattees. A fourth is engaged in the same occupation as the last, or ought to be, but is flirting instead with a man who sits beside her.

Below this group is an altar, with the sacred Chatta over it, under which two boys stand in attitudes of prayer, and around it are grouped buffaloes, oxen, sheep, and goats. Are they being blessed? or are they worshipping? On the right hand stands a man on the edge of a pond, into which a girl is pouring water; he has a wreath (or is it a net?) in one hand and a pole in the other, and beside him another man with his hands joined in an attitude of prayer. Next to him stands a woman with a water-pot under her arm. Above them other men and women, and at the top of the picture a man with a bundle driving two oxen either to field or to market. It seems almost impossible to make a story out of so disconnected a picture as this. It may after all be merely meant to represent the family and the pastoral wealth of the giver of the Gateway, in the same manner as the pictures on the tombs round the Great Pyramid represent similar scenes in ancient Egypt. But whether this or any more recondite meaning should be given to it, it is a curious illustration of costumes, and life and manners in India in the first century of the Christian era.

This bas-relief occurs at the top of the left-hand pillar of the Eastern Gateway on the inner face (Plate XIV.).

SANCHI. PLATE XXXVI.

FIG. 1.

FIG. 2.

L^T COL. MAISEY DEL. A. GRIGGS, LITH.

FOREST SCENE.

PLATE XXXVI.

The scene represented in the lower figure of this Plate may possibly be an early version of one of the most favourite legends of the Buddhist chroniclers. It is mentioned by Fa-Hian,* and is narrated at length with the most miraculous accompaniments both in the Ceylonese Atthakathâ† and the Tibetan Lalita-Vistara.‡ It is briefly this: when the Prince Siddhârtha had reached his sixteenth year, his father sought a wife for him among the daughters of the neighbouring Rajas. All refused, however, because the Prince, though handsome, had not been taught any martial accomplishment, and was therefore incapable of controlling women. To prove his power in this respect, he strung a bow that no one else could string, pierced with his arrows iron targets thicker than those of the Warrior or Minotaur, and at distances which neither Armstrong or Whitworth could face; and lastly, shot an arrow an inconceivable distance, and where it lighted a spring of water gushed forth, which afterwards Fa-Hian tells us was formed into a fountain for travellers.

The only points of resemblance between the picture and the legend are, that a young warrior is shooting across a river, apparently at a rock, out of which a spring of water is gushing. If this is the Prince Siddhârtha, the man on horseback, with the Chatta over his head, must be the Śâkya Daṇḍapâṇi, the father of the lovely Gopâ, and the man seated above his head, talking to the monkey, one of his defeated rivals. Two others are standing behind him. These three may be Ânanda, Devadatta, and Saundaranda.§

In the foreground are three warriors armed with bow and sword, and beside them the usual accompaniment of drums and fifes.

The scene in which the action takes place is represented as a wood, inhabited by monkeys, who are gamboling among the trees, or seated in holes in the rocks. Through the picture runs a river, full of fish, and on its further bank two deer are lying. In none of the versions of the legend are we given to understand that the scene of the competition was in a forest; but we must recollect that the oldest written version we possess, which gives the details of the scene, is at least 400 years more modern than the sculpture, and in India far less time is sufficient to overlay the simplest facts with the most preposterous fables. It may, however, be that by representing a forest and a river, as intervening between the place where the prince was standing and the object he was shooting at, the artist intended to convey an idea of distance.

The bas-relief is the upper one on the standing pillar of the Western Gateway on the front face. (Plate XIX.)

---

* Foĕ-Kouĕ-Ki, XXII. p. 198.
† J. A. S. B., VII. 804.
‡ Lalita-Vistara, XII., 147, et seq. See also Cunningham, Bhilsa Topes, p. 219.
§ Ibid., 147.

The upper picture in this Plate represents one of those transactions between the Hindus and Dasyus, which have probably only a local meaning, and to which, therefore, it is improbable we shall ever be able to affix any definite meaning. It occupies the corresponding position to that last described, but on the fallen pillar of the Western Gateway.

In the centre of the upper part of the picture a Hindu Chief or Raja, accompanied by his minister, is conversing with a Dasyu, whose two wives or daughters are seen beyond him on his left hand. On the Raja's right are two of the ordinary circular huts of the Dasyus, in front of which a man and woman are seated naked. They are sitting on their lower garments, and their upper cloaks are hung in their huts. Two monkeys are playing above them. Between these two huts is seen the fire-pot, which is almost an invariable accompaniment wherever these Dasyus are represented. Below it is the water-pot, and beside it the ladle or pincers. From their position here, they would seem to be the sacred implements of the tribe. Did Fire and Serpent Worship go together? Whatever these implements may be, their universal presence in every scene where the Dasyus appear, and their absence in every representation in which the Hindus are the principal actors, point to a distinction which the sculptors of the Gateways meant to be typical. Whenever they can be identified with certainty, we shall know who the people were who employed them. One only thing, at present, seems clear—that they have no connexion with Buddhism, or with any Buddhistic ceremony with which we are at present acquainted.

The middle of the picture is occupied by deer, below which is a scene which it seems impossible to interpret. A Hindu, apparently of rank, is addressing, with his hands joined as in supplication, a stout Dasyu boy, who bears a large waterpot on his shoulder. To their right two Hindu soldiers, in full equipment, are standing, one of whom is deliberately shooting a Dasyu boy, who is half concealed in the water. There is nothing in the picture to explain why the poor boy should be shot, and I know of no legend which could throw any light on the transaction.

The dress of the soldiers is worthy of remark. They wear a kilt, and the usual cummerbund or waistband, and cross straps to carry their quivers. Their bows are bows of double flexure, which we usually associate with the Parthians or Amazons, but it is doubtful whether any ethnographic distinction can be founded on this peculiarity.

SANCHI.

PLATE XXXVII.

FIG. 1.

FIG. 2.

LT. COL. MAISEY DEL. W. GRIGGS LITH.

GARDEN SCENE.

PLATE XXXVII.

If the two scenes depicted in this Plate can be considered as anything like a fair representation of Buddhist feeling or Buddhist manners in the first century of our era, they present this faith in a marvellously different aspect from anything we have hitherto been taught to believe. If these had been found on a Palace Gateway, it might have been said that the manners of the Palace were not those of the Temple; but the upper one of these is that carved on the front of the Northern Gateway (Plate XII.). The other is the upper compartment in front of the fallen pillar of the Western Gateway.

In the first we have on the right hand a Hindu gentleman playing on a harp, and singing to a lady who is sitting beside him, with her feet in the water of a fountain, and listening with no unwilling ear to her lover's song.

In the opposite compartment the lady is sitting on the gentleman's knee, and he is drinking something out of a cup which certainly is stronger than water.

In the foreground some ladies are disporting themselves in the water with two elephants, and the whole scene is one of pleasure and sensual enjoyment. The only costume of the ladies, except their chignons, is their head belt and their bangles, but they have not all of them even this. The men are slightly better clad, but even they have more cloth in their turbans than in any other part of their dresses.

The lower bas-relief is of a very similar character. It is divided practically into four compartments, in each of which two persons, male and female, are seated on couches. Two of these groups are close to the waters of a lake, in which lotus are shown as growing; two others are on a terrace, in the centre of which a flight of steps leads from the lake. On each of the couches a man and woman are seated in close conversation, to use the mildest term, and all are drinking. Below, or in front of the couch of the couple in the left-hand upper corner, is the wine pot or jar, which continually recurs in the lithographs from the first (Plate XXIV.), but nowhere can it be so distinctly surmised that it contains an intoxicating liquid as here.*

On the top of the steps, between the two upper couple, stand a man and woman, evidently servants, the woman giggling most unmistakeably, and holding her hand to her mouth to prevent an explosion of hilarity, and not without reason. The man, too, turns up his eyes in amazed astonishment.

---

* We ought not to be surprised that drinking should be a favourite indulgence in these days. The Mahâ Bhârata is full of drinking scenes, and many of its episodes turn on the results of intoxication. Even the gods in those days got drunk on Soma juice; why not poor mortals? In addition to this, we must bear in mind that though the Hindus of the plains are so remarkable for their temperance, all the hill tribes drink joyously to the present day. No ceremony, civil or religious, takes place without drinking and dancing, and the festival generally is brought to a close by all—the men, at least—being so drunk as to be unable to continue it.

The arbours under which two of the couples are seated, are curious instances of that sort of summer-house which may be found adorning tea gardens iu the neighbourhood of Loudon at the preseut day.

It is scenes like these that make us hesitate before asserting that there could not possibly be auy connexiou between Buddhism and Wodenism. As we shall see iu the next Plate, Buddhists could also fight—for a religious purpose, it is true,—but still if Hiudus of that faith could fight and drink even to the modified extent to which we find them practised here in the first century after Christ, it requires only a moderate knowledge of political arithmetic to calculate what may have taken place a few centuries earlier. The authors of the Mahâbhârata gloat as joyously over the slaughter of the myriads that lay unburied ou the fatal battle field of Kurukshetra after eighteen days fight, as any Scandinavian scald could have done over the deeds of auy of Wodin's companions; and if Hindus could then drink and fight, as we have every reason to suppose they did, the gulf between the two religions was not at one time so impassable as it afterwards appears to have become. If we would understand the subject, we must turn from those books which have hitherto been our only sources of information, and look back to a time before the iron of asceticism had eaten into the souls of the followers of Śâkya Muni.

SANCHI. PLATE XXXVIII.

FIG.

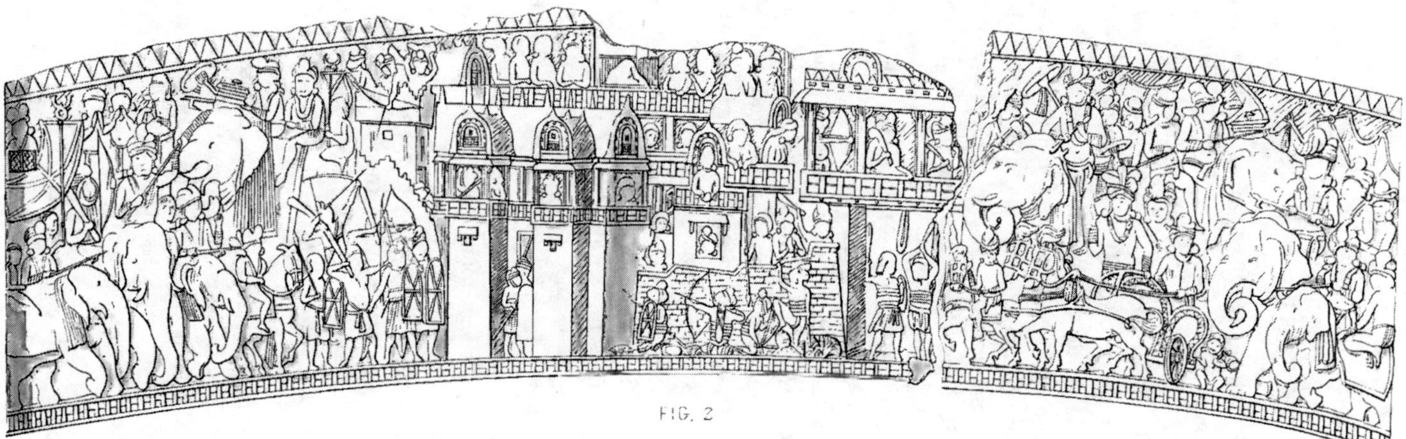

FIG. 2

L^T. COL. MAISEY DEL. W. GRIGGS. LITH.

SIEGE AND RECOVERY OF THE RELICS.

PLATE XXXVIII.

From love to war the transition in the history of most nations is easy and direct, but we hardly expect to meet either in the annals of Buddhism. It is not difficult, however, to see from the upper bas-relief in this Plate taken from the fallen fragments of the Southern Gateway what was the cause of the war thereon depicted. It represents a siege, but on either side an elephant is escaping, bearing a relic casket on his head, and that casket shaded by the sacred Chatta, denoting its importance. It is impossible to say, of course, what these relics are, or what the city that is besieged, but it is at least curious that the caskets are almost perfect pictures of those which contain the relics of Śâriputra and Moggalâna, which were deposited in the neighbouring Topes close at hand. Nothing can be more probable than that the acquisition of these important relics should form the subject of a bas-relief, but we have no record of when they were originally deposited, or whether they were stolen from Sanchi and again recovered, nor by whom they were finally enshrined in the Tope from which they were so lately exhumed.

No. 16.

Relic Casket of Śâriputra, from Satdhara Tope.
From a Drawing by Colonel Maisey.

No. 17.

Relic Casket of Moggalâna, from No. 3. Tope.
From a Drawing by Colonel Maisey.

On the right we have three Princes, or at least three Chattawallahs. The principal of these seems to be the one in the chariot; but none of them are armed, or seem inclined to take any part in the fight. On the left, also, we have a chief, without a Chatta on his elephant, with a smaller one in either hand; but he too looks more like a spectator than a sharer in the fight.

In the centre the siege is carried on vigorously. Two men on the right with the kilt and a breastplate like a Roman soldier, are acting as slingers. A body of archers and spearmen are assaulting a low outwork in the centre, aud bowmen and spearmen are storming the gateway, at which two of the assailants seem to have effected an entrance.

The besieged defend themselves with arrows and spears, and throw down large masses of stone on the heads of their assailants; but what seems strange, no engines of war are nsed,—neither ladders nor battering rams,—nor is any attempt made to set fire to the place. In all these respects the Hindus seem to have been very much behind the stage we know from the Nineveh sculptures that the Assyrians reached at a mnch earlier age.

The other bas-relief, from the fragments of the Western Gateway, forms part of a larger subject, the first part of which has not been drawn, and we therefore qnote Colonel Maisey's description of it. "It represents a long procession approaching a "city whence it is watched by numerous spectators. First, march four standard bearers, "then come musicians, men with spears and shields, others with palm branches, "some look backwards, and seem to be adoring their elephants, which come after "them. These carry Mahouts, with Chaori and Chatta bearers, and are attended "by numerous pedestrians, some with swords and shields, some with bundles, and "one with a spouted vessel. After these come a two-horsed chariot, containing a "man attended by Chatta and Chaori bearers, the hero of the procession, which "is probably a triumphal return from some warlike or religious expedition. The "rear is brought up by horsemen, and two more mounted elephants."

The upper lintel contains what seems a continuation of the above, and is shown in the lower figure of this Plate. On the left is seen a city, into which the head of the procession has already penetrated. Four men, with horse-tail standards, next approach, then a horse led by a boy. The procession is here interrupted by a sacred Tree behind an altar, behind which come the usual array of musicians, led by a man bearing a shield with the union jack upon it. Behind the musicians comes the elephant of state, with three riders, one of whom bears the relic casket on his head, the other two the Chatta and Chaori. The rear is brought up by more elephants and horsemen, one of whom looks remarkably like a modern jockey!

It seems quite clear that the object of these bas-reliefs is to represent the acquisition or recovery of some important relics by the community at Sanchi, and as the sculptures are the gifts of private individuals, the events depicted probably occurred at some date considerably anterior to that of the sculptures themselves. My impression is that the relics are those of Śâriputra and Moggalâna, and the hero of the triumph, Aśoka himself. But this, in the present state of our knowledge, to say the most of it, is little more than conjecture. Be this as it may, these two bas-reliefs are of great interest, in the first place, as showing the state of the arts in India in the early centuries of the Christian era. They certainly are superior to any of the Assyrian sculptures depicting similar scenes, and can hardly be said to be inferior to contemporary sculptures on Trajan's column or similar subjects at Rome.

As illustrations of costume, they are also of great value; but perhaps their most curious peculiarity is their being illustrative of a religious Buddhist war! So far as we know, no war was ever undertaken by a Buddhist community for the sake of propagating their faith or extending the area of their religion. But the desire to possess relics seems to have roused passions antithetical to the usual form of their faith, and they fought either to acquire or to recover these most valued treasures, and they triumphed gloriously when they brought back these treasures to the sanctuary, where they reposed till disturbed by the antiquarian curiosity of two Englishmen in 1854!

SANCHI

PLATE XXXIX.

FIG. 1

Lt. Col. Maisey del.

FIG. 2

W. Griggs, Lith.

LION CAPITALS.

SANCHI. PLATE XL.

FIG. I.

FIG. 2.

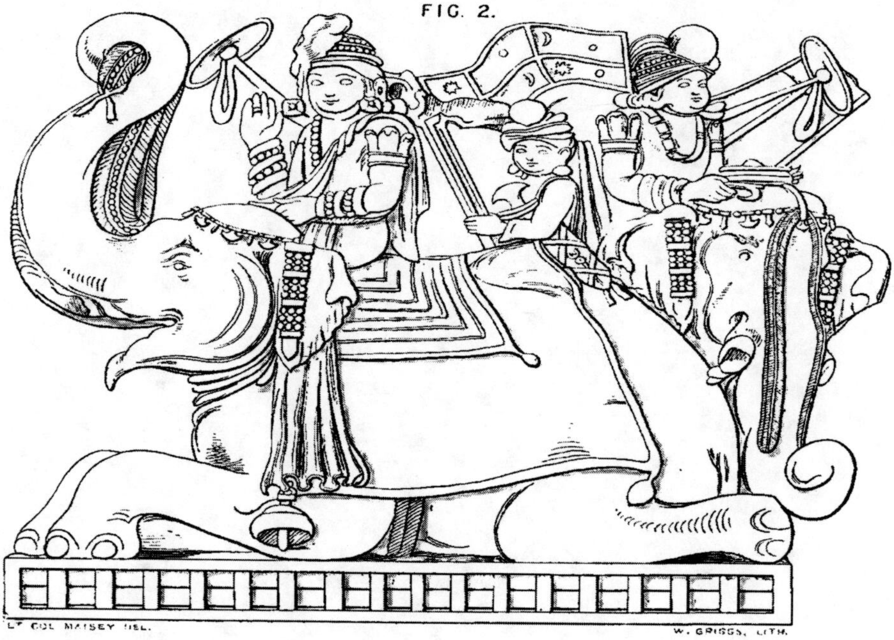

LT COL MAISEY DEL. W. GRIGGS, LITH.

ELEPHANT CAPITALS.

FIG. 1.

FIG. 2.

FIGURES OF BUDDHA AND DWARF CAPITAL.

PLATES XXXIX., XL., AND XLI.

PLATE XXXIX.

THE lion capital (Fig. 1.) in this Plate once adorned a lâṭ that stood immediately in front of the Southern Gateway of the great Tope. From a comparison of the style, and especially of the honeysuckle ornament and the sacred geese of its abacus, with what we find on pillars at Allahabad and Tirhoot, which undoubtedly were erected by Aśoka, we may feel quite confident that this too was erected by him. If this is so, it proves either that the great Tope was erected by that monarch, or that he erected this pillar as an additional ornament to a pre-existing monument. For reasons above given, my conviction is that the Tope was erected by him also, and its date consequently is not far from 250 B.C.

The other capital is that of the fallen Southern Gateway, and seems evidently to be imitated from the older one in its immediate proximity. The honeysuckle ornament has become Indianized, and the execution of the lions is stiff and conventional. It may be suggested that this inferiority may be partly owing to the circumstance that the original lion sculptors came from the north-west—from Bactria—where lions abounded, and that Malwa afforded no models from which the true nature of the animal could be studied. But, on the whole, it seems as probable that they indicate a decay of art from the time when it was first introduced into India under Grecian or rather Bactrian influence, till about the Christian era. Unfortunately we have very little that was executed between these two periods that would enable us to settle this question. The one thing at present known that seems to belong to the period, is the sculpture in the Caves at Cuttack,* but they have not yet been drawn with that critical accuracy which would enable us to reason regarding them. Against this view, on the other hand, we have the superior elegance of the figure sculpture at Amravati three centuries later. It is of course rash to generalise from the very few data we have, but judging from them alone, it may be said that animal sculpture declined from Aśoka's time till the Christian era, but that figure sculpture improved, or at least became more refined, between the epochs of Sanchi and Amravati.

It may be observed, *en passant*, that the winged lion on the abacus of Fig. 2. is much more nearly allied to his Assyrian, or rather Persian prototype, than his degenerate descendants at Amravati.

---

* J. A. S. B., vol. VII., plates XLII. and XLIV.

PLATE XL.

The lower group of elephants in Plate XL. is likewise from the Southern Gateway; it is on one of the blocks over the pillars which separate the architraves into parts (Plate XVI.). It is another indication of the greater antiquity of the Southern Gateway, inasmuch as though not a capital itself, it is evidently just such a suggestion as might lead to the design of the elephant capitals of the Northern or Eastern Gateway, one of which is represented in the upper figure of this Plate.

The figure on the elephant in front of the lower one appears to be royal, from the Chatta borne over his head, and to be followed by another elephant, bearing a relic casket on his head, over which the Chatta of State is displayed. The standard which is borne behind him is of the stars and stripes pattern, while that on the upper capital from the Eastern Gateway is the union jack design; both have the Buddhist Trisul emblem, though in the lower one it is partially broken away. The truth and vigour with which the elephants are sculptured in both these groups go far to disturb the theory just hinted at of a general decline of art at the period they were sculptured, and must rather favour the idea that it was in the representation of lions only that the sculptors of Sanchi had broken down.

PLATE XLI.

The lower figure of the Plate represents the capital of the Western Gateway, which is identical in design with those of the smaller or No. 3. Tope (Plate XXI.), and therefore probably of the same age, though, as before hinted, it is a little difficult to determine what that age may be. I have before stated my reasons for believing that the Western Gateway was the last erected, though it is difficult to understand how, after executing anything so beautiful as the lion and elephant capitals of the other Gateways, they could perpetrate anything so detestable as these. A desire of novelty may have led to the adoption of the dwarfs, after their introduction on the middle architrave of the Northern Gateway (Plate VII.), or they may have a mythological meaning we fail to detect.

The figure of Buddha (Plate XLI. Fig. 1.) from the Vihâra is introduced here because it is similar to four figures which now stand against the Tope inside the Rail, and on which it has been attempted to found an argument as to their antiquity. This one, however, has upon it the familiar "Ye hetu dharma" inscription in the Kuṭila characters of the tenth century, and these, with other indications from the locality where it is found, prove that it cannot be earlier than that date. This is, besides, about the date that must be assigned to it from its style, by anyone familiar with Indian sculpture. The others may be earlier, but not by any long period, though without photographs or drawings it is impossible to say what their exact age may be.

PLATE XLII.

SANCHI.

FIG. 1

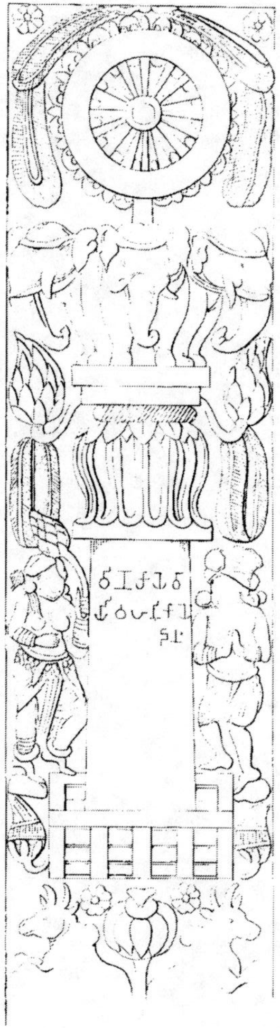

FIG. 2

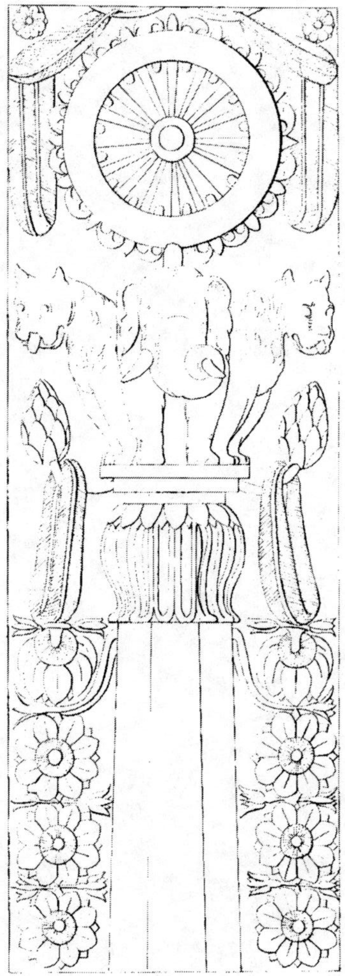

FIG. 3

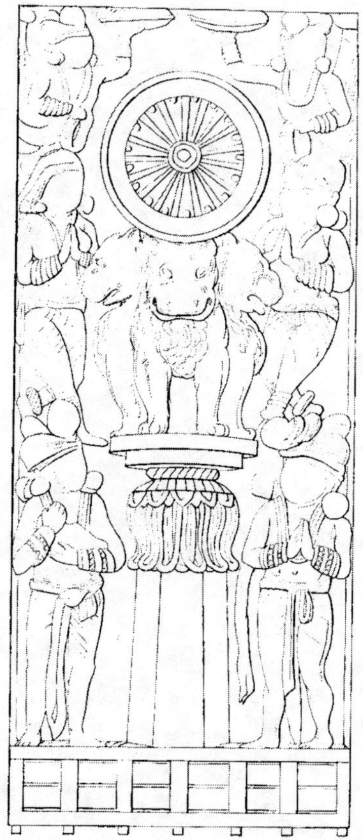

LT. COL. MAISEY DEL.

W. GRIGGS, LITH. INDIA MUSEUM

CHAKRA PILLARS FROM SMALLER TOPES.

FIG. 1.

FIG. 2.

FIG. 3.

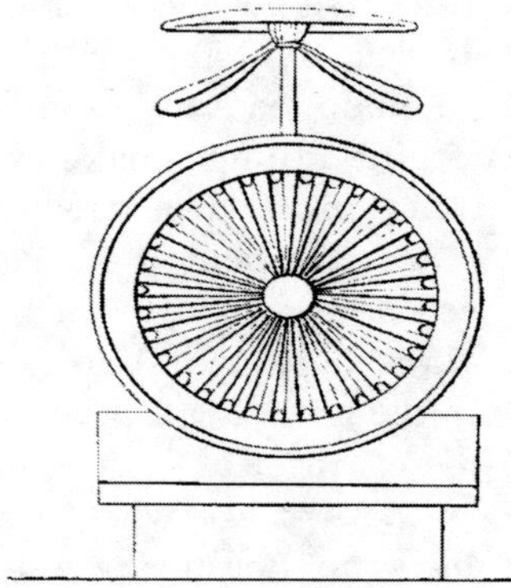

FIG. 4.

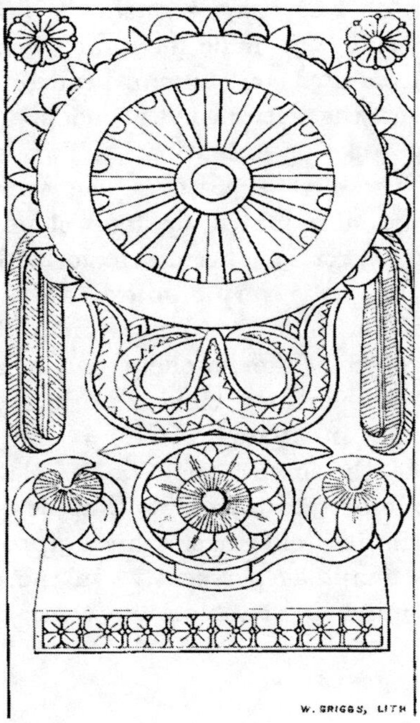

FIG. 5.

Lt. Col. Maisey del. W. Griggs, Lith

DETAILS OF SCULPTURE.

PLATES XLII. AND XLIII.

For reasons given above, page 91, it seems probable that the Rail of the smaller Tope (No. 2., in plan, Plate I.), is intermediate indate between that of the Rail of the great Tope and of the Gateways which were added to it in the first century of our era. Were it not, however, for the form of the characters in which its inscriptions are written, there are circumstances which might induce us to ascribe to it a date even more modern than their erection. Eventually it may turn out that it is so, but for the present we must be content to assume that it was erected about one century before the Christian era.

There are no bas-reliefs, properly so called, on the Rail, but all the discs on the pillars are sculptured (Figs. 2. and 5., Plate XLIII., are examples) "either with "rosettes, human or animal figures, monsters, emblems, and other objects, very "poorly executed, and, with one or two exceptions, not worth a detailed description." Among these, Colonel Maisey enumerates "elephants, seated female with lotus, bull, "monster with alligator's head and fish's tail, five-headed Naga, wheel, tortoise,— "emblem of Kâśyapa,—monster half lion half fish, lion, lion with bull in his mouth, "woman riding a male centaur, horseman, female centaur, snake, canopied female "figure mounted on human-headed animal, bird killing snake, &c." "The angle "pillars of the entrance," he adds, "are rather more decorated, and some of them "of very superior execution." Two of these are represented in Plate XLII. Figs. 1. and 2. The first represents the sacred wheel adorned with garlands, and standing on a pillar, surmounted by four elephants; three only are shown, of course; and on one side a woman offering a lotus bud, on the other a man in the attitude of prayer. No. 2. is very similar, except that there are two lions and two elephants on the top of the pillar, and no human figures. Both these wheels are adorned externally by objects like hatchets, but which I have no doubt are meant for the Trisul emblem so frequently alluded to above.

Fig. 3., in Plate XLII., is a representation of a similar object from the Gateway of the small Tope No. 3. (Plate XXI.). It is hardly distinguishable in design from the other two, except that it is more crowded with figures, and Garuḍas or Devas bringing offerings, which apparently do not occur at No. 2. Tope. There is also an attempt at perspective in the capital, and on the whole it looks more modern, but how much it is impossible to say.

PLATE XLIII.

Fig. 1. in this Plate is from one of the gate pillars of No. 2. Tope, and represents two men apparently turning the wheel and two women in attitudes of devotion. Is this the original of the prayer wheel of the Thibetans? Fig. 4. is a combination often met with of the Wheel, with the Trisul emblem. If I am not mistaken, it means Buddha and the Law, or it may be the Law of Buddha. Fig. 3. on this Plate is a similar combination of a wheel on an altar, with the ennobling Chatta over it. Figs. 2. and 5. have already been described. The first is one of the pillars of No. 2. Tope, the second a rosette, which replaces the five-headed Naga on another of these pillars.

One of the most interesting points connected with these wheel pillars is, that they almost exactly reproduce the pillars that stand in front of the Caves at Karlee and Salsette; not only is their architectural form identical, but the four lions which surmount them are the same, and my impression is that the Karlee pillar once supported a metal wheel, which has now disappeared; but be this as it may, if we are correct in assigning the Karlee Cave to the first century B.C.—which I see no reason for doubting—it is a satisfactory confirmation of the date to find identically the same architectural forms at Sanchi at the same period.

At Amravati, three or four centuries later, the wheel pillars became even more important, and also infinitely more elaborate, and are among the most prominent ornaments of that building.

In Fa-Hian's travels (A.D. 400) we have a description of two pillars, 70 feet high, which adorned the entrance of the Jetavana monastery, outside the gates of Śrâvastî, the old capital of Kośala in Oude, in the time of Śâkya Muni. One of these was surmounted by a wheel, the other by an ox.* So at least he says; but Hiouen Thsang corrects him. When he saw the pillars, more than 200 years afterwards, he calls the ox an elephant, which is much more likely; but the wheel had been replaced by a Dagoba†—a very common form. If the wheel was of metal, it may have been stolen during the reign of some Brahminical king.

It is curious that we almost lose sight of Tree Worship in the sculptures of these smaller Topes, though it forms so prominent a feature in those of the great one. It does occur in No. 3. (see Plate XXI.), but in a very subordinate manner, and I can find no trace of it in Colonel Maisey's descriptions of No. 3. Tope. I do not, however, know that any argument can be based on this. Tree Worship certainly did prevail long before they were erected; but their preference for the Serpent and neglect of the Tree is worthy of attention, and may hereafter lead to some interesting conclusions.

---

* Foĕ-Kouĕ-Ki, p. 171.

† Si Yü Ki, I. p. 296. It is curious, however, to remark that even he was mistaken at Sankissa, where he describes an elephant on the top of a pillar as a lion, when it was an elephant with only his trunk broken off. It was drawn by General Cunningham, and is engraved from his drawing in my History of Architecture, Woodcut 970.

SANCHI.

PLATE XLIV.

ARCHITECTURAL DETAILS.

BHILSA. PLATE XLV.

NAGA CAPITALS.

PLATES XLIV. AND XLV.

THE statue and capital (Figs. 1. and 2.) represented on Plate XLIV. were found lying near the North Gateway, with only a fragment of the shaft that once supported them, the rest having probably been used for sugar mills long ago. The execution of the statue is so extremely good that it would be interesting to fix its date, if possible; but there is no inscription and no indication on the spot to enable us to do so directly. There is, however, at Eran, not far away, a pillar bearing a Gupta inscription, with a capital and statue so nearly identical with this, that the probability is that they may be of about the same age. If I am correct in the date, I assign to the Guptas A.D. 318 to 490; this would place the statue with its pillar in the fourth or fifth century, which, from its style, I am inclined to think is by no means an unlikely date. What adds to this probability is the knowledge that Chandragupta was a benefactor to the Tope at Sanchi. His inscription is seen on the Rail, Plate VIII., and will be found translated in the Journal of the Bengal Asiatic Society, vol. VI. 455, and is just such as would lead us to expect some additions to the fane by him about the year 400.

The rays round the head, the absence of a Chatta, or anything indicating kingly state, render it possible that it is intended as a statue of Buddha; in that case one of the earliest known. There are no statues of the great founder of this religion either at Karlee nor the early Caves of Ajanta, and I fancy we must come down to the age of Buddha Ghoso, A.D. 420, before any free standing statues were carved in his honour. But we know too little as yet to express any distinct opinion on such a subject. It is more probable that it represents one of the Gupta kings, or perhaps it is only some other benefactor to the shrine.

The two pillars, Figs. 3. and 4., are from the portico to the Chaitya hall, photographed, Plate XXII. They are very elegant examples of Hindu architecture. Colonel Maisey suggests that the portico may have been added afterwards, and that this may account for their more modern aspect. Applying to them the same test as to the capital and statue, it would seem that they too belong to the Gupta age. If at least the fragments of architecture which are found at Eran belong to the fifth century, which I see no reason to doubt, these must also certainly be ascribed to the same date. It would be extremely interesting if this could be established, for we have no other structural remains in Central India which are known to belong to that age, and the gap so formed is one it would be most desirable to fill up.

The two Naga shrouded statues represented in Plate XLV. are found in the immediate neighbourhood of Sanchi—No. 1. at the village of Ferozepore, the other on the Nagore hill, not far off. They are both probably more modern than the Topes or their sculptures, and, like the statue in the last Plate, may date from the time of the Guptas. Fig. 2. is evidently the most modern of the two. Neither are remarkable as examples of sculpture, but are curious as exemplifying the belief in the efficacy of the protecting hood of the Naga.

Our lithographed illustrations began with a representation of this snake hood on Plate XXIV., which is nearly as old as the Christian era. They terminate with it here, at a period probably as late as the sixth or seventh century. After this period it seems to have faded out of use as applied to mortals, but to have been appropriated either to the Jaina Tirthankars, or to some of the forms of Vishṇu. It is the common accompaniment of the image of that god even to the present day.

Although it died out in India, the custom still exists elsewhere. In Nepaul, for instance, when it was desired to do honour to one of the late kings, a statue of him was placed on the top of a tall pillar, exactly as is done here; and a cobra, standing on his tail, is represented as spreading his protecting hood over his sacred head.

All this, as well as many other things advanced in the preceding pages, will be much more clear and intelligible when we have described the sculptures at Amravati. The two together form a nearly complete illustration of the arts and architecture of India during the first five centuries of the Christian era; but Amravati is scarcely intelligible without Sauchi, and the contrary is equally the case. Many things which the older and simpler forms leave obscure, become clear when they are read by the light of the more modern gloss. We have hitherto been wholly dependent on the rock-cut examples for all we know on the subject, and they, as before explained, are rude, from the nature of the material in which they are carved, and imperfect from the exigencies of their situation. These two Topes supply their deficiencies, and when the sculptures at Amravati have been described, we shall have a tolerably clear conception of the earliest forms of lithic art in the peninsula of Hindostan.*

---

* All the emblems which adorn these Gateways, and which are alluded to in the preceding descriptions, are found with more or less distinctness on the coins of the period. In the annexed example, for instance, Woodcut No. 16, borrowed from Mr. Thomas's paper in the 1st vol. New Series of the Journal of the Royal Asiatic Society, we have nearly all of them.

No. 16.

Coin of Kraṇanda.

In the centre of the left-hand figure is the conventional representation of a Dagoba surmounted by a Chatta, and above this the circle, and over that the Trisul. If the interpretation suggested in the Woodcut, No. 13, is correct, these symbolize water and air. On the right of the Dagoba is the Tree, very similar in form to the Persian example, Woodcut No. 5, and in the field on the left the swastica, and below it an emblem which is found in the necklace, Plate III., Fig. 4. It may be an altar. Below the Dagoba is seen the Serpent, which is hardly ever omitted from these early coins, and often occupies a more prominent place than he does here. On the other face of the coin the field is occupied by a conventional representation of a deer, attended by a female as lightly clad as those in the bas-reliefs generally are. Over the deer what seems intended as repetition of the Tree emblem, or it may be only the symbol of a sacred enclosure with the ennobling Chatta over it.

The inscription on the two faces of the coin, in old Pali and in Aryan characters, reads, "This is the "coin of the great king, the king Kraṇanda, the brother of Amogha." On the strength of the name, and other indications, Mr. Thomas ascribes this coin to one of the nine Nandas who reigned before 325 B.C. My own impression is that it is more modern, probably subsequent to Aśoka, but certainly anterior to the sculptures of the Sanchi Gateways.

THE TOPE AT AMRAVATI.

CHAPTER I.

Unlike that at Sanchi, the Tope at Amravati has been so completely destroyed that a traveller might ride over the mouuds in which it is buried without suspecting what they covered, any more than those who, before the discoveries of Botta and Layard, looked on the monnds of Assyria guessed what treasures of antiquity were concealed beneath their green slopes. In some respects it is fortunate that it is so, for so soon as a slab is uneovered, either by the monsoon rains or an accidental excavation, it is taken away to be used as a door-step, or more frequently to be burned for lime by the incurious natives. The consequenee of this is, that nothing of the central building probably now remains on the spot, and hardly anything of the inner enclosure; but of the outer Rail there may still be enough to enable us to complete our restoration of it, and to fill up many of the laeunæ which the imperfect materials now available have left in our descriptions.

Although two of the Gateways at Sanchi have fallen, two others are still standing, almost quite perfect; and a quadrant of the Rail is entire, and so is the bulk of the Tope itself. We have consequently no diffieulty in assigning their proper place to all the fragments of sculpture, nor any in comprehending the general appearance or form of the building. At Amravati the case is widely different. It is probable that many of the slabs which Colonel Mackenzie first saw in 1797, and afterwards drew in 1718, were then *in situ*, but he has left no written deseription of his excavations,* and it is only in the rarest possible instances that he has written in pencil on his drawings such brief indications as "inner circle" or "outer circle." Beyond this, there is no explanation of his plan. The slabs recovered by Sir Walter Elliot, which form the bulk of the available materials, had all been removed probably iu the twelfth or thirteenth century from their original site, and built into a little chapel, of which they formed the walls, so nothing was to be learned from them. The task, however, is by no means so difficult as it at first sight appears. First, there are nnmerous analogies with other buildings which are

* The late Professor Wilson, who had long charge of the Mackenzie MSS., and knew more about them than anyone else, says, in his Ariana Antiqua, p. 32., "I have not found any description of it (the Tope at Amravati) "amongst his papers, but from a few brief memoranda it appears to have been visited by "him repeatedly, and in 1816 to have been measured and surveyed."

evident at a glance; but the circumstance that rendered the restoration most easy arose from the practice common to Indian architects of repeating everywhere representations of their main buildings as ornaments to the various parts of it. These, as will afterwards be explained, not only suggest the form, but confirm the restoration in a most satisfactory manner.

The Amravati Tope first attracted the attention of Colonel Mackenzie when on a tour of duty in the district in the year 1797. It seems that some two or three years previous to his visit the Rajah of Chintapilly, attracted by the sanctity of a temple dedicated to Siva, under the title of Amareśvara,* determined to erect a city on the spot, and on looking for building materials for his new capital, opened this and several other mounds in the neighbourhood, and also utilized the walls of the old city of Durnacotta or Dharaṇikoṭṭa, which stood about half a mile to the westward of the site of the new city.† Many of the antiquities perished in the process, and large quantities of the stones were used by the Raja in building his new temples and palaces, but several sculptured slabs still remained *in situ*. These attracted the Colonel's attention so strongly that he subsequently communicated an account of them to the Asiatic Society of Bengal,‡ and afterwards returned to the spot in 1816. Being now Surveyor-General of Madras he employed all the means at his disposal during the two following years to the elucidation of the principal temple, which he now styles Dîpaldinna, and translates as meaning "Hill of Lights." The results of his labours are careful plans of the building and maps of the surrounding country, together with eighty very carefully-finished drawings of the sculptures. These were made by his assistants, Messrs. Hamilton, Newman, and Burke, and are unsurpassed for accuracy and beauty of finish by any drawings of their class that were ever executed in India. Three copies were made of all these drawings. One was sent to the Asiatic Society of Calcutta, another was deposited in Madras, and the third sent home to the Court of Directors, in whose library it still remains. As no text or description accompanies these drawings, they have attracted but little attention, probably because of this deficiency, and the consequent difficulty of understanding the form of the monument or the position of the fragments.

At the same time Colonel Mackenzie sent several specimens of the sculptures to the three museums just mentioned, and they have remained their principal ornaments to this day. But, except an attempt to translate two of the inscriptions, which appeared in Prinsep's Journal in 1837,§ very little notice seems to have been taken of them.

Fortunately, however, when Mr., now Sir Walter Elliot, was Commissioner in Guntur, in 1840, he determined to follow up what Colonel Mackenzie had so well begun. He excavated a portion of the monument which had not before been touched,

---

* Hence the full-length name of the place is Amareśvarapuram. Anglice, Amresbury.

† These and many other historical particulars in this paper are gleaned from two letters communicated by Colonel Mackenzie to Mr. Buckingham, published by him in the "Calcutta Journal," in March 1822. They were afterwards reprinted in "Allen's Asiatic Journal," in May 1823, and as the latter publication is generally accessible while the former is not, all my references to these letters will be taken from it.

‡ See Asiatic Researches, vol. IX. p. 272, et seq.

§ Journal Asiatic Society, Bengal, vol. VI. p. 218.

and sent down to Madras a large collection of the sculptures, where they lay exposed to the sun and rain for fourteen years,* till they were ultimately sent home to this country about the year 1856. Unfortunately they arrived here in the troublous times of the Indian Mutiny, and just in the interval between the death of the old East India Company and the establishment of the new Indian Council. There was no proper place for their reception, and the greater part of them were consequently stowed away in the coach-house of Fife House, where they remained buried under rubbish of all sorts till accidentally I heard of their existence in January 1867. With the zealous co-operation of Dr. Forbes Watson and the officers of his establishment, I had them all brought out into the open air and photographed to a scale of one-twelfth the real size, and this was done so exactly that the photographs can be fitted together almost as well as the real stones could be. With these materials I set to work to restore the building; but though I had considerable knowledge of similar buildings, both older and more modern, I should not have succeeded but for the circumstance just mentioned, that among the sculptures themselves there are numerous miniature representations of the building itself and of its different parts, quite sufficiently correctly drawn to be recognized. With all these aids I believe I can now assign the true place and use to at least nine-tenths of the 160 fragments the India Museum possesses, and feel very little doubt that I might be able to recognize the position of all; but the process is slow and difficult, and requires more time and study than perhaps the value of the additional information now to be obtained would justify.

The position of the Amravati Tope will be easily understood from the map (Plate XLVI.). It is situated on the right or south bank of the Kistnah river, about sixty miles from its mouth, and nearly opposite to its junction to the Moony Air river. The Tope itself stands about half a mile to the eastward of the old town of Daranacotta, or Dharaṇikoṭṭa—the magic city—and unfortunately in the middle of the modern town of Amravati, to which circumstance it owes its destruction. To the westward of the town, a little more distant, is another mound, called Cootchtippa, which has not yet been explored; and to the south a third, called Nuckadeverdinna, which was dug up, and the materials used in building the new town. To the westward of the old town, near the Cootchtippa mound, are a great number of those rude circles of stone which were the burying-places of at least some of the inhabitants of the old city. A still greater number of these, however, are found at a distance of between four and five miles to the south-eastward, where they cover the roots of the hills in great numbers.† They range apparently from 24 to 32 feet in diameter, and when dug into have always yielded cinerary urns, burnt bones, and other indications of being burying-places. One of these has already been given from Colonel Mackenzie's work (Woodcut, No. 7.), where several of those at Amravati are drawn. They are, however, all alike in character, not only

* Selections from the Madras Records, 2nd series, vol. XXXIX. p. 195.

† In the map they are called "Circular Tumuli." This they certainly are not, as they are not raised in the centre. They are literally stone circles, but as the map is a fac-simile, I have thought it better to alter nothing. I have also generally retained the spelling of the map, though it certainly is not in all instances correct.

here, but, so far as I can ascertain, all over the south of India as far as Cape Comorin.

We are still very far indeed from any such knowledge of the modes of sepulture among the aborigines, as to be able to speak regarding them with anything like certainty. Ample materials, however, exist in India, and so soon as anyone will take the trouble to collect and classify them, we shall from their graves be able to discriminate between the different races, and assign to each its proper locality with a precision now entirely wanting to such researches. Nothing of the sort can of course be attempted here, but one curious feature may be alluded to, as it has not yet been suspected by European antiquaries; it is, that these rude megalithic monuments are of all ages; some no doubt of extreme antiquity, but many others of quite recent date; many, in fact, have been erected within the limits of this century, and it is not possible, either from their design or their form, to distinguish between those which are really old and those which are quite modern. In the meanwhile, however, I may be allowed to state that, to my mind, it does not appear doubtful but that the great Rail of the Amravati Tope is a Hindu sublimation of these Dasyu models, though we are still unable to trace the various steps by which so wonderful a transformation took place.

Besides these antiquities in the immediate vicinity of the town, there is a very extensive excavation near Datchapully, forty miles westward, covered with sculpture in a most masterly style, and another on the road leading from the river to the pagoda of Srichallum, ten miles further on. There seems also to be a four-storied cavern at Oondavully in Guntur, and another series in the Ellore districts, at a place called Jilkaragoodum. All these, however, are quite unknown to Europeans, though, if carefully examined, they would probably prove as interesting as the better known Caves of Western India.*

* The following curious memorandum, in a clerk's handwriting, is pasted into one of Colonel Mackenzie's volumes with some pencil marks of his own. I fancy it belongs to 1798, though that date on it is erased. Speaking of the Amravati sculptures, he says, " The most curious and most complete is to be found further on " (from the Dipaldinna), close to the outside walls of the Pagoda enclosure, on the south, and going towards " the river. Here is a small Pagoda of the Lingam, formed by three rough stones or slabs set on end and " covered on the top by another placed transversely " (exactly like Kits Coty House, as shown by a little sketch on the margin). " On this stone is represented the escalade of a fort, a figure ascending a ladder, another " from a turret on the walls shooting an arrow. Before the gate of the place a figure with a round shield " prostrating himself before a chief seated on an elephant, and followed by others on horses, bullocks, &c. " The whole forms a group in a very different style from anything observed anywhere else in this country; " and as the attitudes, profiles, &c., differ from the common Hindu style, a correct drawing would be desirable."

This apparently was never made, and the slab is not in the Museum collection. The description reads almost as if intended for the Sanchi (Plate XXXVIII.), but the scaling ladder is an addition to the siege materiel there represented.

CHAPTER II.

History of Monuments.

So much of the interest and the value of the sculptures at Amravati depends on the age that may be assigned to them, that it is very desirable, in so far as it is possible, to fix the date to which they belong. In the present state of our knowledge this cannot be done with absolute certainty; first, because none of the inscriptions bear dates, nor, with one doubtful exception,* do any contain names that can be recognized as those of historical personages; next, no history or reliable tradition mentions the place by name, with either a date or the founder's name attached to it. A considerable degree of vagueness also prevails, and always must, because the buildings are not all of one age, but certainly extended through one, it may be through two or even three centuries. Notwithstanding all this, their date may, I believe, be fixed with fair approximate certainty, quite sufficient for our present purposes.

Taking, in the first instance, the architecture of the Sanchi Tope as the base of our argument, no one I think can examine the two without seeing that considerable progress had been achieved between the erection of the two monuments. According to the Indian chronometric scale, I would value the interval as at least two or three centuries, taking the sculptures of the great outer Rail at Amravati as the base for comparison with those of the Gateways at Sanchi. On the other hand, if we turn to the temples at Bhuvaneśvar in Cuttack, which dates from 657 A.D., we feel that we have passed into a new and much more modern architectural world. The question is, to determine where between these two poles lies the epoch of the execution of the principal parts of the Amravati monument.

There seems, however, no difficulty with regard to a final date before which it must have been erected. When Hiouen Thsang visited "Dhanakacheka," about the year 640, he describes the principal monument in the following terms, from which I quote at length because of the many interesting points the description contains:— "Un ancien roi de ce royaume l'avait construit en l'honneur du Bouddha et y avait "déployé toute la magnificence des palais de Ta-hia (de la Bactriane). Les bois "touffus dont il était entouré, et une multitude des fontaines jaillissantes, en faisaient "un séjour enchanteur. Ce couvent était protégé par les esprits du ciel, et les sages "et les saints aimaient à s'y promener et à y habiter. Pendant l'espace des mille

* This is the name of the Andhra king Yajnaśrí, read doubtfully on a fragment of an inscription copied by Colonel Mackenzie and reproduced, Plate XCIX. No. IX. This king was most probably the Yue-gnai of the Chinese, who we learn from Des Guignes was a zealous Buddhist, and is stated to have sent ambassadors to China in the year 408. If it really is this king who is mentioned in the inscription, his date would perfectly accord with all we learn from other circumstances. His coins and those of Gotamiputra are said to have been found in quantities in and about Amravati.

" ans qui ont suivi le Nirvâṇa du Bouddha, on voyait constamment un millier de " laïques et de religieux qui venaient ensemble y passer le temps de la retraite pen- " dant la saison des pluies. Mille ans après (le 'Nirvâṇa') les hommes du siècle et " les sages vinrent y demeurer ensemble. Mais depuis une centaine d'années les " esprits des montagnes ont changé de sentiments et font éclater sans cesse leur " violence et leur colère. Les voyageurs justement effrayés n'osent plus aller dans " ce couvent. C'est pour cela qu'aujourd'hui il est complétement désert, et l'on n'y " voit plus ni religieux ni novices."*

Before applying this description, the first point necessary to establish is, that Amravati is really the place of which Hiouen Thsang was speaking. The name he gives is of some value for this purpose, for Dhanakacheka is as like the modern Durnacotta or Dharaṇikoṭṭa as we can well expect a name to be after the corruptions of twelve centuries, and Avaraśilâ for the name of the monastery may also be considered as indicating Amareśvara. Such nominal similarities are hardly sufficient in such a case as this ; but if General Cunningham's reading of the inscription, No. XX. Appendix E., is correct, which I see no reason whatever for doubting, this alone would suffice to settle the question. The slab on which it is found formed part of the inner Rail, and is stated to be a gift to the Mâhâ Chaitya of Dhankakata. Another proof is found in his route, as described by the traveller himself, which even taken alone would suffice for the purpose. After leaving Orissa he reaches Kalinga,—the Kalinga-paṭṭana of the present day,—a well-known spot on the coast. From this he diverges 1,800 li in a north-west direction, say 260 miles, to Kośala, the southern country of that name. This must have brought him either to Wyraghur or Chanda, or more probably to Bhuddrack, between Chanda and Hinghenghat, where there are extensive ruins; all these were important places in ancient times in the Nagpore territories. The distance quoted would not take him so far as Nagpore, but it might to Nirmul, which offers many points that render it probable it may be the place indicated.† In his next stage he retraces his steps to the south-east, and reaches a place which it can hardly be doubted was Warangal, the capital of Venga or Ping-ki-lo. Thence he journeys 1,000 li in a southern direction (143 miles) to Dhanakacheka.‡ The distance and direction both agree as closely as any of those given in his travels with what we find in our modern maps. The coincidence is indeed so close as to leave it hardly open to doubt but that this is the place indicated, even if the nominal similarity were not in itself sufficient.

With regard to the date, I am afraid that very little reliance can be placed on the 1,000 years twice mentioned in the passage quoted above from Hiouen Thsang. First, because he is evidently speaking loosely and in round numbers; but more because we cannot feel sure when he placed the Nirvâṇa. If we assume the Ceylonese date

* Histoire de Hiouen Thsang, 188.

† It may be worth noticing here that Nâgârjuna, in his old age, when Śâlivâhana was on the throne, is said to have resided in this capital of Kośala which our traveller visited, which is another reason why we should try to ascertain its position, if possible.—Histoire de Hiouen Thsang, 186.

‡ Vivien de St. Martin, in his valuable memoir, takes him from Warangol to Rajamendri on the Godavery, though admitting that this would make his route south-east instead of south. He was not then aware of the existence of Durnacotta, which is in the exact direction and distance indicated. He probably would now adopt this rectification. See Mémoires de Hiouen Thsang, vol. II. p. 396.

(543 B.C.), which we now know to be the correct one, it would place the period of prosperity 457 A.D., which would accord perfectly with what we gather from other circumstances. Although, however, this indication may not be of much value, it seems evident from this passage that about the middle of the sixth century Buddhism had suffered such a blow as to prevent any such work as this being undertaken. Even if it is contended that Dhanakacheka may not be Dharaṇikoṭṭa, the facts remain the same. From what our author says of what he saw in Kalinga on the one hand and Djourya* on the other, it is evident that, in the century before his visit, war, pestilence, and famine had swept over the three Kalingas, and nearly obliterated the original population. We know, too, that in the neighbouring province of Orissa the Keśari family, worshippers of Śiva, had raised themselves before that time (A.D. 473) on the ruins of the Buddhist dynasty; † and we also know that in the year 605 the Châlukyas conquered Venga,‡ the country in which Dharaṇikoṭṭa was situated, and they were neither Buddhists nor Snake worshippers. From all these circumstances it may therefore fairly be assumed that it was at some time before the middle of the sixth century, or before 550 A.D. at all events, that all the buildings around the Tope were completed.

If we can thus fix, at least approximatively, the period before which our buildings must have been completed, we can with equal probability ascertain the date when they were commenced. In the first place, we find that Colonel Mackenzie collected a considerable number of coins about "Durnacotta." Some of these were Roman, others of the Bactrian Kadphises type,§ showing that the place was probably of some importance about the Christian era; but as none of these were found in the Tope itself, they have no direct bearing on our investigation. Those coins which were found in the Tope were all of lead, but their date not having yet been ascertained they at present afford us no assistance in our enquiry.|| Among the slabs, however, from the Tope, sent home by Colonel Mackenzie, there is one which bears directly on this point. It is photographed in Plate LXXVIII., Figs. 2. and 3. The sculpture on the front is of the age of the inner Rail, probably the fifth century, but on the back of the same slab is a bas-relief evidently of about the same age as those of the Sanchi Tope. This confirms the evidence we acquire from the coins that a city and buildings did exist here as early as the Christian era, but proves at the same time that none of the buildings we now find there are so early. Some centuries must have elapsed between the times when the sculptures on the back and front of that slab were executed.

Colonel Mackenzie also collected a number of traditions referring to a Mokunti Maharaja¶ who, among the Hindus on the spot, is the reputed builder of the

* Histoire de Hiouen Thsang, p. 185 and 189, and Mémoires, vol. II p. 116.

† Stirling's Account of Cuttack, Asiatic Researches, vol. XV. p. 264.

‡ Journal R. A. S., N. S., vol. I. p. 254.

§ Asiatic Researches, vol. XVII. p. 561 and 582, Plate II. Fig. 29, c. 41.

|| Asiatic Journal, vol. XV. p. 471. Madras Journal, vol. XIX. p. 220, et seqq.

¶ On the spot it is called the Doop Mogaśâla of Mokunti Maharaja. Mogasâla, in the Telinga language, signifies a court for public affairs, and the distribution of justice. "Doop" is Hindostani for sun, or rather sunshine; translated into architectural language this would be "Hypethral Basilica." This would perhaps be the best term that could be applied to it; but it involves a theory it is as well to avoid at present. See Asiatic Journal, vol. XV. p. 469.

Tope,* and curiously enough among his own manuscripts there is one which places a Mokunti Raja exactly where we want him, if looking for a founder of the central building, which, from the evidence of the architecture, seems almost certainly to date from about the year 200, which is the date given to this king in that document.† On examination, however, these traditions are found to refer either to Rudra Deva of Warangal (A.D. 1132), or more probably to Pratâpa Rudra of Orissa (A.D. 1503), and have, consequently, no bearing on the date of the monument. They are all of Brahminical origin, and Benares is the scene of action, but like most Puranic traditions they are foolish and fabulous in the extreme, and refer to a persecution, when the last feeble remnants of the Bauddhas, here called Jainas, were finally expelled from India. It is curious to find Buddhists in India as late as the beginning of the sixteenth century; but though this has little reference to our present enquiry, we must bear in mind that the inscription translated by Mr. Prinsep,‡ and Sir Walter Elliot's excavations, prove that Amravati was a temple of the Buddhists at least as late as the twelfth or thirteenth century. My impression is that the Tooth relic again visited the place in 1187, but of this hereafter.

Turning to the monument itself, we find upon it a great number of inscriptions, and my friend General Cunningham has kindly undertaken to investigate this branch of the subject. The result of his labours will be found in Appendix E. Unfortunately they merely record that the pillar, or bas-relief, or object on which they are found, is the gift of some piously-disposed persons whose names are given; but these names, with one doubtful exception, are, unluckily for our purpose, all unknown to fame. At present, therefore, it is only from the form of the characters that the inscriptions aid in ascertaining the date of the monument. Generally this may be described as the Gupta alphabet, as used either immediately before or after A.D. 318. No trace of the Lât character occurs, though that was used in a modified form at Sanchi on the northern limits of the province certainly after the Christian era.§ The inscriptions in which the form of the letters most closely resembles that found at Amravati are those of the Kenheri and Nasick Caves. If Dr. Stevenson‖ is right in ascribing these to the first half of the fourth century, and I see no reason to

---

* Asiatic Journal, vol. XV. p. 470, et seq. Wilson's Catalogue of Mackenzie's MSS.. vol. I. p. cxxiv., and Taylor in Madras Selections, Second Series, No. XXXIX. p. 229, et seq.

† Madras Journal, No. 19, April 1838, p. 352.

‡ It is to be regretted that the Daladâvansa has not been completely translated, for it appears that in the twelfth or thirteenth century the tooth relic was taken back to India at a time apparently when (1187) a Kirti Nissanga, a prince of Kalinga, was one of the many Indian princes who held sway in Ceylon. It is said to have been conveyed to the banks of the Ganges (Upham's History of Buddhism, p. 32), but as Landresse suggests (Foĕ-Kouĕ-Ki, p. 345) this more probably was tho Godavery, or, in other words, the Kistnah. From some particulars furnished me by Sir Walter Elliot, it seems that the part of the monument he dug into was a chapel formed of old slabs arranged unsymmetrically by some prince about that time, so as to form a chapel for some unexplained purpose. It may have been to receive this relic. The inscription translated by Prinsep (J. A. S. B., vol. VI. p. 218) shows that Buddhism was flourishing at Amravati in—say the twelfth century. Altogether nothing would surprise me less than to find that the Tooth relic sojourned here for seventy-six years before its recovery by the Ceylonese, about 1314 of our era. The materials exist for settling this question, but they have not yet been made available.

§ Cunningham, Bhilsa Topes, p. 264.

‖ J. B. B. R. A. S., vol. V. p. 39, et seq.

doubt his correctness in this respect, this evidence, "valeat quantum," would assign to the Amravati Tope the same epoch.

The evidence derived from the architecture of these Caves confirms this attribution to the fullest possible extent. Two drawings have already been given (Woodcuts 11. and 12.), and more will appear in the sequel, but meanwhile, if I am correct in ascribing the Nasick Cave to Gotamiputra (A.D. 309) and the Kenheri Cave to the age of Buddhaghosa (A.D. 410), this evidence, as far as it goes, would fix the erection of the great Rail at Amravati within the limits of the fourth century.

A good deal has yet to be accomplished before this branch of the investigation can be said to be complete; but everything that has yet been brought to light tends to confirm the assumption that the extreme elaboration of ornament which placed sculptured discs on the intermediate bars, as well as on the pillars of Buddhist Rails, was not introduced before the third century, and every building where it is found must consequently be dated subsequent to the year 200 at the earliest. In so far, therefore, as either paleographic or architectural evidence is concerned, the great Rail belongs to the fourth century. The central building, as will afterwards appear, is older, and the inner Rail more modern.

Notwithstanding all this, there is so much of Greek or rather Bactrian art in the architectural details of the Amravati Tope, that the first inference is that it must be nearer to the Christian era than the form of the inscriptions would lead us to suppose. On the other hand, we do not know how long the classical influence prevailed, and how much it may have been nourished by intercommunication with the West. Down to the age of Constantine, Rome seems to have maintained its intercourse with India, and we must pause before we draw a line as to the time when classical feeling may have ceased to exert an influence on Indian art. Certainly, in this instance, the expression of Hiouen Thsang, that this Tope was ornamented with all the art of the palaces of Bactria, is borne out to the fullest extent; but there seems no reason to suppose that this classical influence may not have endured till the break down of the Roman Empire in the fourth and fifth centuries, though it could hardly have lasted beyond that time.

The one point which it seems necessary to insist upon at this stage of the inquiry is the strong Bactrian influence which is manifested in all the details of the monument. As has been explained, the sculptures, with scarcely an exception, refer to a Naga people and to a Naga worship; and since, as pointed out above, p. 44, Taxila and Cashmere were the head quarters of that faith at this age, that circumstance alone would almost suffice to indicate the north-west as the source from which we must expect information regarding its origin. But, again, how long did the Bactro-Parthian kingdom exist? and how long did it continue to influence the politics and arts of India Proper? These are questions to which no very definite answer can be given in the present state of our knowledge; my own impression is, that the influence continued to a much later date than has hitherto generally been supposed; but there is nothing in all this sufficiently definite to enable us to found on it any argument as to the date of the Amravati Tope.

Although, therefore, it must be confessed that neither these classical influences nor the Mackenzie traditions seem to throw any steady light on our subject, the information collected by Mr. Stirling, and published in his invaluable history of Cuttack, does seem to bear on its origin.

The following extracts from his memoirs* are those which seem most to the point:—"In the reign of Bajra Nath Deo the Yavanas are said to invade the "country in great numbers from Babul Des—explained to mean Iran and Cabul—"but are finally driven back." "In the reign of Huns or Hangsha Deo (query, "Hushka) the Yavanas again invade in great force from Cashmere, and many bloody "battles ensue." In the reign of Bhoja, the Yavanas from Sindhu Des invade the country in great force, but are driven back. Then follows Vikramâditya. If, therefore, the dates are to be depended upon, these invasions took place before the Christian era. Other Yavana invasions occur in the next four reigns; but the most important of all occurred in the reign of Subhan Deo, who ascended the throne 318 (the year of the Ballabhi era). In the ninth year of his reign a Yavana, Rakta Bâhu, invades the country by sea, and conquers it. The king escapes with the image of Juggernath, which he buries under a ber tree, and flies farther into the jungle, where he dies. His son succeeds to the title, but is murdered by the invaders. "A Yavana dynasty then ruled over Orissa for a space of 146 years, or "down to A.D. 473." If these dates are to be depended upon,—and I see no reason for doubting their general correctness,—the period of the supremacy of this Yavana dynasty in Orissa exactly coincides with the dates which from other circumstances I would ascribe to the principal buildings at Amravati. No Stirling has yet visited Guntur, and we cannot therefore assert it, but it seems more than probable that the foreigners who conquered the northern, would also take possession of the southern Kalingas.

This account of this last invasion, being derived from Brahminical sources, would hardly help us much; but, fortunately, we have two Buddhist accounts of the same transaction, which are much more complete and detailed, and which do, I fancy, throw great light on our researches. The first is contained in the Daladâvansa, partially translated by the Hon. G. Turnour, and published in the J. A. S. B. vol. VI. p. 856, et seq.; the other is abstracted by Colonel Low from the Siamese Phrâ Pat'hom, and published in the same journal, vol. XVII. part II. p. 82, et seq. Unfortunately, neither work has been completely translated, and the extracts having been made with reference to other objects, do not give us all the information we want. The following abridgment of the story will, however, suffice for present purposes:—

The left canine tooth of Buddha had been preserved in Dantapura, the capital of Kalinga, probably at or near the spot where the celebrated temple of Juggernâth now stands, for 800 years, when Gûhasîvo, the king, early in the fourth century, was converted to Buddhism from the Brahminical faith, which he had professed up to that time. With the zeal of a convert he dismissed and persecuted the Brahmins, who had hitherto enjoyed his favour. They repaired to Pâṭaliputta (Patna) to complain of this to the paramount sovereign, here called Pâṇḍu, but who, as it appears from the context, most probably was the Gotamiputra of the Śâtkarṇi

---

* Asiatic Researches, vol. XV. p. 254, et seq. J. A. S. B., vol. VI. p. 756, et seq.

dynasty. He orders Gûhasîvo to repair to his court, bringing the relic with him. It is then subjected to every sort of trial. It is smashed on an anvil, thrown into the gutter, and everything conceivable done to destroy or dishonour it. It comes triumphantly out of all its trials. The king is converted, and finally devotes himself to a religious life.

While all this is going on, a northern king—it is not quite clear whence he came*—named Khîrâdhâro, attacks the capital, in order to possess himself of the wonder-working relic. He was defeated and killed in battle, and Gûhasîvo returned, it is said, with the sacred tooth to his capital. Some time afterwards the nephews of Khîrâdhâro, allying themselves with other kings, march against Gûhasîvo. He, though seeing that resistance is hopeless, prepares for defence; but, before going to the combat, he enjoins on his daughter Hemachalâ, who was married to a prince of Oujein, called Danta Kumâra, that in the event of his falling, they should take the relic, and escaping by sea, convey it to Mahâsena, king of Ceylon, who had been for some time negotiating for its purchase.†

The prince and princess fly from the city before its fall, bury the relic in the sand, in the same manner as the image of Juggernath is said to have been concealed in the Brahminical account, and, afterwards returning, the princess conceals it in her hair, and escaping to the coast, they take ship apparently at Tamralipi or Tamlook, and sail for Ceylon. Half-way between the place of embarkation and Ceylon they are shipwrecked, at a place called the Diamond Sands.‡ From the context I do not think there can be much hesitation in fixing this locality on the banks of the

---

* Probably Śrâvastî, then the capital of the northern Kośala, the modern Oude. See General Cunningham's Report for 1862–63, p. 40.

† Some years ago Dr. Bird opened a small Tope in front of the Kenheri Caves in Salsette. In it he found a copper plate recording that a canine tooth of Buddha had been deposited there. The plate is dated in the year 245. From the expression "Samvat" being used, Dr. Stevenson (J. B. B. R. A. S., vol. V. p. 13) assumes that it must be from the era of Vikramâditya. I believe, however, it is correct to assert that no Buddhist inscription is dated from the era of the hated opponent of their religion. If, on the other hand, we assume the era of Śâlivâhana, it brings the date to almost the exact time—A.D. 323—of these events on the east coast; and though it is not directly stated in the inscription, it seems that the tooth was deposited there by Gotamiputra, the very king who played so important a part in the narrative just recorded, and what is more, it seems extremely probable that the Kenheri tooth was, or was supposed to be, the identical one which performed so many miracles in Pâṭaliputta.

This might seem paradoxical had not the same thing happened to the same relic in similar circumstances more than twelve centuries afterwards. When the Portuguese conquered Ceylon, Constantine de Braganza seized the Daladâ and conveyed it to Goa. The king of Pegu sent an embassy after it, and offered any amount of ransom for it. But the bigotry of the priesthood was proof against any such temptation. The tooth was consumed by fire in presence of the Archbishop and all the notables, and the ashes cast into the sea. The result was peculiar. The Ceylonese pretended that the one so destroyed was a counterfeit. A true one was discovered and sold to the king of Pegu, and as soon as he was gone and had paid for it, another true one was found concealed in Ceylon, and is probably the crocodile's tooth that is now so honoured in that country. To complete the parallelism, both the Burmese and the Concani teeth have disappeared, and only their empty Chaityas remain. The Ceylonese tooth still remains with the oldest pedigree of any such relic that the world possesses.

The particulars of this second great attempt to destroy the Daladâ will be found well stated in Sir E. Tennent's Ceylon, vol. II. p. 199. Translations of the original authorities are there given also.

‡ *Dinne* means sand bank in Telugu. This may be the origin of the name Dîpal dinne, which certainly does not mean "Hill of Lights." Can Dîpal, by any synonym, be assumed to mean diamond?

Kistnah. First, from its position half-way;* next, because here only, so far as I know, are those diamond† mines near the coast; but more because, as will be abundantly proved by the sequel, it was the residence of the Naga Raja.

The Naga Raja steals the relic from the princess when she is asleep, but he is forced by the power of a Thero, from the Himalaya, to restore it, and the wanderers again embark, and after various adventures reach Ceylon in the year 312.‡ Mahâsena had been dead nine years, but the fugitives are received with open arms by Meghavarṇa,§ the reigning sovereign; a brick and mortar Chaitya is made, and the relic brought by the prince and princess enshrined with great solemnity (Colonel Low, p. 86).

The narrative then proceeds:—" Three years had passed away, when the king " of Laukâ perceived from an ancient prophecy that in seven years from that date " a certain king, Dhammâśoka Raja, would erect a temple on the Diamond Sands; " and he likewise recollected that there were two Donas of relics of Buddha still " concealed in the country of Naga Raja. He therefore directed a holy person to " go and bring these relics." The Naga Raja's brother swallows the relics, and flies to Meru, but they are taken from him and brought back. " Soon after this Naga " Raja arrived (in Ceylon), in the form of a handsome youth, and solicited a few " relics from his majesty, which were bestowed upon him accordingly."

His majesty now ordered a golden ship to be made. It was one cubit long and one span broad. The relics were put into a golden cup; this was placed in a vase, and the whole put into the golden ship. A wooden ship was next built, having a breadth of beam of seven long cubits.

Danta Kumâra and Hemachalâ being desirous of revisiting their country, the king of Lankâ sent with them ambassadors to one of the five‖ kings who now ruled there, requesting him to show them every attention. The vessel reached the Diamond Sands in five months, and the prince and princess went on shore, accompanied by the priests. An account is then given of the building of the temple, and the mode in which the relics were placed. The vessel now set sail for Dantapura, which it reached in little more than three months. The ambassadors of the king of Lankâ landed with the prince and princess. They were treated with much distinction, and remained in the country.

* The Siamese, as Colonel Low points out, wishing to make their own country the scene of these events, have lengthened the periods of the voyage preposterously. They make it three months from Cuttack to the Diamond Sands, and three more from thence to Ceylon.—J. A. S. B., vol. XVII. pt. II., pages 86 and 87.

† One of the objects of Colonel Mackenzie's surveys was to mark the diamond mines in the locality. He plots the diamond district as extending to about eight miles north of Amravati, but it seems there are no mines elsewhere. Their position is marked on the map, Plate XLVI.

‡ It does not seem quite clear how far the Ceylonese dates are to be relied upon as quite correct about this time. Avowedly there is an error to the extent of at least sixty years in the date their annals assign to Asoka. This has subsequently been adjusted, to some extent, by Mr. Turnour, but not, so far as I can judge, in such a manner as to inspire entire confidence. My impression is that the dates in the fourth century are all from ten to fifteen years too early.

§ Is not this the Varâja of the Western Cave Inscrip. ?—J. B. B. R. A. S., vol. V. p. 42.

‖ Those who, according to the Daladâvansa, had combined with the nephews of Khirâdhâro and conquered the country.

After this follows a third tradition which Colonel Low treats as if referring to another king and to different circumstances, but both from the name he bore and the whole of the circumstances mentioned in the context seems undoubtedly to have been the same person. In the legend he is called Dhammâśoka* and ruled the country of Arvadi, apparently Avanti (Ougein) with strict justice, but is forced by a famine to emigrate with his followers, amounting to 31,000 able-bodied men. The wanderers proceeded southward for seven months. After various adventures they reach a place where water and fish were abundant. Next day the king mounted his horse and reached the Diamond Sands. Here he meets the Naga Raja, builds a Chaitya, and founds a city.

" Dhammâśoka reigned here quietly for seven years, but mortified and unhappy " because he could not reach the relics. His Majesty accordingly offered a high " reward to any one who should find the relics and disinhume them. But this proved " of no avail. It so happened that, in the dilemma, a Putra or son of the king of " Róm or Roum, named Kâkabhâsa, who happened to be trading to the country of " Takkhasilâ, encountered a violent storm. He had 500 souls on board, who, suppli- " cating the gods, were rescued from death. The ship, with much difficulty, reached " close to the Diamond Sands, and observing signs of population cast anchor with " a view to refit."

The Prince of Róm† assists the Naga Raja to recover the hidden treasure, and to build a wonderful nine-storied Chaitya over it, many particulars of which are given; but as they are too long to extract, and either are imaginary or do not refer to the particular building we are engaged upon, it is hardly necessary to quote them here. These quotations might be multiplied to almost any extent; but enough has probably been adduced to show that, in the beginning of the fourth century—about the time when the struggle for the tooth relic was convulsing all India—Buddhist tradition points most distinctly to the Diamond Sands, on the banks of the Kistnah, as the place where a great temple was being built. The kingdom of the Naga Raja certainly was there; and so far as can be judged from every indication as to the locality, if it was not at or near Aṁravati, it could not possibly have been far from the spot.

Though all this tends to confirm the idea that the building referred to is the Amravati Tope, the inference rises almost to certainty when we come to examine the sculptures with which it is adorned. In one bas-relief a ship is represented with

* This is evidently a title, though from the similarity of the name Colonel Low confounds him with the great Aśoka, and places him 321 B.C.

† It would be absurd to found any serious theory on the mention of the name of Rome, if it stood alone and unsupported. The circumstance mentioned in the narrative of the strangers being white men, and coming by sea, is a small confirmation that the people here mentioned were really Europeans. My impression, however, is that few who are familiar with the arts of Rome in Constantine's time, and who will take the trouble to master these Amravati sculptures, can fail to perceive many points of affinity between them. The circular medallions of the arch of Constantine—such as belong to his time—and the general tone of the art of his age so closely resemble what we find here, that the coincidence can hardly be accidental. The conviction that the study of these sculptures has forced in my mind is, that there was much more intercommunication between the east and west during the whole period from Alexander to Justinian than is generally supposed, and that the intercourse was especially frequent and influential in the middle period, between Augustus and Constantine.

two persons on board, bearing relics, and is being welcomed by a Naga king on approaching the shore. In another an ark, in the form of a ship, like that described above, is being borne in state on men's shoulders; and in numerous scenes there are conferences between the Naga king and a prince or king accompanied by a lady, neither of whom nor any of whose suite are Nagas. Of course these may represent other similar scenes which have happened to other people; but a careful examination of the whole presents so many points of coincidence that I hardly think they can be accidental. One point which the sculptures undoubtedly reveal is that Amravati was the capital, or, at least, the residence of the Naga Raja. In all the sculptures which do not relate to the life of Buddha, and in many of these, the Naga king appears with his hood of a seven-headed snake, and all his women have also single snakes at the back of their heads. As will be presently shown, Naga worship almost supersedes Buddhism in the religious representations, so much so, indeed, that it is sometimes difficult to say to which religion the temple is dedicated.

It may be quite true that no single part of this evidence is sufficient to prove the case, but, taking the whole of it together, I think it must be admitted to be sufficient to justify the presumption that the beginning of the fourth century was the great building epoch at Amravati. When all the evidence about to be advanced in describing the Plates is added to what has been adduced, few, I fancy, will be inclined to doubt but that the two great Rails at Amravati are part of the Temple at the Diamond Sands, which, according to the Ceylonese computation, was commenced in the year 322. Judging from the elaboration of the outer Rail, it may have taken fifty years to complete. If this be so, the date of its completion may be about the year 370 or 380 of our era, and the principal part of the building may thus have remained complete for 150 or 200 years after that time, before it was deserted, as mentioned by Hiouen Thsang. From evidence which will be brought forward hereafter, it would appear that the central building or Tope itself is at least a century older than the great Rail, and that the inner or smaller Rail is at least as much more modern, so that, like our own cathedrals, the erection of this Tope may have lasted for two or three centuries, or say from 200 to 500 A.D. Even beyond this, however, there are reasons for believing—as will be shown in describing Plate LXXXIII.—that a building of importance existed here as early as the Christian era, or contemporaneously with the gates at Sanchi. On the other hand, we know for certain that it was afterwards repaired and used for Buddhist purposes as late as the twelfth or thirteenth centuries; but the particulars of this restoration are less interesting, and further explorations on the spot are necessary before they can be made intelligible. All this, however, will be clearer and more easily intelligible when we have gone through the description of the 54 Plates, which are devoted to the illustration of the architecture and sculptures of the Amravati Tope.

PLATE XLVI.

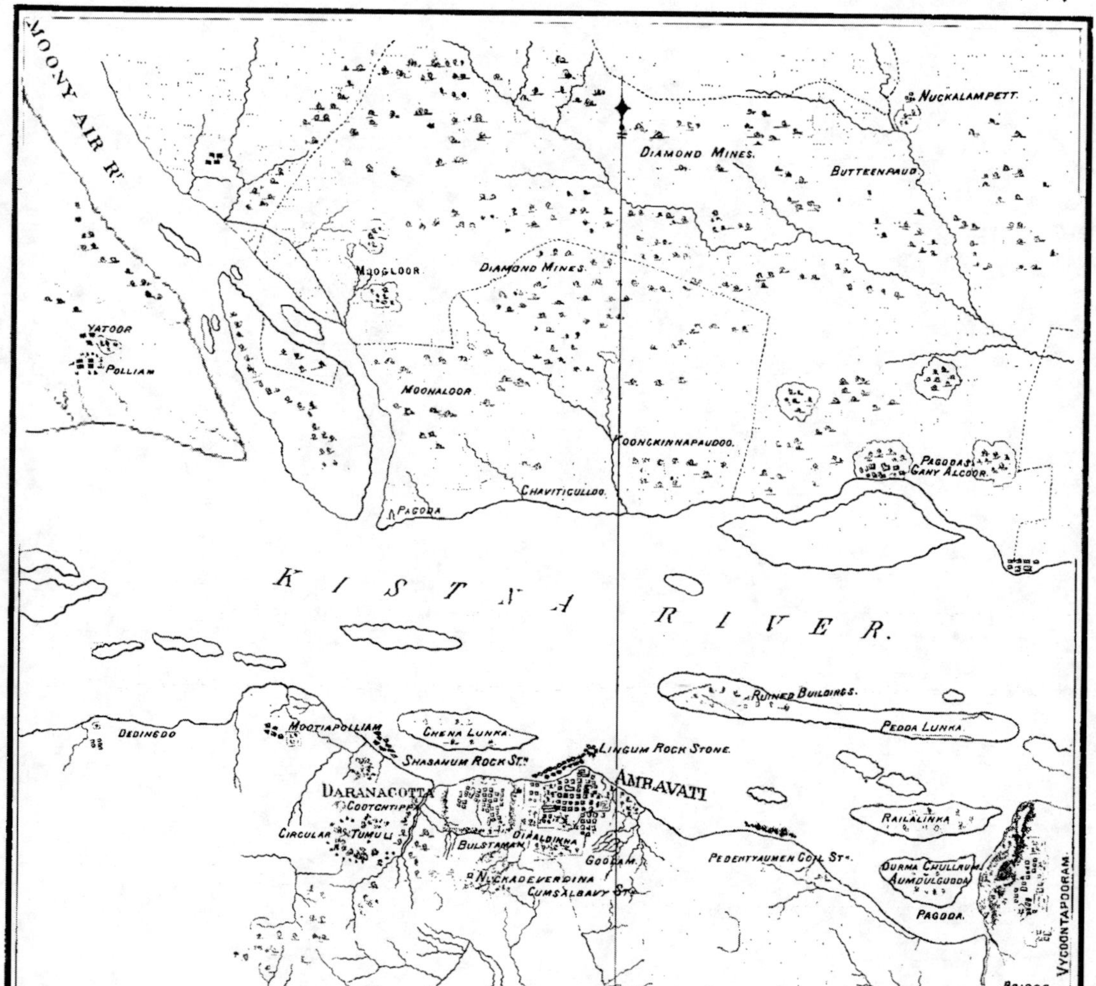

W. GRIGGS LITH.

INDIA MUSEUM

MAP OF AMRAVATI IN GUNTOOR

& OF PURTYALL & THE DIAMOND MINES

WITH THE VILLAGES ADJACENT REDUCED FROM THE ORIGINAL SURVEY.

IN 1816.

SCALE OF 1 MILE TO AN INCH.

FURLONGS.

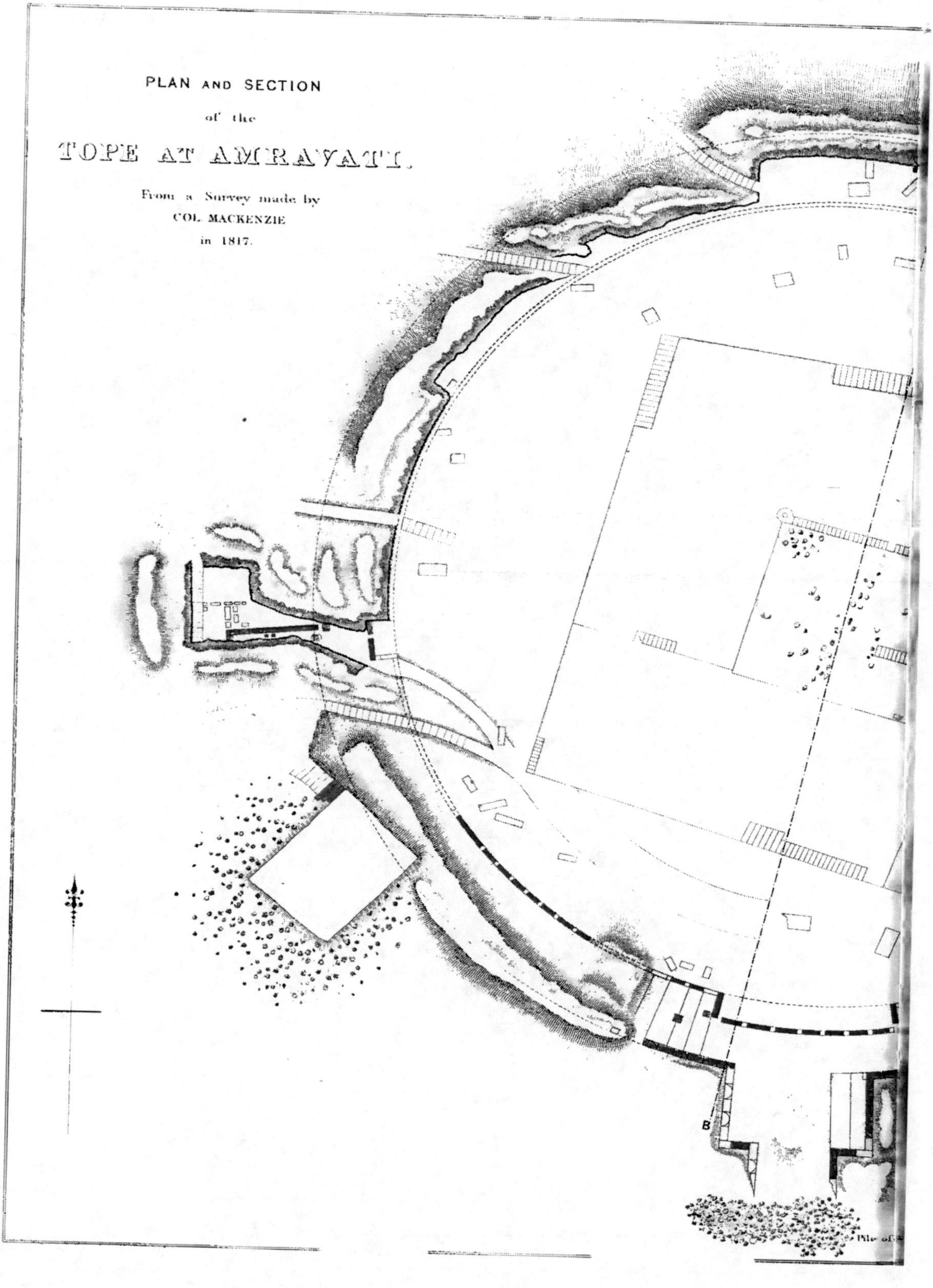
PLAN AND SECTION
of the
TOPE AT AMRAVATI.
From a Survey made by
COL. MACKENZIE
in 1817.
B

PLATE XLVII.

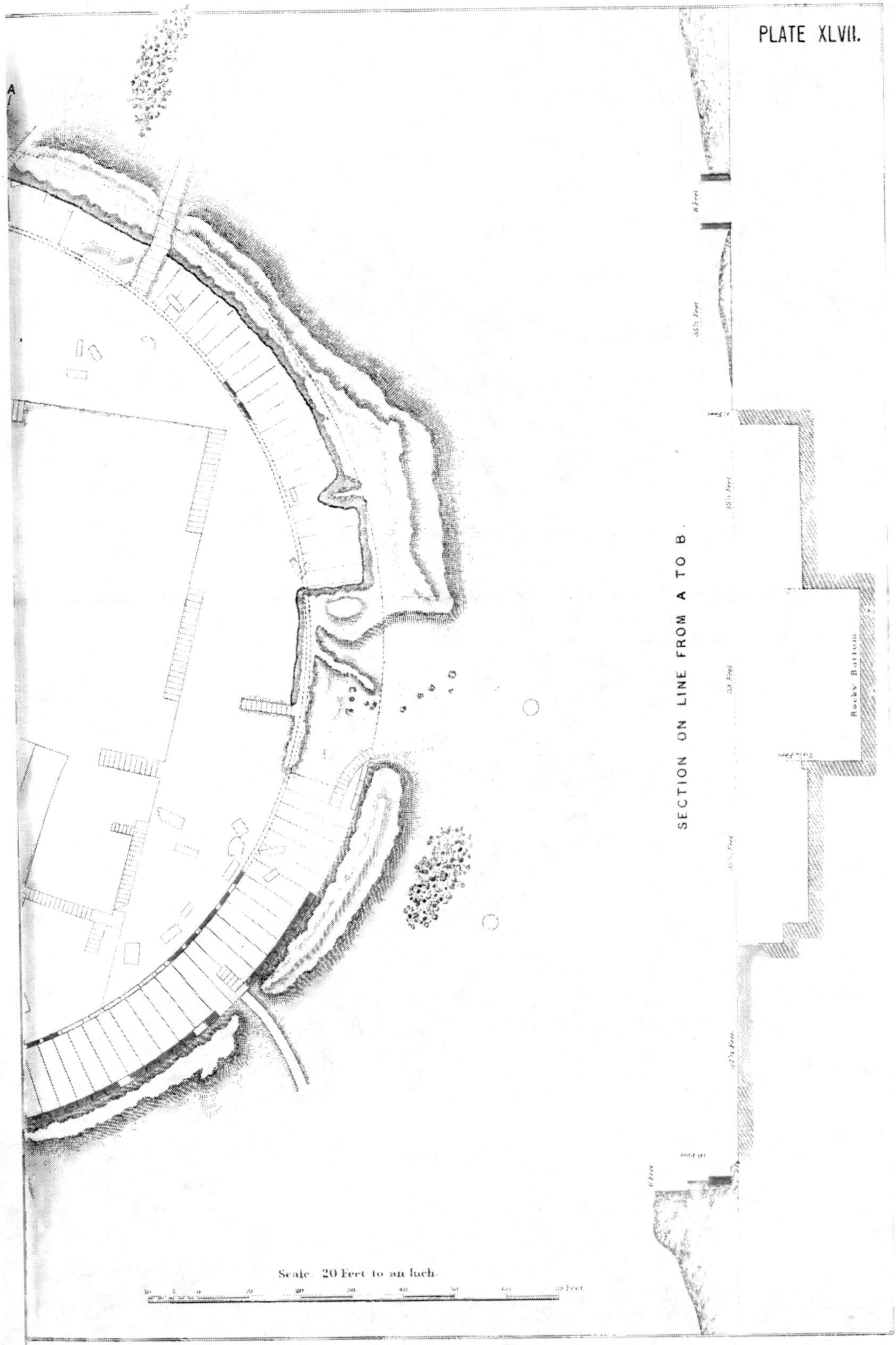
A
SECTION ON LINE FROM A TO B.
Rocky Bottom
Scale. 20 Feet to an Inch.

DESCRIPTION OF THE PLATES.

· AMRAVATI TOPE.

PLATES XLVI. AND XLVII.

Plate XLVI. is copied literally from the survey of the locality made by Colonel Mackenzie in 1816–17, and suffices to explain the exact relative position of the different antiquities already alluded to (page 151). In order to prevent any appearance of adjusting it to suit any theory, the spelling has been retained as found in the original map, though it differs occasionally from that adopted in the text.

The ramparts of the old town of Daranacotta will be observed to the westward of the modern town of Amravati, and the site of the several mounds of Dipaldinna, Nuckadeverdina, and Cootchitippa are also plainly marked. One cluster, though the smallest, of the circular tumuli or stone circles, is close to the old town to the westward; but by far the most numerous groups are gathered round the bases of the hills in the right-hand lower corner of the map, where they are described as existing in hundreds. The diamond mines are all on the left bank of the river, opposite the town.

Plate XLVII. is likewise copied literally from a drawing in the Mackenzie Collection,* and represents the monument as it existed in 1816–17. At that time the slabs coloured dark red were either standing or were lying in such a position that their original site could be identified ; and the paving stones of the procession path, coloured pink, were also *in situ*.

The central building had at that time entirely disappeared, the materials having been utilized by the Raja in building the new town.† Having cleared it away, he was induced to dig deeper in search of treasure, which is always supposed to be buried in these mounds ; and having made a great hole in this pursuit, he afterwards determined to make use of it by forming it into a water tank. This, as will be seen from the plan and section, was not complete at the time it was abandoned, the Raja having ruined himself by extravagance some time before Colonel Mackenzie's second visit. In the process of excavation the earth had fortunately been thrown

* A reduction of it to the scale of 100 feet to 1 inch was published by me in the Handbook of Architecture (Woodcut 9), in 1855.

† "The whole of the inner circle has been dug up, and the stones removed for building purposes. They have been chiefly applied to the repair of Pagodas, and a great many were put to form a flight of steps to the square tank of Shivagunga."—Colonel Mackenzie, in Asiatic Journal, p. 469.

on to the path and rails, so as to protect them to a certain extent; and those slabs which had not been carried away were thus partially protected till some were excavated by the Colonel.* Sir Walter Elliot's explorations were apparently wholly confined to the northern side of the Western Gateway, where a mound of earth concealed the modern chapel, the walls of which furnished nine-tenths of the slabs now in the India Museum.

All that the Raja discovered to reward his search was a small relic casket, which is now in the Madras Museum.† It was apparently similar to those found at Sanchi, but has no inscription and is of no intrinsic value.

The dimensions of the Tope, as shown in the plan, and recorded by Colonel Mackenzie, are 195 feet‡ for the inside diameter of the outer circle, and 165 feet for that of the inner. The procession path is paved with slabs 13 feet long, and the inner rail is 2 feet in width. Each of the four Gateways projected about 30 feet beyond the outer rail; but all are so ruined that the dimensions cannot be ascertained with exactness.

The only addition I have made to the plan is the yellow circle in the centre. This is the site and I believe the dimensions of the enclosing Rail of the central Dagoba. For reasons which will be given when describing Plates XCIII. to XCVIII., it would appear that it did not exceed 30 feet in diameter; and if this were so, it seems nearly certain that other buildings occupied the rest of the enclosure; but as it is nearly certain that all these were erected in wood it is in vain now to hope to find any remains of them. A nine-storied pagoda has already been alluded to (p. 161); and my conviction is that, besides this, there must have been a Vihâra or residence, a Chaitya hall, a Dharmaśâlâ, and other conventual buildings. These, or the greater part of them, must have existed prior to 322; and it was to enclose and unite them that the great Rail was erected. Nothing is so common as such an arrangement as this in the Madras territory. In nine cases out of ten, in their greatest temples, the sanctuary itself is relatively less important, as compared with its surroundings, than this 30-feet Dagoba is to its rails and the other buildings; so that there is at least no *à priori* improbability in the arrangement.§

---

* "In the present state of the mound it is impossible to form any conjecture whether there was any or what sort of building standing in the centre, or for what purpose it was intended."—Asiatic Journal, vol. XV. p. 469.

† The following extract from a letter of 12th June last, from Sir Walter Elliot, contains all the information available on this subject:—"They found in the centre of the mound a stone casket, with a "lid, on opening which a crystal box was found, containing a small pearl, some gold leaf, and other "things of no value. The Raja sent the relics to his tosha khanah, and there they remained. At a "later period I succeeded in securing them for Government, and they are now in the Museum at Madras."

‡ By a curious coincidence this is exactly twice the diameter of the outer circle at Stonehenge. There the inner diameter of the outer circle is exactly 100 Roman feet, or 97/6 feet English. The outer rail in the Indian example is rather more than 14 feet high; that at Stonehenge is, as nearly as it can be now measured, 15/6. These coincidences may be accidental, but though at first sight so different, it does not appear to me doubtful but that they are both simulated sepulchres—cenotaphs—relic shrines, or whatever they may be called, and are utterances of the same primæval faith. What does not appear to admit of doubt is, that they were being erected simultaneously—the western one to commemorate a martyrdom, the eastern to perpetuate the memory of the visit or enshrinement of a relic.

§ So convinced am I of the correctness of the view, that I had prepared a drawing purporting to be a bird's eye view of the Tope, with all these arrangements, and intended it should form the frontispiece to this work. On second thoughts I abandoned the idea. All the other Plates in the work are absolute facts; this would have been said to have involved theories.

AMRAVATI. PLATE XLVIII.

ELEVATION OF EXTERNAL FACE OF OUTER ENCLOSURE.

SCALE 1-3RD OF 1 INCH TO 1 FOOT.

ELEVATION OF INTERNAL FACE OF OUTER ENCLOSURE.

SCALE 1-3RD OF 1 INCH TO 1 FOOT.

PLATES XLVIII. AND XLIX.

When I was first furnished with a complete set of Photographs of the Amravati marbles in the India Museum, I confess that the task of arranging them or of finding out to what parts of the building each belonged, seemed hopeless enough. By degrees, as I became familiar with them, I perceived that they might be classified in three great groups. First, I perceived that in one portion the figures were very much larger than the others, the sculpture coarser, and they had the Sanchi form of Rail as an ornament. These, I afterwards made out, belonged to the central building, and they are found arranged in Plates XCIII. to XCVIII. Once their general characteristics are guessed, there is no difficulty in recognizing them either in the marble or in Colonel Mackenzie's drawings.

A second group consisted of marbles diametrically opposed in style to these. The figures were the smallest, the carving the most delicate, and the ornamentation more elaborate than in any of the others. They were in fact more like ivory carvings than things to be executed in stone. These I discovered belonged to the inner Rail. They will be found in Plates LXXV. to LXXXV.

There only then remained the principal group, which there was no difficulty in recognizing as fragments of the great outer Rail. They occupy Plates XLVIII. to LXXIV. There only then remained a few fragments, Plates LXXXVI. to XCII., which were of no architectural importance, and may have been placed anywhere. Once this assortment was completed, there was no great difficulty in restoring the great Rail. Many of the pillars were entire for their whole height, and some were sculptured both on the back and front; so that, with a little familiarity, that distinction could be easily recognized. In addition to this, each was furnished at the sides with three lentil-shaped mortices, like those at Sanchi, as shown in the frontispiece and in woodcuts 8 and 10. Some also of the intermediate discs still retained their flanges, which fitted into these mortices, though the greater number had been trimmed into circles, apparently for convenience of carriage. There could, however, be no mistake as to their position. The upper Rail was easily recognized by the rounded and weather-worn top, but the animal frieze at the bottom of Plate XLVIII. for a long time puzzled me. Eventually, however, I found fragments which represented the Rail in its complete state. Such, for instance, as Figs. 1. and 2., Plate LXXXVIII., represent the external appearance of the Rail with minute accuracy. They have the waving roll at top, the Zoophorus at bottom, the octagonal pillars, with one central disc and two half discs at top and bottom; and their intermediate Rails with their circular discs and the open spaces between.* With these aids and the sculptures themselves, as I became familiar with them, the task became easy, and the restorations were made which are shown on a reduced scale in

* Compare these with Woodcuts 11 and 12, from Nasick and Kenheri.

Plates XLVIII. and XLIX., and so perfectly do all the parts fit together that I do not think there can be any doubt as to their correctness.

Plate XLVIII. represents the outer face of the great Rail, and is plainer than the inner face, as shown in the next Plate. This was an arrangement singularly consistent with good taste and architectural propriety, as it is evident that those who wished to study the sculptures could do it with more facility in the quiet and seclusion of the interior than from the outside. The only additional ornament on the exterior was the lower animal frieze, which forms a base to the whole. As that was raised two feet above the level of the country outside, something was necessary to hide its external face, while it would be difficult to design anything more elegant or better adapted to its purpose than this frieze of animals. This was not wanted internally, as the pillars there rose from the paving stones of the procession path.

Plate XLIX., Fig. 1., represents the inner face of six pillars of the great Rail, with their intermediate discs and the upper frieze; the whole, as will be observed, were elaborately covered with sculptures. The lower range of sculpture is omitted, as it apparently represented on the outside the height of the solid pavement in the interior. Fig. 2. represents a portion of a frieze of the same dimensions, but from a different part, probably one of the gateways or projections.

There were apparently twenty-four pillars in each quadrant, and eight at least in each Gateway, say 112 to 120 in all. This involves 230 to 240 central discs, all of which were sculptured; and as each of these contains from twenty to thirty figures at least, there must have been in them alone from 6,000 to 7,000 figures. If we add to these the continuous frieze above and the sculptures above and below the dises on the pillars, there probably were not less than 120 to 140 figures, for each intercolumniation, say 12,000 to 14,000 in all. The inner Rail contains probably even a greater number of figures than this, but they are so small as more to resemble ivory carving, but except, perhaps, the great frieze at Nakhon Vat.* There is not, perhaps, even in India, and certainly not in any other part of the world, a storied page of sculpture equal in extent to what this must have been when complete. If not quite it must have been nearly perfect, in all probability less than a century ago.

---

* History of Architecture, vol. II. p. 713, et seqq.

ELEVATION OF THE EXTERNAL FACES OF TWO PILLARS OF OUTER ENCLOSURE.
SCALE 1 INCH TO 1 FOOT.

ELEVATION OF THE EXTERNAL FACES OF TWO PILLARS OF OUTER ENCLOSURE.
SCALE 1 INCH TO 1 FOOT.

ELEVATION OF THE EXTERNAL FACES OF TWO PILLARS OF OUTER ENCLOSURE.
SCALE 1 INCH TO 1 FOOT.

ELEVATION OF THE EXTERNAL FACES OF TWO PILLARS OF SMALLER RAIL.
SCALE 1 INCH TO 1 FOOT.

DISCS ON INTERMEDIATE RAILS OF OUTER ENCLOSURE.

SCALE 1 INCH TO 1 FOOT.

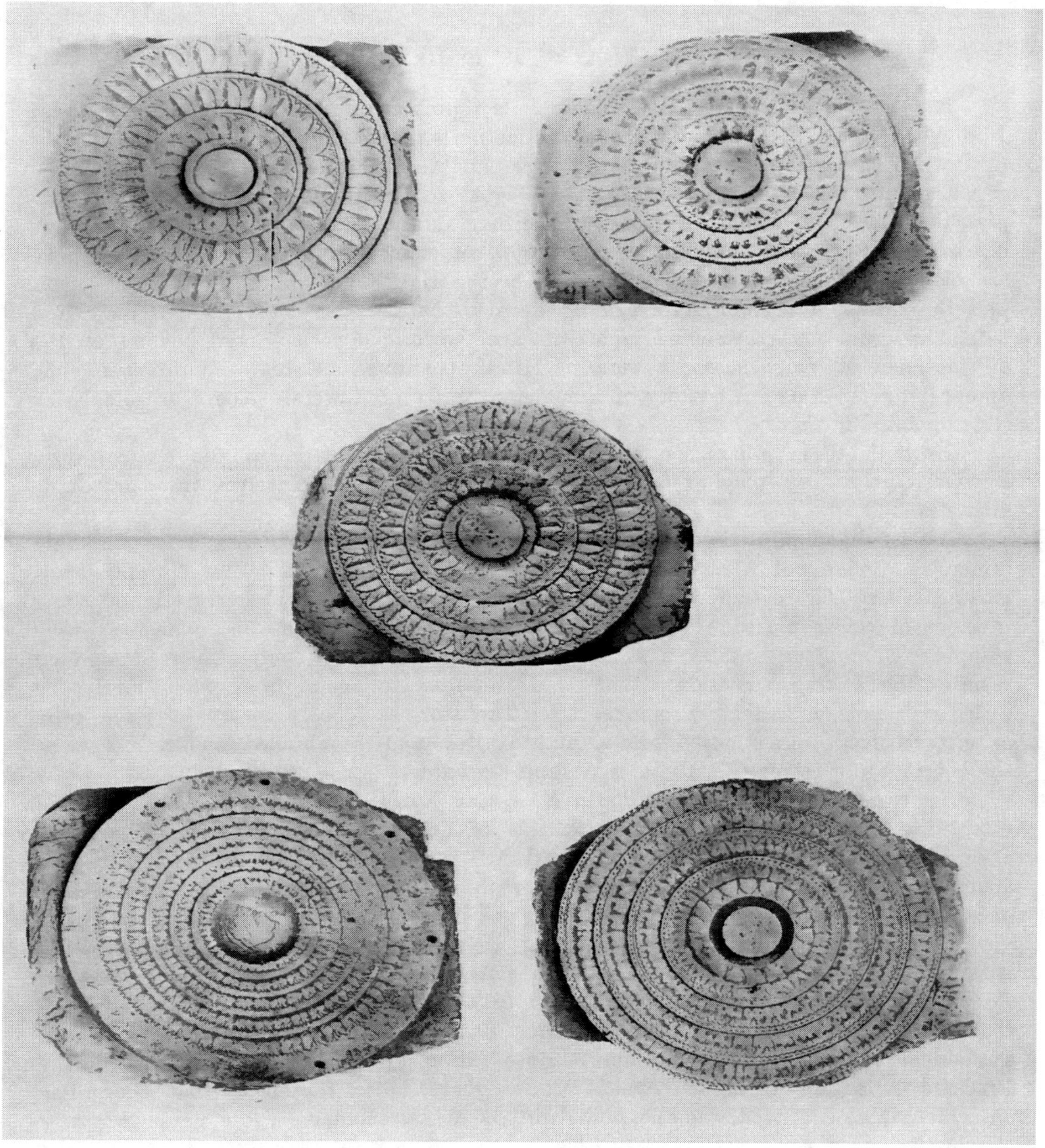

DISCS ON INTERMEDIATE RAILS.
SCALE 1 INCH TO 1 FOOT.

PLATES L. TO LV.

THE six Plates contain all the fragments representing the outer face of the great Rail which exist in the India House collection—with the exception of the friezes (Plates LVI., LVII.),—and are all photographed to the same scale, 1 inch to 1 foot.

The left-hand pillar (Plate L.) is dedicated to the five-headed Naga, who occupies the place of honour in front; on either side of him are two female figures bearing offerings, and standing on two reptilian monsters, apparently dead. Above are elephants worshipping the Dagoba. On the right-hand pillar the Dagoba occupies the principal position, crowned by eleven Chattas. On either side a male and a female figure are represented in attitudes of ecstatic devotion; and beyond, on the outside faces of the octagon, a man in Hindu costume and his wife on each side, approaching the Dagoba, bearing offerings apparently of flowers. Above are elephants worshipping the Tree.

On both these pillars, on the octagonal compartment below the central disc, are Gaṇa or dwarfs, playing and laughing and throwing themselves into grotesque attitudes.

The left-hand pillar in Plate XLI. is so much weather-worn that it is extremely difficult to make out what the story of the sculptures may be. In the upper compartment two figures appear to be upholding a tray, on which a relic or some precious object is placed; and six other figures, floating in the air, appear as worshipping the object, whatever it may be. In the lower compartment two men seem to be seizing something that is descending to them from what might be called a shoot or vessel of some sort.* The story evidently refers to some relic or gift received miraculously below, and exalted and worshipped above, but what the precious object may be there is nothing to show.

The three following pillars (Plates XLI. and XLII.) contain no novelty, but are interesting as exhibiting the endless variety of detail with which these pillars are executed, and the grotesque form of the dwarfs with whom they are adorned. The drum, it will be observed, is here beaten with two crooked sticks; at Sanchi only one was employed.

The two pillars (Plate LIII.) belong to a somewhat smaller Rail, and the patterns upon them are of a somewhat purer and less exuberant style of art. Possibly they may be older, but hardly materially so; and I am clearly of opinion that they are only parts of the great outer Rail, perhaps the old part, or perhaps some detached portion or projection. Both are inscribed. The inscription on the left-hand pillar, according to General Cunningham, is to the effect that the pillar on which it is engraved was the pious gift of a householder—whose name is partly

* There is a drawing of this pillar in the Mackenzie Collection, Plate XXXI., but it does not help us to an explanation of the meaning.

obliterated—together with his wife and son. The other inscription, on the right-hand pillar, is longer, but to the same effect. It records the pious gift of two pillars by Tunulauraka the householder, son of Pusili, together with other members of his family.*

I have before had occasion to point out (page 84) the similarity that exists between the arrangements of the Rail in front of the Gotamiputra Cave at Nasick and that at Amravati. The coincidence becomes even more striking when we compare the pillars in this Plate with one from the same Cave, represented in the annexed woodcut (No. 19). The central circle and the two half-circles at top and bottom are as like as the difference of material would allow; and the lotus buds used to fill up the angles in both examples are nearly identical. It seems to me impossible that the two can differ much in age; and if I am correct in assigning the beginning of the fourth century to the Cave, we cannot be far wrong in assuming that the Rail was erected within a few decades of it either way.

No. 19.

Pilaster in Nassick Cave.
From a Drawing by E. W. West.

Plates LIV. and LV. contain nine of the intermediate discs of the great Rail, as seen from the outer side. The three upper ones in Plate LV. belong to the smaller Rail last described, and fortunately have not been trimmed, like some of the larger ones, so that the flanges by which they were inserted into the pillars can still be observed. The other six, with the six in the centre of the pillars just described, and the eight half discs on the pillar, are sufficient to exemplify the usual form of these ornaments. Every one is different, though all have a general resemblance, and display an exuberance of fancy for such details not probably to be found in any classical or mediæval monument of its class.

In one other point they are interesting as exhibiting a classical tendency, more than any other details at Amravati. They forcibly recall the expression of Hiouen Thsang, "that the Sanghârâma was ornamented with all "the art of the palaces of Bactria,"—an expression the more remarkable because our traveller does not apply it to any other building he saw in India, and we do not know any one in that country where so much classical feeling prevails.† The ornament is the water-leaf of the classical artists, and might be used now on the ceiling of any modern classical hall without anyone detecting that its details were borrowed from any building east of the Bosphorus.

* See Appendix E., Nos. IV. and XV.

† Supra, p. 153.

AMRAVATI. PLATE LVI.

FIG, 1

FIG, 2.

FIG 3

FRAGMENTS OF PLINTH OF OUTER ENCLOSURE.
SCALE 1 INCH TO 1 FOOT.

PLATES LVI. AND LVII.

THE upper external frieze of the great Rail, Plate LVI., is in many respects one of the most pleasing parts of the design. Nothing can well be better, as an architectural ornament, than the wavy flow of the long roll, borne by animated figures, and interspersed with emblems appropriate to the dedication of the Tope.

The three fragments in this Plate, it will be observed, are all of different depth though of the same design, and must therefore have belonged to different parts of the great Rail. Either it was that the deepest were used to eke out the height of the small Rail (Plate LIII.), and so make it range with those parts having taller pillars, or there was one quadrant or some part which had a Rail of a smaller proportion altogether. As we have no knowledge where each fragment was found, it is impossible to say which theory is the true one, either is equally probable, such irregularities being very usual in all Hindu buildings.

Like the last-described features, it seems to be of Bactrian origin. Something at least very like it occurs among the sculptures at Jamâlgiri near Peshawer,* and there so mixed with classical details as to make it appear very ancient. Something very like it is still used, I am told, in Burmah. On the occasion of the funeral of the late High Priest at Rangoon, long rolls, made as lightly as possible of paper, and bound round with rags and coloured decorations, were borne by men on each side of the procession in precisely the same manner as here represented, and probably the same practice will be found elsewhere when looked for. At Amravati the roll is not only most elaborately, but also very tastefully, ornamented, and so interspersed with emblems as to give it all the variety requisite for architectural embellishment. These are generally, of course, the emblems with which we are already familiar, such as the Tree, the Wheel, and the Dagoba, but in the centre of the upper left-hand fragment an ornament is introduced which is new to me, in so far as India is concerned, but is found on the mystic representations of Diana of the Ephesians.†

By far the most curious, however, of the episodes introduced into this frieze is that on the right hand of the upper portion. It represents Garuḍa, the bird of Vishṇu, the dreaded enemy of the Nagas in all ages, holding in his beak, evidently for the purpose of destroying it, a five-headed Naga. It is difficult to guess what this can mean in a temple where the Naga is honoured almost as the chief god, and where everything is at least so mixed up with the honour of this many-headed divinity.

It is interesting, however, as it is just one of those incidental allusions which, when a sufficient number of them are collected together, may enable us to trace

---

* One slab of this frieze was destroyed in the fire at the Crystal Palace in December 1866. A very imperfect representation of it will be found, J. A. S. B., XXI. 606.

† There is a statue of the Ephesian Diana in the Museum at Naples, which has been frequently engraved, which is covered with figures like these. A representation of it will be found in Falkener's Ephesus, p. 286.

the affiliation of Indian religions, and to decide as to their affinities. In the present instance it is another of the indications of the connexion between Buddhism and Vishṇuism so often alluded to in these pages.

The lower frieze, Plate LVII., is not remarkable in a mythological point of view, but curious as a piece of playful fancy, and in perfect keeping with the frolics of the Gaṇa or dwarfs, which are next to it in position. The leading idea throughout the frieze is the humorous one of boys holding on by the tails of animals in a state of greater or less excitement, which they are evidently incapable of controlling.

In the upper figure a boy has got hold of the tail of a bull, very fairly executed, but not so well as the galloping humped animal next below it in the Plate. The latter is as perfect a representation of a bull of purely Indian breed as can probably be found in any Indian sculpture, and the action also is free and animated in an unusual degree. The two-winged lions who follow are by no means so commendable as works of art, but they are curious as lineal descendants of those discovered by Botta and Layard at Nineveh. They are, however, considerably further removed from those prototypes than those which adorn the gates at Sanchi (Plate VII. or Plate XXXIX.), and which still retain many features in common with their Assyrian ancestors.*

The elephant in the last figure shows the same perfect appreciation of the characteristic features of that animal as is done in all the representations of the elephant, both here and at Sanchi. The boy in this instance has got hold of his tusk,—the comic element of the representation, as just remarked, consisting apparently in the absurdity of a boy controlling the largest of animals by such means, or of holding a lion or bull by their tails.

* At the great Pagoda at Rangoon winged lions with human heads guard all the portals leading to the enclosure in which it stands. As may be supposed, from the distance of time and place, they are very different looking animals from their prototypes, but I do not think it admits of a doubt but that they, and a great deal of the architecture of Burmah, were derived from the banks of the Euphrates or Tigris.—See my History of Architecture, p. II. 518.

FIG. 1. FIG. 2.

ELEVATION OF INTERNAL FACES OF TWO PILLARS OF OUTER ENCLOSURE.
SCALE 1 INCH TO 1 FOOT.

PLATE LVIII.

Of the two great pillars of the outer Rail represented in this Plate, that on the left hand was considered as the most beautiful in the Elliot Collection. It was in consequence selected for the honour of being exhibited, and was attached to the outer wall of the India Museum at Fife House. The result has, however, been unfortunate. The frost of our winters has so destroyed the surface of the stone that it has in many places peeled off to such an extent that it is now difficult to trace the design, and the whole is in a degraded and perishing condition.

Its sculptures are wholly devoted to Tree Worship. In the central circle some circular object is placed on the altar in front of the Tree, to which the attention of the bystanders seems to be especially directed. Two men on either hand are making offerings to it, or adding offerings to one already made, and two kneeling figures in the foreground seem trying to catch what may overflow from the right-hand man's offering, which seems to be a liquid presented in a jar. Behind him is a yoke of oxen, indicating that he is a stranger arrived for the purpose of worship. Below the altar are impressions of Buddha's feet.

In the upper bas-relief the altar table is removed. The Tree rises simply behind the representation of the sacred feet, and in the central compartment a number of men are engaged in adoring it. In the left-hand compartment seven men, in standing attitudes, are also paying respect to the sacred Tree. On the right, an equal number, in violent action while in the act of worshipping, seem also to be flying as if driven from the sacred presence.

Something of the same action is repeated in the lowest bas-relief on the pillar. Four women on the left and four dwarfs on the right are worshipping the Tree. On the right stands the king or prince, with the umbrella of state borne over his head in front of another Tree, with a kneeling figure in front of the altar.

On the right an elephant pursues a horseman. His horse has fallen on his knees, and he is being knocked on the head by a dwarf with a mallet.

It is probable that the interest of the story centres in the fallen horseman, who, with his companions in the corresponding compartment above, seems to be driven from the congregation of the faithful; but till we recover a Druma Purâṇa, it is hardly likely we shall know who he is. The Lalita-Vistara and the books we have make no prominent mention of Tree Worship. It belongs apparently to an earlier form of faith, and the legends connected with it are not to be found there.*

---

* The following is a curious instance of the irradicability of local forms, even long after the religion to which they belonged may have perished. At the present day, during the festival of Navarâtri, in honour of Śiva as Amreshwar, the immortal lord, on the third night a brazen tree is carried round the town in procession; on the fifth night a ten-headed serpent in brass. At the close of the festival the worshippers go in great pomp to a tree called Shemmu Veerchum, where the god is made to exercise in shooting an arrow at the sacred tree, followed by a discharge of fire-arms in the air, which closes the ceremony. In the festival called Siva Mahârâtri, the procession to the same tree is the culminating point, to which all previous arrangements are subordinate, and thus the festival closes.—See Asiatic Journal, vol. XV. p. 472 and 473.

The two lower bas-reliefs on the right-hand pillar of this Plate are devoted to the same subject. In the centre a number of women—there are no men—are performing various acts of devotion, and bringing offerings, to the sacred Tree. The scene is laid in the centre of a village, the huts of which are seen both above and on either hand.

In the lower bas-relief all the actors are men. Two in the centre present pieces of cloth or garments to the Tree, and those in the side compartments seem also to be bringing scarfs or similar objects.

The upper sculpture is of a different nature. In the centre a flight of Hansas or sacred geese are winging their way across what appears to be a lake, between two trees. A hand issues from the right-hand tree, with two circular objects in it, and the geese under it look as if falling dead on the shore, but it may be they are only flying downwards. On the sand are five impressions of the sacred feet,—there were probably originally eight,—and two birds, apparently peacocks, are somewhat indistinctly seen strutting on the sand. I have met with no legend that explains all the incidents depicted in the bas-relief, but it seems probable that it is an early form of a Jâtaka, still found in Ceylon. "The royal Hansa assembled all his subjects in an extensive "plain, that his daughter might choose a husband from among them. She chose "the peacock, at which the vain bird was so elated that he raised his tail, and "made such a display as to disgust the king, who in consequence broke off the "match."* If this is the legend, all that can be said is that what is here represented must be an earlier form.† On the left hand are several women presenting flowers in pots, and on the right the Naga Raja with his seven-headed snake hood, and behind him his three wives, over each of whose heads may be seen the single-headed snake, which always marks them.‡

Taken altogether, this is one of the most elegant of the Amravati pillars; and whether as regards its sculptures or its ornamental details, exhibits the progress in elegance and purity of design that has been made since the representation of the Naga Raja and his three wives was carved, which is seen on Plate XXIV., Fig. 2., from Sanchi. The snakes here are so subdued as not to be offensive, and the figures of the women are of great elegance. The ornaments of the circles on this pillar are also of great beauty. Those of the lower semicircle are not surpassed by any in this collection, though the scale of the photographs is rather too small to exhibit them in all their perfection.

---

* Upham's Historical Books of Ceylon, vol. III. p. 289.

† There is another legend quoted by Schiefner (Transactions of the St. Petersburg Academy, 1851, p. 238) from a Thibetan life of Buddha, which may be the one referred to. Devadatta, it is there related, wounded a goose, which fell into the garden of the Bodisattwa. He extracted the arrow, and having cured the wound let it go. It was claimed, however, by the sportsman, and hence arose a serious quarrel. A tree figures as the most important feature in this legend, which may be that one on the left hand; but no hand from another tree, and no peacocks. On the whole the probability seems to be that there was an older legend which is here represented, and which was afterwards broken up into numerous fragments.

‡ The inscription will be found in Appendix E., Nos. XVII. and XIV. They merely record the names of the donors.

ELEVATION OF INTERNAL FACES OF TWO PILLARS OF OUTER ENCLOSURE.
SCALE 1 INCH TO 1 FOOT.

PLATE LIX.

There is no difficulty in recognizing the principal figure in the two central circles of the pillars in Plate LIX. In the first it is the Prince Siddhârtha riding* forth from the city gate, with all the insignia of his rank. The umbrella of state is borne over his head; Chaori bearers attend on either hand, and music and dancing precede him. The glory round his head marks him as the elect—the future regenerator of the world. This is the first time we meet with this distinguishing mark, as there are no glories at Sanchi, though they are found commonly behind the heads of saints in the Peshawer sculptures.

In the circle of the right-hand picture we have the same individual after he had attained Buddhahood, in the robes in which he is always represented after apparently the second or third century of our era. On his right a woman, more fully clothed than any other woman in these sculptures, presents a boy to him, who catches hold of his garment as if entreating him to come with him. The boy's toys are seen in the foreground. It hardly seems doubtful but that this represents Yaçodharâ and her son Râhula entreating the great ascetic to return home to them, and reoccupy the position of his rank and his duties as a prince and a father.

The figures around Buddha are his disciples, among whom will be remarked in the foreground a hump-backed woman (Kubja), who frequently reappears in the sculptures.

The lower bas-reliefs on both these pillars seem to continue the subjects represented in the principal circles. In the centre of the left-hand pillar we have Siddhârtha with the glory round his head; one man kissing his feet, and others in reverential attitudes; and beside him "the Horse," to whom we shall frequently have occasion to revert hereafter. On the left of this a man bearing a relic in a tray; the same as seen in Plate LI., whatever it may be. Below him is a Naga Raja in a kneeling attitude. On the right is the worship of the Chakra or Wheel, with the usual accompaniments, and two antelopes in the foreground.

The story told in the lower bas-relief of the right-hand pillar is easily made out. A prince is seated on a couch, surrounded by his attendants, and a boy with a bow seems to ask him to join in the chase or some martial exercise. In the central compartment he resists the temptations of the daughters of Mâra;† and in the third, having assumed the priestly robes, teaches a multitude under a Bo Tree. It looks at first sight as if intended for an epitome of the life of Buddha, but it may be doubted whether he is really the person intended here, as in none of the three compartments has he a glory round his head, and it is hardly probable that in the same

---

* It is worthy of remark that at Sanchi the prince is always in his chariot, at Amravati on horseback. There is only one chariot in all the sculptures at Amravati, Plate LXXXVI., and the subject of that bas-relief is singularly connected with Sanchi.

† This scene occurs again more in detail, Plate LXIII., where it will be more especially referred to.

pillar he would be represented with and without this accompaniment. It may be some Bodhisattwa, but on the whole I am inclined to believe that it may represent scenes in the life of Râhula, who seems certainly to be the hero of the central bas-relief; and if this is so nothing can be more natural than that his story should be continued on the same pillar. This prince, according to the legend, at the age of twenty, assumed the garb of a priest, and shortly after, by his father's teaching, rose to the rank of a Rahan.* It will be observed that the old woman who appears behind the boy in the central picture reappears in the left-hand lower picture. Is she the mother of Yaçodara?

The two upper bas-reliefs are too completely destroyed for their subjects to be made out. We can just see in the central bas-relief of the left-hand pillar that some person or object is being worshipped by women in the usual attitude, and on the right-hand pillar that Buddha himself is seated in the usual cross-legged attitude, and being worshipped by his followers. We can, however, restore with tolerable certainty the upper representation on the left of the left-hand pillar by comparing it with the left-hand pillar, Plate LI., or Plate LXXIII., Fig. 2. The man whose legs only appear, almost certainly bore a tray on his head, on which stood a cup or some similar object, and the others are reverencing it, whatever it may have been.

It will be observed the representation of Buddha here is very far in advance of anything found on the Gateways at Sanchi, and much more nearly resembling the modern representations found everywhere. The whole scene, indeed, shows a progress which fully accounts for the 300 years that elapsed between the execution of the two monuments.

---

* Bigandet, Burmese Legend of Buddha, p. 229, Journal Amer. Or. Soc. III. 69. His having entered the priesthood by no means precludes his having succeeded to the throne of Kapilawastu on the death of his grandfather. In Burmah, at the present day, nothing is so common as for members of the upper classes to become priests. Some remain so, but many more resume their civil status after three or four years' probation. A young Burmese gentleman looks on entering the priesthood very much as an undergraduate in one of our monastic colleges at Oxford or Cambridge regards his wearing a surplice in chapel. Many in our country remain in the priesthood, but as many return to civil life.

ELEVATION OF INTERNAL FACES OF TWO PILLARS OF OUTER ENCLOSURE.
SCALE 1 INCH TO 1 FOOT.

PLATE LX.

THE palace scenes pourtrayed on the two pillars in this Plate are among the most elegant of the Amravati sculptures, and interesting as pictures of life in India during the fourth century, though it is not easy to affix any particular story to the scenes they represent. Still, as the seated figure in the upper part of the central circle of the right-hand pillar has a glory round his head, we cannot refuse to recognize him as the Prince Siddhârtha; and if so, the scenes represent the Harem at Kapilawastu, which he deserted to devote himself to save his fellow creatures from sin and death.

In front of him, two of the ladies of the Harem are playing at Pachîsî, or drafts, or some such game, while others are looking on; and in front of them a very graceful figure is dancing, while another plays on the flute, a third on a guitar, and one on a drum. Others are listening or applauding, and one child (is it the infant Râhula ?) appears in the foreground.

In the lower bas-relief the same Prince is seated on a couch, in conference with a Naga Raja, and in front of them two women are seated, apparently as attendants. On the left are the Naga Raja's people. On the right the country people are bringing presents of cattle, fruit, &c to the seated Rajas.

The head of the principal figure of the circle of the left-hand pillar is so completely destroyed that we cannot now know whether he had a nimbus round his head or not, nor consequently whether he is the same as the person represented on the right-hand pillar. Most probably he is. The object of the sculpture is to represent the entertainment of two distinguished guests. They are seated on a dais, on the King's right hand, with a table in front of each. The major domo stands between the Raja and his guests, and presents something to the nearest; while a girl in front offers apparently something to drink. In front of her, with his back to the spectators, is a man seated in one of those square-backed chairs which are common in these sculptures. The Queen sits on the Raja's left, in a chair of another and more elegant pattern, but extremely like the modern chairs we now use. To those familiar with Indian habits at the present day, few things are more curious than the fact that all dignitaries in these sculptures are always seated on chairs or sofas, like Europeans; never on the ground or on cushions cross-legged, as is the universal practice now-a-days. The only difference seems to be that the seat of the chair or throne must always have been made wide enough for the sitter to put up one leg on it, which seems to have been the fashionable attitude.

In the central picture some of the women are seated on stools, some on chairs; but in both the circular bas-reliefs, as in the lower one on the left hand of the left-hand pillar, the Raja is seated on a throne with a square back, ornamented with lions' heads.

In the centre of the foreground of the circular bas-relief of the left-hand pillar, is a child attended by two women, one old and one very much younger.

This would seem to connect the two bas-reliefs as representing the same persons, and if that is so, it scarcely admits of doubt but that the principal figure is intended for the Prince Siddhârtha, and the child in that case must be his son Râhula.

In the central lower bas-relief of the left-hand pillar, the Raja is cutting something with his sword, which a man with a steelyard is standing behind him ready to weigh. What the object is cannot be made out from this representation. In the right-hand lower bas-relief a man, with a curious tall mitre or hat, is seated outside the palace gate, doing justice. The same head-dress is repeated several times in the sculptures, but whether it indicates that the wearer is always the same person is not clear. The central picture looks as if intended to represent the hero of the right-hand bas-relief cutting the Gordian knot which his legal acumen could not untie.

The Gateway in this bas-relief is curious, as almost literally reproducing those at Sanchi. There are at Amravati at least a dozen representations of the same thing, all nearly though not exactly alike, but all evidently intended to represent a wooden erection, such as it can hardly be doubted suggested those at Sanchi. Though these are in stone, this material did not at once supersede the wooden form which continued to be employed long afterwards in India, as it is at the present day in China.

FIG. 1. FIG. 2.

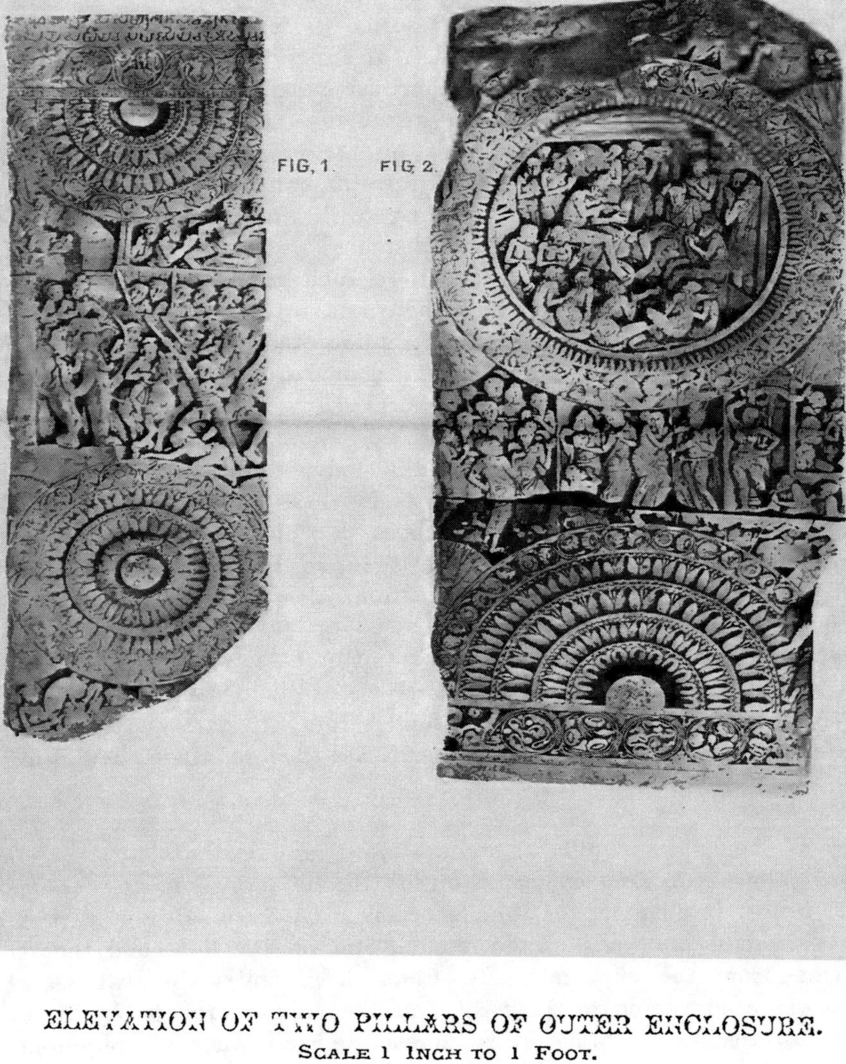

ELEVATION OF TWO PILLARS OF OUTER ENCLOSURE.

SCALE 1 INCH TO 1 FOOT.

PLATE LXI.

THERE does not seem to be any sign or symbol by which we can attach a name to any of the actors in the scenes portrayed in the principal circle of the right-hand portion of Plate LXI., though it is easy to describe the action. It is evidently a disputation held between two men, one of whom, of superior rank, sits in the middle of the picture, and lays down the law in an authoritative manner. The other, on a lower seat, is evidently represented as beaten in argument. Between the two disputants sits an old man with something like a book on his lap, the arbiter in the contest, and behind him an attendant apparently with refreshments. Another man is standing in a gateway of the Sanchi type, and turning to listen. The rest of the audience are all women, ten of them are there as listeners only, an eleventh bears a fan, and a twelfth food. This presence of women in such scenes as these is one of the remarkable features of the sculptures, both here and at Sanchi. Not only do they take part in every action almost without exception, but seem almost as important as the male actors. Certainly the idea of a veiled or Purdah woman had not occurred to the Hindus when these sculptures were executed.

In the lower bas-relief the king or prince issues from one of these Sanchi portals, followed by his wife, to meet or feed a body of mendicant friars or monks. It is the first appearance of these noted priests in these sculptures, and is the more remarkable as there are only two other instances in which they appear at Amravati, and as before mentioned no trace of them is to be found at Sanchi. Both in costume and appearance they differ entirely from the people I have there designated as Dasyus, so that with the knowledge we now possess it seems impossible to confound the two, but this will become more apparent as we proceed. The absence of priests is the more remarkable, because if we were to believe Buddhist books, they flocked in thousands and tens of thousands from all parts of India to attend the great convocations held five or six centuries before these sculptures were commenced.

The story of the left-hand pillar is perhaps more graphically told than almost any other on these pillars. A king is seated on his throne, to whom a messenger with clasped hands brings intelligence or solicits orders. In front of him a part of the army is seen defending the walls of the citadel, and on the left hand the moveable force is sallying from the city gate. In front the infantry, in attitudes of great excitement, are seen advancing to the fight, and the rear is brought up by horsemen and elephants, all remarkably well drawn foreshortened. In the foreground one of the enemy falls on his knees to beg pardon and mercy.

If the lower part of the pillar had been preserved, we might have seen the result of this sally. It no doubt was successful, and as women appear in the fragments that remain the whole ended probably in triumph.

According to the Lalita-Vistara* and other Indian works, a perfect army always consists of four arms, elephants and horsemen, chariots and infantry. Three of these are represented here, but strange to say the chariots are absent, as they always are at Amravati, though, as before remarked, they are so prominent at Sanchi. This probably is owing to some local peculiarity which could only be discovered on the spot. It can hardly be that they had gone out of fashion, because in the great temple of Nakon Vat, in Cambodia, built probably eight centuries after Amravati,† chariots are everywhere used by the chiefs in war, and with wheels as perfect and as light as could be made now by a London coach-builder. Those who know how much civilization is involved in a perfect wheel will acquire a higher estimate of the stage reached by the snake worshippers there, from these mechanical appliances, than even from their sculptures themselves.

Taken altogether, this pillar, both in its decorations and its sculptures, is one of the most elegant at Amravati, and it would consequently be extremely interesting if its inscription told us something of its story. All, however, we gather from it is that the pillar was the gift of three men and their three wives.‡

It is so much narrower than the others just described, that it evidently did not form one of the regular pillars of the outer Rail, but as it is the same height and the circles are the same distance from centre to centre, it probably belonged to one of the projecting Gateways, either as an angle column, or on some return where narrower pillars only could be introduced.

---

* See also the Niti-sâra, or Elements of Polity, by Kâmandaki. Calcutta, 1861, ch. 19.

† See History of Architecture, by the Author, vol. II., p. 713, et seqq.

‡ See Appendix E., No. XIII.

INTERNAL FACE OF TWO DISCS ON INTERMEDIATE RAILS OF OUTER ENCLOSURE.
SCALE 1 INCH 3-4TH TO 1 FOOT.

PLATE LXII.

THE two circular bas-reliefs represented in this Plate are the two most perfect of their class in the collection, and have consequently been photographed to a larger scale in order to make their details more easily visible. The upper one Colonel Mackenzie considered as the most elegant of the Amravati sculptures,* an opinion in which he probably was not far wrong. It is somewhat weather-worn, however, now, and was very seriously damaged on its return from the late French Exhibition.

The action is simple. A casket containing a relic is placed on the throne under an elaborate canopy, and is being worshipped by the Naga Raja and his people. The Naga Raja stands in the centre, with the seven-headed snake hood over him, and the two attendants on either hand, with Chaoris, have also the same canopy. It is not easy to see whether the two men with their hands clasped over their heads are Nagas also, but the probability is that they are. The men behind him have none of them the snake hood, but the twelve females in the foreground have all of them a single snake on the back of their heads. The whole is, however, arranged so much more elegantly than at Sanchi (Plate XXIV.), that it is not offensive, and the snakes would not, indeed, be noticed unless attention was directed to them. The two standing female figures on either hand are singularly elegant, especially the one buying the wreath to present to the relic, or at least she was before her visit to Paris.

It is probably in vain to inquire what the relic is that is enclosed in this casket. If the conjectures hazarded above with regard to the visit of the Tooth relic to this place have any foundation, it is by no means impossible that the famed Daladâ may be contained within, and is here exposed temporarily on the throne to be worshipped by the Naga Raja and his people.†

Both the throne and the canopy or umbrella over it are singularly rich and elegant specimens of the furniture of the period. Such thrones frequently occur, but no such canopy in any other of the sculptures.

The lower circle contains no peg on which it will, I fear, be possible to hang a story. It is simply this, two Hindu

No. 20.

RELIC CASKET FROM MANIKYALA.

* From a pencil note in his handwriting on the drawing of this sculpture in his book.

† In the Tope at Manikyala, opened by General Ventura, a casket was found, of which the annexed is a representation. It contained only fragments of amber in a brown liquid, but the inscription not yet having been satisfactorily made out, we are ignorant to whom it belonged. See Thomas, Edition of Prinsep, vol. I. p. 97, et seqq., and Professor Dowson, in vol. XX. p. 244., J. R. A. S. It probably belongs to a date not far distant from the Christian era. The casket represented in Woodcut, No. 6, p. 76, is, perhaps, even more like the one worshipped by the Naga Raja in the bas-relief. It, too, was found in a Tope at Manikyala, and, to judge from the coins that were found with it, should be of about the same age. Its form, however, and other circumstances, incline me to think it may be more modern.

gentlemen,—they are not Rajas, as they have no umbrellas of state borne over them,—not much burthened with clothing, are seated on a sofa of modern form, listening to a concert of music which is being performed by a number of women in the foreground. Eighteen women seem to be engaged in the performance. Three are playing on harps, three or four on drums, some on flutes, one is blowing a horn, and others are performing on instruments, the nature of which it is not easy to make out. One woman, with her back to the spectator, standing in the centre, appears to be the leader, and is beating time with her hands. In front of her, with one foot on a stool or drum, is the *prima donna*, accompanying her voice with a harp. She has short curly hair, and, like all the musicians, rather a sharp Roman nose, extremely unlike the men or any other of their women. It will also be observed, she alone of all the women has no bangles on her ancles, though she has on her wrists. Besides the eighteen performers two others of the same race will be observed on the right of the circle: one with her hands joined is addressing the principal Queen, while another lower down seems to covet the bead belt of a girl she is talking to. Whoever these performers are they are a class we have not met before, nor do we, so far as I know, meet them again. They are very unlike all the other people represented in the sculptures, and very easily distinguishable from the other people in this bas-relief. The latter have all rather flat noses, and a more Tartar-like cast of features than are generally seen in these sculptures. Are they Gonds? The performers, on the contrary, have singularly sharp features and prominent Roman noses, and seem to have curly heads, but nothing in the least approaching the Negro type in any way. Are they Gypsies?

Besides the musicians and the gentlemen on the sofa, there are three ladies of rank, two on the right and one on the left of the picture, who are accommodated with chairs. Their principal articles of dress are their bangles and their bead belt below their waists.* There are two little girls in the foreground, and about twenty others, who seem to be the attendants on inmates of the Harem.

One other point requires notice. Below the sofa are two jars or pots, evidently containing some drink for the refreshment of those seated upon it. The same thing was observed at Sanchi (Plates XXX. and XXXVII.). There it certainly contained some intoxicating fluid. I am afraid that in this instance also they contain something stronger than water.

* "On the east of the Chanda district (the Gond district nearest Amravati) the men wear no covering for their heads or the upper part of their bodies. The women deck themselves with thirty to forty beads, to which some add a necklace of pendant bells. Bangles of zinc adorn their wrists, and a chain of the same metal is suspended from the hair, and attached to a large boss stuck in the ear. But the greatest peculiarity connected with their costume is the practice that prevails, in more remote districts, of the women wearing no clothes at all; instead of which they fasten with a string passing round their waists a bunch of leafy twigs to cover them before and behind." Barring the twigs, which seem to be a modern innovation, nothing can more correctly describe the costumes of the sculptures than the above extract from Mr. Hislop's paper on the Gonds, edited by Sir R. Temple, p. 8.

FIG, 1.

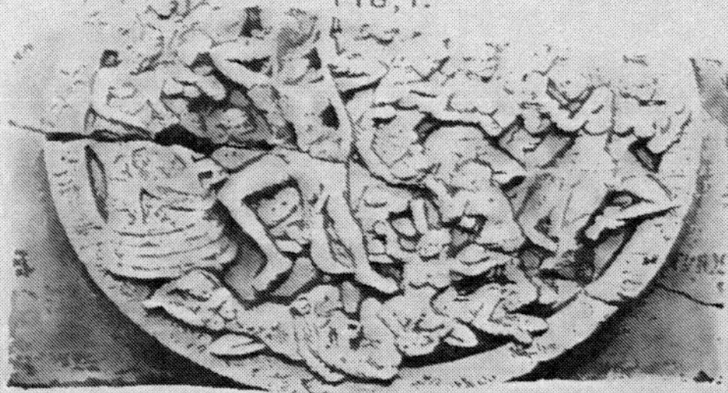

FIG, 2

FIG, 3.

DISCS ON INTERNAL FACE OF INTERMEDIATE RAILS OF OUTER ENCLOSURE.

SCALE 1 INCH TO 1 FOOT.

PLATE LXIII.

THE three circles represented in this Plate are the only other intermediate sculptured circles in the Indian Museum. All three are so much damaged and weather-worn that it is extremely difficult to make out their details, and to feel certain about their story. The subject of the upper one is clearly a temptation scene, and is a more detailed representation of the central bas-relief on the lower compartment of the right-hand pillar (Plate LIX.). A man in great wrath drives from him a number of females, some of whom are in the act of asking favours; some are laughing, some going quietly away, but others have tumbled down, and are being apparently trampled upon. The first impression is, that this is meant to represent the temptation to which Buddha was subjected by the Apsaras, the daughters of Mâra, as described at length in the Lalita-Vistara.* In every respect it would answer for this legend but for the attitude of the main figure. The nearly perfected Buddha replied calmly to all their seductions that he had conquered all the passions, and that love of women had long since ceased to influence him. He looked on them as mere illusions, and their power was gone. It was by calmness and dignity that he repulsed them. This figure is in violent action. He holds a stick—it may be a bow—in his hand, and seems in wrath. All this is so unlike Buddhism that we must probably look elsewhere for a solution of the myth, though it may only be an earlier form of it than that found in the Lalita-Vistara. It might be suggested that the face of the principal and only male figure being destroyed, we mistake the action; but the representation on Plate LIX. negatives this hypothesis. There the face and the figure are complete, and in that instance they can hardly be assumed to be identical with those of the principal figure in the central circle above them. On the whole I am inclined to believe rather that Râhula is the hero of the scene, but the Lalita-Vistara and our other usual authorities on Buddhist tradition, are so singularly silent with regard to him or his connexion with his father's preaching, that I do not know where to look for elucidations. Some one more familiar with Buddhist legends than I can pretend to be, may probably suggest an interpretation.

Though the upper part is broken off, this is one of the few circles that have not been trimmed. It retains the flanges by which it was fitted into the pillars nearly entire.

The middle circle is entire, though weather-worn. It represents a Hindu chief. He has the Chaori, but no umbrella, and is followed by one of his wives on the left hand. Two others are on the right, worshipping a circular object placed on a throne. It is extremely difficult to feel certain what the object may be, though it occurs very frequently in these sculptures; generally, however, there are two of them. Most

---

* Lalita-Vistara, p. 306, et seqq.

probably it is a measure called a Droṇa, or Dona, and contains a relic or relics. Two men like shaven priests stand behind the throne, with their hands joined, in the attitude of prayer, and behind them nine women, also worshipping. Several women in the foreground are in attitudes of violent devotion, one has fallen in her ecstasies quite on her back. This circle also retains a portion of its flanges.

The third or lowest circle in this Plate refers to some legend to which it probably will not be easy to give a name. It may be wholly local. A Raja, with the umbrella of state over his head, stands in a very easy and graceful attitude, leaning on his horse, which issues from the portal of the palace led by a groom in very complete clothing. The Raja is addressing or being addressed by an old lady seated on a couch or easy chair on his right. She is surrounded by her handmaidens, some of whom in the foreground seem to be busy preparing wreaths, while one is taking something out of a box. In front of the hero a number of objects are spread out on a tray or table. They look like lotus flowers, but they may be refreshments of some sort.

At the time the bas-relief was sculptured everyone of course could recognize who the old lady was, and who her son, as easily as we can name at once the Virgin Mary or her Son in any picture of the Italian school, but without some symbol it is difficult to do the same with these Buddhist sculptures. It will be observed that the Trisul ornament surmounts the Gateway in the background precisely as at Sanchi The pillars had, apparently, lion capitals, but the sculpture is too much worn to feel sure of this.

It is to be regretted that a greater number of these circles have not been rescued. Originally there must have been 100 or 120 at least, and judging from the interest of five which the Museum possesses, the whole, when complete, must have formed a very complete picture-bible of Buddhist tradition, as understood at the time they were executed. They are so light and so easily handled, however, that it is to be feared the greater number have been carried away, and either built into walls as ornaments, or what is more probable, burnt for lime.

FIG. 1

FIG. 2

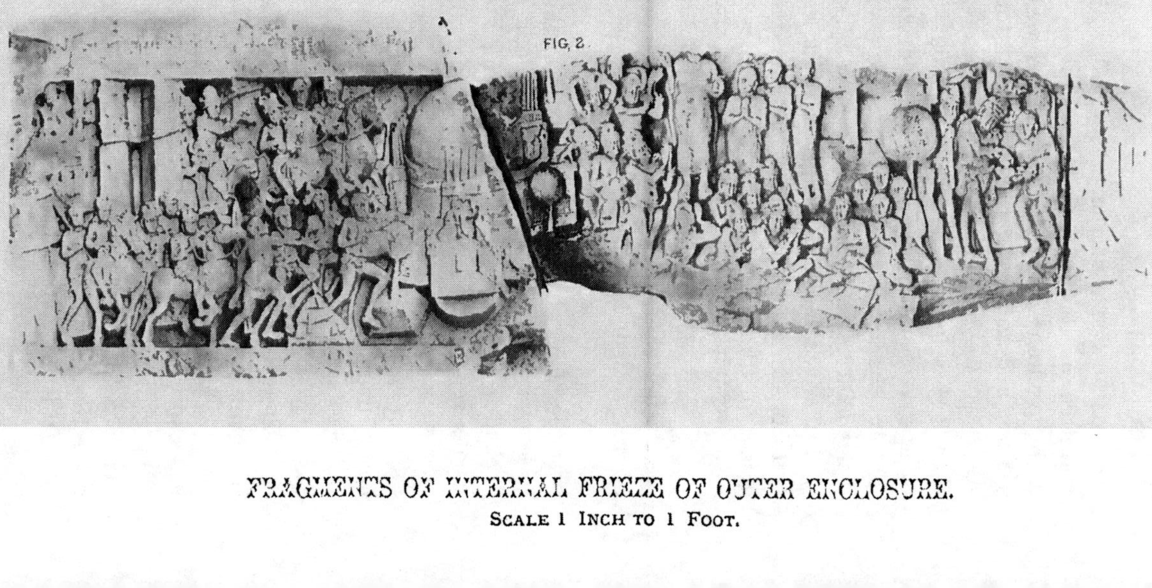

FRAGMENTS OF INTERNAL FRIEZE OF OUTER ENCLOSURE.

SCALE 1 INCH TO 1 FOOT.

PLATE LXIV.

THE photographs on Plate LXIV. represent the only two fragments of the inner face of the frieze of the great Rail which have reached this country. This is to be regretted, as the sculpture is singularly spirited, and a bas-relief 130 feet long, which each quadrant must have possessed when complete, could hardly have failed to tell a story and to give a distinct idea of the arts of the age in which it was executed. As it is, we must content ourselves with two fragments, each only a little more than 8 feet long—17 feet out of 500—and the lower one so much weather-worn as to lose very much of the spirit it originally possessed.

In the upper fragment we have on the left hand a prince seated on a throne inside a city, surrounded by a host of admirers doing him homage; and above, two of his wives looking out of a window. Next we have a procession, with elephants and horsemen, issuing from the city gates, escorting what appears to be the principal object of the ceremonial. From the ruined and worn state of the stone it is not easy to feel sure what this is intended to represent. The lower part of it is certainly an ark or palankeen, shaped like a boat, and borne on the shoulders of men with short curly hair. The upper part may be intended to represent four figures seated in the ark, under a canopy, or if, as I fancy, it is meant to represent a ship, this may be a rude way of depicting the sails and equipment. The boat-like form forcibly recalls the golden ship which the King of Ceylon ordered to convey the relics to the Diamond Sands. It is too big, if the scale is to be depended upon, for the golden ship, and too small for the wooden one, but as the whole representation is conventional, it either represents the identical relic vessel or some similar ark used for a like purpose. As the procession approaches him, the Raja, who is easily recognized in the centre of the picture from the Chatta borne over him, descends from his elephant and proceeds on foot to the sacred Bo-tree, in front of which, and under whose shade the throne is placed for the reception of the relics.

There is another representation in Plate LXXXIV. of a procession bearing what is apparently the same or at least a similar object. In that Plate there are certainly two persons seated in front, and three more inside the litter, or whatever it may be, and they seem bringing a number of presents which are depicted in front. Taking the two together I see nothing in the representation to militate against the idea that this bas-relief may represent Danta Kumâra and Hemaehalâ bringing the relics from Ceylon, as recorded above, page 160.

It is not clear whether the space within the Gateway of the Sanchi type is to be considered as a separate picture, and that the cushion-like ornament at the back of the chair is meant to be represented as already containing the relics or only prepared for their reception. A number of persons are represented as already worshipping either the object on the throne or the Tree behind it. Beyond the tree on the right there is a division where a new subject certainly begins.

There is a very legible inscription on this frieze, but unfortunately it is imperfect at the beginning, and what remains only records that the bas-relief is the gift of the five daughters of Maditi, with their sons and two slaves, whose names are given.*

The lower sculpture represents a procession issuing in like manner from the city gate, and proceeding to a Dagoba with all the accompaniments with which we shall presently become so familiar.

There is the Tee, the five steles or pillars on each face, the Rail with its four projecting Gateways, each with two lions, and on the front of the Dagoba the seven-headed Naga in the place of honour.

Beyond the Dagoba, to the right, are three separate subjects, first, seven men in the usual Hindu costume, listening to a man in priestly robes who is preaching, with three other monks standing behind him. The head of the principal figure is unfortunately broken off, so we cannot be sure who is intended. It may be Buddha himself. In the next division five men are listening to a seated priest expounding, and accompanied by four others of his order. Above them, there is a sacred tree in a square enclosure. The last scene represents the Raja, or Hindu chief, pouring water from the mysterious spouted vessel on the hands of a priest, probably confirming a grant. Behind him are some fragments which seem to represent a monastery. The fragments of marble would, however, require to be very carefully fitted together before they could be reproduced by photography. They are certainly parts of this bas-relief, and when put together may be of some interest.

No women appear on either of these bas-reliefs, except the two in each fragment looking out of the windows on the extreme left of each.

Though so much injured as to make it a little difficult to judge correctly, I look on these two fragments of the frieze with the left-hand pillar in Plate LXI. as the masterpieces of Amravati art. They certainly are more spirited and tell their story more distinctly than any others of those which have been brought to this country.

---

* See Appendix E., No. I.

FIG. 1

FIG. 2

FIG. 3.

FRAGMENTS OF INTERNAL FRIEZES OF OUTER ENCLOSURE.

PLATE LXV.

This Plate contains three fragments of friezes similar in depth to that described in the last Plate, but certainly not part of the same continuous decoration. The first, on the left hand at the top, certainly is not; in the first place, because its style is quite different, but also from its being but three inches less in depth. Fig. 2. may be part of another quadrant; its depth is exactly 2 feet, like the others in the last Plate. Fig. 3. I fancy must have belonged to one of the returns of the Gateways. It is a complete picture in itself, and if it belonged to the outer Rail, could only have been placed in some such detached position.

Fig. 1., besides its inferior style, is dreadfully weather-worn, so that it is difficult to make out the subject. In the first compartment we have a Hindu Raja, with his teapot, pouring water on the hand of a man who carries a parasol, and he is accompanied by another man who likewise carries his own umbrella. Between these figures stands a dwarf, bearing a tray on his head, either to support the spouted vessel when not in use, or to catch the drops of the liquid if they are precious. My impression is, however, that generally speaking the spouted vessel contains most probably water. In the next compartment we have a covered cart drawn by two bullocks, remarkable as being one of the few wheeled carriages at Amravati. The Hindu in the cart meets a man with a parasol, and above him a man with a bangy follows one with a parasol, who is apparently welcomed by a tall figure with two children. In the third compartment three seated figures receive a deputation bearing offerings. Is it possible that these men with the parasols are Chinese, and the subject of the bas-relief the reception of an embassy from China. We know that Fa Hian visited India from China in 399* and travelled in search of Buddhist books and traditions over a great part of India, though he did not reach Amravati. Yadjna Śrí, however, a king whose coins are found frequently at this place, and whose name appears—doubtfully—in one of the Amravati inscriptions (see page 160) sent an embassy to China about the year 408. From its style it is evident that this is among the most modern pieces of sculpture at Amravati, and certainly executed after the dates just quoted. There is, therefore, no *à priori* improbability, and on the whole I am very much inclined to believe that this is the true interpretation of the subject.

Fig. 2. represents in its first compartment the worship of the Dagoba, with its usual accompaniments, and on the right one of those Harem scenes to which it seems impossible at present to attach a name. A noble—he has no emblem of royalty—pats under the chin a lady who is seated on the same sofa as himself. She apparently has a glory round her head, which he has not. It is not, however, Mâyâ, for she died seven days after giving birth to her illustrious son, and I do not know any other female who would be so honoured. Perhaps, however, it is not a glory

* Foë-Kouë-Ki. Translated by Rémusat and others. Paris, 1836.

after all, but something borne by one of the attendants behind. The attendants both before and behind seem to be bringing refreshments, and the chief seems to hold something eatable in his hand. The figures are all elegant, and the sculpture of the best class of those at Amravati.

Whatever may be the difficulty with the two others, there is none whatever in identifying the subjects of the lower bas-relief. In the first compartment Śuddhodana, the father of Buddha, is seated on his throne. In the centre, on his right, sits Mâyâ, this time certainly with a glory behind her head. On his left stands his prime minister, and further on are four seated guests.

The central compartment depicts the well-known legend of the birth of Buddha. When Mâyâ* felt her time approaching, she left the city for the beautiful Lumbinî garden, and gave birth to the future prophet, standing and holding on to a branch of a tree.† Behind her stands her mother-in-law, distinguished by her umbrella, and beside her four men or gods hold a long cloth, which they are prepared to wrap round her. The infant was delivered from her left side. The cradle is prepared in front, and the gods look on and worship above.

The third compartment represents the Prince Siddhârtha seated on a couch under a gorgeous canopy, with a glory behind his head. On the same couch is seated Gopâ, his first wife. In front one woman is playing on a harp, another on a flute. Two in front of them are either listening or singing, and one is playing with a little girl.

All these subjects occur frequently again in the sculptures of the Amravati Tope, and are almost as common in Buddhist iconography as the Nativity, or the Virgin and Child, are among Christian pictures. The mode of treatment varies, however, in all, but excepting that it is somewhat weather-worn, this is one of the clearest and best I am acquainted with.

In both this one and in number 2. above it will be observed that the different groups are cleverly divided from one another by walls, with ornamented ends towards the spectators; these separate without interrupting the action of the piece.

---

* One of the most tempting nominal similarities connected with this subject is suggested by this name. The mother of Buddha was called Mâyâ. The mother of Mercury was also Mâia the daughter of Atlas. The Romans always called Wodin, Mercury, and dies Mercurii and Wodensday alike designated the fourth day of the week. The serpent-formed Caduceus of Mercury seems nearly akin to the serpent-shielded Buddha of our sculptures, and the astronomical sign of Mercury as represented in the annexed woodcut is very like our mysterious Trisul emblem.

No. 21.

These and other similarities have frequently been pointed out and insisted upon, and they are too numerous and too distinct not to have some foundation in reality. All, however, that can be said of them at present is that our knowledge of the subject is not sufficiently advanced to enable us to make use of them as facts for the purposes of our investigation. We have not yet found the thread that is to guide us safely through the labyrinth, but I by no means despair of finding it, and that very shortly.

† The Lalita-Vistara calls the tree a Pipal, "*Ficus religiosa*," p. 86. Others say it was an Aśoka, "*Jonesia Asoka*." In the bas-relief it looks like a Pipal.

AMRAVATI.

PLATE LXVI.

W GRIGGS LITH.

INDIA MUSEUM.

3 Feet 11.2 Inches

ELEVATION OF INTERNAL FACE OF PILLARS OF OUTER ENCLOSURE.

AMRAVATI.

PLATE LXVII.

5 Feet 10 Inches

W. Griggs Lith.

3 Feet. 1 Inch

India Museum

ELEVATION OF INTERNAL FACE OF A PILLAR OF OUTER ENCLOSURE.

ELEVATION OF INTERNAL FACE OF A PILLAR OF OUTER ENCLOSURE.

PLATES LXVI., LXVII., AND LXVIII.

PLATE LXVI.

THIS Plate, lithographed from a drawing in the Mackenzie Collection, represents one of the angle pillars of the great Rail. The tall pillar, with three full and two half circles, is introduced as an angle piece terminating the curved part, and commencing the straight projection of one of the Gateways.*

The subject of the central circle, though much broken, is apparently a Buddhist preacher addressing men and women in the foreground, who listen in attitudes of adoration ; and higher up floating figures, Devas or Devatâs, attend and bring offerings.

The three bas-reliefs in the octagon part below are similar in subject to those described above in speaking of Plate LVIII. On the left a chief, seated on a throne, is listening to the animated eloquence of a warrior, who seems addressing a youth seated cross-legged on the ground. The result of this speech is seen in the central compartment. The King, with the umbrella of state, sallies forth on his elephant, but unarmed, and accompanied by two of his women. His army accompany him in the foreground, and a floating figure above offers a wreath. In the third compartment the enemy fly, apparently without striking a blow !

As the head of the principal figure in the centre is broken off, we cannot feel sure that it represents Buddha himself. If it is he, this bas-relief ought to refer to some legend of his youth. If it is one of the Bodhisattwas, which is possible, it is to him that the event depicted must be referred.

PLATE LXVII.

It will not be necessary to say anything here about the mutilated circle in this Plate, as another representation of the same subject will be found further on in Plate LXXIII., where it occurs on an intermediate Rail.

In the lower bas-relief we have in the centre a Saint or Bodhisattwa seated expounding. From his being accompanied by a horse, it probably may be Avalokiteśwara. One man is embracing his foot, but the principal personage is presenting a cloth.

On the left we have the worship of an emblem, which I have already suggested may mean Buddha himself, though in what combination is by no means clear. It

* Compare it with woodcut No. 19, page 168.

recurs frequently further on, so we shall have to refer to it again and again. Here the Trisul emblem is placed on a tall pillar, from each side of which issues what may be taken for flames. At the bottom are the sacred feet on the Lotus. To the right of the pillar is the Naga Raja with his wife. On the left a saint with a glory round his head, and a bird hovers over him—it looks like a pigeon (?) Behind him is a Naga woman, and above them four women bearing pots on their heads.

On the right-hand side are seven women, looking at the gambols of dwarfs and grotesque figures in front of the Sacred Tree.

PLATE LXVIII.

This pillar, though very much dilapidated, is of considerable interest, first, as a means of comparison with Plate XXXI., representing a similar scene at Sanchi, and secondly, because it may possibly represent the arrival of the relics, in charge of Danta Kumâra, from Ceylon. The upper circle is too much mutilated to be deciphered; but in the centre of the lower compartment we have a boat or ship, in which is one man paddling. In front a man in the garb of a priest, with his hands joined, worshipping a relic or rather two relic bundles or Droṇas, placed on a throne, below which the sacred feet are seen. Above these is the same Trisul emblem as was seen in the last Plate. If I am correct in my conjecture, this would simply mean relics of Buddha, whether or not they were coming from Ceylon.

Below, the Naga Raja is welcoming the arrival, accompanied apparently by two women and a man. In the right-hand compartment a chief bears himself the canopy of state, evidently in honour of the relics, and his wife stands behind in the act of worshipping.

That these represent relics arriving by water at Amravati seems quite clear, but whether those mentioned at page 160 or some others, must for the present I fear be matter for conjecture. My own impressions are in favour of the Ceylonese relics being those here depicted, but the destruction of the upper part of the pillar and the fracture of the sides deprives us of the means of determining the point. I may also add that, notwithstanding the general fidelity of the drawings made for Colonel Mackenzie, it would be satisfactory, in a difficult and important case like this, to see the slab itself.

AMRAVATI.

PLATE LXIX.

ELEVATION OF INTERNAL FACE OF A PILLAR OF OUTER ENCLOSURE.

PLATE LXX.

W. [illegible] LITH INDIA MUSEUM.

ELEVATION OF INTERNAL FACE OF A PILLAR OF OUTER ENCLOSURE.

PLATES LXIX. AND LXX.

THE central circle in Plate LXIX. represents the reception of a Princess and Prince by some one, very important from his size, who stands under a canopy with his hands joined. The Princess presents a piece of cloth, on which is the impression of two feet. If any dependance can be placed on the story in the Râja Tarangiņî,* this would indicate that the strangers came from Ceylon, and consequently they probably were Hemâchala and Danta Kumara. If the person receiving them were the Naga Raja, I should consider this as nearly certain. Unfortunately, his head is so defaced that it is impossible to be sure; but as none of his women have snakes at the back of their heads, it is most probable that he was not a Naga. It may, however, represent the reception of the same persons in Ceylon; and these peculiarities about the head-dresses of the women would lead to the belief that we have got among a new people.

The story of the lower bas-relief is not difficult to make out, though, without knowing who the principal person in the central bas-relief may be, it is not easy to give a name to the principal parties concerned. On the right "a gay and a gallant knight"—a Raja on horseback attended as his body-guard—comes to court a maiden, who sits in a tall round-backed chair on the left. Between the two in the centre sits the stern father with his two wives, with the ladies of his household disporting themselves in front and attending on him behind. One of the attendants of the expectant bride is getting a garland out of a box, and others are ready with refreshments, while the principal ladies-maid reports to her mistress the arrival of the Prince, and describes his person. The shields and helmets of the Prince's attendants are worthy of remark, as they are unlike any others we have hitherto met with in these sculptures.

PLATE LXX.

This is one of the most interesting, in a ritualistic point of view, of the whole series of pillars at Amravati. In the central circle we have a throne, on which are placed two objects I have ventured to call Droņas of relics. At the back is the Trisul emblem on a pillar beneath the sacred Tree, and the feet are in front. If the Trisul emblem is that of Buddha, the combination seems intelligible, but otherwise it seems difficult to suggest what it may in this instance mean.

---

* Mihira Kula, King of Cashmere, made war on Ceylon because the cloth of Sinhala was stamped with a golden foot as the seal of the monarch. (It means evidently the feet of Buddha, as used everywhere.) His wife, wearing a jacket of Sinhala cloth, the impression came off on her bosom, and the king, indignant that the mark of anyone's foot should appear on the bosom of his wife, invaded Ceylon, and forced him in future to stamp his cloth with the golden Sun.—Asiatic Researches, XV. 28. Mihira Kula, it should, however, be observed, lived before the time of these events (his date was probably 200 A.D.), and cloths with the sacred feet stamped upon them are by no means uncommon in the Amravati sculptures, where no reference to Ceylon can be intended.

On the right-hand side is a group of shaven priests in the robes we usually see, even down to the present day, as the ordinary and distinctive dress of Buddhist priests. On the other side the figures appear to be all of the usual Hindu type; but the upper part of the group is so defaced that it is impossible to feel sure.

In the bas-relief below we have, on the left, our old friends the Dasyus or Takshaks worshipping the five-headed snake in a temple precisely as at Sanchi (Plate XXIV.). Their hair is dressed as in Plate XXXII. They are bearded as these, but as no other people are, either at Sanchi or at Amravati. We have also the deer, indicating a forest people, and a Stûpa without a Tee, as in the Plate last quoted.

In the central compartment the same people are worshipping the Trisul emblem on a throne; but in front of it they have placed an object which is identical with one which a figure, in Plate XXXII., on the left hand is roasting in the fire. I am quite unable to form an opinion as to what it may be intended to represent. On the right we have again the Buddhist priests worshipping the Trisul emblem, as in the central circle.

This and the corresponding bas-reliefs at Sanchi seem intended to show that these Takshaks or Dasyus, whoever they may be, were the original and real Serpent Worshippers. This Plate, however, represents the two religions as partly distinct, partly amalgamated. As the work progressed—indeed from the foundation of Sanchi to the destruction of Amravati—the Naga element seems to have become more and more important as years rolled on, and at last to have become predominant. But as both the Topes were built by Hindus, the poor Dasyus and their religion, in its purity, are forced to be content with the slight notice that is taken of it here and in the corresponding sculptures at Sanchi. The juxtaposition, however, of the two religions on one pillar, as is done here, is singularly interesting, especially as so much pains are taken at the same time to mark the antagonism that existed between them. At Sanchi the difference might have been assumed to be local or accidental; but when we find the same distinction maintained three centuries afterwards, in a distant locality, it must be admitted that they were permanent, and that the sculptors meant to mark the differences which characterized the two forms of faith.

AMRAVATI.

PLATE LXXI.

FIG. 1.

FIG. 2.

INTERNAL FACE OF TWO DISCS ON INTERMEDIATE RAILS OF OUTER ENCLOSURE.

PLATE LXXII.

FIG. 1.

FIG. 2.

INTERNAL FACE OF TWO DISCS ON INTERMEDIATE RAILS OF OUTER ENCLOSURE.

PLATES LXXI. AND LXXII. Fig. 2.

THESE three circles from the intermediate Rails of the outer enclosure are lithographed in fac-simile from drawings in the Mackenzie Collection, and represent the Trisul emblem in various combinations. It is a little unfortunate that no stone with this emblem upon it in this combination has reached this country, because, though we may feel great confidence in Colonel Mackenzie's draughtsmen, it might aid us in understanding this emblem if we could touch the real stone, and feel whether that flame-like emanation on each side of the pillars was really intended to represent fire, or what it really was. Flame occurs several times in the sculptures at Sanchi; and if this emblem was found there in that form, it would be easy to say what was intended; but flame does not occur anywhere at Amravati in an unmistakeable manner, and it is impossible therefore to say how far it may have been conventionalized. I can only therefore state it as my impression that flame is here intended.

The upper part of circle, Fig. 1., Plate LXXI., is unfortunately destroyed, and we cannot therefore feel sure how the emblem terminated, but all the rest of the arrangements are easily intelligible. Both in this and in Fig. 2. the cushion-like object which I have ventured to call a "Droṇa of relics" is placed on the throne, and below it are the impressions of the sacred feet.

In the upper circle, on the right-hand side, is a group of Buddhist priests in their yellow robes worshipping. In front there are two supple women in attitudes of adoration, who occur so frequently in these sculptures, and on the left a chief in the ordinary Hindu costume presents his little son to the emblem. Around him are the women of his family.

In the lower circle the same structural arrangements occur up to the Trisul, but the whole is surmounted by the Chakra, or Wheel, which, as above suggested, I believe to be the emblem of Dharma or the Law. Here all the worshippers are men. It is, in fact, one of the very few scenes in these sculptures from which women are entirely excluded. Whether it was considered that the study of the Law was not appropriate for women, or from whatever motive, the fact of all the worshippers being of one sex and of one race is exceptional. The only other peculiarity worthy of remark is the introduction of two antelopes, one on each side of the throne.

Fig. 2. Plate LXXII. represents the Trisul ornament, not on a throne, but behind an altar. The sacred feet are there, but no relics. The principal worshippers in the upper compartment are two men with seven-headed snake hoods, and two women with single snakes. The Chaori bearers and other attendants have not this appendage.

In the centre of the bas-relief sits the principal personage, with a nine-headed snake hood, between two of his wives, and beyond, on the edge of the circle on either hand, is a female figure standing, and holding on to the branches of two trees. A girl attends on each, one of whom has a snake at the back of her head, the other has not. In front are three musicians with snakes, and on their right a lady without a snake seems to require the assistance of a girl with a snake. Whether she is tipsy or merely faint is not clear. There is a pot on a table behind her that looks suspicious.

This distinction between people with snakes and those without is most curious and perplexing. After the most attentive study I have been unable to detect any characteristic either of feature or costume by which the races can be distinguished, beyond the possession or absence of this strange adjunct. That those with snakes are the Naga people we read of, can hardly be doubted; yet they never are seen actually worshipping the snake like the Dasyus, but rather as protected by it. The snake seems their tutelary genius, watching over, perhaps inspiring them; but whether they borrowed this strange emblem from the natives of the country, or brought it with them from the north-west, are questions we are hardly yet in a position to answer satisfactorily.

To revert, however, to the Trisul. It will be observed that in all the six representations of it in these three Plates the central limb terminates in a point. In this it differs essentially from those which crown the Gateways at Sanchi, though it agrees generally with the form found on the coins and elsewhere. At Sanchi (Plates VI. to IX.) it will be observed that a shield-like emblem is introduced between the outer horns. This is represented in the necklace of emblems (Fig. 4. Plate III.), the fourth from the top on the outside of the left-hand string, and the fifth on the opposite one. It occurs above the Swastika on the great Khaṇḍagiri inscription,* and is found by itself painted on the pillars of some of the oldest of the Western Caves. If the diagram, page 106, is to be taken as an explanation of the compound emblem, it represents Ether, and is here omitted. The crescent there meant Air, the triangle Fire, the circle Water, and the square block Earth. As nothing the least resembling the triangle is found in any of these emblems, this would favour the idea that flames were really meant in these representations. The pillar would thus represent the earthy or real body with water and air. Ether was replaced by the soul divine, symbolized by the Tree, the Wheel, or such other emblem as was placed in conjunction with the Trisul on its pillar. All this, however, is so hypothetical that I would willingly refrain from entering upon it if I knew where to look for information elsewhere. Surely there must be Buddhist books that treat of emblems; but as both General Cunningham and Colonel Maisey, whose attention was turned to the subject in India, are quite at sea regarding them, I fear the requisite explanations are not easily accessible.

---

* J. A. S. B., vol. VI. plate LVIII.

AMRAVATI.

PLATE LXXIII.

FIG. 1.

FIG. 2.

W. GRIGGS. LITH. INDIA MUSEUM.

INTERNAL FACE OF TWO DISCS ON INTERMEDIATE RAILS OF OUTER ENCLOSURE.

PLATE LXXII. Fig. 1., and PLATE LXXIII.

With the upper circle in Plate LXXII. we return to one of those domestic scenes which it is easy enough to understand, though it is difficult to assign names to the principal actors.

Above, a Raja, with two females behind him, is seated on an elephant in a boat, being apparently ferried across a stream—the Kistnah? Two of the females who accompany him jump on shore the moment the boat reaches land, and embrace two other females who seem awaiting their arrival. The Raja's ladies are easily distinguishable by their allowing their long back hair to hang loose behind them. Those who receive them have a roll, something like a comb, at the back of their heads.

In the foreground a lady is seated, with her attendants; on the left, as usual, are the musicians, and above the two "dames d'honneur." On the right one attendant offers her something apparently to eat, and another something to drink out of a small pot slung on her arm.

The story seems simply to be, that a certain Raja, whose name we cannot guess, comes across the river to demand the hand of the fair lady in the foreground, but beyond that we cannot at present go.

The story of the bas-relief, Fig. 1. Plate LXXIII., is likewise simple enough, except perhaps the name of the principal figure. From the glory round his head, however, he is either Śuddhodana or his son Siddhârtha, before he became Buddha. If the upper part of the bas-relief were complete, we might speak with certainty, but from what we see I fancy it more likely to be the king than his son.

Whichever it is, he is represented seated on the throne between his two principal wives on high-backed chairs, and surrounded by the ladies of his court, some seated, some standing in pairs, but all collected to witness a wild dance performed by six men in the centre. The left, as usual, is occupied by the musicians, who are all women, and the dancers are certainly exerting themselves in a manner quite unknown in the East in modern times, and which could hardly be surpassed in the ballet of a modern opera house. No religious significance seems to be attached to the ceremony. It appears to be only an amusement of the palace.

This cannot be said of the lower circle, Fig. 2. of Plate LXXIII. Here five men in the centre dance wildly while upholding a tray, on which is a cup, possibly the begging dish of some Bodhisattwa. It may even be supposed to be that of Buddha himself. Seventeen men, with various head-dresses, though in the same Hindu costume, dance wildly in front of these three. The women dance in the background, and behind the tray, in the centre, is seen the head of the principal personage of the ceremony, among the ladies and gentlemen of his court. He has no emblem, so it is impossible to say what his rank may be.

There can be little doubt but that this sculpture is intended to represent a great religious ceremony, on the occasion of the public display of a much-valued relic.* The wildness with which the men dance in these two sculptures is very unlike anything we are accustomed to in India at the present day among the Hindus. All the hill tribes, however, from Beerbhoom westward, to the extreme limits of Gondwana, are passionately addicted to dancing. The young men and women of the villages meet on all festal occasions, and at certain seasons of the year dance all the night through, and with as much zest and as violent action as any Celtic Highlander could display.† We must never overlook the fact that these sculptures do not represent the Aryans—at least certainly not in their purity—but the aborigines, or tribes of very mixed blood, and dancing with them was a passion. I am afraid drinking was so also.

As before remarked, this bas-relief is an exact reproduction of the central circle of the pillar, Plate LXVII., except that there a man with a seven-headed snake hood appears among the performers. From this circumstance, and others to be mentioned further on, I am inclined to believe that if we had the whole Rail we should find the same subjects repeated possibly as often as four times, once in each quadrant, and with very little variation. This I think is almost certainly the case with the inner Rail, but this is the only instance of a duplicate which I have yet found belonging to the outer enclosure.

---

* Fa-Hian mentions having seen the begging dish of Buddha in Afghanistan, and also "un vase où Foë a craché ; il est de pierre et de la même couleur que le pot de Foë" (page 27), and he describes the honours paid to them and to other relics which he saw, but he does not mention dances as part of the ceremonies. According to the usually received tradition, the form of the pot here displayed is not that of the begging dish of a priest, but it may be his spittoon !

† Campbell's Ethnology, J.A. S. B., Special Report, 1866, page 182., et seq., and the Government Reports on the Central Provinces, passim.

AMRAVATI. PLATE LXXIV.

PORTION OF INTERNAL FACE OF FRIEZE OF OUTER ENCLOSURE.

PLATE LXXIV.

THIS bas-relief* is the pendant to that represented in the photographs, Plate LXV., Fig. 3. It is indeed earlier in Buddhist chronology, as that represented the birth of Buddha, this only the annunciation. It is divided into three compartments. In the first sits Śuddhodana, the father of Buddha, surrounded by the gentlemen of his court. There are no ladies present, which is unusual.

In the central division, Buddha, symbolized by the white Elephant, descends from the Heaven Tûshita,. borne by celestial dwarfs and surrounded by Devatâs. An umbrella of state is borne before him, and music and dancing accompany him. In the third division, Mâyâ is represented asleep on her couch. Four men guard the four angles of her bed, and her women stand or sit on either side. She dreams she sees the white Elephant descend from Heaven and enter her womb. As this same subject has already been presented in Plate LXV., and will occur again, it is not necessary to describe it more particularly here. It is evidently as great a favourite with the Buddhists as the Annunciation is with early Christian painters.

The preceding twenty-six Plates may be sufficient to convey a correct impression of the form of the great outer enclosure of the Amravati Tope, and of the mode in which it was decorated; but in extent they can hardly be considered as representing more than a tenth or a twelfth of the whole. Even supposing that some of the subjects may have been repeated in different quadrants of the Rail, still the whole conveys a marvellous impression of the fertility of invention and patient labour with which the Indians in all ages decorated their religious edifices. There are temples both in India and in Cambodia which equal Amravati in this respect, but in none of these, so far as I am aware, is the art so dramatic, or the story told with such distinctness or such elegance, when looked at from an outside point of view.

It would be extremely interesting if any ancient traveller had left us even an indication of what such a monument was intended by its founders to express; none such, I fear, exist. Yet when Fa-Hian visited Ceylon in the year 410, he describes the preparation made for the great annual festival in honour of the celebrated Tooth relic; on which occasion it was conveyed in procession, from Anurâdhapura to Mehentele, a distance of about six miles. After the preliminary ceremonies, he goes on to say, " The king thus disposes or hangs up on the two sides of the route representations " of the 500 successful manifestations in which Buddha had assumed various forms, " such as the transformation into lightning (?), into the stag-horse, or the king of " the elephants, &c. These, painted in different colours, are executed with care, and

* The slab from which this drawing was made was presented by Colonel Mackenzie to the Museum of the Asiatic Society of Bengal, where it now is. It was engraved for M. Foucaux's Translation of the Lalita-Vistara, Plates III. to VI.

"look like life."* I have already had occasion to remark† that the Ceylonese mode of making Rails seemed to depend on some such arrangement. Instead of a continuous stone screen, as at Sanchi or Amravati, they consist of stone posts adapted to hang tapestries or pictures upon, and I fancy that this pictorial display described by Fa-Hian is the counterpart of what we see in stone on the banks of the Kistnah. The Amravati Rail may have been in progress while Fa-Hian was in Ceylon, and both displays were, if I mistake not, got up in honour of the sacred Tooth.

The sculptures of the Amravati Rail were at one time painted, and traces of colour may still be detected in the recesses of the sculptures. When this was the case, the difference between the temporary decoration along the path through which the Tooth was borne in triumph in Ceylon, and the permanent procession path at Amravati, would not be so great in appearance.

We must wait, however, till all the Rails known to exist in India are published before these and many other points can be settled in a satisfactory manner.

Perhaps the most interesting point, regarding it at least for our present purposes, is that it is a purely original and Buddhist form of art. It hardly seems doubtful but that the unhewn circles of stones that exist at Amravati and all over the western world are the rude originals out of which it grew, first into such a circular enclosure as we find at Stonehenge, then into such a Rail as we find at Sanchi, and lastly into such a screen as this. It is the blossoming of a long series of attempts which probably would have for ever remained rude in the hands of the western nations, but which Indian taste fashioned into beauty, as we see it here.

Besides its history, however, and its originality, this outer Rail at Amravati is to be admired for its elegance and appropriateness. I do not know of any architectural form which, in such a climate, is or could be more beautiful than this. The sculptures on the walls of a temple could not be so well lighted or so well displayed, and to a certain extent must always be subordinated to the architecture. Here the two are perfectly in accord, helping one another, and as the "temenos" enclosing a sacred spot, and uniting without hiding a group of sacred buildings, I do not know where to look for anything combining so many excellences of design as this encircling screen of the great Temple of the Diamond Sands.

---

* Foĕ-Kouĕ-Ki, p. 335.

† Ante, p. 82.

RESTORATION OF A PORTION OF INNER ENCLOSURE.

SCALE.

1 2 3 4 5 6 FT.

PLATE LXXV.

The inner Rail of the Amravati Tope that bounded the procession path on the side next the centre, was richer and more elaborately carved than the great outer Rail, though inferior both in dimensions and in architectural design. It was, in the first place, only half its height, or 6 feet above the path, as compared with 12 feet on the other side. It had, however, some metallic finishing on the top, which is now lost, and must have added not only to its height but to its architectural effect. The holes by which the metal cornice was fastened to the marble still remain, but no trace of the metal itself; and I have failed to detect any representation of this inner Rail from which it might be restored. My impression is that it must have been a range of Trisuls, not unlike fleurs de lys; but this is only a guess.

A portion of this Rail is restored in Plate LXXV., from fragments that undoubtedly belong to it, and its vertical dimensions and arrangements are certain, so far as it goes; but I cannot feel certain how far the Dagobas were apart, nor whether the other parts were arranged exactly as I have placed them. The arrangements probably varied in parts, but could not have been very different from what is here suggested.

My impression is that there were twelve representations of the Dagoba in each quadrant, and that they were spaced about 10 feet apart from the centre, and that the same representations were repeated four times, or once in each quadrant. My reason for this supposition is, that in the Elliot and Mackenzie Collections we have thirty different representations of Dagobas, of which twenty-seven or twenty-eight certainly belonged to this Rail, and the principal emblem on the front of each is repeated as follows:—

Buddha seated on the Naga, with hood - -	3	times.
Ditto, without Naga - - - - -	3	,,
Ditto, standing preaching - - - -	4	,,
Ditto, with Horse - - - - -	1	,,
The Chakra or Wheel emblem occurs - -	4	,,
The Horse - - - - - -	3	,,
The Feet enfolded in the Naga - - -	3	,,
The Tree - - - - - -	1	,,
The Relic Casket - - - - -	1	,,
The Naga Raja, with attendants - - -	1	,,
The great five-headed Naga alone - - -	6	,,
	30	,,

It is with reference to the last alone I am in doubt. Some of the Naga Dagobas do undoubtedly belong to this Rail; others in the Mackenzie Collection may not. It is a little difficult to judge from the drawings; from the sculptures it is always easy to determine to which Rail any bas-relief belonged, or whether it formed part of the decoration of some other building.

Looking at the above list, it will be seen that some subjects are repeated four times, several thrice, others, it is true, only once, and we miss one subject to make up our twelve. Still, considering how small a portion of the Rail we have, and that the subjects were not selected, but picked up by accident, the inference seems fair that there may have been twelve subjects, and each was repeated four times.*

Whether the Chakras with their pillars, or the steles terminating in Dagobas, were placed exactly as shown in the restoration, must for the present be an open question, but one not of much importance. The frieze was certainly arranged as shown, but alas its metal crowning ornament is gone and cannot be restored. All these parts are repeated in the following Plates, where they will be again referred to. The central object has not been repeated, being too much damaged to be of much artistic importance; but it is one of the most interesting fragments of the Rail, and if it was repeated, as I suppose, in each quadrant, it would be interesting if another copy could be found. It contains the whole creed of Amravati. At the bottom we have the throne, with the relic Droṇa; behind that the Tree. In the central compartment the Wheel with garlands, upon or behind the throne, and men worshipping; and the whole crowned by the Dagoba with its Rail, its five steles, its lions, and the five-headed Naga in the place of honour. The worshippers, both terrestrial and celestial, have been so defaced as to be hardly perceptible in the photograph, though plain enough in the marble. We miss both Buddha and the Trisul, except around the Wheel; but otherwise this one sculpture contains a fair epitome of the religious faith to which this gorgeous monument was dedicated.

This inner circle has been so ruined that it is difficult to make out now where the entrances were, by which access through it to the interior was obtained. Judging from what we find at Sanchi and elsewhere, we may feel certain it could not be direct. Care was taken to hide from those outside what was passing in the interior, so as to add mystery to sanctity. My conviction would be, that the entrance was past the ends of the small advanced segment shown in front of the Southern Gateway, were it not that Colonel Mackenzie's plan (Plate XLVII.) shows two slabs placed there, blocking the passage. I do not, however, gather from his descriptions that the stones marked red were actually standing *in situ* when he was there, but only that they were found lying about, and that their places could be recognized. Joining the two segments, as shown in the plan, is just such a suggestion as an over-clever draughtsman would make; but if so, it is a mistake I am afraid there is now no means of rectifying. All I know of the subject would lead me to suppose that they did not exist there, and that the seven detached stones originally stood alone in the centre of the procession path and unconnected with the rest of the Rail.

---

* If this theory is correct, the two standing Buddhas in the restoration in this Plate would not have appeared in the same quadrant. Unfortunately, they are the only two slabs in the collection which are perfect and of moderate width, so as to fit my scale.

ELEVATION OF A PORTION OF INNER ENCLOSURE.

SCALE. 1 2 4 FT.

ELEVATION OF A PORTION OF INNER ENCLOSURE.

SCALE. 1 2 4 FT.

PLATES LXXVI. AND LXXVII.

THESE two Plates represent the two most perfect Dagobas from the inner Rail which are now in the India House Collection. They were sent home by Colonel Mackenzie, and were among the principal ornaments of the old museum in Leadenhall Street, which they reached about the year 1820. It is probable that other slabs of the same description exist in the museums at Calcutta and Madras. As their details are so minute they have been photographed to twice the scale of the others, or 2 inches to 1 foot.

For reasons to be given hereafter, when describing the central building, I believe these Dagobas to be free copies, "mutatis mutandis," of one which existed in the centre of the circle, and which, having become pre-eminent for some reason or other, in the fourth century, these Rails were erected to enclose it; but whether this is admitted or not, they are interesting as showing how Dagobas were ornamented, or how at least the Buddhists thought they ought to be ornamented, at the time this enclosure was built. If we compare the very plain Rail at Sanchi with the very elaborately sculptured enclosure at Amravati, we ought to expect the same progress towards elaboration in the Dagobas themselves. Even if we assume that the older Dagoba was as little ornamented as it now appears, it seems natural to expect from comparison with the Rails, that in the fourth century the Dagobas may have been as richly sculptured as these representations would lead us to expect they were.

All these sculptures represent the Dagobas as surrounded by a Rail four discs in height, whereas the great Rail has only three. The Rail in these representations is surmounted by a frieze, sometimes of animals, sometimes of wreaths. Inside the Rail, and to the same height, the Dagoba is perpendicular, and ornamented by pilasters, between which are the usual emblems, terminating upwards in the Dagoba, the Wheel, the Serpent, or the Tree, as the case may be. Above this are two rows of sculptures, divided into panels, the lower generally single figures or emblems, but sometimes also groups; the upper always historical groups, generally three on each quadrant. Among these it is not difficult to recognize many of the scenes described above. For instance, on each side of the five steles in Plate LXXVII. we recognize the subjects already depicted in Plates LXII. and LXV., and others may be made out. The central right-hand upper panel in Plate LXXVI. represents a battle scene, which ought not to appear on a Buddhist monument, but seems the same as that on the small pillar, Plate LXI. The medallions, also, higher up in the dome, all contain subjects which are repeated over and over again elsewhere.

One of the remarkable peculiarities of these sculptured Dagobas is the five steles which occur over the principal figure in each face, twenty in all. What they symbolize it is difficult to say. It may be the five Buddhas of the present Kalpa, or the five Dhyâni Buddhas, or the five Elements. Everything in Buddhism goes by fives.

Generally the central one is crowned by a Dagoba, and on their lower parts are represented Wheels, Trees, Dagobas, and other emblems, sometimes singly, sometimes in pairs. In Plate LXXVII. by an inscription recording the donation.*

Inside the Rail are generally four other pillars or lâts, bearing figures or emblems.

The dome is always surmounted by a Tee with an umbrella and flags, and when the slab is perfect, floating figures, but without wings or griffins to ride upon, as is generally the case at Sanchi, are always represented as worshipping the Tee. That they are intended as celestial beings is certain, and this being so, perhaps the best name to give them is Devas or Devatâs.

As before mentioned, the principal figure is generally varied. On Plate LXXVI. it is Buddha seated on the folds of a great Naga, with an inner hood of seven and an outer of fourteen heads, with the usual worshipping figures. In Plate LXXVII. it is Buddha standing with his right hand raised. The worshipping figures on his left are Nagas, on his right a man and woman in the usual Hindu costume.

Outside the Rail a man or a woman on either side of the entrance is always represented either as purchasing offerings from persons who are selling them, or are bringing offerings, generally borne on the heads of dwarfs. On either side of the entrance is always placed a vase,† which will be alluded to hereafter.

All this is practically new to Indian antiquaries. Hitherto our ideas regarding structural Dagobas have been derived from the present appearance of those at Sanchi or Manikyala, or from the very imperfect representations we possess of those in Afghanistan, and these are all now at least plain or nearly so. The one which it seems was intended to have been as richly ornamented as these was that at Sârnâth; but it was left incomplete, probably in the tenth or eleventh century, which seems to be the age to which its decoration belongs.‡ Had it been completed it would have been even more elaborately decorated than those at Amravati. Those in Caves hardly help us in this respect; they probably were painted, and the colours having perished, there is nothing left from which to form an opinion. Those in Ceylon, too, are in much too ruinous a state to aid in this inquiry, so that these representations on the inner Rail are really the only authentic documents we have, and they thus become in this respect invaluable.

---

* Appendix E., No. VIII.

† One which belonged to the central building is shown on Plate XCVI. It is photographed to the usual scale.

‡ Asiatic Researches, IX. 203.

FIG, 1.

FIG, 2.

FIG, 3.

ELEVATIONS OF PORTIONS OF INNER ENCLOSURE.

SCALE 1 INCH TO 1 FOOT.

PLATE LXXVIII.

THE upper figure in this Plate is the only slab in the India Museum representing the Naga in the place of honour on the Dagoba.* But there are among the drawings in the Mackenzie Collection six others similar to this, with merely such variations of detail as occur in all these representations. Generally speaking, the Naga Dagobas are less profusely ornamented with sculpture than those more essentially Buddhistical in their arrangements, but the subjects all belong to the same class. In this one, for instance, we have Mâyâ's dream, the birth of Buddha, and other well-known subjects in the medallions on the dome, and the Wheel, the Tree, the Trisul, and other familiar emblems on the band under the five steles. The Serpent of course occurs there also. The Rail, too, is identical with that of the other Dagobas. The frieze is generally of the roll pattern (Plate LVI.), and there are the four Lions as usual, belonging to each entrance.

What we really do miss, and what seems the characteristic distinction between the two, is the absence of worshippers. As will be observed, the panel under the Naga is blank. In a more purely Buddhist Dagoba it would have had two or more kneeling or worshipping figures. There are no persons outside the Rail bearing offerings, and there are no historical bas-reliefs.. The Nagas had no history apparently. All this makes it difficult to say whether these purely Naga Dagobas were worshipped generally or were appropriated to a particular class like the Dasyus or Takshaks.† My impression is, that at the time these sculptures were executed the Naga and the Buddha were so mixed up together, and so nearly equal, that it is impossible to draw any distinction between them, either as to the worship or their worshippers.

The two lower photographs in this Plate represent the obverse and reverse of the same slab. The Dagoba itself is the duplicate of that represented in the last Plate, and is so very nearly similar that at first sight they might be mistaken for the same. On close examination, however, the differences are easily detected. The Rail in Plate LXVII. has an animal—this has a roll frieze. The Naga worshippers are on Buddha's right instead of his left. The position and character of the upper range of bas-reliefs are slightly altered. The subjects of the medallions are changed. In the last Plate the subjects represented in them were Buddha seated, and on either hand the men dancing, and bearing the relic trays on their heads. In this Plate the scenes are the Annunciation and the birth of Buddha. The two may, however, be taken as a fair example of the extent of variation with which the same design was repeated four times, once in each quadrant of the Rail.‡

---

* I of course except the central slab in Plate LXXV., and such representations as occur in Plate LXIV., and elsewhere, where the Dagoba with the serpent occurs in conjunction with other objects.

† In the Mackenzie Collection, Plate XIII., two Hindus are worshipping a Naga Dagoba; but from their position it is not quite clear that they are worshipping the Naga.

‡ The reader will of course bear in mind the scale to which the one is photographed is double that of the other.

The great interest of this slab, however, resides in the sculptures on the back of it. They are very much larger and ruder than anything else at Amravati, and so different in design that they must evidently belong to another age than those we have been describing. On the other hand the figures, the tree, even the flying harpy-like figures above, are so nearly identical with what are found at Sanchi (Plates XXIV., XXV., XXVI., XXVII., XXVIII., and XXIX.), but not found elsewhere at Amravati, that we can hardly help ascribing them to the same age; obviously executed by an inferior artist, but still nearly identical.

The question thus arises, Was there an older building at Amravati, contemporary with the Gateways at Sanchi, which was desecrated when the inner Rail was erected, and its slabs used up for the new buildings? Or was it *in situ* when the elaborate sculpture of Fig. 3. was added on the other side of it? Taking all the circumstances of the case into consideration, my impression is that the latter may be the true solution of the difficulty. According to this hypothesis, that which is now the inner Rail was originally the outer Rail of the Tope, sculptured, like Fig. 2., on the inside, but probably plain on its outer face. When the great outer Rail was added in the fourth century, and the procession path carried outside this Rail, then these elaborate sculptures were added to match those of the great outer Rail then being erected. All this is so completely in accordance with what we find being done in Hindu temples in the south of India down to the present day, that I can hardly bring myself to doubt that this was what took place in this instance.

On the other hand, however, it may also be that both these Rails are parts of an entirely new design commenced only in the fourth century, and that this slab belonged to some building which may have been removed in order that it might not interrupt their alignment. Whichever hypothesis we adopt, the conclusion is the same as regards the age of the sculptures on the front and back of the slab. It proves incontestably that there was at Amravati a building as old as the Gateways at Sanchi, if not older. My impression, indeed, is that this sculpture is the most ancient of any represented in this volume. It is so difficult, however, to know what allowance should be made for locality or the personal equation of the artist, that it is impossible to speak positively on such a subject.

As before remarked (page 155) the coins found by Colonel Mackenzie would lead us to suppose that Amravati was a place of importance as early at least as the Christian era; this sculpture, therefore, not only tends to confirm that surmise, but aids us materially in understanding the history of the place.*

---

* A curious piece of collateral evidence to the same effect is obtained from the inscriptions at Karlee and those Western Caves which date from about or before the Christian era. The name of Yavana Dhanaka cheka frequently occurs in them either as an artist or a benefactor, but whether as one person or several has not been determined. Dr. Stevenson (J. B. B. R. A. S., vol. V., pp. 11, 20, &c.) translates the name as the "Greek Xenocrates." General Cunningham, with much more probability, makes it the "Yavana of Dhanaka cheka"! The first reading we may safely reject. If the second is established, it will be interesting to find our city on the Kistnah sufficiently important and artistic to have lent assistance to these great undertakings. At present, however, the indication is too vague for much reliance to be placed upon it.

FIG, 1.

FIG, 2.

FIG, 3.

ELEVATIONS OF PORTIONS OF INNER ENCLOSURE.

SCALE 1 INCH TO 1 FOOT.

ELEVATIONS OF PORTIONS OF INNER ENCLOSURE.
SCALE 1 INCH TO 1 FOOT.

FIG. 1.

FIG. 3.

FIG. 2.

ELEVATIONS OF PORTIONS OF INNER ENCLOSURE.

SCALE 1 INCH TO 1 FOOT.

PLATES LXXIX., LXXX., AND LXXXI.

THESE three Plates contain nine photographs of fragments of the Dagobas of the inner Rail, all to the scale of 1 inch to 1 foot. They are not all the examples which the Museum Collection contains, but they are probably sufficient to illustrate the variety as well as the monotony of these representations.

In Fig. 1., Plate LXXIX., the principal object of worship is the Wheel, but the Naga appears very prominently on the Dagoba.* The same object is repeated in Fig. 3., which, though very much broken, is a better and more perfect piece of sculpture than the other, tending to show, as other circumstances do, that the different quadrants were not all exactly of the same age.

The lowest figure on the left hand of the same Plate contains a form we have not yet met with. The principal object here is a representation of the sacred feet enveloped in the folds of the Naga, and worshipped by Naga men and women.

The emblem has unfortunately disappeared from Fig. 1., Plate LXXX. This is to be regretted, as it seems a beautiful fragment, and the two children below, the panel in which it ought to appear, betoken something new.

Fig. 2. and 3. of this Plate, and Fig. 3. of Plate LXXXI., instead of the emblems we are usually accustomed to, contain two medallions. The upper, representing the worship of the Horse, the lower Buddha seated cross-legged, surrounded by listeners or adorers.

As we have frequently had occasion to remark, the Horse plays an important part in the sculptures at Amravati. It is once represented as honoured at Sanchi (Plate XXXV.), but this form of worship occurs here several times, but nowhere so prominently as in these three Dagobas. (It is to be presumed that there was a fourth.)

It is not easy to say what we are to understand from the prominence of the Horse in such a position as this. Is it an importation from Scythia, brought by immigrants from that country? Is it the Horse of the Sun, or of Poseidon? Is it the Avalokiteśvara of the Thibetan fables? Some one must answer who is more familiar than I am with Eastern mythology. At present it will be sufficient to recall to memory how important a part the Horse sacrifice or Aśwamedha plays in the Mahâbhârata, and in all the mythic history of India. What is still more curious is that the worship of the Horse still seems to linger in remote parts of India. At least in a recent work by Mr. Hislop, missionary at Nagpore, edited by Sir R. Temple, he describes the religion of the Gonds in the following nine words:— "All introduce figures of the horse in their worship." Other instances might no doubt be found if looked for, but the subject is new and unthought of.

In all these Dagobas in which the horse occurs, the objects next in importance

* This slab has been so long exposed on the external wall of Fife House, that it is nearly destroyed, and its details can but with difficulty be made out.

are the sacred feet. They occur on each side of the five steles under a great umbrella, but what the connexion between the two may be is by no means clear.

The principal representation on the Dagoba, Fig. 1., Plate LXXXI., is a repetition of the scenes depicted in the upper circle, Plate LXII.,—the worship of the relic casket by the Naga Raja; but so far as can be made out, there does not seem to be anything in the other bas-reliefs on this Dagoba which would enable us to identify the relic, or say whence it came. So far as execution is concerned, this is one of the most delicate as well as one of the best preserved examples belonging to the series.*

The remaining Dagoba, Fig. 2., Plate LXXXI., is the most essentially Buddhist of the whole, using the word in the sense in which we now understand it. Buddha is seated in his usual cross-legged attitude in the place of honour, and reappears in easily recognizable forms in the sculptures above. Yet, if I mistake not, on the very top of the dome there are the remains of a great Naga, in a position more prominent than on any other Dagoba of this class.

In all these Dagobas, when sufficiently perfect to enable the emblems to be made out, it appears that the central stele of the five was crowned by a miniature Dagoba. But on the lower part of the steles (Plate LXXX.), on the left-hand lower corner, there are in the centre a Dagoba, on each side of that the two Wheels, and then two Trees, and in others, a figure adorns the base of each stele, but without any mode by which he or they can be distinguished. Other combinations are found, both on those represented here and on those in the Mackenzie drawings, but all of the same character, and apparently without any important significance.

We shall have occasion to refer again to these miniature Dagobas when speaking of the central one, for the restoration of which they are most important. Even in themselves, however, they are as interesting as any of the slabs at Amravati, and as important as illustrations of the form of Buddhist art in the fourth or fifth century of our era.

* After they were photographed, the marbles were returned to the coach-house, and afterwards were transferred to the Military Stores, when the Fife House establishment was broken up. In neither position were they, nor are they accessible; there are, consequently, many points which my more educated eye might enable me now to detect, which I overlooked when I had access to them.

FIG, 1

FIG, 2.

FIG, 3.

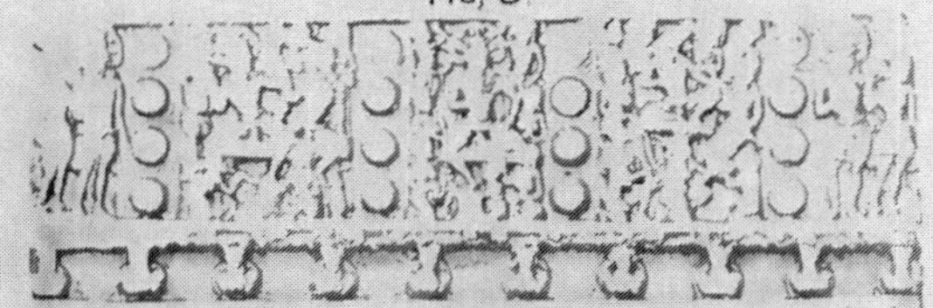

FIG, 6.

FIG, 7.

FIG, 4.

FIG, 8.

FIG, 5.

FRAGMENTS OF FRIEZES OF INNER ENCLOSURE.

FIG. 1 ENLARGED SCALE, FIGS. 2 TO 8 1 INCH TO 1 FOOT.

AMRAVATI.

PLATE LXXXIII.

FIG. I.

FIG. 2.

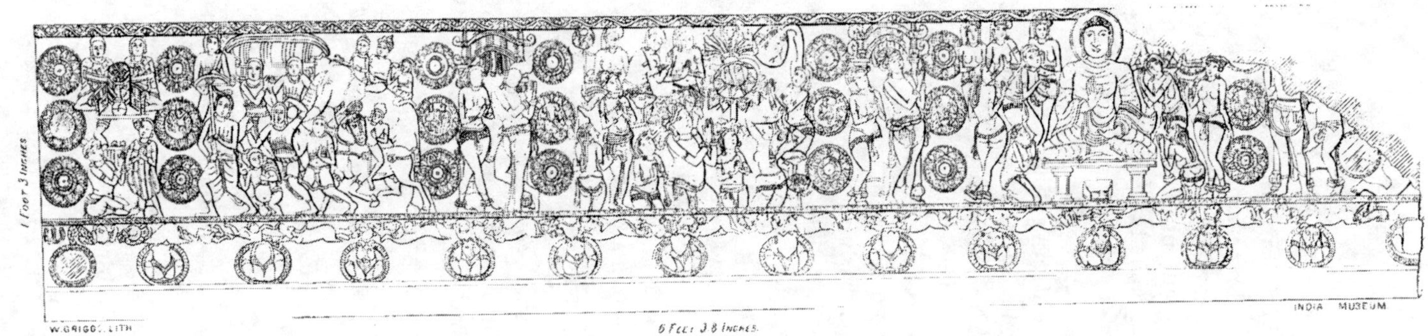

FRAGMENTS OF FRIEZES OF INNER ENCLOSURE.

PLATES LXXXII. AND LXXXIII.

We have unfortunately very few fragments of the frieze that crowned the inner Rail. Like that of the outer, it seems to have been one of the most elegant as well as interesting parts of the whole. The India Museum contains no specimen of the best quadrant, but one found its way by accident into the British Museum,* and is photographed to an enlarged scale in Fig. 1. Plate LXXXII. Two others are represented by drawings in the Mackenzie Collection, and are reproduced in Figs. 1. and 2. Plate LXXXIII. Figs. 6. and 7. Plate LXXXII. belong probably to a different quadrant, and Figs. 2. and 3. on the same Plate are certainly from another part of the enclosure from that represented in the three fragments just enumerated.

The whole frieze was very ingeniously divided into compartments by conventional Rails, with three discs or knobs. The central one is sculptured, but the upper and lower knobs are merely lotus flowers, like those of the great Rail. Between each of these pillars is a small compartment, containing a man and a woman or an object of worship, while the larger compartments always contain a historical subject. I am not aware that any more ingenious or pleasing mode of treating such a sculptural representation is to be found in any other building in any part of the world.

In Fig. 1. Plate LXXXII. we have, first on the left, the man bearing the relic on his head, and men, women, and Nagas following in wild dance (vide ante, Plates LXVII., LXXIII.). In the centre we have Buddha, or rather Prince Siddhârtha, with his horse, apparently blessing little children. In the third a Bodhisattwa—he has no glory—expounding to a Naga people, all of whom have snakes at the back of their heads.

In the small compartments we have on the left a Hindu man and woman in the usual costume; on the right a man and woman in a costume betokening a colder climate; but in order to prevent its being understood to be in a colder country, a palm tree is introduced between them. Are they Scythians? Do they bring the

* The history of this slab is so curious that it may be worth recording. When I was at the Crystal Palace, Monti the sculptor one day asked me to come to his place in Great Marlborough Street to see a piece of Indian sculpture which belonged to a friend of his, and had been left in his charge. I was so struck with its beauty that I got it moulded, and three casts were taken. One was presented to the Crystal Palace, one to the Asiatic Society, and a third to the India Museum. The two first were destroyed in the fire in December 1866; the third luckily was safe. When I became familiar with the Amravati marbles, I at once recognized this slab as belonging to that Tope, and immediately set to work to try and find out what had become of it, but for a long time in vain. One day, however, talking to Mr. Vaux, of the British Museum, about the Amravati discovery, he said, "We have a slab with a Gupta inscription on it in the cellars," and sent a man with me to point it out, when I at once recognized my old friend. It seems an officer of the Museum was getting his hair cut in Great Marlborough Street, when the barber, knowing who his customer was, asked him to look at a piece of marble lying in the back yard. The officer had the good taste to see its value, got a grant from the trustees for 10*l*., and purchased it. I may mention that there is also in the British Museum a figure from one of the Gates at Sanchi, though how it got there nobody knows. There is nothing from Sanchi in the India Museum. This therefore is the only opportunity that exists in this country of comparing the two styles from actual examples.

horse? The man who kneels in front of it is in the same costume, and the whole may be parts of one story or one symbolism.*

It was on the top of the Museum slab that I first perceived the holes into which the crowning metal finish was fixed. From their form and position I would have had little hesitation as to what they were intended for, but the fact that every ridge in the great Serpent temple of Nakhon Vat in Cambodia was originally adorned by a metal ornament, removes at once any doubts that might exist. This inner Rail being apparently the last thing erected, there are no representations of it in any other part of the building, and till one is found the exact form of the ornament must remain doubtful. As before suggested, my impression is that there was a repetition of Trisuls.

Fig. 1. Plate LXXXIII. contains in its two compartments what are evidently intended as parts of the same story. On the left hand a man steps into the scale of a steelyard which another is holding in his hand, while another in the foreground holds a bird in his hand as if intending it should be weighed against the man. In the second compartment the first man seated on a throne holding the bird in his hand expounds the moral of the transaction for the delight and benefit of his hearers, if not for that of modern mankind, though I have no doubt the legend might be traced.†

In the lower lithograph we have, first, the Trisul emblem on the throne, with two priests behind (compare Plates LXVIII. and LXXI.). Then a procession, with a palanquin, elephant, horsemen, &c. (compare Plates LXIV. and LXXXIV.). In the centre the sacred feet on the lotus shaded by the Naga, and worshipped by Naga people (compare Plate LXXIX. Fig. 2.). Then Buddha, in his usual attitude, preaching to a female congregation. There does not seem to be any attributes by which the figures in the smaller central compartment can be identified.

Fig. 2. Plate LXXXII. is scarcely historical. It only contains figures of the Naga Raja in various attitudes and with various accompaniments. The principal object in Fig. 3. is the adoration of Buddha by the white elephant. It unfortunately is very much weather-worn.

Figs. 4. and 5. are portions of two smaller friezes. In the first it is the horse that is honoured (compare Plate LXXX.). In the other the relic borne on a man's head. This is so well preserved that if it were not so small we might almost hope to make out what is intended. Till access can be obtained to the slab itself it must remain a puzzle.

Figs. 6. and 7. belong to the principal frieze, but are so weather-worn and so fragmentary that their subjects can hardly be made out.

Fig. 8. belongs to another frieze, and does not seem to form part of the Rail, but belongs apparently to some detached building.

---

* The inscription in Fig. 1. will be found, Appendix E. Fig. XX., and translated in so far as its weather-worn character will allow. It is one of the most interesting of the series, as it records a gift to the Mâhâ Chaitya of Danakakata. If this is established, it settles the question of this being the place described by Hiouen Thsang as Danakacheka. The other long inscription, Plate LXXXIII. Fig. 1., will be found in the same Appendix, No. II. It is unfortunately only known from a transcript by Colonel Mackenzie's draughtsman, who did not know the character, but it can be made out tolerably satisfactorily.

† Is it the legend. J. A. S. B. vol. XVII. part II. p. 73.

AMRAVATI.

PLATE LXXXIV.

FIG. 1.

FIG. 2.

FIG. 3.

W. GRIGGS LITH

INDIA MUSEUM

FRAGMENTS OF FRIEZES.

FEMALE FIGURES FORMING PORTION OF INNER ENCLOSURE.

W. GRIGGS, LITH. INDIA MUSEUM

FRAGMENT OF BAS RELIEF.

PLATES LXXXIV., LXXXV., AND LXXXVI.

PLATE LXXXIV.

FIGS. 2. and 3. of Plate LXXXIV. represent two other portions of the frieze of the inner Rail. From the style of sculpture and the arrangement of the lotus discs, they evidently belong to a different part of the Rail from those previously quoted, and have all the appearance of being the most modern of the sculptures at Amravati. From their character I should guess that they might belong to the sixth century, but as something of this appearance may be due to the draftsmen, this indication must not be implicitly relied upon.

The figure seated on the couch between his two wives in Fig. 2. is probably the same as is depicted in Plate LXXIII. Fig. 1. The interest of the story evidently hangs on the three old women in the foreground, whoever they may be.

In Fig. 3. we have Buddha represented in the usual attitudes in which he appears in all sculpture subsequent to the fourth or fifth century, but in which he hardly appears before that time.

Fig. 1. is also of an inferior character as a piece of sculpture, but is curious as representing what appears to be a kind of litter borne on men's shoulders, in which five persons are seated. Two men only are represented as carrying it, though it must have required at least a dozen. It is introduced here not because of its beauty, but because it may serve to illustrate a somewhat similar representation in Plate LXIV. Fig. 1. If, however, it is only a litter or palanquin, this would seem to militate against the idea expressed when describing that Plate, that it was the boat-shaped ark bearing relics from Ceylon. In this case the difficulty of ascertaining what this action may represent is very much augmented by the fact that the marble is only a fragment, and we do not see to whom or towards what object the procession is tending. So far as can be made out, the persons in the litter are bringing as presents those objects—jewels or relics—which are displayed in front of them, to some person or shrine that was depicted in the front part now broken off; and it may be that Danta Kumara and Hemachalâ were thus borne on their return to Dhanakacheka. At present, however, I am afraid the materials do not exist for determining this question.

PLATE LXXXV.

These two female figures, with several others, were used as pilasters either at the angles of the inner Rail or in the centre, when it was desirable to separate the subjects into groups. They cannot be said to be pleasing, showing all the defects of the style in an exaggerated manner, but they are certainly curious. That on the left bears apparently a torch in her right hand, and behind her head is seen the familiar snake. The figure on the right holds a dagger run through a human head, and in her left another head held up by a handle. Whether these are to be considered as heads severed from human bodies, or as vessels in the form of heads, is by no means clear. If the figure were Durgâ, or any shadowing of her appearance on the stage, we would at once acknowledge them as skulls, but in the absence of the marble itself, we must not speculate too boldly.

The niches in which these figures stand are curious reminiscences of the Sanchi Gateways.

PLATE LXXXVI.

The principal interest in this piece of sculpture centres in the bearded figure in the lower division. Except those represented in Plate LXX., he is the only man with that appendage* at Amravati.

That he is of the same race as those I have called Dasyus or Takshaks at Sanchi is evident, not only from this, but from the form of his kilt and his mode of dressing his hair. From the animals that accompany him he is intended to be represented as a dweller in the woods, and his hermitage is seen behind him—no longer a circular thatched hut, but a square-built cell. Beside it is a tumulus, in a square enclosure, similar to that represented in Plate XXXII., and with a pot of flowers at each angle. Still, from the absence of a Tee, it remains uncertain whether we are to consider this as a Dagoba, or a Tomb, or a Temple of the older people, from whom the Buddhist may afterwards have adopted this form for their Dagobas. My own impression is, that the latter is the most likely hypothesis. From the reverential mode in which the women approach him, and the manner in which the man in the chariot brings his gift, it is evident that the bearded man is considered a holy hermit. So far, however, from this reflecting a priestly character on those of his race at Sanchi, it appears rather that the race had become nearly extinct, and that the first time the Hindus approach one of them with reverence is on one of the latest sculptures at Amravati, when the few who remained had acquired a character of sanctity from their scarcity.

I am afraid from the style of drawing, that this bas-relief has been entrusted by Colonel Mackenzie to an inferior artist to copy, which is to be regretted, as it is one of the most interesting in the series. So far as can be judged from the style, it is one of the most modern of the whole. The chariot, the hermit, and the head-dress of the king do not occur in any other sculpture at Amravati. The altar in front of the Pipal tree is peculiar, so is the mode in which the women dress their hair. Besides all this, it does not seem, either from its style or dimensions, to belong to either of the Rails or to the central building. It probably was part of some later erection, of which no other fragment now remains, but with such evidence as this drawing affords it is not possible to say what that was or when erected.

The head-dress of the Raja in the upper division of this bas-relief is also worthy of remark. We have only once met with it before, in Plate LX., but is similar to some that are found in the Caves at Badamee, belonging probably to the ninth or tenth century. A similar head-dress is also represented by Colonel Abbott, as found in a fragment of a statue at Mullote, in the Punjab.† My impression is, that it is of Persian or rather Yavana origin.

---

* The Scythians, in Fig. 1. Plate LXXXII., ought perhaps to be excepted, but they are evidently strangers.
† J. A. S. B., vol. XVII. Plate IV. Fig. 2.

FRAGMENTS OF SCULPTURE.
SCALE 1 INCH TO 1 FOOT.

FIG, 1

FIG, 2.

FIG, 3

FIG, 4.

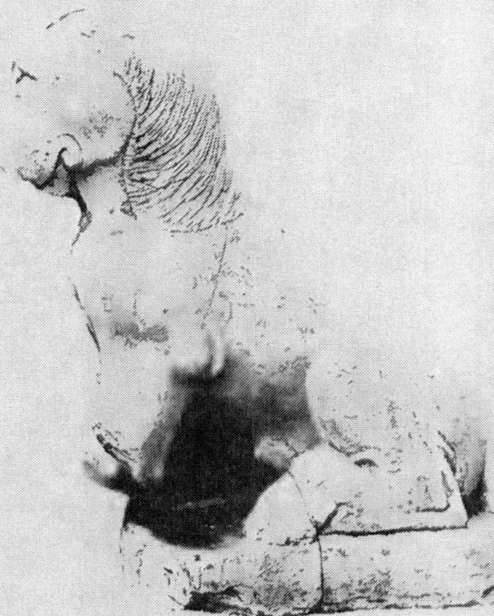

FIG, 5.

FRAGMENTS OF SCULPTURE.

SCALE 1 INCH TO 1 FOOT.

DETACHED PILLARS WITH EMBLEMS.

SCALE 1 INCH TO 1 FOOT.

PLATES LXXXVII., LXXXVIII., AND LXXXIX.

THESE three Plates contain representations of various details, some of considerable interest, but which do not belong to either of the Rails, and to which, except the lions, we cannot at present assign any definite position in the building. They are all to the scale of 1 inch to 1 foot.

No. 1. Plate LXXXVII. is a figure of Buddha, as he is usually represented in the fifth and sixth centuries. It is of no especial merit, and probably is among the most modern sculptures of the place, coeval with the fragments of the frieze (Plate LXXXIV.).

Fig. 2. represents a fragment of a frieze of the Trisul emblem, of the best age and very good execution. It did not belong to either of the Rails, nor to any building of which we have now any knowledge.

Fig. 3. represents the sacred feet of Buddha, probably of the same age, and it may be from the same building as the last. In the centre of the soles is the Chakra; above it the Trisul emblem reversed, with a swastika on each side. Below the Chakra is the swastika again, with an ornament like the crux ansata on each side. On the great toe is the Trisul, on each of the others a swastika. The whole, however, is in such low relief that it is extremely difficult to bring it out in the photograph.*

Fig. 4. is the Chakra, with the swastika and foliage, all of very elegant sculpture.

Fig. 5. is one side of the abacus of a pillar, meant to bear a lion or some other emblem. The representation on it is one we have frequently met with before of two elephants bringing offerings to the Dagoba. This is not only a favourite subject of Indian sculptors, but of Indian legends. Fa-Hian, for instance, tells the following legend of a Dagoba at Râma Grâma, about twenty miles eastward from Buddha's birthplace. The place being sterile, and there being no inhabitants, troops of elephants were continually seen bringing water in their trunks to moisten the earth, and gathering all sorts of flowers and perfumes to perform the service of the tower or Dagoba, which, by the way, was guarded by an enormous Dragon or Naga. The legend goes on to say that certain followers of the doctrine of Tao-sse were so struck by the reverential behaviour of the elephants, that they were converted to Buddhism.†

Fig. 6. represents a seven-headed Nâga of more than ordinary perfection of sculpture.

Figs. 7. 8. and 9.—An architectural fragment of great elegance, but which could not belong to any building we now know. These, with other sculptures in the collection, suffice to prove that there must have been several different edifices within the enclosure, which have been so utterly swept away that it is impossible to say now what they may have been.

---

* The worship of the sacred feet, or footprints, is one of the favourite forms of Vishnuism at the present day. At Gaya the Vishnu pud is the principal temple, and wholly devoted to this form. It succeeds Buddhism in its original seat as Juggernath superseded the Tooth relic at Puri.

† Foĕ-Kouĕ-Ki, p. 227.

PLATE LXXXVIII.

Figs. 1. and 2. in this Plate are curious as being exact elevations of the outer face of the great Rail, used evidently as a frieze to some building in the enclosure. On comparing it with the elevation in Plate XLVIII., it will be seen at once how exactly they tally. The pillars are octagon, with a central complete lotus disc, and a half-circle at top and bottom. Between the pillars are three Rails, each with a complete foliated disc or circle. Above them is the roll ornament, and below the Zöophorus or animal frieze. With such pictures the restoration, though sometimes puzzling, becomes when done perfectly authentic.

Fig. 3. is made up of fragments of one of those curious columns on which the Chakra is usually placed. A similar one, but much smaller, is shown in Plate LXXV., and another from the Mackenzie Collection is lithographed in Plate XCVIII. Four other representations of similar columns exist in that collection, all differing, but all equally fantastic. They all commence at the bottom, with the throne and the relics upon it. Behind them rises a central column of varied and fantastic design, and on each side are men riding on horses, lions, oxen, giraffes, and human-headed monsters of most varied design. This one, when complete, must have been about 13 feet in height.

Figs. 4. and 5. represent two of the lions that adorned the portals of the great Rail. If we may trust the bas-reliefs, there must originally have been four to each Gateway, or sixteen to each Rail.

PLATE LXXXIX.

This Plate represents four faces of a very beautiful octagonal pillar that once stood probably within the enclosure, and supported a statue or an emblem; most probably the former, as all the principal emblems are on its faces. There is the sacred tree in its circular enclosure, and easily distinguished as a Pipal from the form of its leaves. The wheel on its pillar is a square one,—the Lion-pillar and the Dagoba.

The foliage on three sides is the flowing lotus pattern, executed with great delicacy and elegance. On the side with the wheel it is different and more complicated, but equally beautiful. It seems, however, that the wheel should always crown a complicated arrangement of this sort, but from what motive we do not now know.

Above the emblems the pillar changed into a polygon of sixteen sides, and may have been as high again—it is now about eight feet high—before terminating with the capital, on which the crowning object stood.

The inscription merely records that it is the gift of Hagha of Gadhika, together with his son and daughter. (See Appendix E., No. V.)

AMRAVATI. PLATE XC.

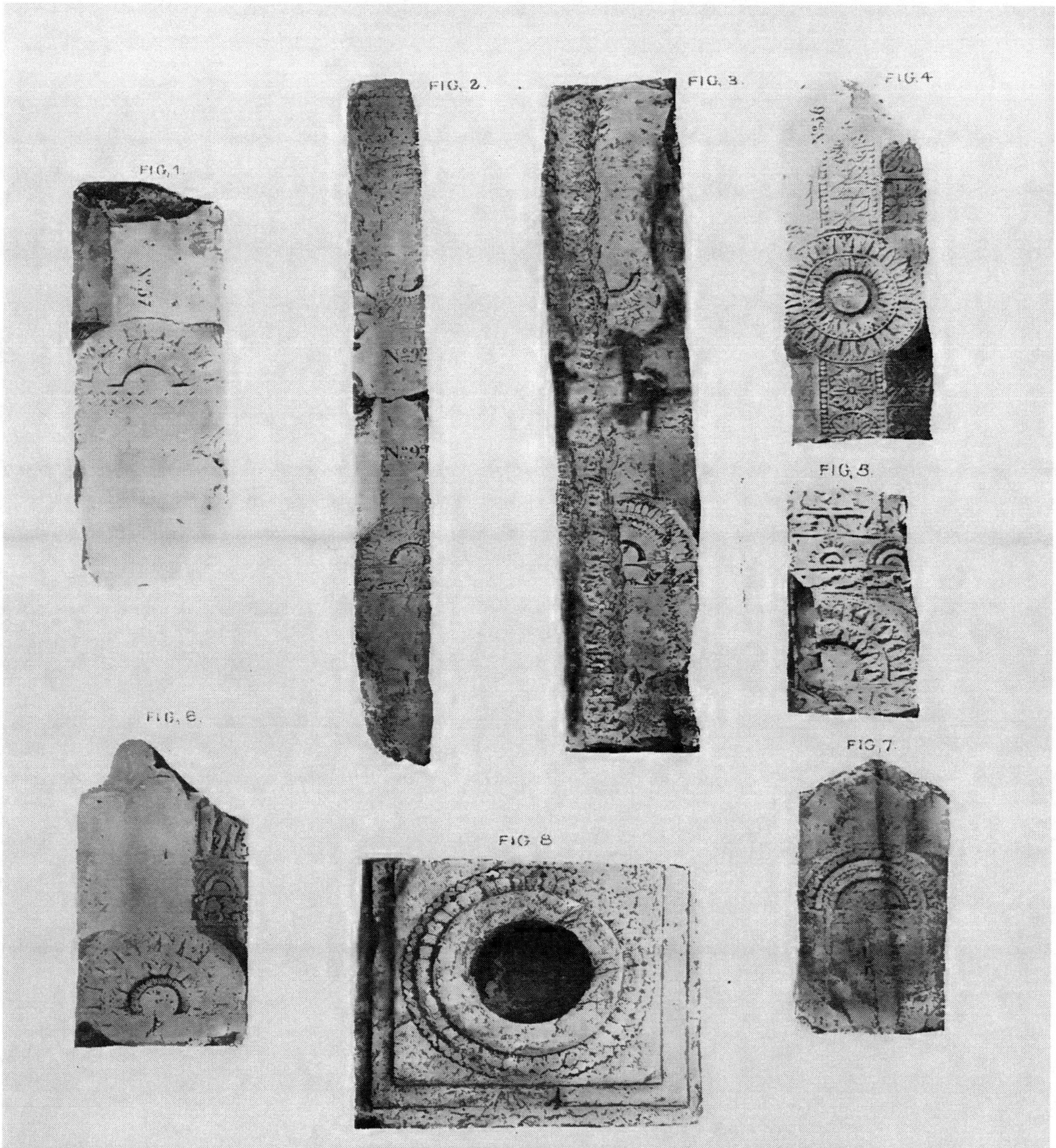

FRAGMENTS OF PILLARS.
SCALE 1 INCH TO 1 FOOT.

FIG. 1

FIG. 2.

FIG. 3

FIG. 4.

FRAGMENTS OF SCULPTURE.

SCALE 1 INCH TO 1 FOOT.

FIG, 1.

FIG 2.

FIG, 3.

FIG, 4.

FIG, 5.

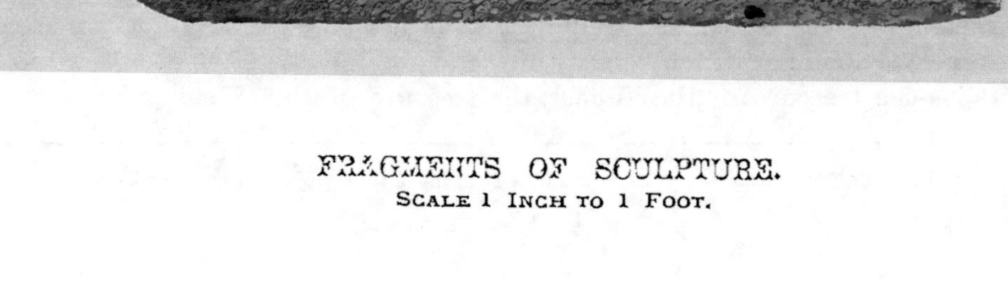

FRAGMENTS OF SCULPTURE.

SCALE 1 INCH TO 1 FOOT.

PLATES XC., XCI., AND XCII.

PLATE XC. contains seven fragments of other pillars and one base. Two of them, the first and last, have inscriptions, but so faint that it is difficult to make them out. Fig. 2. has an inscription at the top, the letters of which are beautifully legible, but unfortunately it is split down the middle, so as to be utterly unintelligible. It is not easy to say whether these are fragments of the five steles which ornamented each face of the great Dagoba, or whether they were "Stambas," bearing emblems which may have stood in various places in the enclosure. From their form and style, as well as the minute character of the inscriptions, which could not have been seen at that height, it would seem probable that they may have stood on the ground. On the other hand, however, the position of the inscription on the columns of the Dagoba, Plate LXXVII., would favour the idea that they once occupied a similar position.

PLATE XCI.

Contains four fragments of considerable interest, though it is at present impossible to say what position any of them may have occupied in the buildings within the enclosure.

The first is a Dagoba divided into compartments by pilasters, with double Lion capitals of a curious Persepolitan type, but altogether of considerable elegance. The pillars themselves, however, are of the same form as those used in the Rails, with one central circular disc, and two half circles at top and bottom. The cushion capital also recalls what we find afterwards at Elephanta and Ellora. Between them, in the place of honour, is the five-headed Naga; on the right the Wheel, and on the left the Tree. With the Dagoba, these form the four principal objects of adoration in this place. Were it not for the very wooden form of the Tee, I fancy this sculpture would be of comparatively modern date. No. 2. is simpler, but certainly more modern. The Naga here reigns supreme on the Dagoba, without any compeer. The crowd of umbrellas that crown the Tee is a curious ebullition of Hindu fancy.

The upper part of Fig. 3. is so defaced that it is difficult to make out whom it represents. It is probably, however, the same scene as recurs in Plate XCV. Fig. 1. Whatever his name may be, he is a man who possesses two wives, two friends, a horse, and an elephant, and is probably meant to be contrasted with the Raja as in the lower compartment of the bas-relief, who is a Chakravarti Raja possessed of the seven precious things which constitute human greatness, according to the Lalita-Vistara,*—the treasure of the Wheel, the treasure of the Elephant, the treasure

* Foucaux's Translation, p. 14, and plate II., where this subject is engraved.

of the Horse, the treasure of a Wife, the treasure of a Pearl, the treasure of a Major Domo, and of a Counsellor. The sequence is curious, but characteristic.

Fig. 4. is another edition of a legend more frequently repeated than almost any other in Buddhist scriptures. As mentioned above, it was with their artists as great a favourite as the Annunciation and Nativity were with Christian painters. In the left upper compartment we have Śuddhodana and his friends, and on the right Mâyâ's dream. The upper part of the slab being injured, his umbrella and her elephant have both disappeared. Below we have on the right the scene in the Lumbini Garden, which immediately preceded the birth of Buddha. It is not quite clear what the fourth compartment is intended to represent, as it is not to be found in any edition of the legend I am acquainted with. It looks as if it were intended that the old woman who appears in the first compartment should announce to the King in his bath the birth of the miraculous son. The cloth she carries in her hands bears the same impression of the sacred feet as that which is wound or to be wound round Mâyâ, in the next compartment.

PLATE XCII.

The upper figure in this Plate once formed part of the frieze of some Rail. It may have been one of the returns of the great Rail, but it is difficult to see, if that is so, where it would fit. It is the now familiar subject, the adoration of the wheel, by men, behind the throne on which the cushion or relics are placed (compare Plate LXXI. Fig. 2.). The inscription upon it merely records that it is the pious gift of Akasavâdi and Samiriti householders.*

The three fragments in the centre certainly belong to the outer frieze of the great Rail. Fig. 4. shows its commencement. Fig. 5. is a portion of another Rail belonging to some unknown building. It is very carefully executed, and though the "motivo" is the same as the first frieze, still the introduction of the dwarfs and the arrangement of the whole is novel and of great beauty.

---

* Appendix E., No. XVI.

RESTORATION OF A PORTION OF CENTRAL BUILDING.

SCALE. 1 2 3 4 8 FT.

PLATE XCIII.

Looked at from an architectural point of view, the most difficult question connected with the Amravati Tope was to ascertain whether any building occupied the centre of the enclosure, and if any, whether it was a Dagoba or a Chaitya hall, or a Vihâra or monastery. Owing to the excavation of the tank in the centre of the mound, as mentioned above, absolutely no trace of its foundation remained, and it might as probably have belonged to one as to any other of these classes. *À priori*, both from what Hiouen Thsang says * and the general probabilities of the case, I should have felt inclined to restore it with a Sanghârâma or Buddhist choir, like that at Stonehenge. But on looking carefully through the Mackenzie drawings, I soon perceived there existed among them representations of a class of sculpture which certainly did not belong to either of the enclosures; and from some pencil memoranda on the drawings, some of these were identified with the loose stones lying in the centre of the enclosure (Plate XLVII.). In the Elliot Collection, also, there are some twenty fragments, some of which are those drawn by Colonel Mackenzie's assistants, others so exactly in the same style, that it was easy to group them apart. Having got so far, it was not difficult to see that these fragments formed part of a Dagoba similar in design to those of the inner Rail, and which consequently must have formed the central object of the group of buildings.

If anyone will look carefully at any of the Dagobas represented in Plates LXV., LXVI. to LXXIX., he will perceive that the solid part to the height of the Rail is divided into slips by long pilasters, between which are various sculptures, generally hid by the Rail, but terminating upward by a Dagoba, with the three umbrellas on each side, or a Wheel or some such emblem, as in Figs. 1., 3., and 5. of Plate XCIV.

The historical subjects belonging to this group of sculptures were all found to be two-storied—if such an expression may be used. The lower group stand in a simple three-barred Rail of the Sanchi type; above them is a flat band, variously ornamented. Besides these, there are a considerable number of fragments, which all terminate upwards by a cornice or battlement of Trisuls, evidently forming the crowning ornament of a wall.

All the principal fragments of this class have been arranged in this manner in Plate XCIII., and, if compared with any of the Dagobas of the inner Rail, it will be seen, I think without doubt, that the one is a copy of the other. There is first the perpendicular part, terminating in the Wheel or Dagoba. Then the two stories of sculptured panels, and then the rich cornice, which invariably terminates the whole before the springing of the dome.

Arranged in this manner, these fragments make up a wall 22 feet high, and taking the widest of those of the Rail as our model, this would make the central

---

* Voyages, 188.

Dagoba 30 to 35 feet * in diameter, and its height, including dome and Tee, about 50 feet.

To those who are not familiar with the architecture of the country where this Tope is situated, it may appear strange that so magnificent an enclosure should have been erected to enshrine so insignificant a casket. Such an arrangement is, however, there rather the rule than the exception. Take, for instance, the great temple at Seringham. The outer enclosure measures more than 2,500 feet each way. Each of its Gateways is 130 feet in width, 100 feet in depth, and would, if completed, have risen to 300 feet in height. The inner six enclosures, though less than the outer, are all of great magnificence ; but the central building is smaller and less in magnificence than nine-tenths of the village temples in the neighbourhood. The cause of this inversion of the usual rule is easily explained. A village temple becomes famous from some miracle performed by its god, or rich from the endowment of some dying sinner. To pull it down would be desecration, but to add enclosure after enclosure and gateway to gateway was easy, and has happened in nearly all the great temples of Southern India, and did, I fancy, happen at Amravati.

In Egypt, too, something of the same sort occurred at Karnac. The little sanctuary of Orsortasen became there the nucleus of all the subsequent magnificence, and, though overshadowed by the palace of Thothmes and the great hall of Menephthah, it still remained the most venerated, though the smallest of all the erections in that vast enclosure.

---

* The yellow circle in the plan, Plate XLVII., which is meant to mark its site, is 50 feet in diameter. It was made so to include a terrace or procession path, with or without a Rail, which I conceive must have surrounded it.

AMRAVATI. PLATE XCIV.

PORTIONS OF SCULPTURE OF CENTRAL BUILDING.
SCALE 1 INCH TO 1 FOOT.

FIG. 1.

FIG. 2.

FIG. 3.

FIG. 4.

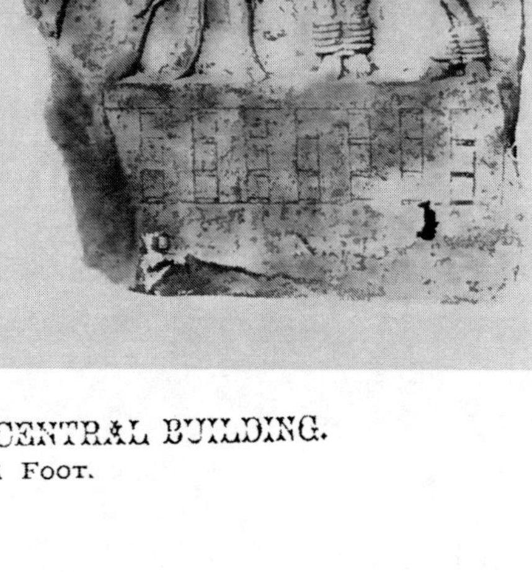

PORTIONS OF SCULPTURE OF CENTRAL BUILDING.

SCALE 1 INCH TO 1 FOOT.

FIG, 1.

FIG, 2.

FIG, 3.

FIG, 4.

FRAGMENTS OF SCULPTURE OF CENTRAL BUILDING.

SCALE 1 INCH TO 1 FOOT.

PLATE XCVII.

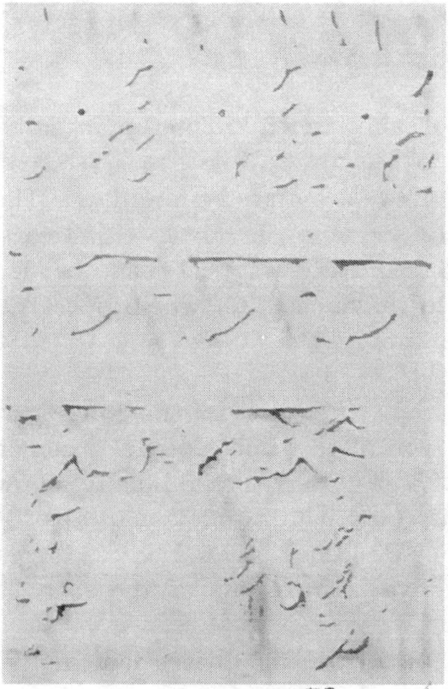

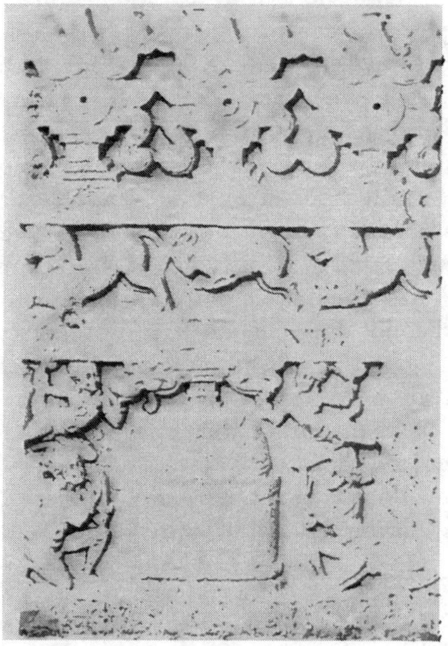

PORTIONS OF FRIEZE OF CENTRAL BUILDING.

SCALE 1 INCH TO 1 FOOT.

PLATES XCIV. TO XCVII.

There is very little in the sculptures of the central Tope that calls for any particular remark after what has been said in the preceding pages. The emblems employed in its decoration are those with which we are already familiar. The Throne, with the relics upon it, the Tree, the Wheel, and the Dagoba. In two instances, at least, (Plate XCIV. Fig. 3.* and Plate XCVII. Fig. 1.) the five-headed Serpent is in front of the Dagoba, and in both these instances the worshippers are unmistakeably Hindus, and the same who are worshipping the Wheel and the Tree in the same sculptures.

The Naga people also occur in at least one instance in the lower part of the bas-relief, Fig. 1. Plate XCVI. The slab was complete when Colonel Mackenzie drew it, but even without that, enough remains of the lower bas-relief to show that it represented one male and three female Nagas, but who were essentially Buddhists, if we may judge from the seven figures of Buddha,† seated cross-legged, which appears immediately over their heads, and the five impressions of the sacred foot that are placed between the snakes' heads.

The Horse, too, forms an important element in the decoration of the central monument. In Plate XCV. Fig. 1. and Plate XCVI. Fig. 1., he may be merely the favourite charger of the man who is leaning against him, but in Plate XCV. Fig. 4. he is introduced in mid air alongside the Wheel as an object of equal reverence; and on a piece of sculpture where the Wheel just above him is the especial object of worship; and in Plate XCVI. Fig. 3. he issues from the portal with the umbrella of state borne over him, the hero of the representation. The same subject is repeated on another slab, Plate XCVIII. Fig. 2., from a drawing in the Mackenzie collection, but which is easily recognized as belonging to the upper or sculptured part of the central building. The first impulse, on looking at these and on the last-quoted illustrations, is to consider them as representing the commencement of an Aśwamedha, or horse sacrifice; but one of the essentials for that is wanting in both. The story of the Aśwamedha is easily understood. A Raja, who claimed to be lord paramount in India, let loose a steed to wander wherever he listed, and followed close behind him prepared to fight anyone who dared to meddle with the horse, and to release him if anyone took possession of him. If he accomplished this, and brought the steed back in safety, he was acknowledged a Chakravartti Raja. If he failed, the sacrifice did not take place.

In the bas-relief at Sanchi, Plate XXXV. Fig. 1., a Raja is following the steed in his chariot, and that may therefore be the commencement of the Aśwamedha. At

---

* This slab has been so long exposed on the outer wall of Fife House that its sculptures are nearly obliterated.

† That is, assuming the figures of Buddha to be cöeval; but they have very much the appearance of being added afterwards.

Amravati the challenger is in all instances absent, and it seems difficult to account for this if such a sacrifice were intended. On the whole I am much more inclined to believe that the Horse was an object of reverence, if not exactly of worship, at Amravati, and that those bas-reliefs on the Dagobas (Plates LXXX. and LXXXI.), and those on the central building, as well as those elsewhere, all shadow forth that faith and that only.

I would require that much more attention should be paid to this subject than I can pretend to have done, and also that more materials should be available for the investigation, before any confident opinion could be expressed regarding the real position of the horse in these sculptures. Meanwhile I may state that the inference I draw from the representations of the horse in the sculptures is that the reverence paid to him is the counterpart of the worship of the Bull Nandi by the Sivites. The two sects are and always were the antipodes of each other in India, and each seems to have adopted an animal as their emblem, the Buddhists taking the horse as theirs. This does not of course preclude the idea of this form of worship being borrowed from Scythia. On the contrary, everything we learn from either Sanchi or Amravati points to the north-west and to countries beyond the Indus as the source whence everything took its origin. What the Buddhists derived from those countries was, however, directly antagonistic to anything which we know that the Aryans either possessed or affected, and must consequently have been derived from some other race. Whether, therefore, we call the people Turanian or Scythian, we come back to the same thing. The Buddhists must have derived the foreign influences from a northern Turanian race, occupying the countries both to the north and to the south of the Himalaya chain, being the people who were Buddhists in India and are Buddhists in Thibet. If Sivaism arose among the Dravidians, they were of a different race, and must have come into India by another route, probably across the Lower Indus.

One indication of the age of the central building should not be passed over without notice. The principal string course under the lower range of panels, is throughout of the plain Sanchi type of Rail. This, if not an absolute test of age, is at least one of the best indications we possess, and would go far to prove that the central building is older than the Rails that enclose it. Wherever a Rail is represented on the enclosures at Amravati, it is always of a more ornate and more complicated character than that on the central building.

Another test is the form of the characters of the inscriptions. Both General Cunningham and Mr. Thomas are of opinion that those on the central building are the oldest, but cannot, from their limited extent, feel sure how much more ancient they may be.

The principal inscription—No. XIX. Appendix E.—merely records that the sculpture on which it is found is the pious gift of Agheya, the pupil of Buddha Rakshita.

PILASTER INNER ENCLOSURE.

PILASTER CENTRAL BUILDING.

PLATE XCVIII.

The Wheel pillar represented in Fig. 1. of this Plate contains no novelty, or anything which is not found in those represented in Plates LXXV. and LXXXVIII., but it is more distinct than the first and more complete than the last of these, and is consequently useful towards understanding one of the most characteristic features of the inner Rail to which it belonged.

The slab, Fig. 2., which is also from the Mackenzie Collection, is extremely useful towards completing the restoration of the central building, inasmuch as it carries us direct from the three-barred Rail to the Dagoba frieze. It will be observed in Plate XCIII. there is a hiatus between the upper range of sculptures and the Dagoba, which, as far as any evidence went, might be of any dimensions. In this slab we have the Rail, the two ranges of sculptures, and the crowning Dagobas, all in one slab, and fortunately with the dimensions written upon them, which settles the question.

The upper sculpture is also interesting as illustrating the legend of King Dharma Aśoka, alluded to above, page 160. "After reaching the Golden Sands, his majesty " had a dream in which Devatâs appeared to him and said that underneath the temple " were relics which had been deposited there by order of the king of Lankâ. Next " day the king directed people to dig into the Chaitya, but the crows, or spirits in " their shape, compelled them to desist.

"It happened that at this time the Naga with seven heads and as many tails " guarded the Chaitya, but no sooner had the king, accompanied by Mahâ Tuli " (sent by Indra to assist) and a large retinue, approached close to it, than this " mighty snake king was observed to be majestically disentwining himself from " the huge fold with which he had encompassed the relic shrine."* As already related, with the assistance of the king of Róm he was eventually successful, and founded a city, and built a new Chaitya to enshrine the recovered relics. Was this the temple we now see? and are the relics those so frequently represented in the foregoing Plates?

It is, of course, extremely difficult, if not absolutely impossible to arrive at anything like certainty in such a case as this, but after what has been said above, I think the history of the Amravati Tope may be made out with very tolerable precision. First, we have indications from the coins collected by Colonel Mackenzie, and also from the slab, Plate LXXVIII., Fig. 2., that buildings did exist on this spot as early as the Christian era, but we have now no means of knowing what they may have been. In the next place, judging from the character of the sculptures, as well as from such shadowy traditions as exist, it does not seem that any part

* J. A. S. B., XVII. p. 90.

of the buildings which have been described above were undertaken till more than a century after the Gateways at Sanchi were completed.

About or after the year 200, however, the central Dagoba may have been commenced with an enclosing Rail, of which, however, nothing has reached this country. Subsequently, in the beginning of the fourth century, either in consequence of the visit of the Tooth relic on its way to Ceylon, or from some other local cause, the place acquired celebrity, and the great outer Rail was commenced, and it may have continued during the remainder of that century before being completed. The sculptures of the inner Rail seem then to have been taken in hand, possibly were not completed till the year 500, after which time decay seems to have set in, and nothing further was done.

All that we know of Indian art is perfectly in accordance with this, and now that we are enabled to study the sculptures at Sanchi we can speak with some confidence on this subject. Before they were known, everything as we traced the history of art backwards seemed to become more and more elegant and perfect. Now that we have got hold of the earliest examples, we find that the art began in rude vigour, but without any of that refinement it afterwards attained. About the fourth century seems to have been the culminating point, and from that period the rock-cut temples, and those at Bhuvaneswar and elsewhere, carry us on without intermission till we reach such temples as those on Mount Abu, 1032; those around Hullabeed, dating from 1200 to 1300; or those at Kanaruc in 1241. We know that in this period there was no retrocession nor any age of decay which would account for the inferiority of the sculptures of the central building compared with those of the enclosure, on the supposition that these were the more modern of the two.

The architecture, as far as it goes, bears out the same conclusion as the sculpture. At Sanchi it is careless and wooden, the string courses seldom horizontal and occurring at every different level. It is the same in the central building at Amravati, especially in the crowning cornice, Plate XCVII. In the Rails, all afterwards became precise, almost finicking, and that remains a characteristic of Hindu art to the present day.

CONCLUSION.

Architecture.

There are few of the subjects mooted in the previous pages regarding which it would uot be easy to say a great deal more than has been said, nor would it have been difficult to find illustrations from other monuments which would have rendered the subject much more complete. It has, however, been thought better, in the first instance at least, to confine the work to the representation of the two monuments named on the title page, with only such introductory matter and descriptions as were requisite to render them intelligible, and to leave their application to a future time, and probably to other hauds.

In so far as the History of Architecture is concerned, we do not learn much from these Topes that had not previously become known to us from an examination of the rock-cut examples, but there is a great deal in them that confirms what was previously only suspected, while a knowledge of their forms fills up some important gaps which existed in our history of the early styles of Indian art.

Irrespective of this, however, these two Topes are interesting, inasmuch as they are the two oldest structural buildings which, so far as we yet know, are to be found in India in anything like an intelligible state. If the Tope at Sanchi was really erected by Aśoka—and there seems no good reason for doubting that it was so—it is the only one of the 84,000 Stûpas he is traditioually said to have erected of which a vestige now remains, and its Rail is the oldest and simplest in form of all those of which any fragments uow exist. Its gateways, too, are unique, as no other example of such a form is known to exist anywhere in India, though judging from the frequency with which representatious of them occur at Amravati, they must have been at one time very common. All those, however, that occur in the bas-reliefs of the Southern Tope seem to have been of wood, and those at Sanchi, though of stone, are very slightly removed in form from their wooden prototypes.

The whole of the superstructure is so essentially wooden in construction that we rather feel inclined to wonder bow men dared to attempt its erection in stone, and are equally astonished that it should have stood for eighteen centuries nearly uninjured. The pillars, too, are evideutly imitations of carved logs. The irregularity in spaciug the divisions, the mode in which the dividing string courses stop, without running all round, and the wavyness of the lines, all betray the workmanship of people unfamiliar with the even bedding requisite for stone masonry in such positions, though the irregularity may be rather pleasing in wood carving.

All this is changed when we come to the age of the Great Rail at Amravati. There the architectural details are carved with sharpness and precision. The string courses are horizontal, and the general construction so truly lithic, that it requires some study and some knowledge to detect the wooden forms that still remain. The examples of Rails at Muttra and Buddh Gya are probably intermediate between these two, and when published may perhaps enable us to render our history a little more complete. Enough remains at Gya to enable it to be restored with certainty when anyone will take the trouble to do so. That at Muttra is probably too far ruined, but meanwhile, till casts or photographs can be obtained, it is impossible to speak with any certainty regarding them. These four Rails, however, are nearly all that now remains to enable us to write the history of structural architecture in India anterior to the building of the great Bhuvaneswar temple in 627 A.D.* We may eventually be able to eke out this meagre list by hints borrowed from the Topes in Ceylon and Afghanistan, but they, I fear, are either too modern or too much ruined to be of much service. The real complement to our scant knowledge must be derived from the Caves. We have in Behar some nearly as old as Aśoka, though more modern than the Rail at Sanchi, and at Bhâjâ and Karlee in the Western Ghats we have others which were excavated before the Christian era. From that time to those at Junir and Nassick there are probably a hundred examples, including those of course at Kundana, Ajanta, and elsewhere, which may have been executed in the first three or four centuries of the Christian era, and those at Cuttack may be even earlier than those of the western side of India. All this makes up an amount of evidence probably sufficient for present purposes, but the caves being all interiors, do not supply all the information required. Even if the Topes at Sanchi and Amravati do not suffice to complete our knowledge, they and other bas-reliefs add immensely to our stores, and when the whole is combined together we can form a very fair idea of what the architecture of India was from the time when stone was first employed till the inhabitants acquired that perfection in the art which is exhibited in the carvings of the Rails at Amravati.

The fact, however, of our having been obliged hitherto to rely to such an extent on rock-cut examples for our knowledge of the early arts of India, has prevented our being able to ascertain how far the history of sculpture and decorative art has coincided with that of architecture. There is very little sculpture in the early Caves, and what there is, is generally carved in a coarse unsuitable material, and frequently in situations where it is badly lighted and imperfectly seen. It was therefore perfectly open to anyone to argue that these sculptures were not a fair test, and that the Hindus may have been proficient in representations of the human form and in decorative sculpture at a time when their architectural knowledge was still in its infancy.

The great fact that we learn from a study of the sculptures of the Topes at Sanchi and Amravati is, that the plastic arts followed the same law as those of

* I am doubtful about the age of the Takht-i Sulimán temple in Cashmere, but it may be older, A.D. 290 ?

construction. We can now assert with confidence that all the permanent forms of art arose in India after its inhabitants were brought into contact with western civilization, by the establishment of the Grecian kingdom of Bactria. It seems probable that such sculptures as we have of Aśoka's reign were actually executed by Grecian or at least by Yavana artists; but from his time to the present day we can now trace the rise and fall of Hindu art almost without a break. We can assist at its first rude but vigorous attempts. We can follow it till it reached its highest point of manipulative dexterity, in the fourth century, at Amravati. We see it maintaining itself nearly at the same level—with some fluctuation, of course—till the decline of Buddhism, and the irruption of the Mahomedans. From that point the history of Hindu art is too surely written in decay, and we can trace its gradual deterioration to the present day.

In a few words, what we have gained by the study of the arts of the two Topes, is the assurance that the whole history of permanent art in India is comprised in the last twenty-one centuries, and that we now possess a sufficient number of examples, and have sufficient knowledge, to grasp the subject as a whole. There may be some gaps still to fill up, some details that require rectification, but for the first time it can now be said that we know the beginning, the middle, and the end of the history of the arts of that great Indian branch of the family of mankind.

Religion.

The picture which the sculptures of the Topes at Sanchi and Amravati afford us of the religious faith of the inhabitants of India at the time they were erected is perhaps more novel, and also more interesting, than the information they afford regarding the arts of the country. Before they were discovered, the only contemporary record we possessed of the early forms of the Buddhist faith was that derived from the inscriptions of Aśoka, engraved on pillars at Delhi, Allahabad, and in Tirhoot, &c., and those on the rocks at Orissa, Gujerat, Peshawer, and elsewhere. What we find in them is Buddhism without Buddha. Except in the short inscription at Bhabhra (App. C.), the founder of the religion is not once mentioned, nor any of his doctrinal formulas. That marvellous tenderness towards everything that has life is strongly inculcated; respect for parents and superiors, mutual kindness and forbearance, and above all, toleration of other faiths, are insisted upon, and many moral doctrines common to Buddhism and other forms of faith; but we scarcely gather whether they emanated from some Solon or some Socrates or from Ŝâkya Muni. The faith was then the rival of that of the Vedas, and affected their purity and absence of all human agency or miraculous manifestations.

At Sanchi, 300 years afterwards, we find the state of affairs altered, but not to any very great extent. Buddha, the great ascetic, as we have always hitherto known him, nowhere appears. In his place we have only the Prince who forsook parent, wife, and child, and threw aside his royal state and all worldly advantages, that he might devote his life to the benefit of his suffering fellow men. But even this is, as it were, only incidentally announced. It requires some knowledge and a great deal of study to detect it. On the other hand the religious observances which the sculptures of Sanchi reveal to us are, that in those days the old ancestral worship of a Turanian people had been refined from reverencing the sepulchres of their forefathers into a veneration for relics and relic shrines, the Dagoba or Tope being the object most frequently and most prominently worshipped there. Next to the Dagoba, if not indeed more important, is the worship of the Tree. It occurs quite as frequently, and often in more prominent positions in the sculptures, but against this we must bear in mind the fact, that the great Tope itself was there, and those Gateways were themselves erected to do it honour.

Next in importance to these, but very much less frequent, is the worship of the Wheel, and next to it the Trisul emblem, though it is very doubtful whether this last ought to be considered as an object of worship at Sanchi, and not merely as an hierogram, expressing a sacred meaning, but not an idol.

The Serpent is only once worshipped at Sanchi, and then apparently by a people totally distinct from the governing race, who erected the Gateways and carved the representations upon them. But groups occur six, or it may be ten, times in which a man sits shielded by the seven-headed Naga, and surrounded by women who have the strange accompaniment of a single snake at the back of their heads.

The most remarkable circumstance, however, connected with the bas-reliefs at Sanchi is the total absence of anything approaching asceticism. No priests appear anywhere; and though we have palaces, there is no building that can be taken for a monastery. On the other hand, the sculptors revel in depicting regal state. Music and dancing take the place of divine service, and drinking and love-making fill up the time of the Buddhists of those days. Most strange of all, we have war! It is true it may have been undertaken to acquire or recover some valued relic, or for some such Buddhist object, but fighting on a Buddhist monument is at strange variance with usually received opinions.

When from these we pass on over another three centuries to the time of the sculptures at Amravati, we find a state of affairs much more nearly approaching to the usually received formula of Buddhism. Buddha, the ascetic, occasionally appears in the usual attitudes and the usual costume, but much more frequently in the more modern than in the older bas-reliefs of this Tope. His statue does not apparently occur among the fragments of the central Dagoba,* and only twice on the fragments we possess of the great Rail. On the smaller Rail, however, such representations become frequent, and very similar to what we are accustomed to on the Caves and Buddhist temples after the fifth century.

The actual worship of the Dagoba occurs as a rule only on the central building. It is frequently represented afterwards, and with more elaboration, on the inner Rail, which I take to be the last important addition to the Tope, but it can hardly be said that it is there represented as worshipped by the people of the sculptures. It is more like a frame to contain pictures to be reverenced by the people. The purely abstract symbol of Relic Worship has become a storied page of legendary lore, and, if I read it rightly, the picture has to a very great extent obliterated the original idea of the relic shrine.

---

* I do not feel quite sure about Fig. 1., Plate LXXXVII. It may belong to the central building, but I rather think it was a detached statue.

On the other hand, Tree Worship maintains nearly the same relative position of importance at Amravati that it did at Sanchi, but with this important qualification. Where the two Topes have anything in common, it is most apparent in those points in which they approach nearest in age. We find, consequently, the Tree Worship most important in the central building, next in the great Rail, but nearly evanescent in the sculptures of the inner Rail. It only occurs once in the place of honour on any Dagoba in our collections, and never on the frieze nor on the wall. The change is so gradual that it can hardly be accidental, and I am on the whole inclined to believe that Tree Worship was to some extent losing its importance before the sculptures at Amravati were complete.

The Chakra or Wheel, on the contrary, seems to have gone on growing in importance. Nothing at Amravati exceeds the fanciful elaboration of the pillars which support this emblem, and it is introduced so frequently and so prominently that it was evidently considered one of the principal emblems of the faith.

The Trisul emblem seems also to grow in importance as we descend the stream of time. As before mentioned, it does not seem to have been directly worshipped at Sanchi, nor is it so treated in the central building at Amravati, but on the great Rail it occurs several times elevated on what appear to be fire pillars, and most decidedly as a thing to be worshipped.

The greatest change that took place between the two epochs seems to have been in the position of the Naga. As just mentioned, he appears only once as an object of worship at Sanchi, and from six to ten times as spreading his seven-headed hood over some important personage.

At Amravati he occurs certainly ten or twelve * times in the place of honour on the Dagoba or on pillars as the principal object to be worshipped. Twice he occurs in a similar position shielding the head of Buddha, thrice protecting the sacred feet, and at least thirty, it may be fifty times spreading his hood over Rajas or persons of importance, exclusive of course of the women with their single snakes, who are always more numerous. There is of course some uncertainty in stating these figures, as we have only so small a portion of the Amravati sculptures at our command, but on the whole I am inclined to think that what we possess is a fair representation of the whole, and if so, it is not too much to assert that the Naga is the great and ruling idea at Amravati, and seems to have been growing in importance from the oldest buildings there till the time when additions ceased to be made, and the place became deserted.

The Horse is another animal which was certainly honoured at Amravati to an extent that we are justified in calling worship; it hardly, however, seems to have been a growing faith, and probably was more prominent in the central building than in subsequent erections, though it appears prominently on the inner Rail.

Another important change is, that at Amravati we have shaven priests, such as we easily recognise and such as we find at the present day on the other side of the Himalayas, or in Ceylon or Burmah.

---

* I am forced to state the numbers thus rather vaguely, because I cannot always feel quite sure whether some of the drawings in the Mackenzie Collection may not represent sculptures in that of Sir W. Elliot; generally, the difference is easily recognized, but not always.

Music and dancing are still represented at Amravati, though rarely. Drinking hardly occurs, and love is kept in the background. In fact we cannot but feel, in comparing these sculptures, that when we come near the end of the Amravati series we are approaching very nearly to the state of affairs which existed when the Ceylonese and Thibet books were first composed. At Sanchi we were in another and an older world, but by degrees religious forms assumed a state more nearly resembling what we now find. Another century, and the sculptures of the Tope might have served literally as illustrations of the Mahawansa or the Lalita-Vistara. Meanwhile the great interest resides in the fact that they represent a state of affairs that existed before these or any Buddhist books we now possess were reduced to their present legendary form.

Ethnology.

It is more difficult to speak with anything like precision regarding the ethnology than as to either the architecture or religion displayed in the Topes. This does not arise so much from any want of distinctness in the sculptures as because the countries of Hydrabad and Berar have never yet been scientifically explored. We are almost entirely ignorant regarding the different races who inhabit the vast central plateau of India, on whose outer edge these two Topes were erected, and we neither know whence they came nor when they settled in their present locations. Now that the Nagpore territory has escheated to British rule, there is a prospect of something being done to clear up these difficulties, but the only result hitherto obtained from the labours of the Nagpore Antiquarian Society is to show us how much remains to be done, and at the same time what a vast amount of valuable material exists on the spot and is available for the inquiry.

The people most distinctly characterized in the sculptures of these two Topes are those I have designated Dasyus or Takshaks. They are infinitely more important at Sanchi than at Amravati, but appear in both places as a quasi aboriginal race, and treated as inferiors by the builders of the Topes. They appear at the same time to be the real and original Serpent worshippers, and if their connexion with Taxila and the Punjab can be satisfactorily established, it will throw considerable light on the principal features of the present inquiry. Meanwhile it is curious to observe, as we pointed out before, that as a straight line drawn from Taxila to Amravati passes through Bhilsa, Nagpore, and other localities where Snake Worship was especially prevalent, it does look like the central line of such a migration. If any such ever took place, it was long anterior to Buddhism, possibly before or in consequence of the great war, celebrated in the Mahâbhârata.

Another race, who seem almost as distinctly marked, are those with short curly hair. There are only two men so distinguished at Amravati, and the sculpture on which they are found is of such inferior execution (Plate LXXXIV.) that no argument can well be founded upon it. In Plate LXII., Fig. 2., several women are so distinguished, but no men. At Sanchi the case is different. The drummer boys generally have curly hair, so have the charioteers and menials in many instances, and in one bas-relief (Plate XXVIII.) these curly-headed people seem to be the principal actors. From their costume they seem to come from some colder country, and I have suggested Bactria, though there are no doubt many difficulties in such an attribution. At first sight it might be supposed they came from Africa—Zanzibar—like the Hubschees at present in the Nizam's service, but in the absolute silence of all tradition the difficulties in the way of such an hypothesis seem greater than as regards the other. The question has rather a curious interest in an artistic point of view, as there seems little doubt that it was from this people—whoever they were—that Buddha derived the negroid hair by which his statues are always distinguished, and which has given rise to so much speculation. In so far as we now know, sculpture, taught by the Greeks, was practised in the North-west long before it penetrated into India Proper, and it is probable that the earlier statues of Buddha were fabricated there. If this is so it would favour the idea that the curly heads may have belonged to that country.

Even supposing it were possible to locate and name these minor groups, the great question would still remain, Who are the people who in the preceding pages have been designated as Hindus? From the appearance of Śâkya Muni, and their being so generally associated with him, I think that there can be very little doubt but that the sculptures meant to represent the inhabitants of the province now known as Upper Bengal, more especially of the districts of Tirhoot and Behar, which were assuredly the cradle of Buddhism. At first sight it might appear that a distinction ought to be drawn between the followers of Buddha at Sanchi, and those at Amravati. The figures, especially of the women at the former place, are so much fuller, it may be said coarser, and so much more like what we are accustomed to call Scythians or Tartars, that it might be assumed that they could not belong to the same race. On the whole, however, I am inclined to believe that the difference is more artistic than ethnographic. From the earliest sculptures in the Caves to a late period, there seems to be a tendency to refine and attenuate, and my impression is that this difference is due to that cause.

If this is so, the people who are associated with Buddha in both Topes are the mixed race of Bengal,—a people with a certain infusion of Aryan blood in their veins, but which had become so impure from mixture with that of the aboriginal tribes who existed in Bengal before the Aryan immigration, that the distinctive features of their higher civilization were almost entirely lost. Of this no greater proof could be given than that Buddhism was able to rise on its ruins.

Another important question is, Are the people who wear the snake-hoods of the same race as the others? Sometimes I have thought I could detect such distinctions as would enable a separate classification to be made, but on the whole it is probably safer to assume, for the present at least, that the differences are only artistic. Their costume, their mode of wearing the hair, and their features are certainly generally the same, with only such distinctions as may be accounted for by fashion or local peculiarities, and we ought therefore to consider them as two different nations rather than as two distinct peoples.

The people whose manners and customs appear to present the closest affinities with what we find on the monuments, are those now known as the Gonds and other closely-allied tribes inhabiting the country to the south of the Vindhya hills. From their language we learn that they were allied to the Dravidians, now occupying nearly the whole of the Madras presidency, but ethnologists have not yet determined whether they occupied also the great basin of the Ganges, or whether another race more nearly allied to the Thibetans and Burmese originally inhabited these plains. From such indications as we gather from the sculptures of the Topes, I am inclined to the latter view, but it is perhaps better at the present stage of the inquiry to be content with stating the problem and its difficulties, rather than to attempt to solve it from the very imperfect data at our command. Be this as it may, everyone will probably be inclined to admit that the Plates published in this volume are a most important contribution for the elucidation of many of the difficulties connected with Indian ethnography, but the real value of this evidence will never be extracted from them till they are carefully examined by persons on the spot, who have local experience and personal knowledge of the tribes of Central India. When this is done the Topes at Sanchi and Amravati may contribute as much to our knowledge of the ethnography of India in the early centuries of the Christian era as they have certainly done towards completing the history of the architecture and illustrating the religious forms of the faiths of India at that early period of time.

FINIS.

APPENDIX.

APPENDIX A.

THE following two extracts are taken from a work entitled "Der Ehsten abergläubische Gebräuche Weisen und Gewohnheiten, von Johann Wolfgang Boecler, weiland Pastor zu Kusal in Ehstland und des Consistorii in Reval Assessor. Mit auf die Gegenwart bezüglichen Anmerkungen beleuchtet von Dr. Fr. R. Kreutzwald. St. Petersburg, Buchdruckerei der Kaiserlichen Akademie der Wissenschaften. 1854."

The first is curious, not only as showing the prevalence of Tree Worship in Esthonia at a very recent date, but more so as containing a form of prayer addressed to the Tree God which I have not met with elsewhere.

Dr. Kreutzwald's account of the Serpents, and their annual parliaments, accords with that reported by Castrén as occurring in Sweden (vide supra, p. 25). He does not profess to have seen snakes worshipped himself, but he quotes the late Provost Masing (I. 39.) as having in his boyhood seen tame snakes (unterirdishe Hauswirthe), who were fed and nourished by the peasantry, and honoured as household gods:—

" Die *Baumverehrung* der Esten lässt sich aus der jüngsten Vergangenheit nachweisen und wird ohne Zweifel auch heutiges Tages manche Anbeter finden, obzwar — seit die ungläubige Spottsucht unter den Nationalen selbst grösseren Spielraum gewonnen, und durch Aufhebung der Leibeigenschaft manche frühere Verhältnisse verändert worden, die Zahl der baum- und quellgläubigen Seelen jährlich mehr einschmelzen und bei Ausübung ihrer alten Gebräuche noch vorsichtiger werden dürfte, wodurch nach wenigen Jahren vielleicht alle sichtbaren Spuren verschwinden. Indessen möchten wir nicht verbürgen, dass bei dieser spiegelglatten Oberfläche auch der Meeresgrund überall ein ungetrübter sei. In den beiden ersten Decennien des laufenden Jahrhunderts, wo in solchen Dingen weniger Zurückhaltung herrschte, haben wir in Allentacken, Wierland, Jerwen uud Harrien heilige Bäume mehrfach gesehen; sie standen unweit des Wohnhauses an einem geschützten Orte, genossen eine sorgfaltige Pflege und wurden gegen Beschädigungen in Acht genommen. Es waren in der Regel alte Linden, Eichen oder Eschen, erstere am häufigsten. Nach der Mittheilung eines glaubwürdigen bejahrten Nationalen wurden solche Bäume wenigstens einmal im Jahre mit frischem Thierblut begossen, desgleichen musste, wenn eines geschlachteten Thieres Herzschlag zur sogenannten "frischen Suppe" *würske leem* — benutzt worden war, bevor ein Mensch davon gekostet hatte, eine Portion über des heiligen Baumes Wurzeln verschüttet werden, damit der Viehstand besser gedeihe. Am Johannis — Abend hing man in Wierland einen mit "Glücksblumen" *õnne lilled* — durchwundenen Farrenkraut-Kranz in des heil. Baumes Zweige. Am folgenden Morgen wurden die "Glücksblumen" aus dem Kranze genommen und auf jegliches Hausgenossen Glück ein Blümchen zwischen Wandritzen gesteckt, um zu erfahren, wessen Glück in diesem Jahre am schönsten sich entfalten werde. — Der Farrenkraut-Kranz blieb am Baum hängen bis er verwelkte, dann erst ward er abgenommen und bis zur Neujahrsnacht sorgfältig aufgehoben, wo der Abends unter das Kopfkissen gesteckte welke Kranz die Träume dieser Nacht ominös machte. Zu gleichem Zweck streute man in der Johannis-Nacht blühende Blumen unter das ruhende Haupt, die hier, wie der welke Kranz am Sylvester-Abend, für den Schläfer weissagende Vorbedeutung gewinnen sollten. Die Auslegung der Traumorakel besorgten hier — wie's auch anderweitig geschieht — alte Weiber, denen selbst im Volksliede das Prädikat "*targad*" (weise) beigefügt wird, wenn's etwas zu rathen giebt, was über den kleinen hausbackenen Verstand hinausgeht. Es ist uns nicht erinnerlich, Steine unter den heiligen Bäumen bemerkt zu haben, auch wussten wir damals keine besondere Aufmerksamkeit diesem Gegenstande zu widmen, daher, falls wirklich welche vorhanden gewesen, sie leicht unbeachtet können geblieben sein. Nach den Mittheilungen des *Herrn Lagus* aus der Fellinschen Gegend, soll unter dem "Linden-Altar"—*pärna altari al* — immer ein Stein gestanden haben, auf den der Opferbringer seine Gaben hinstellte, nachdem er vorher auf blossen Knien drei Mal von Osten nach Westen, und drei Mal wieder zurück gerutscht war, wobei er sprechen musste: "Empfange die Speise zur Opfergabe." Dann wurden dem Stein zur Besiegelung des Bundes noch drei Küsse gegeben und nun konnte man fortgehen. Auch sollen die Fellinschen Linden — was in Estland nicht der Fall war — auf einem "Hügelchen" gestanden haben. In einem darauf bezüglichen Volksliede hören wir den Opferbringer sprechen:

Saada ônne sarwikuile,	Sende Glück du den Gehörnten,
Kaitse meie kabjajalad,	Wahre unsre Hufenfüssler,
Warja meie warwaskannad,	Schirme unsre Zehenhacken,
Sôrgaliste sigidusta.	Das Gedeihen auch der Klauer.

Wir wollen hier einen Estnischen "Opfergebrauch" ausführlicher beschreiben. Der Opferbringer musste aus seinem Zeigefinger einige Blutstropfen ritzen und dabei sprechen: "Ich nenne Dich " mit meinem Blute und verlobe Dich mit meinem Blute, und bezeichne Dir meine Gebäude zum " Segnen, als Pferdeställe und Viehstadeln und Hühnerstangen; lasse sie gesegnet sein durch mein " Blut und deine Macht."

"Sei mir zur Freude, Du Allermächtigster, meiner Eltern Erhalter, mein Beschützer und " meines Lebens Beschirmer! Ich flehe zu Dir aus Fleisches und Blutes Kraft: Empfange die " Speise, die ich Dir darbringe zu Deinem Unterhalt und zu meines Leibes Freude; bewahre mich " als Dein gutes Kind, und ich werde Dich dankend preisen. Bei des allmächtigsten, meines " eigenen Gottes Hilfe, erhöre mich! Was ich aus Nachlässigkeit etwa Unvollkommenes gegen " Dich gethan habe, das vergiss! Aber bewahre es treu im Gedächtniss, dass ich meine Gaben " auf ehrbare Weise meinen Eltern zu Ehren und zur Freude und zur Vergeltung abgetragen habe. " Ueberdies küsse ich drei Mal niederfallend die Erde. Sei mit mir schnell im Thun und Friede " sei mit Dir bis hierher."*

In Wierland wurden die heil. Bäume *Hie-* oder *Pelgepuud*, in Harrien *warjo-puud* — "Schutzbäume" genannt. Das *hie* wird von unsern Sprachkennern gemeiniglich durch *heilig* übersetzt, andere wollen darunter einen Hain verstehen; von unserm Nichtkennerstandpunkte müssen wir bemerken, wie letztere Erklärung bezüglich auf den einzelnen Baum durchaus unstatthaft erscheint.† *Pelg*‡ soll nach *Herrn Lagus Taara's* Namen in der Kindersprache bedeuten."

The following two invocations to the Serpent are translations from the Finnish, which is given in the original work in parallel columns.

"O du Schlange, Unterird'sche,
Erdkuchen, Erdbrötchen,
Unter die Erd' hinab neun Klaftern,
In den Fels hinein acht Ellen!
Hülfe, Kehl', Hülfe, Seel',
Hülfe, lieber Herr Gott!
Hülfe, Hülfe helfe dir,
Den gesund *Taara* geschaffen
Von der Mutter Leib bis sum Lebensend'!
Silber auf des Argen Zipfel,
Weisses Silber sei dem Feinde!

Spruch gegen den Unterirdischen.

Erdväterchen,
Erdmütterchen,
Erdjüngferchen,
Rasengrossmütterchen,
Euch des Silbers Weisses bring' ich:
Gebt mir Helle gegen Schmerzen,
Gebt Gesundheit ihr dem Siechen,
Bringe dann euch meinen Dank dar!

---

* Wortgetreu aus dem Estnischen übersetzt, wie Hr. Lagus das Opfergebet aus dem Munde eines Fellinschen Esten niedergeschrieben.

† Das Wort *Hie* hängt mit dem Finnischen *Hiisi* zusammen. Vgl. *Neus*, Ehstnische Volkslieder S. 208. *Sj.*

‡ *Pelg* bedeutet eigentlich "Furcht," im Dorpater Dialekt. *S.*

Streckt sich jemand erhitzt auf den feuchten Erdboden, oder setzt er sich oder ein Glied seines Leibes im heissen Dampfbade dem kalten Luftzuge aus, so entsteht nicht selten ein feiner, brennend juckender Hautausschlag, der ausschwitzt und später eine Kruste bildet. Mit dem Abfallen dieser ist die Krankheit beendet und ohne weiteres Genesung eingetreten (vgl. *Hupel*, nord. Miscel. III. 227). Diese Krankheit schreibt aber der Ehste dem Anhauche der Unterirdischen zu, die er gestört zu haben vermeint, und soll sie nach ihnen *maa alused* oder *maa hingamine* (Erdhauch ; das norweg. *alvgust*, Elbhauch, s. *Grimm* a. a. O. S. 430) benennen (s. *Rosenpl.* a. a. O. I. 33 f.). Um den Zorn der Unterirdischen zu besänftigen und von ihnen Heilung zu erlangen, schabt er nun als Opfer auf die Stätte etwas von seinem Silberschmuck oder einer Silbermünze, nachdem er sie dreimal mit der Sonne um den erkrankten Theil bewegt (vgl. unten die Anmerkung zu No. 31, welches letztere jedoch auch scheint unterlassen zu werden (s. *Hupel*, topogr. Nachricht, II. 141). Dazu spricht er dann die Formel. Dieses Opfer geschabten Silbers ist bei ähnlichen Anlässen auch in Schweden üblich ; der Opfergebrauch indess umständlicher, s. E. M. *Arndt*, Reise durch Schweden III. 15 f.

Dass aber zu diesem Opfer das edle Silber genommen wird, scheint sich aus der Vorstellung zu erklären, welche Ehsten und Schweden von den Unterirdischen haben. *Lagus* erhielt von den felliner Ehsten folgendes Bruchstück:

Sie, die kleinen Unterird'schen,
Die geheimen Schmid' Allvaters,
Schafften ihr Geschäft in Nächten,
In den Nächten Mühgeschäfte ;
Tags, da war der Ruhe Weile.

Nach anderer Angabe hört man in schweigsamer Mitternacht, hält man das Ohr an die Erde, das Schmeiden der Unterirdischen in den sieben Nächten von Weihnachten bis zum Neujahr und kann selbst unterscheiden, ob unter den Hämmern Eisen, Silber oder Gold erklingt. Nach einer dritten Angabe, die auch als Lied vorhanden war, waren es wieder die Unterirdischen, welche dem Schlangenkönige seine Krone geschmiedet hatten. Der blendende Glanz dieser Krone lockte sämmtliche Schlangen heran, dass sie in dem Sirtsosoo westlich vom Peipussee um den Konig einen Haufen von der Höhe eines grossen Heuschobers bildeten, aus welchem das Haupt des Königs gleich der Sonne hervorleuchtete."

APPENDIX B.

Abstract of the Níla-Mata, by Professor E. B. Cowell.

It is mentioned in the Rájatarangini that "the Bauddhas, in their hatred of the Śástras, abolished the ceremonial laid down by the Níla-puráṇa ;" but the work entitled the Níla-Mata can hardly be the puráṇa there alluded to.* It is written in a very modern style, but, like other similar recent compilations, it may be founded on old materials. Much of it is occupied with the instructions of the Snake-king Níla to the people of Kashmir ; but it is singular that Snake Worship is hardly alluded to in the copious list of offerings there enjoined throughout the Hindu year. The earlier portion of the work wears a partially Vaishṇava character, but some Śaiva legends occur in the latter portion.

---

* Similarly the *Nandi-puráṇa* mentioned in the Rajat. I. 123., can hardly be the work described by Professor Aufrecht, in his Catalogue of the Bodleian MSS. p. 81.

The two manuscripts used for the present analysis contain respectively 81 pages and 312 pages; each manuscript has 15 lines in a page, but in the latter manuscript the pages are much smaller and the letters much larger. Both are very inaccurately written, and there are many variations in their respective texts. The poem seems to contain about 1,450 ślokas. It is written in the ordinary Anushṭubh metre, and is supposed to be a continuation of the Mahábhárata, and consequently to be recited by Vaiśampáyana to Janamejaya, the great-grandson of Arjuna.

The poem opens with Janamejaya's asking Vaiśampáyana why the king of Kashmir is not represented as joining in the Mahábhárata war, although the maṇḍala of Kashmir was the principal one in the world. Vaiśampáyana replies by relating that the king of Kashmir, Gonanda, had been slain by Kṛishṇa among the Gándháras on the Indus. Kṛishṇa appoints his rival's widow as regent, and her son (Gonanda according to one manuscript, Govinda according to the other,*) did not join either Páṇḍavas or Kauravas on account of his youth. This leads to some questions on the mythological history of Kashmir, and Vaiśampáyana then repeats a dialogue which had taken place between King Gonanda II. and the sage Bṛihadaśwa. This dialogue is properly the Níla-Mata.

Bṛihadaśwa commences with an account of the destruction of the world by water at the end of the previous Manwantara, the preservation of Manu and his seeds in a ship which is fastened to the mountain now called Nau-bandhana, in the west of Kashmir; and when the world of living creatures is created again, Deví, as Kaśmírá, becomes the land of Kashmir. The snakes, persecuted by Garuḍa, take refuge in the lake Satídeśa, and anoint Níla as their king. Kashmir is subsequently ravaged by a demon named Jalodbhava, who is at length killed by Vishṇu. Kaśyapa then asks Vishṇu that the country may be inhabited by gods and men, but the Snake-king demurs. Kaśyapa threatens him with Piśáchas as his neighbours, and tells him that there is an island in "the sea of sand" inhabited by Piśáchas, Daityas, and Yakshas. Their king, Nikumbha, always sets out on the full moon of the month Chaitra, for an annual expedition of six months against his rebellious subjects; he passes the remaining six months in peace on the Himálaya. In future, he threatens, these six months will be passed with the snakes. Níla is in great distress, until at last Vishṇu, pitying him, promises that the arrangement shall only last one set of four ages, and after that time the snakes shall be allowed to have only men as their neighbours. "In whatever place "belonging to any snake men shall dwell, men shall honour him with flowers, incense, and unguents, "with various offerings of food and dances. And whatever people shall keep the good customs "declared by thee, they shall dwell in this country, blessed with cattle, corn, and wealth." The country is thenceforward inhabited for six months in every year by men who come in on the full moon of Chaitra, and sow and reap their corn, but clear off in Áśwayuja, when the country is again given over to the Piśáchas. The various deities become the different rivers; thus Umá becomes the Vitastá, Lakshmí the Viśokí, &c.

This predicted occupation of Kashmir by the Piśáchas continues for four ages. At the end of that time the human inhabitants had, as usual, reaped their grain and cleared off from the country before the full moon of Áśwayuja; but a certain Brahmin named Chandradeva remained with the Piśáchas. One day he wanders disconsolate, till he comes to the place in the mountains where Níla holds his court. He propitiates the Snake-king by a hymn of praise, and Níla grants him a boon. He asks that Kashmir may thenceforth be inhabited by men without fear of perpetual emigrations. Níla grants it: "Thus be it, O best of Brahmins; let men always dwell "here, but observing my words, revealed to me by Keśava." The Brahmin dwells at his court until the month Chaitra comes round, and the human inhabitants flock in from all sides with their king, Víryodaya. Chandradeva goes to him and declares what he has seen and heard, and the king and his people agree to observe the words of Níla, and thenceforth they dwell undisturbed in Kashmir (cf. Rájat. I. 182), which gives a somewhat different legend.

---

* This is the Gonarda II. of the Rajat. I. 62-82.

Gonanda then asks Bṛihadaśwa what "the words of Níla" were. The sage then repeats the lesson as it was uttered by Níla himself to the Brahmin. Here follows a long list of the principal rites and ceremonies throughout the year, beginning with the full moon of Áśwayuja; it contains some curious matter, but the Nágas are hardly ever mentioned.

At the close, Vaiśampáyana interrupts the original dialogue by the remark that Gonanda did not obey these laws, and consequently fell at Mathurá, being slain by Balabhadra (cf. Rájat. I. 59–63).

Gonanda then asks for some account of the principal Nágas who dwell in Kashmir. A long list of names follows, and some legends; and also a list of the principal deities worshipped there, and the benefits derived from visiting their shrines. Bṛihadaśwa then relates some legends connected with several holy places in Kashmir.

The poem winds up with a return to the original interlocutors. Janamėjaya asks Vaiśampáyana to eulogize the glory of the river Vitastá, which closes the work.

APPENDIX C.

THE following translations of the rock-cut edicts of Aśoka are reproduced here without note or comment, but literally, as they have already appeared several times in print. None of those yet given to the public can be considered as either perfect or complete, but the sense can in all cases be gathered from them, and they are sufficient for our present purposes. Two other copies of these edicts have been discovered since these translations were made,—one at the foot of the Himalayas, north of Meerut, and another in Cuttack. When these are published a more perfect translation may be possible. Those who desire further information are referred to Prinsep's translation, J. A. S. B., VII. p. 219. et seqq.; to Professor Wilson's J. R. A. S., XII. 153, et seq.; to Burnouf, "Lotus de la Bonne Loi," Appendix, p. 659, et seqq.; and to Mrs. Speir's Life in Ancient India, p. 230, et seqq. The object for which they are introduced here, is neither to explain their text nor to comment on their doctrines, but to afford the reader of the previous pages a picture of Buddhism as it existed B.C. 250, in the words of its most ardent devotee and its principal promoter. This is done in order that he may compare it with Buddhism as presented 300 years afterwards in the sculptures at Sanchi; or as it appears 300 years after that time, in A.D. 350 at Amravati. This completes the means of comparison in so far as this work is concerned; but, as already mentioned, the frescoes at Ajanta afford a fourth picture 200 years more modern than Amravati; and again, 300 after that we have the Thibetan Lalita-Vistara. Unfortunately we still want, and it is feared are little likely to obtain, any contemporary record at the beginning of our series, 300 years before Aśoka, but it is satisfactory to know that materials now exist for illustrating the other five epochs of Buddhism.

TABLET I.

This is the Edict of the beloved of the Gods, the Raja Piyadasi. The putting to death of animals is to be entirely discontinued, and no convivial meeting is to be held, for the beloved of the Gods, Raja Piyadasi, remarks many faults in such assemblies. There is but one assembly, indeed, which is approved of by the Raja, * * * which is that of the great kitchen of Raja Piyadasi; every day hundreds of thousands of animals have been slaughtered for virtuous purposes, but now, although this pious Edict is proclaimed that animals may be killed for good purposes, and such is the practice, yet as the practice is not determined, these presents are proclaimed, that hereafter they shall not be killed.

TABLET II.

In all the conquered territories of the Raja Piyadasi, even unto the ends of the earth, as in Chola, in Pîda (the kingdom of Satyaputra), in Keralaputra (or Malabar), and in Tambapanni (or Ceylon), and to Antiochus the Yona Raja, and to those Princes who are allied with him, it is proclaimed that two designs have been cherished by Piyadasi,—one regarding men, and one relating to animals,—that everywhere wholesome vegetables, roots, and fruit-trees shall be cultivated, and that on the roads wells shall be dug and trees planted, to give enjoyment for both men and animals.

TABLET III.

King Piyadasi says:—This was ordained by me when I had been twelve years inaugurated in the conquered country; that amongst those united in the law, whether strangers or my own subjects, quinquennial expiation shall be held for the enforcement of moral obligations, as—duty to parents, friends, children, relations; Brahmins, and Sramans. Liberality is good, non-injury of living creatures is good, abstinence from prodigality and slander is good. The Assembly itself will instruct the faithful in the virtues here enumerated, both by explanation and by example.

TABLET IV.

In past times, during many hundreds of years, there have prevailed destruction of life and the injury of living beings, want of respect for kindred, Brahmins and Sramans. But now King Piyadasi practises the Law, the drum sounds, and the Law is proclaimed by processions of cars and elephants, and displays of fireworks. That which had not been seen for centuries, is now seen * * * in consequence of King Piyadasi's commands that the Law be practised * * * And Piyadasi will cause the observance of the Law to increase; and the sons and grandsons and great-grandsons of Piyadasi will cause its observance to increase until the *Kalpa* of destruction.

TABLET V.

They (the Mahâmâtra) shall also be spread among the warriors, the Brahmins, the mendicants, the destitute, and others, without any obstruction, for the happiness of the well-disposed, in order to loosen the bonds ot those who are bound, and liberate those who are confined, through the means of holy wisdom disseminaeed by pious teachers, and they will proceed to the outer cities and fastnesses of my brother and sister, and wherever are any other of my kindred; and the ministers of morals, those who are appointed as superintendents of morals, shall, wherever the moral law is established, give encouragement to the charitable and those addicted to virtue. With this intent this Edict is written, and let my people obey it.

TABLET VI.

Hitherto attention has not been given to reports and affairs incessantly, or at all times, and on this account I decree that at all times,—even when I take recreation in the apartments of the women and children, or in conversation, or in riding, or in gardens, in all places,—there shall be informers (*Prativedaka*) to make known to me the wishes of the people; and everywhere I will occupy myself with the welfare of the people; and whatever I declare, or whatever the Mahâmâtra shall declare, shall be referred to the Council for decision. Thus shall reports be made to me. This have I everywhere and in every place commanded, for to me there is not satisfaction in the pursuit of worldly affairs; the most worthy pursuit is the prosperity of the whole world. My whole endeavour is to be blameless towards all creatures, to make them happy here below, and enable them hereafter to attain *Swarga*. With this view this moral Edict has been written: may it long endure; and may my sons and great-grandsons after me also labour for the universal good; but this is difficult without extreme exertion.

TABLET VII.

The beloved of the Gods, the Raja Piyadasi, desires that the ascetics of all the different beliefs (the *Pâshaṇḍa*) may everywhere dwell (unmolested): they all aim at moral restraint aud purity of disposition; but men have various opinions and various desires, and the ascetics obtain either all or merely a part (of what they want). However, even for him who does not obtain a large gift or alms, purity of dispositiou, gratitude, and steady devotion is desirable.

TABLET VIII.

In past times Kings were addicted to travelling about, to companions, to going abroad, to hunting, and similar amusements; but Piyadasi, the beloved of the Gods, having been ten years inaugurated, by him easily awakened, that moral festival is adopted (which consists) in seeing and bestowing gifts on Brahminas and Sramanas, in seeing and giving gold to Elders, and overseeing the country and the people; the institution of moral laws and the investigation of morals. Such are the devices for the removal of apprehension, and such are the different pursuits of the favourite of the Gods, King Piyadasi.

TABLET IX.

The beloved of the Gods, the Raja Piyadasi, thus says:—Every man that is, celebrates various occasions of festivity, as,—on the removal of incumbrances, on invitations, on marriages, on the birth of a son, or on setting forth on a journey,—on these and other occasions a man makes various rejoicings. Such festivals are fruitless—are vain; but the festival that bears great fruit is the festival of duty (the *dharma mangala*), such as the respect of the servant to his master; reverence for holy teachers is good; liberality to Brahmins and Sramanas is good. These and other such acts constitute verily the festival of duty, and this is to be cherished as a father by a son, or a dependant by his master; * * * for the establishment of this object virtuous donations are made, for there is no donation equal to the gift of duty; * * * benevolence contracted between friends * * * is mere chaff; * * * by these means let a man seek *Swarga.*

TABLET X.

The beloved of the Gods, the Prince Piyadasi, does not esteem glory and fame as of great value; and besides, for a long time it has been my fame and that of my people that the observance of moral duty and the service of the virtuous should be practised, for this is to be done. This is the fame that the beloved of the Gods desires; and inasmuch as the beloved of the Gods excels (he holds) all such reputation as no real reputation, but such as may be that of the unrighteous,—pain and chaff; for it may be acquired by crafty and unworthy persons, and by whatever further effort it is acquired it is worthless and a source of pain.

TABLET XI.

Thus says the beloved of the Gods, King Piyadasi: There is no gift like the gift of virtue, whether it be the praise of virtue, the apportionment of virtue, or relationship of virtue. This (gift) is the cherishing of slaves and dependants, pious devotion to mother and father, generous gifts to friends and kinsmen, Brahminas and Sramanas.

Respect for the life of creatures is good; this is what ought to be said by a father, by a son, by a brother, by a friend, by an acquaintance, by a relation, and even by mere neighbours: this is well; this is to be done. He who acts thus is honoured in this world, and in the other world infinite merit results from this gift of the Law.

TABLET XII.

Piyadasi, the beloved of the Gods, honors all forms of religious belief, whether professed by ascetics or by householders, both by giving alms and by other modes of showing respect. But the beloved of the Gods does not esteem alms and marks of respect so highly as the increase of that which is the essence of renown. Now the increase of that which is essential for all forms of belief is of many kinds, but nevertheless the base of it is, for each of them, praise in words. Further, a man must honor his own faith without blaming that of another, and thus will but little that is wrong occur. There are even circumstances under which the faith of others should be honoured, and in acting thus, according to circumstances, a man increases his own faith and injures that of others. He who acts differently diminisbes his own faith and injures that of others; he, whoever he may be, who honours bis own faith and blames that of others out of devotion to his own, and says, moreover, Let us make our faitb conspicuous; that man, I say, who acts tbus merely injures the faitb he holds: concord alone therefore is desirable. Further, let men listen to each law and follow it with submission, for such is the desire of the King, beloved of the Gods. Further, may men of all faiths abound in knowledge and prosper in virtue! And those who have faith in this or that religion should repeat this:—The King, beloved of the Gods, does not value alms or marks of respect so much as the increase of that which is the essence of renown and the multiplication of all beliefs. To this end great ministers of law, and superintendeuts of women * * * and other officers are appointed, and the fruit of this institution will be the speedy increase of all religions, as well as the illumination of the law.

Extract from Tablet XIII., the rest being so injured that it does not admit of continuous translation:—

" There is not in either class of the heretics of men, a procedure marked by such grace * * * nor so glorious, or friendly, nor even so extremely liberal as Devánampiyo's injunction for the non-injury and content of living creatures; * * * and the Greek king besides, by whom the kings of Egypt, PTOLEMAIOS and ANTIGONOS and MAGAS, * * * both here and in foreign countries, everywhere wherever they go, tbe religious ordinances of Devánampiyo effect conversion. Conquest is of every description, but the conquest which bringeth joy, springing from pleasant emotions, becometh joy itself. The victory of virtue is happiness * * * such victory is desired in things of this world and things of the next world. (J. R. A. S., XII. 233.)

TRANSLATION OF THE BHABRA INSCRIPTION, BY PROFESSOR WILSON.

Piyadasi, the King, to the venerable Assembly of Magadha, commands the infliction of little pain and indulgence to animals.

It is verily known, I proclaim, to what extent my respect and favour (are placed) in Buddha, and in the Law, and in the Assembly.

Whatsoever (words) have been spoken by the divine Buddha, they have all been well said, aud in them verily I declare that capability of proof is to be discerned; so that the pure law (which they teach) will be of long duration, as far as I am worthy (of being obeyed).

For these I declare are the precepts of the Law of the principal discipline (Vinaya), having overcome the oppressions of the Aryas and future perils, (and refuted) the songs of the Munis, the Sûtras of the Munis, (the practices) of inferior ascetics, the censure of a light world, and (all) false doctrines.

These things, as declared by the divine Buddha, I proclaim, and I desire them to be regarded as the precepts of the Law.

And that as many as there may be, male and female mendicants, may hear and observe them, as well also as male and female followers (of the laity).

These things I affirm, and have caused this to be written (to make known to you) that such will be my intention.

APPENDIX D.

The Hindu races worship three classes of deities,—the Grâma devatâ, or village god; the Kula devatâ, or household god; and the Ishṭa devatâ, the personal or patron god.

Snake Worship is general throughout peninsular India, both of the sculptured form and of the living creature. The sculpture is invariably of the form of the Nag or Cobra, and almost every hamlet has its Serpent deity. Sometimes this is a single snake, the hood of the Cobra being spread open. Occasionally the sculptured figures are nine in number, and this form is called the "Nao nag," and is intended to represent a parent snake and eight of its young, but the prevailing form is that of two snakes twining in the manner of the Esculapian rod.

Some Hindus hold that the living snake is not worshipped as a devatâ by any Hindu sect, but is reverenced in commemoration of some ancient event. If this be correct, it has, perhaps, relation to some astronomical occurrence. Others, however, maintain that it is as a devatâ that it is worshipped; but whatever be the origin of the adoration, the living snake is worshipped everywhere throughout Southern India. On these occasions the worshippers resort to the snake's residence, called in Urdu the سانپ كي هوٹ Sāmp kī hūṭ, which they ornament with streaks of vermilion and daubs of turmeric, and of wheat flour, and they hang garlands of flowers near, strung on white cotton thread, and laid over wooden frames. Also, in the ninth Sravan, which occurs in the rainy season, the "Nâg panchamî" festival occurs, on which Hindus go in search of snakes, or have them brought to their houses by the "Sanpeli," the snake charmers who snare them. The snakes are then worshipped, and offerings are made to them of milk, and in nearly every house figures of snakes, drawn on paper, are fixed on the walls and worshipped. Those who visit the snakes' būts, plant sticks around the hole, and wind white cotton thread around and over the sticks. The Mahratta women go, a number together, to the snakes' hūt, and, joining hands, circle five times round and round it, singing songs, and then prostrate themselves. They pour milk into the hole (they ought to give it to the snake). They hang festoons of Chernhela flowers and cucumber fruit, and sprinkle a mixture of sugar and flour (Sakr Suji).

On the 25th January 1868 I halted in the temple of the Grâma devatâ of Assaye, where Sir A. Wellesley defeated the Bhonslah. I there saw Hanuman with a lingam, and Basava, the bull, and the tulsi plant, and on the western wall of the temple was a cobra snake, drawn in white, which the worshippers said was travelling to Ceylon or Lankâ. They laughed when I said he would be long on his journey.

In Southern India the deity under whose name the snake is worshipped is Subrămănī, whose shrine is said to be in the western part of Mysore, and the image there is described as a shapeless lump of earth.

I have only once seen living snakes in the form of the Esculapian rod. It was at Ahmednuggur, in 1841, in a clear moonlight night. They dropped into the garden from over the thatched roof of my house, and stood erect. They were all cobras, and no one could have seen them without at once recognizing that they were in congress. Captain Havelock, to whom I showed these remarks, mentioned in reply that he once, in broad daylight, in the jungles, saw pythons, just as I have sketched them,* in the singular form of the Esculapian rod, but many natives mention having seen this sight. Natives of India believe that it is most fortunate to witness snakes so engaged, and they believe that if they can throw a cloth at the pair to touch them with it, the cloth becomes a representative form of Lakshmi of the highest virtue, and is taken home to their houses and preserved as such.

---

* A sketch of the serpents in this attitude accompanied the letter, but not sufficiently perfect to enable a woodcut to be made from it.—J. F.

No Hindu, ordinarily, will kill a snake, but turns aside on seeing it. Young men who have been educated at English schools, however, have no such reserve, and a Mahratta Brahmin has informed me that he has killed three of them.

Snakes are kept in houses in Ceylon and Guzerat, partly seemingly as objects of worship, and partly to destroy rats, but no similar practice prevails in the south-eastern parts of peninsular India.

CH. ED. BALFOUR, M.D.

Secunderabad, 23d January 1868.

MEMORANDUM ON SNAKE WORSHIP.

On the Nâg Panchmee festival, which occurs, I think, on the fifth day of the Hindu month Bhadoon, in the rainy season, Nâgs (Cobras) are worshipped by most of the lower classes of the people in the Deccan, and more particularly in the Shorapore country. The principal of those classes in Shorapore are the Beydars, who are decidedly an aboriginal tribe, which is numerous in Mysore and in the southern Mahratta country. The Shorapore class came from Mysore and settled in Shorapore and the Rachore Doab, under chieftains who were originally servants of the Rajahs of Beejanugger, but who became subjects of the Kings of Golburgah and Beeder, and of Beejapoor after the fall of the Beejanugger state. The Beydars have not mingled with other Hindu castes, and though they profess to be Hindus, they adhere to many of their original superstitions and ceremonies, which have nothing to do with Hinduism; they have little or no reverence for Brahmins, what there is indeed being sparingly afforded, except by the higher classes among them, who have adopted them as priests. The Snake festival, therefore, has very little of the elements of Brahminism in it, if there are any. The ceremonies are very simple: the worshippers bathe, mark their foreheads with red colour, and in small parties, generally families who know each other, go to places where Cobras (Nâgs) are known to live or to frequent. There are generally sacred stones in such places, to which offerings of flowers, ghee, &c., are made, and the stones are anointed with red colour and ground turmeric, prayers and invocations being made to the local spirit of the place and to the Serpents. Small new earthen saucers, filled with milk, are then placed near the stones, or near the Snake's hole, if there be one. Cobras are fond of milk, and are believed to watch the ceremony, coming out of their holes and drinking the milk, even while the worshippers are near, or sitting at a little distance to see if their offering is received. Should the Snake appear and drink, it is esteemed a very fortunate circumstance for the worshippers. Should the Snake not appear, the worshippers, after waiting awhile, depart, and visit the place next morning, when the result is anxiously examined; if the milk has disappeared, the rite has been accepted, but not in so marked a degree as if the reptile had come out at once. These ceremonies end with a feast.

Snake Worship is especially resorted to on behalf of children; and the women and children of a family invariably accompany the male head, not only at the annual festival, but whenever a vow has been made to a Serpent Deity. The first hair of a child which is shaved off when it has passed teething, and other infantine ailments, is frequently dedicated to a Serpent. On such occasions the child is taken to the locality of the vow, the usual ceremonies are performed, and with other offerings of flowers, &c., the child's hair is combined. In every case a feast follows, cooked near the spot, and Brahmins who attend receive largess and alms, and relations and friends receive invitations.

In the Shakti ceremonies, Poorna-abhishék, which belong, I think, to aboriginal customs, the worship of the Snake forms a portion, as emblematical of energy and wisdom. Most of these ceremonies are, however, of an inconceivably obscene and licentious character. They are not confined to the lowest classes, though rarely perhaps resorted to by Brahmins; but many of the middle class sects, of obscure origin and denomination, practise them in secret, under a strange delusion that the divine energy of nature is to be obtained thereby, with exemption from earthly troubles.

Although Snake Worship ordinarily belongs professedly to the descendants of aboriginal tribes, yet Brahmins never or rarely pass them over, and the Nâg Panchmee is observed as a festival of kindly greeting and visiting between families and friends—as a day of gifts of new clothes or ornaments to wives or children, &c.

The worship of Grâm Deotas, or village divinities, is universal all over the Deccan, and indeed I believe throughout India. These divinities have no temples nor priests. Sacrifice and oblation is made to them at sowing time and harvest, for rain or fair weather, in time of cholera, malignant fever, or other disease or pestilence. The Nâg is always one of the Grâm Deota, the rest being known by local names. The Grâm Deota are known as heaps of stones, generally in a grove or quiet spot near every village, and are smeared some with black and others with red colour.

Nâg is a common name both for males and females among all classes of Hindus, from Brahmins downwards to the lowest classes of Sudras and Mléchhas. Nâgo Rao, Nâgojee, &c., are common Mahratta names, as Nâgappa, Nâgowa, and the like among the Canarese and Telugoo population.

No Hindu will kill a Nâg or Cobra willingly. Should any one be killed within the precincts of a village, by Mahomedans or others, a piece of copper money is put into its mouth, and the body is burned with offerings to avert the evil.

It is, perhaps, remarkable that the Snake festival is held after the season or at the season of casting the skin, and when the Snake, addressed or worshipped, is supposed to have been purified. Some Brahmins always keep the skin of a Nâg in one of their sacred books.

In reference to the lower castes alluded to, I may mention those who practise Snake Worship with the greatest reverence:—1. Beydars. 2. Dhungars or shepherds, Aheers or milkmen, Waddiwars or stone-masons, Khungins or rope-makers, Brinjaras and other wandering tribes, Mangs, Dhérs, and Chumars, Ramoosees, Bhils, Gonds, and Koles, all which I believe, with many others, to be descendants of aboriginal tribes, partly received within the pale of Hinduism.

Lingayets, who are schismatics from Hinduism, and who deny *in toto* the religious supremacy of the Brahmins, are nevertheless Snake worshippers, many of them bearing the name Nâg, both male and female.

I cannot speak of the North of India, but in the whole of the South of India, from the Nerbudda to Cape Comorin, Snake Worship is now existent.

MEADOWS TAYLOR, Col. M. N. I.

The festival of the Moonsa Poojah takes place each year about the end of August.

The tribes that I have seen present at it were Bhowries, Dhangas, and Santhals, and the locality was at a large jungle village beside a range of low hills, to the west of the hill Beharînath, and to the south of the hill of Pachete.

The snake catchers and charmers, at this period of the year, assemble and make a tour of the neighbouring villages, carrying snakes twisted around their necks and bodies, the chief of the procession being either carried on men's shoulders, or riding on a buffalo. He generally has a rock boa or python hanging over his shoulders. The usual amount of beating of the Nagara, playing the flute, and singing, attends the procession, and large quantities of the favourite spirit "Mowha" and sweetmeats are consumed.

Presents are also made to the snake bearers, and general dissipation prevails.

A. VANS BEST, M.D.
Bengal Establishment.

NOTE.

In August last, when this work was going to press, Professor Goldstücker brought me a note on the Naga tribes of Cashmere which he had received from H.S.H. Prince Frederick of Schleswig-Holstein, who was then residing in the valley. My intention was to have added this note to this Appendix, but it now turns out most unfortunately that it has been mislaid and cannot be found. This is to be regretted, not only because it was an account of the Nâgas of the present day by a most intelligent and competent observer, but also because the Prince insisted most strongly on the medical qualities of the tribe, and their possession of nostrums which had been handed down from remote antiquity. This retention of the Esculapian character by the snake worshippers is one of the most curious points connected with the subject, but it is one that, now that attention is directed to it, will I trust meet with full elucidation from some inhabitant of the valley.

J. F.

APPENDIX E.

THE Amravati inscriptions are similar to those on the Railings and Gateways of the Buddhist Stupas and Monasteries at Bhilsa and other places. They are all written in the Pali language; and, where not injured by weather or breakage, they are generally clear and legible. With two exceptions they have been all copied by myself from the sculptured slabs, and have since been compared with the photographs. The two exceptions are Nos. II. and XI., which have been taken from Colonel Mackenzie's drawings. The former is a good copy, and is mostly legible; but the latter is unfortunately a very corrupt transcript of the most important of all the Amravati records, as it certainly contains the name of a King, which, if it had been faithfully copied, would most probably have enabled us to fix the date of the inscription.

The following translations are not offered as critical renderings of the inscriptions, but simply as free versions conveying their general meaning, which is usually confined to the specification of certain gifts made to the sacred edifice by various individuals, both priests and laymen, in which they were frequently joined by their wives and children. The same practice is still common in Burmah and in other Buddhist countries.

Some of the words which are of unusual occurrence require explanation. In No. IV. I have rendered *gharani*, by "wife," that is, the mistress of the house. The present Hindi form is *gharwâli.* The word *paṭâ* occurs three times in Nos. II., XI., and XX., and the word *pataka* three times in Nos. IV., XIV., and XX. As both words are combined with figures in No. XX., I take them to be the names of the particular gifts thus recorded, and consequently that they refer to the sculptured stones themselves. *Paṭâ* is most probably the same word as the present Hindi *Paṭao,* which means a "broad stone slab," and is specially applicable to the Amravati railing stones, in which the breadth is equal to three times the depth. Both names are derived from the Sanskrit *pâṭa,* breadth, from the root *paṭa,* to spread or extend. The word *pataka,* or in No. XX. *bataka,* is spelt with the dental *t*, and is most probably therefore not connected with *paṭa,* which invariably has the cerebral *ṭ*. I conclude that it must be the name for a railing pillar, because it is found in Nos. IV. and XIV. recorded on the tops of two of them. The name used for a square or octagonal pillar is *thabho* (see No. III.) from the Sanskrit *stambha.* In No. XX. we have a record of two *Paṭas* and three *Patakas,* which I believe to refer to three broad slab pillars of the railing, and the two architrave slabs that covered them. I cannot suggest any explanation of the word *vetika,* which occurs in No. XI., but I conclude that it is the name of some one of the sculptured slabs, as it is coupled with *paṭa.*

AMRAVATI TOPE.

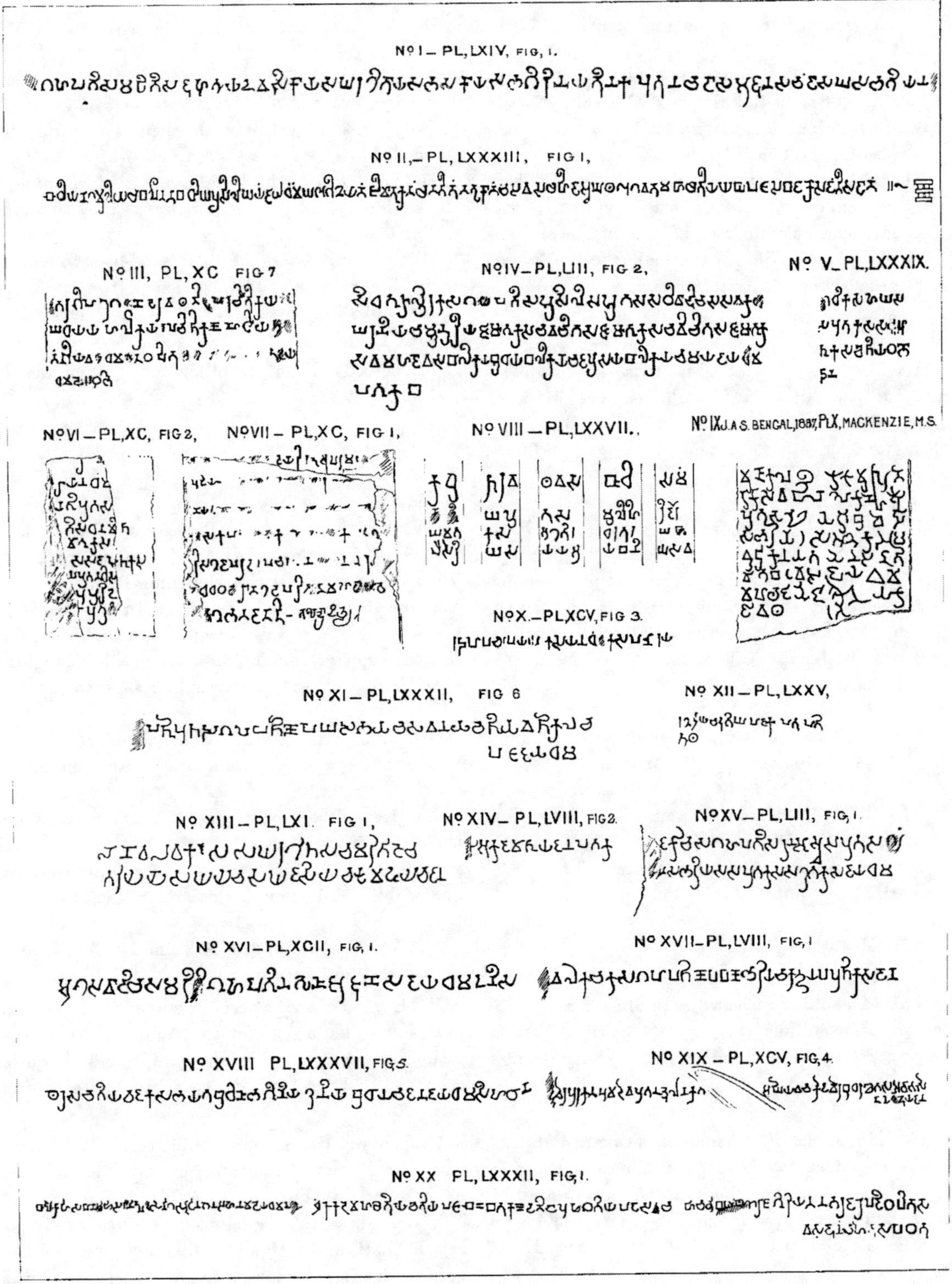

INSCRIPTIONS.

The small figures in the text mark the beginnings of the lines of the different inscriptions.

I. . . . . gahapatisa Maditisa duhutuya Uvasikâya, Sagha-Rakhitâya, Sabhâsakâya, Sabhagirinaya, tina ka putana cha Dâsa Ajunasa, cha Dâsa Ghasa, bhatiyâna . . .

I. (Gift) of the householder *Maditi's* daughters *Urvâsika*, *Sangha-Rakshitâ*, *Sabhâsakâ*, (and) *Sabhâgirinâ*, together with their sons, and the slave *Arjuna*, and the slave (*San*)*gha*, . . .

II. Bodhiya Nâgamuliya cha Balinada Bodhiya Pusiliyayam deya dhama. Bhagineyânam, Jâmâtukânam, cha natitam natukânam, cha savasa cha hidâswa, ghatha Bhagavata mahâchetiye yaghâ patâ sabada kosa dantisa dâuam.

II. Pious gift of the Buddhist *Nâgamuli*, and of the Buddhist *Balinanda*, Pusiliyas (? descendants of Pusili).

Gift of their sisters, of their sons-in-law, and of their (—?—), and of all friends, to the great Chaitya of Bhagavata of a slab . . . . enshrined tooth (?) . . . .

III. . . . . tara giha rega . . nadera vathadi parachitikaya (2) ghadhayaya hâlikaya napachitika . . hodiyada . . (3) nâgiyatama dhamateri thapita (6 letters) ta deya (4) dhama d(—?—) thabho.

III. Pious gift of a pillar (the remainder is unintelligible).

IV. Sidham! Tunulaurakasa Gahapatisa Pusilisa-putasa, Sethivadi-cha Sasivakasa, (2) gharaniya cha Mununiya, Jâmâtukasa-cha Vachitasa, jâmâtukasa-cha Vichitasa, jâmâtuka-(3)sa cha Mahajevasa, Bâlikaya Budhâya, Bâlikaya Chandapusaya, Bâlikaya Chamaya, deya-dhama (4) pataka ba.

IV. Be it auspicious! Pious gift of two slab-pillars of *Tunulauraka*, the householder, son of *Pusili*, and of *Sasivaka*, the chief Banker, and of his wife *Munuri*, and of his son-in-law *Vachita*, and of his son-in-law *Vichita*, and of his son-in-law *Mahajeva*; his daughter *Budhâ*, his daughter *Chandrapusa*, (and) his daughter *Charmâ*.

V. Gadhikasa haghasa, (2) saputakasa, saduhu-(3)-tukasa chetiya thabho (4) dânam.

V. Pillar gift to the Chaitya of *Hagha* of Gadhika, together with his son and his daughter.

VI. . . (Nâ) râyana dhama . . . latiputasa . . gahapatisa Dhana Mi(trasa) . . (j)âmâtrika . . . . sa saduhu(trika)sa putana dhisa . . prapuri . . . putra.

VI. Imperfect,—but enough remains to show that the inscription is of the usual form, and records the gift of the householder *Dhana-mitra*, and of his son-iu-law, his daughter, &c.

VII. Mostly illegible.

VII. At tbe end of the last line but one I read the word *Mahâchetiya*.

VIII. Kabu 5 ravatha vasa Budhi sama . . . ya putasa mulihiri Sagha-Mitrakasa Akhatisa Dhawa Siriya Ba- . . siriya Saghaya Ayabaniga sava.

VIII. This inscription is engraved on five small pillars or stelæ, on one of the sculptured representations of a Stupa. Many of the letters are quite clear and distinct; but no part can be read with certainty.

IX. Munâkala . . kumudaputa rakasa Vâhilasa Kanhiya putasa ta . . ye . . Budhika sa Bhâriya . . . sa . . . Kusuma dhudu Kanayatasa dâsadati mita badavasa deya dhama. Maharaja Yâdnya Siri Sadakani vatha.

IX. This is the most valuable of all the Amravati inscriptions; but uufortunately the slab has not come to England, and there is only a copy made by a draughtsman to refer to. The title of Maharaja is distinct in the last line but one, and the name following it appears to be *Yâdnya*, who was one of the last of the Andhra kings.

X. radahapachepaya . . kasayanadha . . . kasapanoraya.

X. Not read.

XI. . . patiputasa gahapatino Haghasabhaya cha Savanaya Chetiya vetika cha paṭâ deya dhama.

XI. Pious gift to the Chaitya of a *Vetika* and a slab, of the householder ——*patiputra*, and of *Haghasabhâ*, and of *Savanâ*.

XII. Rakhadiya cha Datiya padaka pata patitatha.

XII. Not read.

XIII. Lonavalavakasa, Saghirakhitasa-cha, Maritisa-cha, Bhâriyayo Saghaya-cha, Sagha-dâsiya-cha, Kumadaya-cha, danam.

XIII. Gift of *Lonavalavaka*, and *Sanghirakshita*, and *Mariti*, aud of their wives *Sanghâ*, and *Sanghadâsi*, and *Kumâdri*.

XIV. Akarâ Mâtriya dânam patika.

XIV. Gift of Akarâ's mother of a slab-pillar.

XV. . . daki chasa gal.a] atisa rana aswas, putasa . . . . na, saBhariyasa, sa-Putakasa sakhatakasa deya dhama.

XV. Pious gift of ——*dakicha*, the householder, son of *Rana-Aswa*, . . . together with his wife, and his son, and his (—?—).

XVI. Akhasavâdi cha Samariti gahapatina tuno Ajunasa deya dhama unisa.

XVI. Nineteen pious gifts of *Akhasavâdi* and *Samariti*, householders.

XVII. Valikachakasa gahapatino Pâpino bhâriya-cha Kanhâya paputikasa dânam.

XVII. Gift of *Pâpi*, householder of *Valikachaka*, and of his wife the grand-daughter of Kanhâ.

XVIII. Therasa Chetiyavadakasa Bhayata Budhino, Bhaginiya Bhikhuniya Budhaya-cha dana deya dhama Siha-thâna.

XVIII. Pious gift of a Lion-pedestal of the *Thera* (*Sthâvira* or Elder) *Bhayata Budhi*, the enlarger of the Chaitya, and of his sister the Nun *Budhâ*.

XIX. . . . virapurakana puma devaputana dulena krita.

Agheya Vachakiṭa Vira Budharakhitasa atevasinaya deya dânam.

XIX. ——(first part not read.)

Pious gift of *Agheya Vachakita Vira*, pupil of Budha Rakshita.

XX. Bâlikâhi sahina tihisa nitya sanigama Khatana gena sahadama deya dhamana Dhankakata mahachetiya chetiya paṭâ be 2, bataka 3, datisa pupha gatiya paṭasa . . cha . . hâ cha nebatasa tha . . ṭha Râjagiriyanam nata vadâre paditha pita sanasa dânam chahitasa pathati.

XX. Parts of this inscription are not intelligible; but enough has been made out to show that it records the gift of two slabs and three slab-pillars by certain persons of *Râjagiri*, the ancient capital of Bihâr.

A. CUNNINGHAM,
Major-General R.E.

NOTE.

The principal points of interest in these inscriptions, with reference to the preceding text, are the allusions to the Tooth relic in No. II., to Yâdnya Śrí in No. IX., and to the Mahâ Chaitya of Dhanakakata in the last. If on further investigation their correctness should be established, the history of the monument can hardly be considered doubtful.—J. F.

APPENDIX F.

The two following tables contain the results of my lucubrations in the chronology of the principal Indian dynasties who are recorded to have reigned for seven centuries before and as many after the Christian era. As mentioned in the body of the work (page 63), it is my intention to submit a paper embodying these facts, together with the data on which they are founded, to the Royal Asiatic Society, and perhaps it would have been prudent to have awaited the remarks and criticisms which might arise in discussing it before printing it in the naked form in which it is here given. It was absolutely necessary, however, in a work involving so much history as this, that some system of chronology should be adopted, and as my investigations have led me to results in many cases widely different from any published tables, the work must either have been left incomplete in this respect, or my views stated in some form or other. All I ask of the reader, at present, is to believe I have a reason to give for every date and every synchronism in these tables; whether it is a good reason or not must be determined hereafter. The whole, however, appears to me to hang so well together and to accord so well with what we learn from coins or inscriptions, or from the architectural remains, and historical traditions, that I feel confident that the scheme will be found correct within very narrow limits of error.

All the dynasties here quoted will be readily recognized as those published by Prinsep,* Wilson,† Thomas,‡ and others. No novelty in this respect has been attempted. It is only the arrangement that is, in some instances, somewhat different from that usually accepted. The newest list is that of the Sâh kings, which is copied with its dates from one by Mr. Justice Newton, which appeared in the "Bombay Times of India" in July last.

There are several of the dates in these tables which I would like to adjust arbitrarily to the extent of four or five years, and when I can give my reasons I shall probably do so. For the present I prefer leaving them as I have found them. They are near enough the truth for the purposes of the present work.

---

* Useful Tables, Calcutta, 1834. † Vishṇu Purâṇa. London, 1840.
‡ Prinsep's Indian Antiquities. London, 1858.

20 Descents from Kaliyuga.	37 Descents in 600? Years from Yudhishṭira.		
Kritanjaya, 1st emigrant from Kośala.	Śaiśunâga Dynasty.		
Raṇanjaya.	Śiśunâga	691	
Sanjaya.	Kâkavarṇa.		
Śâkya.	Kshemadharman.		
Śuddhodana.	Kshetraujas.		Buddha born, 623.
	Bimbisâra	603	,, attained Buddhahood sixteenth year of this king.
Râhula, son of Śâkya Muni.	*Kaṇwâyana*, 9.		
	Bhûmiputra, 14.		
Prasenajit.	Ajâtaśatru	551	,, died eighth year of this reign 543. First Convocation held that year.
Kshudraka.	Udayâśwa	519	
Kuṇḍaka.	Daśaka	503	
Suratha.	Nâgadâśoka	495	
Sumitra.	Śiśunâga	471	
	Kâlâśoka	453	Second Convocation 100 years after Buddha's death.
	Mahâ Nanda	425	
	Sumâlya.		
	7 Nandas.		
	Interregnum, Kauṭilya.		Alexander in India, 327.
	Maurya Dynasty, 137 *years.*		
	Chandragupta	325	
	Bimbisâra	301	
	Aśoka	276	Third Convocation, 255 B.C. in 17th year after his inauguration. Stûpa at Sanchi.
	Suyaśas	240	
	Daśaratha	230 ?	Caves at Behar.
	Sangata	220 ?	
	Indrapâlita	212 ?	
	Somaśarman	210	
	Śaśadharman	203	
	Vrihadratha	195	
	Śunga Dynasty, 112 *years.*		Caves in Cuttack ?
	Pushpamitra	188	No. 2 Tope at Sanchi ?
	Agnimitra	152	
	Sujyeshṭha	144	
	Vasumitra	137	
	Ârdraka	129	
	Pulindaka	127	Caves at Bâjâ ?
	Ghoshavasu	124	
	Vajramitra	121	
	Bhâgavata	112	
	Devabhûti	86	Great Cave at Kárlee.
	Kâṇwa Dynasty, 45 *years.*		
	Vâsudeva	76	
	Bhûmimitra	67	
	Nârâyaṇa	53	
	Suśarman	41	
	,, died	B.C. 31	

ANDHRA DYNASTY.	SÂH KINGS.	KINGS OF MAGADHA.	KINGS OF CASHMERE.	
	Nahapana - B.C. 57			Great Caves at Karlee.
Śipraka - B.C. 31			Hushka, Jushka, Kanishka } Tartar Princes established Buddhism	
	Ushavadâta - 11			
Krishṇa - A.D. 8	Swâmi Chastana - A.D. 10	Śakrâditya.		Nâgârjuna.
	Jaya Dâmâ.			
Śâtakarṇi I. - 10			Abhimanya, A.D. 21	Gateways at Sanchi.
Pûrṇotsanga - 28	Jiva Dama - 38		GONARDAYA DYNASTY.	
			Gonarda. *Naga worshipped.*	
Śrîvaswâmi - 46	Rudra Dâman.			
	Rudra Sinha - 45–47		Vibhishaṇa.	
Śâtakarṇi II. - 64	Rudra Sâh.	Buddhagupta.	Indrajita.	Śâlivâhana, A.D. 78.
	Srî Sâh.			
Lambodara - 120	Sangha Dâman.		Râvaṇa.	Early Caves at Ajanta.
	Dâman Sâh.			
Apîtaka - - 138	Yaśa Dâman.		Vibhishaṇa.	
	Dâmajâta Śrî - 97		Nara.	
Sangha - - 150	Vîra Dâman.			
	Îśvara Datta.		Siddha.	
Śâtakarṇi III. - 163	Vijaya Sâh - 115	Tathâgatagupta.		
	Dâmajâta Srî.		Utpalâksha.	
Skandhaswâti - 186	Rudra Sâh - 131, 141		Hiraṇyâksha.	
	Viśva Sinha - 143			
Mrigendra - 193	Atri Dâman - 153, 157		Hiraṇyâkula.	
Kuntalaswâti - 196	Viśva Sâh - 160, 168			
	22. Rudra Sinha - 173 or 213		Vâsûkulo.	
Swâtîkarṇa - 204	Âśâ Dâman.	Balâditya.	Mihirakula, 200 ?	Central building, Amravati.
	Svâmi Rudra Sâh - 223, 235			
Pulomâvit - 205	Svâmi Rudra Sâh II.			
Gorakshâśwaśrî 241	Svâmi Rudra Sâh - 223, 235		Vaka.	
	Svâmi Rudra Sâh.			
Hâla - - 266			Kshitinanda.	
Mantalaka - 271			Vasunanda.	
Purîndra sena - 276		Vajra.	Nara.	
Râjâdaswâti - 6 ms.			Aksha.	
Sivaswâti - 281			Gopâditya, 290 ?	Built Takht i Suleiman?
Gautamiputra - 309	GUPTA, or BALABHI Era - 318		Gokarṇa.	Cave at Nassick.
Vâsithi putra 330			Narendrâditya.	Outer rail, Amravati.
Pulomat - - 355	Gupta.		Yudhishṭhira.	
Sivaśrî - - 383	Ghaṭotkacha.	Kings of OUGEIN and CANOUGE.	ÂDITYA DYNASTY.	
Skandaswâti - 390			Pratâpâditya, 350 ?	
Yajnaśrî - - 397	Chandra gupta I. - 400, 411	Vasudeva.	Jalaukas.	
Vijaya - - 406			Tunjina.	Inner Rail, Amravati.
			Vijaya.	Buddha ghosha.
Vadaśrî - - 412	Samudra gupta - 420 ?	*Bahram-gour.*	Jayendra.	Great Cave at Kenheri.
Pulomat - - 422			Ârya Râja.	
„ died - 429 or 436	Chandra gupta II. - 430 ?	Ramadeva.		
			GONARDAYA LINE *restored.*	
	Kumâra gupta - 442	Harsha.	Meghavâhana, 434?	
CHÂLUKYA KINGS.				
Jaya Sinha Vijayâditya - 430 ?	Buddha gupta - 463		Sreshṭasena.	
		Vikramâditya - 490 ?		
Râja Sinha.	Toramâṇa - 498		Hiranya, Toramâṇa } 498	Buildings at Eran.
Vijayâditya II.				
Pulakeśi I. - 489		Silâditya - - 530	Mâtrigupta, 525	
Kirtti Varman I.				
Mangalîśa.			Pravara sena, 530	Zodiac Cave, Ajanta.
	BALABHI KINGS.	Prabhâkara.	Yudhishṭhira II.	
	Nine kings from Bhaṭârka Senâpati 493 ?		Nandravat.	
	Śrîdhara Sena.	Râja varddhana 607 ?	Raṇâditya.	Temple at Martand.
		Silâditya - 610	Vikramâditya, 30th year, 622	
Vishṇu Vardhana founds Vengi 605	Dhruva Sena II. - 628	„ died - 650	Balâditya, cotem. Yezdigerd and Hiouen Thsang.	Temple at Bhuvaneśwar.
	Dhruva Sena III. - 640			
Pulakeśi II. founds Kalyân 607	Silâditya - 656			
	Silâditya - 666			

APPENDIX G.

BIRTH OF ŚÂLIVÁHANA.

THE following two extracts from a paper by Colonel Wilford in the ninth volume of the "Asiatic Researches" are of little value from any historical point of view, but being derived from Brahmanical sources, they are curious as an unconscious testimony to the prevalence of Nâga traditions at the time the Sanchi Gateways were being erected.*

"Towards the end of his reign, Vicramarca sent secret messengers through all the world to "inquire whether a child were born of a virgin one and half year old. The messengers returned "to Ujjayini with the news that a male child was born of a virgin, the daughter of a potmaker, "begot by the King of Snakes (called Tacshaca or the Carpenter in the original), while she was "in her cradle. They informed him also that the child named Śâliváhana had attained the "age of five years, and that his grandfather had made numberless figures of soldiers to amuse "him.

"Vicramarca marched at the head of an army, but the protecting Snake came to the "assistance of the Child, and inspired the figures of clay with life, who started up as able "warriors, attacked Vicramarca and his army, and defeated them" (p. 120).

"There were two Brahmans, who had a sister who lived with them in a state of widow-"hood—her husband having died while she was yet very young. She conceived by a Nâga "Cumâra (or Tacshaca), and the brothers, ashamed of this seemingly disorderly behaviour of "their sister, left the country. The unfortunate young widow thus deserted found an asylum "in the humble cottage of a pot maker, where she was delivered of a male child, whom she "called Śâliváhana."

After some irrelevant matter, the story reaches the battle, and goes on thus:—"They "fought on both sides with courage, but the Nâga Cumâra, or son of the Great Serpent, "stupefied Vicramarca's army, who, finding his soldiers asleep, implored the assistance of the "Serpent, Vâsuki, who gave him some Amrit, with which he revived his troops, and Śâliváhana, "hearing of this, sent two of his men for some of it, and Vicramarca complied with his request, "and here ends the legend" (p. 130).

* Śâliváhana died A.D. 78. His capital was situated 300 miles south-west from Sanchi, but his kingdom extended to the eastward of Nagpore (vide supra, p. 154). If I am not very much mistaken, Nâgârjuna, Kanishka, and Śâliváhana are the three persons who had the greatest share in engrafting on Buddhism that Serpent Worship which gave rise to those forms which it has been the object of the preceding pages to develope.

NOTE.

The following footnote was inadvertently omitted on page 94:—

Professor Wilson, quoting from the Mahâ Bhârata, says, "The King Sagara, in obedience to his Guru, "Vasishta, deprived the Mlêchch'has of their institutes, and imposed on them these marks: the Sacas had "half the head shaved, the Yavanas and Cambojas the whole of the hair taken off, the Paradas were ordered "to wear beards."—Asiatic Researches, XV. 49.

INDEX.

A.

B.

C.

D.

E.

F.

G.